WITHDRAWN

Family Fictions

FAMILY FICTIONS

Narrative and Domestic Relations in Britain, 1688-1798

Christopher Flint

Stanford University Press
Stanford, California
1998

Stanford University Press
Stanford, California
© 1998 by the Board of Trustees of the
Leland Stanford Junior University
Printed in the United States of America
CIP data appear at the end of the book

To my family.

And to the memory of Thomas Edward Yingling,

"Bind us in time."

Acknowledgments

Over the course of its lifetime, *Family Fictions* has generated a number of intellectual debts, and I would like to acknowledge them here. From its early inception to its more mature form, this book has benefited immeasurably from Ellen Pollak's attention to the language and argument; without her calm counsel it would never have materialized. John Richetti provided crucial guidance, and just the right touch of wry perspective, and has continued to be a generous and critical resource. Michael Seidel offered seasonable advice and encouragement, and enlivening baseball anecdotes, when the project was still a fledgling work of criticism.

At the University of Pennsylvania, I was lucky to encounter a group of friends and scholars who have continued to be a rich source of intellectual and emotional sustenance. Both collectively and individually, I owe an inestimable debt of gratitude to Michael Awkward for his sage responses to my ramblings and his wicked backhand up the alley; to Steve Goldsmith, whose generosity and spirit seem limitless; to Celeste Langan for her sustaining humor and penetrating criticism; to Joe Valente for his voracious intellectual curiosity; and to Tom Yingling, who, despite his absence, still serves as one of my most cherished interlocutors. My thanks, for their bracing encouragement and support all those years ago, also go to Peter Dorsey, Frank Hoffman, Susan Greenfield, and Pidge Molyneaux.

I would also like to thank several colleagues at the University of Michigan who steered me away from rickety sentences and specious reasoning: Lincoln Faller, Jonathan Freedman, Marjorie Levinson, Marlon Ross, Patricia Yaeger, and especially Elizabeth Barnes, Anita Norich, and Adela Pinch for their conversation, wit, and camaraderie. In the final stages of manuscript preparation Paul Rodney helped me stay abreast of an alarming mass of criticism on both the history of the family and eighteenth-century fiction. Theresa Braunschneider cheerfully logged countless hours of patient and meticulous proofreading, source-hunting, and bibliographical tracking.

At Stanford University Press I found in Helen Tartar a humane and resourceful editor, in Jan Spauschus Johnson a patient and understanding associate editor, in Janet Mowery a thorough and unerring copy editor, and in John Feneron a remarkably accommodating production editor. I thank them for their rigor, expertise, and assistance. The anonymous readers for the press supplied such cogent and detailed suggestions that the final revision seemed almost to write itself.

In keeping with the subject of this book, I reserve some of my deepest gratitude for more personal connections. The Flint family—Nomie and Wes (who made it all possible) and Rob and Lucy (who made it lively)—have watched the genesis of this book (as so many other things) with bemusement, encouragement, and interest. To Gray Flint-Vrettos, who appeared during the latter stages of revision, I owe inordinate thanks for instilling the discipline needed to complete the book by constantly enticing me away from it. Finally, my most extensive obligations go to Athena Vrettos, who nurtured so many of the book's surviving arguments, scolded unruly sentences into decorous behavior, and trained ideas to follow their most logical order. Without her unfailing support, wisdom, and editorial skill, this book would have made a sorry entrance into the world.

Fellowships from the National Endowment for the Humanities and the American Society for Eighteenth-Century Studies, and a Faculty Recognition Award from the University of Michigan supplied crucial money and time for the research of this book. A portion of Chapter 3 was originally published in *ELH* 55, no. 2 (1988) and is reprinted by permission. A portion of Chapter 4 is reprinted by permission from *SEL Studies in English Literature* 29, no. 3 (1989).   C.F.

Contents

A Note to the Reader

In anthropology, sociology, demographics, and genealogy, words such as "family," "house," and "kinship" have rigorously defined meanings. Given, however, that eighteenth-century British culture relied on fluid terminology, I will be using such words in a more conditional sense than these other disciplines demand. In most of what follows, context will define the particular usage. But in general, by "family" I mean the group of people who share close biological, affective, and economic ties that individuals in the group regard as binding them to a dutiful code of conduct toward one another. "House" and "household" are meant to signify the architectural space and social relations whose relatively unified structure serves to regulate the needs of a family living together with whatever other figures it can afford to include in its places of residence. In some special cases, "family" and "household" may be virtually synonymous, as when a small family lives in one domicile without servants. I reserve "kinship" to designate that set of blood relations dictated by genealogical history. These terms will, I should add, have different inflections at different historical moments and according to variations in class and geography. Finally, I usually employ "domesticity" or "household government" when referring to an interest in and attachment to maintaining the economy of a household. "Domestic ideology," though closely related, signifies the practices and belief systems connected to the social and economic management of family, house, household, and kin.

Family Fictions

Introduction

to familiari´ze. (1) To make familiar; to make easy by habitude.
(2) To bring down from a state of distant superiority.
—Samuel Johnson, *Dictionary*

Familiar Fictions

At the center of Oliver Goldsmith's *The Vicar of Wakefield*, the
Primrose family commission a family portrait "so very large" that
they have "no place in the house to fix it" (83). The picture's unwieldy bulk suggests that the family's symbolic act, originally aimed
at improving their own social image, both distorts their domestic
appearance and, paradoxically, reveals its hidden nature. As the vicar
observes, "The picture . . . instead of gratifying our vanity, as we
hoped, leaned, in a most mortifying manner, against the kitchen
wall, where the canvas was stretched and painted, much too large to
be got through any of the doors, and the jest of all our neighbours"
(83). In failing to envision the unfitness of the portrait, the Primroses manifest a compulsion about representing familiar household relations that vexed eighteenth-century prose fiction in general. Like
many other fictional families, the Primroses are caught in a chastening process that exposes them to the dissonance of eighteenth-century household iconography. Here, Johnson's dual definition of the
verb "to familiarize," as both a comforting and a diminishing term,
captures the narrative's, as well as the period's, contrary need to
make the family appear both normal and mythical, bourgeois and
aristocratic, private and public. Ironically matching form and function, the very content of the picture duplicates this state of incoherence and excess:

My wife desired to be represented as Venus, and the painter was desired not to be too frugal of his diamonds in her stomacher and hair. Her two little ones were to be as Cupids by her side, while I, in my gown and band, was to present her with my books on the Whistonian controversy. Olivia would be drawn as an Amazon, sitting upon a bank of flowers, drest in a green joseph, richly laced with gold, and a whip in her hand. Sophia was to be a shepherdess, with as many sheep as the painter could put in for nothing; and Moses was to be drest out with an hat and white feather. Our taste so much pleased the 'Squire, that he insisted on being put in as one of the family in the character of Alexander the great, at Olivia's feet. This was considered by us all as an indication of his desire to be introduced into the family. (82–83)

A picture of chaos, in which a clergyman confronts his Venerean wife with textual admonitions about monogamy while their children appear in the guise of irreconcilable literary types, the painting reveals those dangers to the household that the Primroses doggedly ignore: the incompatibility of husband and wife, secret fantasies of power or virtue in the children, the incommensurability of family aspirations and financial means, and a predatory aristocracy. The vicar himself, as both narrator and member of the household, embodies the contradictions that the entire clan refuses to acknowledge. Consumed by their own domestic obsessions, the family's individuals are thus oblivious to the way in which their particular history intersects with the larger history of the family as a contested social structure.

Goldsmith's rendering of a family struggling to create a picture of itself indicates the complexity of making domestic images that both promote and accurately record household behavior. Wanting either to affirm Rousseau's observation that "there is no more charming picture than that of family" (12) or acknowledge that, in Charles Fourier's words, "all family relations are corrupt" (28), the book manifests the representational tensions of eighteenth-century domestic relations and their participation in a process of "defamiliarization," where what is familiar is made strange and exotic.[1] That is, in the process of standardizing family structure, the very reverse of Johnson's familiarization obtains: the conventional household becomes the site of aberrant and heightened relations. Goldsmith's portrayal of a domestic scene riven by competing representations of the household thus raises questions about the correspondence between eighteenth-century fiction's depiction of the family and its mode of storytelling. To what degree did the fiction's conventional emphasis on family life indicate that it popularized actual historical changes in how the family behaved? In other words, how were these changes of a nature to encourage a developing domestic structure commonly associated with novelistic plot? And how often, as the Primroses' embarrassing experience implies, did the fiction participate in an extensive cultural pretense about reconfiguring domestic relations that simply produced incoherence? Ultimately, the prose fiction seems to exemplify the ways in which several maneuvers for organizing household relations intersected—at times sharing approximate ideological objectives, at other times moving in radically different directions.[2]

The popularity of prose fiction in eighteenth-century Britain has, of course, been traced to an extraordinary number of cultural events. These include advances in printing technologies, the modernization of journalism, changes in readership and education, the development of circulating libraries, shifts in the institution of literature, the impact of philosophic realism and empiricism, the emergence of a leisured middle class, the feminization of discourse, and penal theories of social containment.[3] But the urge to align the history of the family with the history of prose fiction has been particularly acute. In one way or another, recent critics have often assumed that the popularity of the fiction in this period was partly a response to the development of the affective nuclear family (as distinct from the "extended family"), a modern normative ideal of social organization.[4] Indeed, one of the central issues that eighteenth-century fiction raises obsessively is the extent to which kinship binds the individual to natural obligations.[5]

The purpose of this book is to explain how eighteenth-century prose fiction used the family as an instrumental concept in a struggle to resolve cultural tensions that were themselves dependent on competing representations of kinship. It contends that by the time late-eighteenth-century writers looked back at their century's prose fiction and called it "the novel" they saw with eyes conditioned paradoxically to align "novelty" and "family" (which often implied tradition). Certainly, families are in their way conducive to novelistic form, but the period's domestic paradigms were as unwieldy as the fiction that both represented and enabled them. Early prose fiction, perhaps more than any other genre, merged its interest in family history with its own prolonged form. The encyclopedic nature of the works allowed for the minute examination of family concerns to an extent not usually or easily sustained in other literary genres. The critical term for this book is, consequently, "familiarization," which I use to denote how a novel representation of the family, made familiar through literary portrayal, modified preexisting and sometimes conflicting conceptions of domesticity. A distinctive attribute of this process is that a habitual set of relations must be alienated in order to undergo a compelling sequence of transformations back into ordinary experience. It takes "defamiliarization" a step further, returning the critical object to the ordinary. Traditional notions of the family are estranged, reconstituted as novel concepts, and then finally presented as natural social norms.

Ideally such an investigation would link the fictional material to established historical claims about the development of the family. Whether actual changes in family structure occurred in anything resembling a distinctive social transformation depends, however, upon how one characterizes historical process in eighteenth-century domestic relations. Ironically, the social institution perhaps most aimed at harmony has mostly produced contentiousness among its many commentators. This disagreement is reflected particularly in the argument over the modern constitution of the family. For better or worse, one of the most persistent historiographical claims is that at some point roughly in the seventeenth century the growing cultural emphasis on "individualism" and "affective" relations caused a shift in family structure from a relatively porous one that stressed kinship, lineage, and economic concerns (while repressing affection, marital choice, sexual pleasure, and children's needs) to a more limited one that encouraged individual gratification and intense loyalty among the "elementary" members of the family (husband, wife, and children). This historical account generally asserts that in the Early Modern Period barbaric forms of extended kinship gradually evolved into the liberal "modern family."[6]

The study of eighteenth-century domesticity, however, has been conditioned by a troubling and persistent disparity about how to interpret historical data concerning household relations. The nuclear family, in particular, has been an acute source of territorial positioning among historians and sociologists. Demographic analysis and social history have frequently relied on organic theories of cultural transformation to explain a multitude of tensions within the British family. Such approaches tend, in fact, to reproduce the exclusionary tactics of which families themselves have often been accused. Lawrence Stone's *Family, Sex and Marriage*, for example, provides a particular historical plot based on a spatial metaphor, according to which the family as a social grouping advances from an "open lineage" system between 1450 and 1630 to a "restricted patriarchal nuclear" formation between 1550 and 1700 and finally to a "closed domesticated nuclear" grouping between 1640 and 1800 (67–299). While Stone acknowledges the gradual and overlapping nature of these changes, he nevertheless describes the process as an inexorable and mostly progressive "walling-off of the nuclear family" (149). This forward movement is reflected, he asserts, in both statistical evidence and literary material, both of which, he implies, are mutually reinforcing. That is, different sources of evidence operate in a relatively unified field of cultural production, creating what he calls "a coherent composite picture" (25). Stone's theoretical assumptions about history thus mirror the type of family he regards as the culmination of the process he examines; like the closed domesticated nuclear family itself, his account strives for a reassuring and compartmentalized structure of relations.

In what amounts to a long and peculiarly fruitful divorce in the scholarship about family history, Stone's argument, which extends theories offered by earlier writers such as Philippe Ariès, Lewis Henry Morgan, and Talcott Parsons, challenges an equally popular view that reduces the household to a social and historical constant.

Viewing the family as more a function than a space, one related to the development of the state, historians such as Peter Laslett, Keith Wrightson, and Ralph Houlbrooke argue that the British nuclear family has always been a persistent historical paradigm. The family may have been differently figured at different times, but intimate conjugal and nuclear relations have remained constant or, if anything, diminished in effectiveness in the wake of modern industrialization.[7] As a group, these historians tend to be skeptical of accounts that rely on nonstatistical information. In *The World We Have Lost*, Laslett cautions against relying on imaginative literature to support claims about sociological behavior, isolating evidence that emerges out of a critical and statistical approach from that which derives from "deceptive" literary sources (90).[8] Laslett's model thus admits different and, at times, incompatible explanations of historical events, but also segregates and ranks them according to their apparent empirical persuasiveness or ideological bias; one is fully capable of disinterested reflection, the other is always potentially engaged in calculated misrepresentation. Such a model of historical investigation implicitly ratifies a relatively inflexible theory of discursive specialization. As I show in Chapter 1, however, the full range of published work on family relations in the period engages qualitative as well as quantitative assessments of the household that, in turn, challenge the attempt to dis-integrate literary and nonliterary evidence.

Despite their differences, a peculiar complementarity between the antithetical claims that the nuclear family either progressed or regressed at a critical phase roughly in the eighteenth century is reflected in the continuing justifications of these twin findings. In an attempt to accommodate both positions, Françoise Lautman has argued that "the extended family was found only among the ruling or wealthy classes" because they alone had the power to accumulate, protect, and transfer patrimony: "The real structure and function of the family have not changed. The change lies in the way society views a certain ideal that the ruling classes once practiced effectively" (252–53).[9] By demoting the extended family to a more limited position in the development of Western patterns of kinship, Lautman preserves a transhistorical view of the nuclear family while justifying the pervasive impression that the open lineage system exerted determinate influence as a historical force. Lautman thus shifts attention to the symbolic and often variable functions that different family types served in establishing "the social organization as a whole" (254). In doing so, however, she retains a generally monolithic assessment of the nuclear family, which she associates with a socially ineffective lower class; as a result, the nuclear group seems to lack the supple adaptive qualities of more "coherent" systems of kinship (259).[10]

The project of assessing specific conjugal behaviors in the eighteenth century while trying to clarify general cultural patterns that might account for them is a difficult task in itself. But it is compounded by the limits of structurally isolating the nuclear family from other household practices in the first place. This issue has, to some extent, been addressed by Nancy Armstrong and Leonard Tennenhouse, who view the opposing positions represented by Stone's evolutionary account and Laslett's functionalist one as reducible to a single ideological claim that is "exempt from history." In *The Imaginary Puritan* they observe that such histories of the family "reduce a rich variety of kinship relations and domestic practices down to a sentimental discourse that reflects present-day common sense, or popular psychology" (83). Although they do not provide an alternative account to these histories, Armstrong and Tennenhouse usefully suggest an approach according to which history functions as a network of shifting cultural behaviors that respond to various ideological pressures. Yet Armstrong's own pioneering work on "domestic fiction" charts a specific and ultimately dominant plot for the period's construction of family relations, in which the "domestic woman" assumed an exalted role in generating an ideal of the "modern individual" that "was first and foremost a woman" (*Desire and Domestic Fiction*, 8).[11] Her radical and transformative reassessment of domestic politics thus proceeds, in a deliberately polemical way, by foregrounding a particular domestic practice and form of kinship from among the "rich variety" of behaviors she and Tennenhouse later acknowledge.

Some of the most persistent controversies associated with domestic history derive from the tendency of many scholars to insulate an unchanging private domain of personal intimacy from a public sphere of work and government. This presumed fixity of household behavior allows the family either to dictate modes of public experience while being protected from them or to remain exclusively detached from such influences. By maintaining the essentially stationary role of the nuclear family, historians such as Alan Macfarlane, Ferdinand Mount, and Linda Pollock thus finesse both progressive and regressive domestic histories. Macfarlane, for example, claims that the nuclear family's unchanging contours over time—dating possibly back to early medieval England—suggest that such a family type is a "necessary, if not sufficient, cause of capitalism." Capitalism, in turn, becomes an ineluctable force that shapes British culture from its very beginnings and that emerges largely from the very family type it is supposed to have produced (see Macfarlane, *Marriage and Love*, 329–36). Pollock, in a similar though less-expansive vein, admonishes others to "ponder just why parental care is a variable so curiously resistant to change" (*Children*, 271).[12] Like Laslett, Macfarlane and Pollock regard the nuclear family as a well-established feature of human conduct, but they extol it not so much to bewail the erosion of its power as to defend a particular social and economic norm that continues to govern human behavior. Here, the variety of material and discursive practices that constitute the "nuclear family" is again subjected to definitional constraints.[13] These contending interpretations of family history thus produce not only a range of paradigms that run from the universal and conservative to the revolutionary and progressive, but also, within each paradigm, an equally ramified set of implications. Individually, despite their profound differences, each treats family history in terms of exclusive patterns of deployment; taken together, they indicate the "rich variety" that each seems constructed to deny.

In order to engage these compelling but apparently incompatible appraisals of the eighteenth-century British family, we need an explanation of how both fictional and nonfictional representations of the eighteenth-century family could produce the fierce polemical debates that have appeared. The teleological impulse behind the theory that domesticity followed a consistently linear trajectory toward the modern nuclear family is both its strength and its limitation. Because it links the history of the family to a culture's awareness of its own past, it demonstrates that the family can be treated as an institution, at least partly aware of its own historical position and construction. It also implies, however, that the family is the site only of revolution and never of conservation, isolating one definition of family from the wide array of domestic practices that the word historically signifies. It elides the very problem that Jacques Donzelot articulates in *The Policing of Families* in his discussion of eighteenth-century responses to interfamilial breakdown: "[H]armony between the order of families and the order of the state was more the result of a tactical collusion than that of a strategical alliance. . . . [T]here was indeed a temporary convergence on . . . the family's undesirable members; but whereas for families this concentration served the purpose of exclusion, for the state it was valuable as a means of checking the costly practices of the family, as a starting point for a policy of conservation and utilization of individuals" (25). Donzelot's remarks here can be extended to suggest that the progressive, regressive, and stationary arguments about the family's historical conditions mask certain complicating features of social interchange: that individual families themselves experience diverse structural transformations within a lifetime, that the correlation between the family and state is never a fixed one, and that any given culture will consist of a dynamic exchange among different types of domesticity, none of which can be fully understood in isolation.[14]

The historiographical construction of household behavior (with its enabling division of family groups into "extended" and "nuclear" types and its productive discussion of the historical process of those paradigms) has thus provided a model of the family that eighteenth-century discourses concerned with the variety of domestic practices and kinship patterns tended to blur. This book, consequently, provides an analysis of two intimately related subjects—family and fiction—that emphasizes competing and coexisting explanations of domestic ideology as part of a process of social reproduction rather than a single historical account of the family's development. It does not assume that the eighteenth-century British family operated according to a set of principles that only modern scholarship could illuminate, but rather that the period itself reveals productive tensions in its own family ideology. Emerging as variant portrayals of household conduct, these tensions are dispersed through a number of different genres and texts that it is the project of this book to examine. I claim, nonetheless, that the single most effective means for the period's own complex theorizing about family relations was prose fiction, largely because of its flexible incorporation of other discourses such as conduct books, philosophical treatises, and demographic studies.

If we look at the so-called rise of the nuclear family at the birth of the modern, industrial, capitalist state in Britain we find that it may have been essentially a semiotic event—what Jeremy Bentham called "a legal fiction" (17–18). It paralleled the efforts of a culture to disseminate an ideal capable of both nurturing an individual's sense of liberty and policing it, without, however, appearing to legislate affective behavior.[15] The belief in such a rise helped provide a context for creating professional and regulative discourses about the family that, without appearing invasive, sought to govern the conduct of individuals, families, and societies. The fiction, I claim, confronted a "new" image associated with progressive forces—the nuclear family—that already had a long history. The narrative prose fiction of the period, then, inscribed a desire to exalt the beginnings of a familial configuration that was neither entirely new nor untouched by historical context. In challenging the claims that the family either experienced a revolution in form or that it remained essentially unchanged, *Family Fictions* explains the persuasiveness of these opposing accounts of family history by arguing that they are among a set of divergent tactics used by eighteenth-century writers to refashion the symbolic and affective power of the family. Aligning a variety of sexual and domestic practices with authorized national interests, the purpose of this refashioning is to affirm the sentimental family's central role in managing civil behavior. At a time, however, when the middle class was beginning to scrutinize itself as a distinct social entity, its most popular form of literature reveals that many felt estranged from the most intimate and yet explosive of social experiences—family life. The prose fiction sought to channel these disturbingly fluid domestic feelings, yet it is itself haunted by the specter of unregulated affect.

One of the central issues I examine, then, is not so much whether the centrality of family relations in prose fiction should be attributed to changed domestic conduct, but whether it can be linked to a persistent reformulation of traditional family relations into other expedient forms.[16] My methodology therefore assumes that both discursive representations of the family and the practices they may have recorded are part of a series of negotiations within the social sphere. In thus arguing for a versatile perspective, I am influenced by Michel Foucault's notion of "tactical polyvalence" in the discourse surrounding the family's and state's deployment of sexuality (*History of Sexuality*, 100). The family, he argues, neither mirrors nor provides a model for society. Instead, it was employed to enable a variety of complementary interests, such as "Malthusian" controls of the birthrate, encouragement of "populationist" expansion, "medicalization" of sexual behavior, and "psychiatrization" of affective conduct (100). Yet Foucault ultimately resolves this interplay of tactics and local strategies into "an over-all strategy" that gains support from those "tenuous relations" as if they were its "prop and anchor point" (99). Here, Foucault transforms the stubborn plurality of various strategies suddenly, and without explanation, into two fixed entities that both sustain and moor an "over-all" form of power. In contrast, I regard those "tenuous relations" as legible but constantly modulating features of the social sphere, part of a network of temporary connections. The concept of "familiarization" is thus useful because a culture so constituted seeks to render habitual—as much through demography as through literature—the behavioral tactics it has itself made disruptive and alien.

Whether the nuclear family was old or new, eighteenth-century prose fiction's insistence on the importance of such a family, as it was either sentimentalized or desecrated, points to an urgent concern over its image that the fiction shared with the nonfictional literature. As a consequence, we can observe how, through fictional representation, writers entered a discursive field that presented dialectical views of the individual's responsibility to the family in order to renew the political force of established forms of kinship. Prose works of the period certainly shared the century's increased desire to regulate and rationalize the way families were created. That need is, perhaps, most visible in Lord Hardwicke's Marriage Act of 1753, which stipulated that the solemnization of marriage was to be limited entirely to marriages that were previously recorded by banns or license. As a result, enforcement of such procedures shifted from ecclesiastical to secular courts. The varied means of instituting marriage were thus reduced, at least in official discourse, to a monolithic system (by increasing secular control of the process). This urge to rationalize affective relations through legal sanctions found parallel expression in narrative conventions. In the same way that the Marriage Act operated selectively on a variety of conjugal rituals to produce an authoritative version of the family, eighteenth-century prose narratives frequently sought to separate themselves from other discursive practices in order to produce a unified domestic ideology. Thus the eighteenth-century writer's persistent assertion of the novelty of his or her domestic fiction, as opposed particularly to the romance, may have paralleled the century's desire to lend coherence to affective and sexual behavior by distilling a "new" form of matrimonial contract from the manifold practices that preceded it. But just as the Marriage Act incited a range of attempts by individuals to circumvent the law (from couples eloping to Gretna Green in Scotland to communities maintaining folk traditions in defiance of new legalities), writers also found ways to refashion the narrative paradigms they ostensibly rejected, reincorporating both familiar and novel forms.[17]

Domesticating Narrative

That there was an intimate link between eighteenth-century fiction and the literature of marital and familial behavior seems indisputable. Both Daniel Defoe and Samuel Richardson wrote conduct literature that not only itemized conjugal, parental, and filial duties but also clearly inspired fictional treatments of those same concerns. Eliza Haywood wrote twin treatises on marital conduct, one entitled *The Wife*, the other entitled *The Husband. In Answer to the Wife*, and the volatile concerns of these books appear in much of her mature fiction. Successful writers such as Elizabeth Singer Rowe, Penelope Aubin, and Fanny Burney were all praised for the moral didacticism of their work, particularly insofar as they affirmed the moral imperatives of domestic harmony and economy. Even so radical and unconventional a thinker as Mary Wollstonecraft wrote fiction that manifested the moral aims of conduct material; *The Wrongs of Woman* dramatized the social conditions of female experience that prompted *A Vindication of the Rights of Woman*, which was both a political document and a manual on domestic behavior. In fact, a number of conduct books, such as *The Domestic Instructor*—which was "selected principally from celebrated authors"—simply extracted particularly effective exhortatory material from domestic prose fiction.

Such apparent collusion between "fictional" and "instructional" discourse inevitably implies a dynamic interchange between conventionally literary and nonliterary works as they purportedly affect social behavior. Recent critics such as Nancy Armstrong emphasize the profitable exchange between these two modes of writing, although Armstrong reverses the customary direction of influence between fictional representations of household economy and nonfictional ones: "In time, following the example of fiction, new kinds of writing—sociological studies of factory and city, as well as new theories of natural history and political economy—established modern domesticity as the only haven from the trials of a heartless economic world" (*Desire and Domestic Fiction*, 8). Such intertextuality suggests, according to Armstrong, that the conventional distinctions that modern criticism draws between the fictional and nonfictional material distorts their effective interplay. This intertextual exchange substantiates the view that a concerted effort was made to refigure domesticity, and that the effort was, at least initially, a largely discursive activity. To see prose fiction and conduct literature as the principal agents of change in domestic economy, however, severely limits modes of production in eighteenth-century culture to terms that privilege the textual over the nontextual and that exclude other symbolic systems, such as architecture, theatrical performance, painting, sculpture, and even the elaborate processions of the royal family. And the extensive affiliation between fictional subject matter and the concerns of conduct literature does not settle the question whether such ideological compatibility indicates "actual" cultural changes. It does, nonetheless, express a pervasive desire (in both the eighteenth and twentieth centuries) to represent the need for such fundamental changes. Amplifying the scientific and philosophic rationalism synthesized by Locke and championed by others such as Bacon, Descartes, Hobbes, and Newton, eighteenth-century writers of prose fiction began to address the problems associated with the newly conceived social, political, and economic status of the individual without necessarily transforming the social contexts that produce individuals. They were concerned with the effect of these intellectual changes on the fabric of everyday life, on how individuals juggled their own intense interests with those of the family, the magistrate, the landowner, the mob, and the crown. At the same time, such writers also wanted to diminish some of the power of the individualism they were, in theory, promoting.

It was especially in the instances of love and family roles that fiction sought to clarify the relation between self and other. Childhood and courtship became imbued with profound ideological significance. These were not new thematic issues, of course, but they were treated differently in prose narratives than in, say, poetry or drama. For example, the figure of the child began to attract greater attention. If writers were to address the problems of what defined and what constituted the natural rights of a human being, they first had to trace the origins of individual desires and impulses and differentiate them from what society provided for or demanded of the individual. As part of this process of differentiation, the relation between a person and his or her family needed to be questioned, not only in terms of the distinction between self and other (which, as Freud suggests, is codified first within kinship paradigms), but also

in terms of developing a social consciousness, of systematically training the child's mind.[18] Prose fiction, at least by the mid-century, had
become a pedagogical tool aimed at normalizing adult relations either through an analysis of successful child rearing, or, conversely,
through an examination of the negative effects of inadequate upbringing.

Similarly, the process of the courtship and marriage of characters
just entering adulthood became a relatively dominant, even exclusive, feature of the prose fiction. The extramarital affairs in the
scandal chronicles, the antisocial behavior in criminal literature, the
exoticism of the travelogue, the random adventures of the picaresque,
the complex erotic alliances of the romance—all fictional subjects
and forms that flourished in the sixteenth and seventeenth centuries—were gradually replaced or absorbed in the eighteenth century
by narratives dealing with the affective experiences of young adults
seeking conjugal bliss in a domestic environment. Even before Richardson, writers like Elizabeth Singer Rowe and Penelope Aubin were
domesticating prose fiction;[19] their work encouraged later writers to
rescue such writing from its reputation for immorality and lack of
realism by producing works that detailed the experiences of heroines
and heroes who affirmed domestic comfort, virtue, and common
sense and that could be read in and for the family. As Jean Baptiste
de Freval wrote about *Pamela* in a letter to Richardson (who
promptly added it to the editorial puffs of the first edition): "[I]t will
be found worthy a Place, not only in all Families (especially such as
have in them young Persons of either Sex) but in the Collections of
the most curious and polite Readers. For, as it borrows none of its
Excellencies from the romantic Flights of unnatural Fancy, its being
founded in Truth and Nature, and built upon Experience, will be a
lasting Recommendation to the Discerning and Judicious" (I, 4). As
the de Freval quotation suggests, prose fiction was, by many, coming to be identified with the family and defined in terms of social efficacy.

An especially protracted form of narrative, domestic fiction could
provide a detailed account of the intricate affairs of the family. In effect, it anatomized the family. Grounding its own language in the

"objective" prose of the educational treatise, conduct book, sermon, and marriage manual, it was admirably equipped to explore the vital concerns of the "modern" family: the duties of children to their parents, the responsibilities of parents toward their children, the standards of conduct husbands and wives should adopt toward one another, the relations that constitute the nucleus of the family. But simply to say that the prose fiction examined the family with a new intensity does not necessarily prove that the family itself experienced profound historical changes in organization. Moreover, the prose fiction's need to expound domestic norms while continuously defending its novelty created an almost intractable aesthetic problem: that is, how to reconcile claims of inimitability with the desire to provide standard models of behavior.

The fundamental questions that prose fiction's exhaustive description of domestic life raises thus have more to do with the family's image than with its historical identity. Did literary depictions precede and enable the changes they portrayed? Or, conversely, did the prose narratives attempt to popularize a change that either never happened or occurred long before? Were they serving ideological aims that simply refashioned images of the family in such a way as to bring a semblance of order to the different overlapping functions of kinship? One way to answer such questions is to regard them as arising from eighteenth-century attempts to rewrite history (domestic as well as "political") in accordance with modern epistemological values that were themselves constantly shifting in ideological function.[20]

What writers in the second half of the eighteenth century and throughout the nineteenth century realized (and sometimes disguised) is that the structural and semiotic patterns of narrative discourse, in addition to describing and giving instruction on familial affairs, formally manifest the complex social mechanisms that constitute blood relations and marital alliances in what is conventionally regarded as the "family."[21] The intense detail of the prose fiction, its protracted form, and its sentence-by-sentence scrutiny of the verbal and familial intricacies of relationships evinces an idealized, self-sufficient community of affective individuals whose relationships to each other are concise and fully legible. Thus, despite its often negative representation of family, eighteenth-century prose narrative reified family structure, constructing a cognitive as well as descriptive framework that by its very nature endorsed "familiar" relations. Eighteenth-century fiction usually treated the family as a given, a natural order, rather than a historically constituted entity, and its literary form—the prosaic treatment of a fundamentally ordinary and familiar world—represents that assumption. Though glorifying the power of the individual to resist oppression, coercion, and social injustice, and frequently depicting the family as an institutional force imprisoning "a strong intelligent offspring" (Paulsen, "Pilgrimage and the Family," 78), the prose fiction of this period was equally concerned with moral instruction, with synthesizing the radical energies of individualism and the pressures to conform to social and ethical standards of behavior.

Representations of the nuclear family thus served at least two important socializing functions: they nurtured the Lockean idea of cooperation and contract that would ideally govern human behavior in the marketplace and the political arena; and they accommodated the new valuation of personal liberty, subordinating the role of parents to one that ensured the child's autonomy. The recurring appearance of the rebellious child opposing an inflexible family signals not simply the conflict between self and society, but the complicated adjustments in the social fabric caused by the constant mutation of authority and liberty in eighteenth-century culture. The prose fiction of the period instructed children and parents to regard the family as an ideological force that refined both individual autonomy and a sense of contractual obligation that would ensure that autonomy, creating a change not so much in practice as in perception. At least in the realm of fiction, the radical break associated with individualism also involved a consolidation and, in some cases, a conservative reevaluation of political or civic obligation. As Carol Kay notes, "the novel defines its political authority by setting up a comparison or contrast of itself with other sorts of discourse that make direct claims of power and influence" (9); texts that ardently differentiate themselves (such as prose fiction) are just as likely to be positioning themselves as objects of power as the forms they seek to dispel (such as the romance).

Eighteenth-century narratives were not merely about the process of self-definition, the birth of the hero, the rise in stature of the individual, or the emergence of "man"; they were also about the social determination of the very concept of "individuality." The luxury of an immutable self able to exert its will freely required an elaborate collaboration among family members, educators, doctors, the clergy, legislators, and politicians. We see documented in the prose fiction of this period not only a cultural shift toward the self, but an increased sensitivity to the signs that would allow that selfhood to come into being. Indeed, the enforcing of "affective individualism," the affirmation of empiricism, and the supposed consolidation of the nuclear family point also to ideological circumstances that constrain individuals by making them seem free-acting agents with autonomous political and social rights. What appears to be subverting "traditional society"—the principle of unrestricted liberty—can in fact be rewriting it. Prose fiction in the eighteenth century chronicles that profound reconception of the individual's relation to community, from the family circle to the national estate. The unstable relations between eighteenth-century protagonists and their families indicate not a simple conflict between traditional values and the values of individualism, but a complex and dynamic modification of existing ideologies by new ideological pressures.

In eighteenth-century fiction, Lockean paradigms of the self are embodied in characters whose peculiar task is to learn to become themselves in some kind of self-conscious way. Pedagogically, the fiction most often dramatizes the actions of a central figure whose alienated energies initially threaten to disrupt social order, but who in the end serves in some way to unify it through his or her acquisition of knowledge. In *Pamela,* Part II, the doctrinal sequel to Richardson's first, enormously popular success, the heroine capitalizes on the "dreadful experiences" of her early history by becoming a model of social deportment and by inculcating the same behavior in her new "peers"—the aristocratic friends and relations of Mr. B. Quoting extensively from Locke's *Thoughts Concerning Education* in the concluding pages of her collected letters, she brings harmony to the aristocratic world, directing both the government of her own family and that of the neighboring gentry by consciously turning her private diary into an edifying public document. Thus Richardson explicitly manipulates his story to express a growing conviction that prose fiction should serve an exemplary domestic purpose.

As Jay Fliegelman has persuasively shown, "the new rationalist pedagogy (and its moral sense and Rousseauistic variations) may be said to have contributed immeasurably to the form of the novel's development" (36). In other words, prose fiction acts as a pedagogical tool, helping to transmit and popularize Lockean doctrine either by positive or negative example. Indeed, if we take this argument one step further, we can see that the very form of domestic narratives, following the injunctions of Locke's civil, philosophical, and educational principles, was becoming the structural equivalent of the new philosophy, linking individualism, contractualism, linear psychology, educative enlightenment, and the association of ideas to achieve representational fullness. The prose fiction did not simply mirror social reality; it was the aesthetic manifestation of the things it examined, fashioning itself on the ideals of the nuclear family. Insofar as the family was itself subject to both internal and external pressures of variable intensity and range, the fiction that modeled itself on the nuclear family tended to produce overlapping models of social interaction.

The relation of narrative form to family structure is not, then, simply one of ideological or epistemological reflection. It is one in which narrative art translates the values of the family into formal precepts. One might say that a significant aim of Western fictional narrative, following Locke's reasoning, is to allow the writer to represent characters and societies as organic entities that complement the world outside the text. Individual characters and the worlds they inhabit manifest a process of engendering, conception, and development that produces a credible universe of human and object relations. By this I mean that prose fiction not only proposes alternative modes of conduct (actions intended to change the reader's epistemology); it also imaginatively reshapes the world as a structure de-

fined by meaningful and, usually, temporal elements. As Edward
Said suggests, prose narratives are aesthetic objects that supply connections to a degree usually lacking in the phenomenal world; they
are defined largely by the extent to which they render complex but
disclosable relations among characters and between characters and
their environment (93). Prose fiction satisfies the writer's (and presumably the reader's) desire to modify reality in the Lockean sense,
to generate not only characters but also causal links, binding genealogies of figures, actions, and motives, which are much more determining in the fictive world than outside of it.

Thus, eighteenth-century prose fiction naturally poses a question
connected to the earlier one of whether narrative is centrally about
the family: do fictional relations take the form of, or generate, family relations? Both narrative and genealogy usually develop in linear
fashion, acquiring coherence by making the relations between characters or kin meaningful and by plotting a beginning and end that
accentuate the continuing temporal (or historical) dimension of human experience (what Said calls "dynastic ideology" and what Locke
calls "personal identity"). This is especially true of the "realistic"
writers of the eighteenth and nineteenth centuries, who used the
family paradigm as a source for both their subject and their technique.

This coupling of family and fiction, I would argue, is a constitutive part of the eighteenth-century writer's narrative procedure as a
whole. In relating stories of a certain length and complexity, relations of a different sort seem to become necessary. Indeed, the word
"relation" has historically conveyed the dual significance of consanguinity and storytelling with which this book is concerned. From
the Latin *referre*, meaning to refer (literally, to be thrust [*ferre*] back
in between [*re*]), the word "relation" originally designated a signifying act by which an object or person was classified or referred. According to the *O.E.D.*, it was employed particularly in terms of
other corresponding objects or persons. With use it eventually
served, in addition to its taxonomic function, as a synonym for narrative activity, presumably because a well-told tale brought disparate
events into cogent relationship, putting episodes logically between

others. Subsequently, it was also used in conjunction with the family, to describe an individual's subordinate place in a network of social and biological connections or to designate a determinate set of resemblances. As in the word "family," which derives from the Latin word for servant (*famulus*), "relation" bears the etymological traces of a process whereby an alien aspect of what appears to be an easily contained and classifiable condition is made to seem normal— that our "blood" should predispose us to people we had never met, that telling one's story required being thrust back between others, or that a household might be defined by its servants.[22]

The coincidence that the word "relation" should denote the act of narrating and the condition of kinship, and the fact that both meanings developed out of the concept of subordination to a larger or corresponding category in a structure of knowledge, emphasizes the strange doubleness of domestic fiction. If, as is often claimed, telling one's story is a means of establishing power and knowledge, of verifying one's independent identity, the etymology of the word "relation" implies that storytelling conversely subordinates and disperses one's individuality by emphasizing the fixed connection between the self and a larger social whole. In the context of prose fiction, which has historically valued its own newness (or novelty) and whose linguistic origins would seem to verify its relationless status, the notion of relatedness seems, then, particularly problematic. As much as narrative fiction appears to empower the storyteller, the protagonist, or the reader, it also seems to subordinate these versions of the self to linguistic relations, to the rigid logic of classification, to, in effect, the conception of the family. Thus the relative context of the prose fiction seems to counteract its theoretical claims of self-generation and novelty, reestablishing a complex idiom of familial determinism. To be in such a position is, assuredly, to obtain an identity, although identity must be understood not as a transcendental condition but as a social necessity stemming from one's apparently natural relations to the world. Prose fiction may have appealed to a wide readership in the eighteenth century because it dramatized in a particularly acute and extended way the complex linear and associative process that eighteenth-century rationalists attributed to everyday experience. At the same time, it seemed to provide the more liberating opportunity to, in Tristram Shandy's words, "tell my story my own way" (41).

In eighteenth-century prose fiction, the desire to conflate genealogical and textual parables is particularly acute. Like the sublimation of commonplace experience in enlightenment aesthetics generally, the fiction expresses concerns about how ordinary family experience can be effectively dramatized. These concerns are, in turn, akin to the eighteenth-century author's anxieties about giving birth to a "new" form of writing. They are motivated by the desire to render surprising the very behaviors they hoped subsequently to make entirely familiar. It is this problem of "familiarization" that shapes my discussions of specific eighteenth-century narratives and their repeated convergence on issues of origin, identity, and continuity. In prose narrative, the storytelling act, which initially seems to be one of empowerment and imaginative freedom, is, as Said puts it, "a desire to create a new or beginning fictional entity while accepting the consequences of that desire" (82). That is, a narrative, once engendered, constrains the writer to a structure that is determined by the coherence of its internal relations and for which the writer has an aesthetic responsibility that approximates the responsibility of a parent to a child. In effect, prose fiction is engaged in the same institutional process as the family: making relations of power and subordination seem natural and neutral. The eighteenth-century view that the novel justly supplanted the romance because it more faithfully reproduced everyday life may be regarded as a contributing aspect of prose fiction's institutionalization. In much the same way that the rise of individualism can be seen as an ambiguous break with the past, one that in certain ways reconstituted the claims of society over the individual, the tendency of realistic prose narrative to glorify a natural representation of the world so that the resulting vision is always new, unique, individual, and liberated, may be regarded as an ironic adjunct to its dependence on relational patterns, its strengthening of expressive force through descriptions of subjugation, filiation, and dynastic continuity.[23]

Family Practice

In this book, I trace the relationship between family and fiction as much in terms of the increased sophistication of eighteenth-century narrative theory and practice as in terms of the supposed historical development of the nuclear family. Each of the following chapters provides a variant of eighteenth-century domestic ideology that exemplifies what Donzelot calls the "tactical collusion" or "temporary convergence" of household doctrines. The works I examine, in other words, demonstrate a preferred mode of representing the family that serves several interconnected functions: reinforcing the specific artistic and ideological aims of each text, positioning that representation of family against competing models of domesticity, and, ultimately, entering a wider network of both literary and non-literary discourses about household government.

The literary texts I discuss—works by Aphra Behn, Daniel Defoe, Samuel Richardson, Eliza Haywood, Horace Walpole, Laurence Sterne, and Mary Wollstonecraft—were not only remarkably popular or controversial but also represent a sufficiently wide range of narrative types, formal devices, and gender differences to support my claims about the competing representations of the family within the eighteenth century itself. These texts are cogent examples of the different manifestations of domestic ideology that recur in eighteenth-century prose fiction. Because they are also the works of both male and female writers, I hope to have avoided the onesidedness that structures many noteworthy approaches to eighteenth-century prose fiction, such as John Bender's, Lennard Davis's, and Michael McKeon's highlighting of male writers in their studies of the origins of the novel, or, conversely, Catherine Gallagher's, Jane Spencer's, and Janet Todd's corrective examinations of the history of fiction in which the works of female writers are separated from those of their male counterparts.[24] In some instances, I have chosen certain works of an author over others—*Pamela* instead of *Clarissa*, *Robinson Crusoe* instead of *Roxana*—because their largely ignored sequels pursue the domestic trajectory of characters beyond the period leading up to marriage and provide a much more comprehensive account of those characters' experiences with marital strife, child rearing, and conflicts with kin.

There are, inevitably, omissions, such as Henry Fielding's *Tom Jones* or *Amelia*, Tobias Smollett's *Humphrey Clinker*, Fanny Burney's *Evelina*, and Elizabeth Inchbald's *A Simple Story*. Indeed, the various accounts of family structure I analyze in this book appear throughout eighteenth-century fiction and are intended to evoke connections to texts and authors beyond those I discuss. For example, although there are enormous differences between Richardson and Fielding (and a long critical tradition examining them), the kind of analysis I would perform on *Tom Jones* or *Amelia* would simply verify that Fielding, like Richardson, regarded the family as an analogue to the novel, consistently linking the structure of his fiction to the language of kinship, household management, and family duty: "we consider a Book," he says, "as the Author's Offspring, and indeed as the Child of his Brain" (Fielding, *Tom Jones*, 2: 568).[25] Similarly, Smollett's narrative echoes points I raise in discussions of both Defoe and Richardson about the need to convert the lack of domestic security into an opportunity to refashion family relations. Burney's and Inchbald's work on the relationship between domestic propriety and limited household revolt reinforces my analyses of these issues as they are more emphatically deployed in Behn and Wollstonecraft.

In Chapter 1, I begin with a variety of discourses about the family with which the fiction was in dialogue. Using sermons, conduct books, legal discourse, medical tracts, philosophical treatises, and demographic and economic works, I discuss eighteenth-century British perspectives on the history of kinship, particularly in relation to the imputed rise of the nuclear family. The chief problem this chapter addresses is the extent to which we can claim that a dramatic change in family structure occurred in the period under consideration. Do seventeenth- or eighteenth-century accounts of the family constitute an "anthropology" that either supports or negates claims made by nineteenth- and twentieth-century studies of family history, some charting a progressive movement toward nuclear affect, others affirming the transhistorical existence of the nuclear family?

As part of a network of related discourses that sought to produce an authoritative model of the family into which it could dispose various forms of domestic and affective behavior, prose fiction frequently reproduced the interaction between different social policies, from those implied in demographic studies to those advocated in sermons. That the British family was, in fact, an object of reformation discourse in this period is indicated by a series of crucial historical events, from Locke's attack in *Two Treatises of Government* (1690) on Robert Filmer's *Patriarcha* (1680) to the Marriage Acts of 1753 and 1835. The relative ineffectiveness of these philosophical, political, and legal attempts to delimit customs governing affective behavior reveals, however, the indeterminate exchange between official familial discourse and cultural practice. That indeterminacy is implicit in the fiction's tendency to pit its reformist purposes against its goal of quantifying, in William Godwin's phrase, "things as they are" (1).[26]

The subsequent chapters trace the engagements of specific authors with the manifold tactics that eighteenth-century culture employed covertly to control the meaning of the family. In analzying this material, I use three heuristic terms to organize the range of narrative practices by which eighteenth-century British prose fiction articulated its contested relation with family ideology. The three terms—"marginalization," "legitimation," and "disavowal"—correspond roughly to three eighteenth-century approaches to the social assessment of the British family: (1) regarding the family as a mere supplement to other social institutions such as the church or the monarchy; (2) affirming its central role in managing civil behavior; and (3) describing its problematic relation to cultural mechanisms of power. I do not claim that these terms function dialectically in the narrow sense of the word: that is, one is not the cognitive by-product (either materially or ideologically) of the "productive" interaction between the others. Rather, they are interactive (and at times conflicting) modes of narrative production, and, while I chart them here in roughly chronological fashion, they do not necessarily appear in a consistent developmental sequence throughout the century. Instead, I intend them as flexible conceptual tools for describing gen-

eral tendencies. They characterize rather than define fictional practice at certain times in the period, and particular works of prose
fiction frequently evince all three in varying degrees. Whereas
previous critical accounts of eighteenth-century British fiction have
often read its descriptions of the family either as part of progressive
historical trends or as evidence of cultural decline, my analysis of
prose fiction narratives emphasizes complementary, and sometimes
contradictory, transformations in eighteenth-century domestic practice and representation. These, in turn, suggest that advancement
and decline are not mutually exclusive patterns of historical social
change but aspects of an epistemology of behavior that, in different
times and places and for different purposes, can just as easily ratify
progressive as regressive (or even static) interpretations of culture.

Chapter 2 addresses the first tactic—marginalization—by discussing how Aphra Behn's conflation of romance and realism in *The
Fair Jilt* expresses her ambiguous response to the necessity of the
family in both the constitution of female identity and the construction of narrative plot. For the most part, that ambiguity serves a
complex rhetorical and ideological purpose; though a necessary constituent, the family in Behn's fiction is denied prominence as a structural component of the text. The family is both an immanent and
an immaterial ideal. In Behn's fiction, nonmarital romantic passion
(of the dangerous sort the jilt Miranda indulges) is ultimately censured; but the family does not, as a result, acquire significant ideological force. While romance simply expends itself, the family is already permanently disabled. In Behn's short scandal narratives,
which constitute the majority of her prose fictions, female rapaciousness underscores the anti-courtship and anti-domestic impulse
of Restoration narrative; they do not validate domestic ideology, in
part because sexual politics in Behn's fiction endorse the fluid sexual
practice of the Stuart court in which the family chiefly signified political alliance. Behn's use of romance may in fact be aimed at demystifying the household implications of an empirical ideology (the
assumption that an intensive examination of everyday experience reinforces rational judgment, for example). Indeed, Behn's fiction already contains a critique of the domestic realism it seems to herald

and the romance it still echoes; in a sense, it renders strange both of these models of narrative and affective relations, only to recuperate them as strategies for creating a more critical definition of the family. If we regard the scandal chronicle as sensationalized romance (that is, as the condensing of romance's heightened passion and decorum into spectacle), then we can see Behn's deployment of feminocentric romance in her narratives as the means by which she couples female transgression with the formal demands of prose fiction. The family appears as an institutional force in these tales, but its marginal status in the various plots indicates both its sublimated function as an organizing element of narration and Behn's antipathy to domestic coercion.

In Chapter 3, I examine an alternative use of marginalization by concentrating on Defoe's symbolic substitutions of family relations in *The Life and Strange Surprizing Adventures of Robinson Crusoe* and *The Farther Adventures of Robinson Crusoe*. Unlike Behn, Defoe marginalized family in an attempt to glorify individual autonomy without sacrificing the benefits of civil government. Crusoe's adventures enact a much more radical displacement of the family than Miranda's, but they ultimately exonerate a paternal economic system that erases female labor and makes desire a supplement to economic, and specifically masculine, efficiency. Yet by retaining the essential features of domesticity, Defoe's male protagonists never fully escape the determining effect of the very social relations they persistently flee. Like the scandal chronicles, travel narratives, and criminal fictions popular in Defoe's day, his narratives produce an apparent disjuncture between the writing self and the family, merely sublimating the role kinship plays in defining both individual identity and narrative form. If *The Fair Jilt* delineates the attempt by a female figure to enter political relations by making her conventional domestic sphere an adjunct to experience rather than an end in itself, Defoe's masculocentric narratives dramatize male attempts to exclude competing domestic relations in favor of subordinate and symbolic ones (like Friday). The familiar realm, already diminished in practice, is figuratively reappropriated and naturalized by the seemingly self-sufficient adventurer in his quest for social and economic power.

The second tactic used to "familiarize" prose fiction—what I call "legitimation"—appears repeatedly in narratives written after the 1740's (though it existed long before then) and is exemplified in the work of writers such as Haywood, Richardson, and Fielding (and earlier in Aubin and Jane Barker). In Chapters 4 and 5, I examine closely the nature of familial ideology in Richardson's *Pamela* and Haywood's *Miss Betsy Thoughtless*. Preserving the essential conflict between self-definition and social coercion that characterizes earlier prose fiction, these writers, instead of sublimating the conflict, examine the psychological, social, and political consequences of kinship in overt and self-conscious ways. In *Pamela, Clarissa, Sir Charles Grandison, Miss Betsy Thoughtless*, and *The History of Jemmy and Jenny Jessamy*, the relevance of the family to narrative acts is explicit. Indeed, much of the difference between Behn or Defoe and Richardson and Haywood lies in the degree to which the family experience becomes the primary issue and unifying force of the work. Fundamentally ordinary conditions, such as the daily employment of a serving girl or the courtship of a young lady, are made to seem alien through overcharged, sometimes sensational, domestic events. Yet the estrangement of household relations in Richardson and Haywood occurs not through the displacement of family ideology but through its profound intensification.

The purpose of these "legitimations" is ultimately to stabilize relations and to establish narrative closure, even when the protagonist's will and identity seem naturally opposed to unity or finality. What is central is the protagonist's relation to the conception of a stable family and the material prosperity that the family embodies. These texts pose a number of questions that arise with stubborn frequency in late-eighteenth- and nineteenth-century fiction. When and how should property belonging to the parents become property of the child? Must the generational transference of domestic authority always be accompanied by strife? And how is the desire to leave one's family rendered in narrative plots as a natural and an ethical desire?

Chapter 4 addresses these questions by closely examining the vexed nature of familial ideology in Richardson's *Pamela* (Parts I and II), viewing the heroine's fraught absorption into an affluent upper-class family as a peculiarly triumphant erasure of self into a legitimate affective symbol. Tracing the verbal and social manipulations of the word "familiar" (as in familiar letter), we can see how Richardson collapses family ideology wholly onto a solitary and usually female icon of domestic propriety. Making lower-class individualism the mechanism (one might say the handmaiden) of social regeneration at the most basic level, *Pamela* converts an abnormal event (marriage between upper and lower classes) into a normal one in order to reform the dominant household norm. In Richardson, then, male rapaciousness replaces the female aggression that appears repeatedly in Behn's work; the victim is instead an already sufficiently domesticated heroine, and her suffering paradoxically produces a stable "self," which in turn generates family harmony. Ultimately, I argue, the blurring of Pamela's letters with her pregnant body and her assimilation into an affluent marriage enable the final reduction of her to a family "Cypher," the ideal image of her incorporation into a domestic economy.

Chapter 5 extends this discussion of self-management in the eighteenth-century domestic woman to examine the moral reformation of a resistant female protagonist, rather than the reformation of discrepant household norms by a model heroine. Where Richardson legitimates the domestic subject by repeatedly exposing her to external dangers, other writers of the period couple such assaults with perilous behavior that originates within the subject. In *The History of Miss Betsy Thoughtless*, Haywood validates both her profession and her heroine by examining the opposition between social expectation and individual desire that is signaled in the title as the contest between "history" and "thoughtlessness." Reproduced throughout the work, this pattern of alternating the remembering and forgetting of one's behavior defines both the characteristic operations of Betsy's mind and the movement of narrative itself. According to eighteenth-century domestic ideology, when vanity and irrationality overtake the female mind—when a woman's self-importance supplants the legitimate desires of men—social anarchy ensues. Betsy's thoughtlessness paradoxically aligns her "progress" with the repetition of folly.

This folly is transformed into justification, however, by the heroine's unusual domestic incorporation in the last quarter of the narrative, where she goes through an unhappy marriage, separation, widowhood, and happy remarriage. Such unconventional legitimation of her shifting marital status (at least by eighteenth-century standards) provides a surprisingly radical complement to the narrative's more conservative mortification of Betsy's desires. To a large extent, her history marks prose fiction's historic shift in balance from scandal chronicle (the corrosion of family ideology) to courtship narrative (the conversion to family ideology). Indeed, Haywood appears to be a significant link between earlier writers such as Behn and Defoe and later ones such as Burney and Austen. *The History of Miss Betsy Thoughtless*, for example, merges the sexual indiscretion and domestic propriety that prose fiction engages throughout the eighteenth century in the heroine herself; combining scandal chronicle, bildungsroman, roman à clef, and domestic fiction, Haywood's work also consolidates diverse generic modes through an inclusive form of legitimation.

Not all the prose fiction written in the second half of the eighteenth century, however, follows the unifying pattern that is represented in *Pamela, Miss Betsy Thoughtless,* or the didactic work of Penelope Aubin. Indeed, Richardson's scathing indictment of the bourgeois family in *Clarissa* helped produce a number of radical texts that began to question the ideals of conventional family life, often delineating them without recourse to the pious religious comforts that Richardson employed to check his own radical impulses. In the concluding chapter, I use Horace Walpole's *The Castle of Otranto*, Laurence Sterne's *The Life and Opinions of Tristram Shandy, Gentleman*, and Mary Wollstonecraft's unfinished work, *The Wrongs of Woman: or, Maria*, to describe the widespread "disavowal" of the family among many authors, some more radical than others, writing later in the eighteenth century. In fact, the latter part of the century is marked by an increased number of narratives that scrutinize the psychological, social, and political consequences of kinship in fundamentally skeptical ways. The anxieties about household government, affective relations, and genealogical imperatives articulated by the mid-century writers become central and disruptive features in the work of Walpole, Sterne, and Wollstonecraft. More than ever before, the "familiarization" of prose fiction discloses an apparent inconsistency between moral purpose and narrative function.

In these later works external factors disrupt the comfortable world of the family, threatening to undo it or turn it into a force of repression. The "growth" of the protagonist is linked to social collapse and realignment—that is, to historical process. Though family serves patriarchal society, its weaknesses become so apparent that patriarchy itself appears to be intrinsically and fatally flawed. This third tactic, then, is characterized by narratives that are both aesthetically and ideologically fragmented and that frequently exhaust themselves in confronting antithetical impulses about the family and fiction. My use of the term "disavowal" is thus akin to Patricia Spacks's analysis of eighteenth-century "plots of affiliation," a term she employs in *Desire and Truth* to describe a sentimental narrative's release from the stringency of "plots of power," where the story is determined by the linear reproduction of family connections instead of a looser alliance of close relations that fall outside biological kin (114–19). Unlike Spacks, however, I regard such plots as invariably entangled by the power they seek to annul. For example, *Tristram Shandy*, probably the most obvious instance of the shift in attitude that I am describing, simultaneously celebrates, exploits, and denudes the sentimental portrayal of the family as it (de)constructs its own narrative order. The rise of sentimentalism was, paradoxically, both the announcement of a new benevolent attitude toward the family and politics and a self-conscious critique of such ideal sentiments.

The resurgence of romance as a tenable mode, particularly in the gothic and sentimental romances late in the century, thus signals both the atavistic persistence of seemingly obsolete genres and the way in which authors sought to adjudicate the politics of kinship even when they seemed determined to disavow the conventional family. This diffusion of radical thought about individual rights, political equality, and self-respect challenged the implicit assumptions that had previously fortified domestic fiction. The narratives of this period are provocative largely for the way in which they use the image of the family both to invoke enlightenment beliefs about the nature of subjectivity, class, and gender and to submit those beliefs to an intense and often withering social scrutiny. The emotional extravagance of gothic and sentimental fiction toward the end of the century, part of a melancholic nostalgia for older forms of social ritual, offers an often strange example of how prose narrative as object of consciousness provides an archeology of the family in which layers of different types of domestic structure persist with the new. By demolishing the family, late-century writers often hoped to reclaim it.

Returning to the moment in *The Vicar of Wakefield* when the members of the vicar's singular household posture before, and ultimately on, the painter's canvas, we can see that their histrionic behavior already anticipates the antithetical impulses that characterize domestic portrayals in later works. Like that disarmingly simple image, fictional families in the eighteenth century do not assume roles in either a straightforward or a consistent manner. They neither imitate nor reflect cultural practice, but rather they function symbolically; their roles are no more reducible to a single coherent historical interpretation than the relationships among the family members in the Primrose portrait.

The readings that follow reveal, I believe, the particularly minute coupling of "familiar" subject and narrative practice and the participation of eighteenth-century prose fiction in a wider dialogue about the interactive nature of domestic relations. Tracing the peculiar correspondence between the creation of families and texts, these chapters examine narrative motives, ranging from enablement to anxiety and from simple confirmation to complex disassociation, that inform the act of writing family relations. As the Primrose portrait indicates, an attempt to fictionalize domestic experience reveals an interrelated set of descriptive tactics, neither fully comprehensible nor entirely incoherent, which condition the strange alliance of meanings in eighteenth-century British depictions of the household.

These fictions are, at once, both familiar and alien, their very strangeness working to reestablish normalcy. They share the curious position of the vicar himself, who must act as an intimate participant in the creation of family fictions and serve as a more objective relater of those fictions. The eighteenth-century narratives I examine in this book similarly attempt to mediate public and domestic spheres. The resulting cultural perspective, however, is not unlike the Primrose painting itself: family relations not only act internally to disrupt the representational field in which they are framed but also imply a complex traffic in models, narratives, and behaviors that crisscross, and thus challenge, the boundaries set around that enclosed domestic space.

1

Toward an Eighteenth-Century Anthropology

The world appears like a great family. . . .
—John Wilmot, Earl of Rochester,
"Like a Great Family"

Family Subjects

It is difficult to assess how members of eighteenth-century British society viewed domestic history since they appear to have had extremely flexible definitions of the words "family," "home," and "household" and were largely unconcerned with interpreting them more rigorously.[1] Indeed, many prose fiction writers of the eighteenth century, interested in how the values of the nuclear family might affect individual experience, shaped their discourse to address complex new attitudes toward subjectivity within traditional structures of social alliance. But the historical grounds for those attitudes—the part they play in larger temporal developments—did not particularly engage them. The family chronicle in prose fictional form, providing an extended representation of a family through several generations, does not appear in any force until the late nineteenth century.[2] This representational emphasis on singular households in the eighteenth century extends to many of the discourses that shaped conceptions of domestic life, from demographic studies to didactic literature.[3] Such works frequently focus on the experiences of a single generation or two; yet they also demonstrate an implicit appreciation of the lasting impact of ancestral lineage and conservative patriarchal values on social behavior. This chapter concentrates on nonfictional commentary about the family in order to situate the fiction as part of a network of related discourses that gave tactical value to affective behaviors. Together, they encoded new symbolic forms of power within household and state that made the sentimentalized nuclear family both the vehicle for and an obstruction to an ideological exaltation of the feeling subject.

That affective individualism as a domain of special scientific, philosophic, ethical, and economic importance was struggling to find suitable form is reflected in the titles of almost all eighteenth-century prose fictions, with their emphasis on the life, history, letters, opinions, experiences, adventures, or travels of a single character whose name denotes both a subject and the fiction that articulates that subject: *The History of Miss Betsy Thoughtless*; *The Life and Strange Surprizing Adventures of Robinson Crusoe*; *The Life and Adventures of the Lady Lucy*; *Evelina, or the History of a Young Lady's Entrance into the World*; *The History of Lady Barton*; *The Life and Opinions of Tristram Shandy, Gentleman*. Commencing with their titles, these narratives confront the vexed relation between historicizing the subject—providing a linear account of a dominating fictional consciousness—and positioning the individual within a set of determining social contexts which by their very nature are nonlinear. We see in these works the urge, on the one hand, to create a new and convincing discourse about individual autonomy, and a desire, on the other hand, to exalt the notions of social obligation and causality. The emblazoned primacy of "Evelina" is pitted against the pragmatic necessity of her "Entrance into the World."

In extending the familial issues pioneered by the mid-century writers, various authors working after 1750 produced narratives that incorporate family dynamics at nearly every point of the story and that are oppressively constrained by relational quandaries. Indeed, a predominant amount of fiction in this period is titled expressly in terms of family relations. A list of 25 representative works from 1750 to 1799 (extracted from a much longer list) contains a collective account of almost every conceivable family-related circumstance, disaster, or complexity:

The Unnatural Mother and Ungrateful Wife. A Narrative founded on true and very interesting Facts (1750); *Memoirs of Sir Charles Goodville and His Fam-*

ily: in a Series of Letters to a Friend (1753); *The Marriage Act* (1754); *Lydia, or Filial Piety* (1755); *The Brothers* (1758); *The School for Wives. In a Series of Letters* (1763); *Family Pictures. A Novel, containing Curious and Interesting Memoirs of Several Persons of Fashion* (1764); *The Exemplary Mother; or, Letters between Mrs. Villars and her Family* (1769); *The Modern Couple* (1770); *The Undutiful Daughter; or, the History of Miss Goodwin* (1770); *The Nobel Family* (1771); *The Divorce* (1771); *Memoirs of Mr. Wilson; or, the Providential Adultery* (1771); *The News-paper Wedding; or, an Advertisement for a Husband* (1774); *The School for Husbands* (1774); *The Orphan; a Novel, in a Series of Letters* (1783); *The Bastard, or the History of Mr. Greville* (1784); *Family Sketches; or, The History of Henry Dinmore* (1789); *The Modern Husband* (1789); *The Predestined Wife: or Force of Prejudice* (1789); *The Posthumous Daughter* (1797); *Family Secrets; Literary and Domestick* (1797); *Saint Julien; or, Memoirs of a Father* (1798); *The Legacy* (1799); *A Piece of Family Biography* (1799).[4]

I do not mean to suggest that English fiction after 1750 was exclusively about the family. Many of the older prose fictional forms continued to be produced—criminal biographies, scandal chronicles, travel narratives—while other relatively new forms flourished that often had little to do overtly with family—the oriental tale, for example. But the majority of extended fictional works in this period were, it is safe to say, dominated by the image of the family. One of the titles above from 1754 is even named after Lord Hardwicke's Marriage Act, which, as I have noted, vitally affected the nature of family development in England, sharpening the prevailing attitude toward endorsing and policing conjugal relations. Moreover, the rise in popularity of domestic conduct books, for both men and women it should be insisted, not only coincided with the rise of domestic fiction but can be seen as part of the same ideological promotion of the family.

Because these narratives were, in part, the fictional equivalent of conduct books, they did not merely express a literary convention; they also consciously manipulated social attitudes concerning the family. The above list suggests that particular obsessions were being exploited. Many of the titles show that fictional characters, instead of being defined by characteristics or actions (as in *The Life and*

Strange Surprizing Adventures of Robinson Crusoe or *The Fair Jilt*) were linked more insistently to their familial roles. Others indicate that schooling was required to indoctrinate certain family members in socially acceptable behavior. Such works drew parallels between an individual's adoption of a family ideology and that individual's adequacy as a legitimate member of society.

It is also apparent from the list that many of the domestic fictions between the middle and end of the century continued to rely on the convention of factuality (whether historical, biographical, or epistolary), reinforcing the notion that prose fiction reflects authentic human experience, and quite ordinary experience at that. Displacing in some measure the epic, tragic, or fantastic bias of "high" literature and using romance paradigms to glamorize affective relations while seeming to reject its privileging, anti-domestic idiom, the "factual" family narrative unifies the presently lived time of the individual and the dynastic continuity of the family. The entire process of life is sentimentalized and exhaustively amplified (it is no coincidence that the detailed analysis of family relations discovered its most hospitable welcome in the dilated form of prose narrative, often a multivolume affair). Even when the ordinary hero or heroine must undergo a period of abandonment, inverted fortunes, or spiritual trial, the fundamental commonness of experience acts as a force that can reverse the protagonist's alienation. The ordinary is elevated to the status of the heroic; everyday life is transformed into a desirable philosophical objective; and family alliances are restored at story's end in what amounts to a triumphant verification of their essential value. In turn, the social needs of the state are nurtured by the familiarization of individuals, who come to see the necessity of forces that encourage them to surrender to or merge with a certain ideology of the family, an ideology that appears to have all the inevitability of birth and death.[5]

Part of an extensive body of textual and social relations, the domestic fiction served to enhance the culture's ability to negotiate compelling and divergent models of the individual's responsibility to the family. In their mixing of education, empiricism, and social engineering we can observe the intersection of the pedagogical and individualistic strains in these works with related and equally charged forms of behavioral discourse. First, they exploit a set of political discourses from John Locke's *Two Treatises of Government* (1690) to Mary Wollstonecraft's twin *Vindications* of men's and women's rights (1790; 1792) that extolled individual liberties within the family, without, however, disrupting what Wollstonecraft calls "the order of society." Second, certain philosophical works provided behavioral models that concentrated nearly exclusively on the dominance of human consciousness, usually at the expense of formative domestic or biological influences. Locke's *Essay Concerning Human Understanding*, George Berkeley's *Treatise Concerning Principles of Human Knowledge*, David Hume's *Treatise of Human Nature*, David Hartley's *Observations on Man*, and Thomas Reid's *Inquiry into the Human Mind*, among others, constitute a corpus of texts written between 1690 and 1763 that viewed the human subject as the repository of truth and value and systematically developed new theories of psychological causality that encouraged that subject's voluntary suspension of personal ambitions, rather than its enforcement through the family. Third, in terms of economic theory, Adam Smith's laissez-faire theories, combined with the persistence of "possessive individualism" in the works of writers from James Harrington to David Ricardo, correspond to the individualist values that dominate so much eighteenth-century fiction, but generate, as well, the comprehensive systems of population analysis, demographic reasoning, and moral management that characterize much late-century economic theory about the family's impact on the national character. Finally, in much of the period's religious doctrine, the emphasis on individuals seeking grace through work and locating religious belief in an individual relationship to God encouraged personal interpretation of scripture to replace a traditional exegesis mediated by Church officials. Such principles again revert to the centrality of human experience in its relation to the external world in order to reproduce an even broader community of belief that works up through the family instead of down to it, as demonstrated in Locke's *The Reasonable-*

ness of Christianity (1695) and less radically in John Tillotson's "Of
the Works Assign'd to Every Man, and the Season For Doing It"
(1690).[6]

Although specific histories of the family were not widely dis-
seminated, one can thus deduce a partial view of how the period understood the institutional "progress" of the family from related discussions such as those in political discourse, philosophy, economic
theory, and conduct literature. In all these discourses we see a double movement in the treatment of an individual's relation to the social, and, specifically, the familial community. Instead of having
principles of coercion work from without in a system of expectations that the family imposes on its members, the individual ostensibly adopts appropriate principles of behavior (originating in and
allied with the preservation of the self) for the benefit of the family.
Simply put, human subjects internalize dynastic impulses that both
generate and obstruct their personal desires. By seeming to oppose
older behavioral norms while also operating covertly through the
individual's voluntary will, such techniques appear to be that much
more compelling; they provide models of governance that could appeal to both self-interest and corporate concerns.

Locke and the Governing Family

In many ways Locke provides the most convenient example of
the period's attempt to refigure human behavior, especially as he
tries to mediate "individualism" and social obligation or, to use his
own word, "contract." While his influence has been increasingly
questioned since J. G. A. Pocock challenged Locke's immediate importance in seventeenth- and eighteenth-century British culture, he
still provides a remarkably succinct example of attitudes toward the
family that eighteenth-century fiction also adopted. Indeed, it is in
his attempt to bring unity to diverse discourses about government,
human psychology (or "understanding" as he calls it), and pedagogy
that makes Locke particularly relevant to a discussion of "familiarization."[7]

Locke is famous in political history for having opposed arguments that made the paterfamilias seem the natural model for all governments to emulate. By refuting Robert Filmer's *Patriarcha, or the Natural Power of Kings* (1680), *Two Treatises of Government* (1690) challenged authority on multiple levels. A primal battle for mastery, what might be called a figural act of patricide, informs almost every aspect of Locke's program in *Two Treatises*: he was attacking the concept of patriarchalism, as argued in a book whose title emblazons fatherhood; disputing a traditional spokesman on that subject; opposing an absolutist king, himself a figure of paternalistic governance; contesting the political establishment; and contravening the Protestant Christian doctrine of political and social authority based on the Fifth Commandment. Naturalizing the nuclear family, Locke suggests that what he is describing, in contrast to the patriarchal family Filmer depicts, has an even more venerable history. Typically, he extols a "revolutionary" concept in terms that invoke a return to the past, a recovery of nature, tenderness, and God. As several scholars have noted, however, both Filmer's revived treatise and Locke's attack on it comprised a curiously fabricated event, focused on what was essentially an obsolete debate.[8] Locke seems to use his quarrel with Filmer to construct an occasion for arguing a paradigm shift that, in fact, was already reasonably established. Moreover, *Two Treatises* constitutes a political act in which a specific historical and family concern—the Exclusion Crisis of 1681—stands for an apparently universal condition. This appearance of universalism is sustained by the artful resuscitation of older political assessments of the family (Charles II's supporters were themselves recycling Filmer's work, which had been written as policy justification for the Royalists during the Civil War).[9] That *Two Treatises*, having finally appeared in print in 1690, came to be regarded as an instrumental means of justifying the Glorious Revolution only emphasizes the adaptive political meaning of domestic relations as they are constantly resituated in the political realm.

Arguing that an affective bond ensuring the just treatment of children by their parents is naturally and divinely sanctioned, Locke inverts the power relations that Filmer advocates to reinforce liberal views of individual conduct: "God hath woven into the Principles of

Humane Nature such a tenderness for their Off-spring, that there is little fear that Parents should use their power with too much rigour; the excess is seldom on the severe side, the strong byass of Nature drawing the other way" (*Two Treatises*, 178). In charting the parameters of individualism, however, Locke was constantly alert to limiting the freedoms he invoked; in this respect his "individualism" functions as much to subject the individual to a system of governance as an end in itself. Thus, Locke corrects the tendency to affirm the inviolable rights of all individuals, which his own theorizing about the arbitrariness of patriarchal rule seems to elicit, by relocating civil governance in a theory of rationality. Though individuals should be free of the arbitrary power exercised by a patriarch over his family or his kingdom, a person's freedom is, according to Lockean doctrine, still constituted in civil society by social determinations based on rational capability.

Defining rationality as the "bond" between reasoning adults, Locke argues that the relations between husband and wife and parents and children are the result of conscious decisions based on reasonable interpretations of scriptural and natural law. Yet this rationality is also the characteristic and native feature of all normal human beings. What Locke does in *Two Treatises* is to emphasize the contractual and artificial basis of the family in order, paradoxically, to underscore its natural constitution. Challenging Filmer's contention that Adam, representing all men, had a title to sovereignty by the subjection of Eve, he states that Eve's subordination is not coincident with political power: "[I]t can be no other Subjection than what every Wife owes her Husband, and then if this be the *Original Grant of Government* and the *Foundation of Monarchical Power*, there will be as many Monarchs as there are Husbands. If therefore these words give any Power to *Adam*, it can be only a Conjugal Power, not Political, the Power that every Husband hath to order the things of private Concernment in his Family, as Proprietor of the Goods and Land" (192). Locke similarly argues that the father holds power over the younger generation only to ensure the rational succession of property: "His Command over his Children is but temporary, and reaches not their Life or Property. It is but a help to the weakness and imperfection of their Nonage, a Discipline necessary to their Education" (329). The conjugal system justifies the subordinate position of children, who "are not born in this full state of *Equality*, though they are born to it" (322). The family Locke depicts here is one in which the husband's conjugal power is not patriarchal but proprietary, however fine that distinction may be. That Locke does not regard this as a political matter suggests the urgency with which he wanted to make the nuclear family the ideal symbol of sexual alliances and property management and to free such relations from the intractable problems associated with political justification. The notion of individuality, while appearing to be the foundation of Locke's doctrine, is actually a principle inferred from social realities. More often than not, those "social realities" are contained in the family and extend from there to civil government, a premise refined by other political philosophers such as Edward Gee and James Tyrrell, who responded to Filmer's criticisms of unrestricted liberty by replacing the individual with the family as the source of political consent.[10]

Locke's fuller treatment of identity in *An Essay Concerning Human Understanding* (written at roughly the same time) is no less motivated by liberal assessments of the individual. But if we compare the two discourses we find that the basic principles of subjectivity and family relations in Locke's political writings correspond in problematic ways to the philosophical ones. The central propositions of the *Essay*—that there are no innate principles in the mind, and that all complex ideas derive from the association of simple ideas based on sensation—may be said to derive from the assumption that an individual begins life without perceived attachments. This is in some ways the epistemological equivalent of Locke's assertion in *Two Treatises* that man is born to a state of freedom.[11] Unlike *Two Treatises*, however, the *Essay* seldom mentions the family, somewhat surprisingly since the burden of the work is to trace the origins of human understanding.[12] Moreover, while the political discourse relies heavily on the presence of certain innate characteristics within all human beings—the inclination to nurture their offspring, the instinct to form a "Conjugal Society," the universal belief in inheritance, and "the Great Foundation of Property"—the philosophical discourse begins by attacking settled ideas, barely allowing that the child has "perhaps, some faint *Ideas* of Hunger, and Thirst, and Warmth, and some Pains, which they may *have* felt in the Womb" (*Essay*, 85). Indeed, the *Essay* often seems purposely aimed at negating the very kind of arguments made in *Two Treatises*. Locke may very well have believed that the nature of political theory necessitated a discussion of social relations and therefore emphasized concepts having to do with interdependence, obligation, and consensus. Epistemology, in contrast, in seeking to identify the characteristic perceptual activities of the solitary mind, relies on a vocabulary of independence.[13]

It is perhaps understandable, given its focus on primary identity, that the *Essay* tends to avoid discussing the role that the family plays in the development of consciousness. The tabula rasa represents an attempt to create a definable point of origin uncorrupted by allegiances, coercion, or contingency, a property that belongs wholly and exclusively to the self. But Locke's neglect of household matters is itself a suggestive sign of their instrumental force in his reasoning. Despite its variance from the familial mode of *Two Treatises* and its relative silence on the subject, his account of the autonomous workings of the mind does finally build implicitly on a principle of familial determinism. The relationship between the two works is thus one of tactical difference: where *Two Treatises* masks its obligations to paternal power by demystifying patriarchy, the *Essay* masks its connection to the author's own political works by nearly erasing family contexts.

Though contesting what *Two Treatises* claims about man's identity, the *Essay* attempts the same difficult negotiation between notions of independence and relation. While Locke's account of human understanding seeks in part to liberate the individual consciousness from the anxiety of precedence, this is true only in the sense that man's understanding is born in a state of nullity, when the self has no powers to recognize its existence. Identity, for Locke, is achieved only after the mind has learned to recall sensations, associate ideas in progressively complex configurations, and relate this acquired knowledge to a unified existence occupying a continuum of time and space. Consciousness and identity become the means to repress the disconnectedness of the ego. The explosive energy of the self, its ability to manifest a variety of psychological states, is arrested by the very processes that define the mind's unique capacity to understand itself.

The idea of "relation" thus becomes a central component of Locke's argument in *An Essay Concerning Human Understanding*, reintroducing the concepts of accountability, pattern, affinity, and alliance that seem so positively absent from the initial rendition of the mind as a blank slate. Familiarizing the terms that had been purposely estranged because of their political connection to patriarchal thinking, Locke rescues them for reuse in a "modern" assessment of identity. The Second Book of the *Essay*, on ideas, for example, is dominated by discussions of relation, from those having to do with ideas to those having to do with power. All consciousness, in effect, is based on a model of association and kinship: Locke traces human understanding from the blankness of birth to a more complex cognitive state characterized by adult thinking in which connections between various sensations and reflections upon those sensations are made. This association of ideas, Locke casually states at one point, grows explicitly out of the familiar experiences of childhood: "[I]t will not perhaps be amiss, to trace our Notions, and Names, from their beginning, and observe by what degrees we proceed, and by what steps we enlarge our *Ideas* from our first Infancy" (411). The names that children give to "*Nurse* and *Mamma*" are made gradually inclusive, until, reaching a point where "a great many other Things in the World, that in some common agreements of Shape, and several other Qualities, resemble their Father and Mother, and those Persons they have been used to, they frame an *Idea*, which they find those many Particulars do partake in; and to that they give, with others, the name *Man*, for Example" (411). Once set in motion, the train of associations, to use Locke's own metaphor, is limited by the nature of the original impressions: "Personality extends it self beyond present Existence to what is past, only by Consciousness, whereby it becomes concerned and accountable, owns and imputes to it self past Actions, just upon the same ground, and for the same reason, as it does the present" (346). There is no room left for sudden ruptures, unexpected mutations, innovations, and reversals in the psychological constitution of identity. As Hume later attests in his *Treatise of Human Nature*, the power of the mind derives from its generative abilities. Thus lineage is even more fixed in the close alliance Hume draws between mental relations and blood relations, as he uses the latter to explain that the strength of a conceptual relation is determined by how "near" the connected ideas are in the mind: "each remove considerably weakens the relation. Cousins in the fourth degree are connected by *causation* . . . but not so closely as brothers, much less as child and parent" (11).

Locke's philosophy of human understanding is restricted to a distinctly modern notion of psychological causality and determinism whose ultimate source is the child's experience within the family. Seeming to undermine a tradition of predetermined character traits, Locke goes on to formalize a theory of identity that just as rigidly confines personality to a legible and familiar form. The radical potential of the tabula rasa is thus rewritten in the form of a tautology. In eighteenth-century fiction that doubleness helps to explain the paradoxical novelty of the fiction itself. Calling those narratives that rely on linear determinacy "plots of power," Patricia Spacks distinguishes them from "plots of affiliation," which rely on a disordering of such linear thinking.[14] Both paradigms, however, seem to derive from Locke and suggest that the two plots are coterminous. If the political discourse manipulated the family as a signifying system in order to substantiate claims about the ideological reordering of English society, the philosophical discourse developed a rational description of the autonomous mind that mostly rejected overt references to the mind's dependence on familial origins, only to relocate dependence, relation, and origin in the defining patterns of human thought. In essence, the two tactics Locke employed in his major polemical works resemble extremes of familial representation, from overdetermination to sublimation, that are also documented in eighteenth-century fictional prose.

Demonstrating the practical applications of his philosophical and political conceptions of identity, relation, and free will in *Some Thoughts Concerning Education*, Locke attempts, in some measure, to link the issues he had already raised in the political and philosophical works. In many respects, this work is most revealing about Locke's epistemological assumptions and about his desire to unify his own disparate theories. It is also *Some Thoughts* that, because of its affinity to conduct literature, and its emphatic desire to apply theory to practice, most closely approximates the discursive nature of prose fiction. Like the fiction, it seeks to normalize political relations by making them a natural attribute of the domestic scene.

Some Thoughts was intended, in part, to address the problem of the relation of the independent mind to the establishment of political ideology. Locke argues in the dedicatory epistle to Edward Clarke, *"Errours in Education should be less indulged than any: These, like Faults in the first Concoction, that are never mended in the second or third, carry their afterwards-incorrigible Taint with them through all the parts and stations of Life"* (79). To manipulate early experiences through education is to manipulate reality; by rigorously supervising how the tabula rasa comes to be inscribed, one can begin to modify the foundation of the political state: *"The well Educating of their Children is so much the Duty and Concern of Parents, and the Welfare and Prosperity of the Nation so much depends on it, that I would have every one lay it seriously to Heart . . . Though that most to be taken Care of, is the Gentleman's Calling. For if those of that Rank are by their Education once set right, they will quickly bring all the rest into Order"* (80). Locke's reforms must be seen, then, as emanating from an ambiguous desire to liberate the consciousness and yet govern it. Though the mind builds ineluctably and freely on experience and sensation, paradoxically, those experiences and sensations can be dictated for the good of the state and a preexisting class hierarchy.

In *Some Thoughts* Locke views education as a means of demystifying knowledge and challenging traditional concepts that seemed to constrain the individual's growth and potential for productivity. Original sin, innate ideas, golden age utopianism, all are in some way or another negated by rational comprehension. Locke insists

that "Mens Happiness or Misery is most part of their own making"
(83), and that constitutional differences are insignificant in comparison with the effect of education. "That the Difference to be found in
the Manners and Abilities of Men, is owing more to their *Education*
than to any thing else; we have reason to conclude, that great care is
to be had of the forming Children's *Minds*, and giving them that seasoning early, which shall influence their Lives always after" (103).
Here Locke makes ideological conditioning seem natural by establishing it in consciousness before the mind can be critical, can imagine somehow standing outside of it. Like wood or food, human understanding gains value as its "original" condition is modified, and
then gradually intensified (or seasoned), over time—as if organic and
artificial states were identical. For Locke, education embodied the
spirit of rationalism and contract; it was an understanding established between teacher and pupil for the pupil's eventual entrance
and useful occupation in the world; it was supposedly an act of
natural deference rather than power.

The parent's or governor's function in this educative process is al-
legedly to aid the child's development toward independence. In the
philosophic as well as the political realm, Locke always perceived
parenthood as an obligation to the child, and filial obedience as a
necessity only as long as the parents were fulfilling their duty to facilitate the child's eventual cognitive and physical independence. Ostensibly, this is also the chief purpose of *Some Thoughts*: "[H]e that
will have his Son have a Respect for him, and his Orders, must himself have a great Reverence for his Son. *Maxima debetur pueris rever-
entia*" (133). And yet the function of the father in Locke's scheme is
frequently reversed. The language and attitude assumed in speaking
of filial obedience, parental authority, and the inheritance of property often reflect the deliberate affirmation of a father's arbitrary
will and of his paternal right to his children's constant submission.
The result is to deprive the political and philosophical discourse of
much of its efficacy in the presence of actual social relations:

Fear and Awe ought to give you the first Power over their Minds, and
Love and Friendship in riper Years to hold it: For the Time must come,

when they will be past the Rod, and Correction; and then, if the Love of you make them not obedient and dutifull, if the Love of Vertue and Reputation keep them not in Laudable Courses, I ask, What Hold will you have upon them, to turn them to it? Indeed, Fear of having a scanty Portion if they displease you, may make them Slaves to your Estate, but they will be never the less ill and wicked in private; and that Restraint will not last always. Every Man must some Time or other be trusted to himself and his own Conduct; and he that is a good, a vertuous and able Man, must be made so within. And therefore, what he is to receive from Education, what is to sway and influence his Life, must be something put into him betimes; Habits woven into the very Principles of his Nature; and not a counterfeit Carriage, and dissembled Out-side, put on by Fear, only to avoid the present Anger of a Father, who perhaps may dis-inherit him. (10)

This seems to be sentimentalizing patriarchy as much as undermining it, especially as it concedes the father's ability to tyrannize over his offspring by granting or withholding property—Filmer *redivivus*. Locke tries to obviate this imbalance by familiarizing the entire process, showing how the relation of property and power among fathers and sons ought to be based ultimately on friendship and understanding. But the recourse to consent and love merely alters the means and not the intent of what the father hopes to gain: "Power over their Minds." By conditioning the child to accept honorable and rational obedience as the unifying principle of family relations, and then conceiving it as mutual respect, Locke makes the individual's conception of self a consequence of the father's willpower (in the sense of both exercising and writing one's "will"). Pedagogy reproduces the cultural tactics that enable a society to incorporate marginal figures by postponing their individual rights without damaging the credibility of its egalitarian aims. By encouraging assimilation, and the willing surrender of due merit, through the individual pursuit of family and self-esteem, Locke makes psychic wholeness the mirror image of social cohesion.

Like his political and epistemological theories, Locke's pedagogical theory builds consistently on a tautology: the liberated self is a natural projection of those social features it is destined to emulate, and freedom in turn becomes the privilege of the indoctrinated. The human subject in his various theories of social conduct internalizes principles of coercion that the nuclear family, as configured in eighteenth-century behavioral discourse, was supposed to supplant. Similar to eighteenth-century prose fiction, which did much to popularize Lockean doctrine, Locke made "individualism" the product rather than the agent of a reimagined social contract. In *Some Thoughts* we can observe Locke's reversal of earlier positions: where the political doctrine seems resistant to governmental sanctioning—a tactic used to bolster its apparent disengagement from ideological or partisan motives—the domestic conduct book subtly endorses such institutional relations in order to substantiate its own discursive authority.

Family and Natural Law

Locke based most of his observations about the family on the Bible and on the work of seventeenth-century philosophers of natural law, particularly Grotius, Pufendorf, Hooker, and Hobbes (the latter about whom he had significant reservations). The Old Testament gave Locke two models, one based on the conjugal relationship between Adam and Eve, the other based on the extended patriarchal family commanded by Abraham. Like many of his contemporaries, Locke argued that the family was the primary social unit and was generally sanctioned by nature. But he and others struggled with the same historical variance that has divided modern anthropology, sociology, and history: whether the nuclear family was a permanent or variable feature of human development.[15] By demonstrating how the family evolved from patriarchal to contractual forms, and going so far as to suggest that patriarchal power was always limited in civil societies, Locke reinforced his own belief in fundamental patterns of human behavior based on contract and free will.[16]

Natural law, however, encouraged the view that man initially existed in a state of near lawlessness. Both Grotius and Pufendorf (referred to by Locke in *Some Thoughts on Education* as essential reading) admit that contemporary evidence from "savage" cultures suggests that "any number of customs might satisfy the bare re-quirements of law." That included polygamy and incest: according to Pufendorf, "no Degrees of Marriage are forbidden by the Law of Nature"; Grotius also admitted that by the "pure law of nature" po-lygamy and incest could not be considered improper, although di-vine law overruled the law of nature on this question.[17] These claims would be reiterated later by Hume, who insisted in "Of Polygamy and Divorces" that earlier households were radically extended. The ancient Britons, he notes, strategically arranged marital customs, providing an "equal number of wives in common" in order to link their society more closely (3: 200).

At the furthest extreme, Hobbes argued that human society de-veloped out of a state of radical uncertainty. His contention that "the condition of man" is "a condition of war of every one against every one" essentially refuted the notion that man originally lived in conventional familial groupings (*Leviathan*, 85).[18] Seeming to fore-shadow Johan Jakob Bachofen's theory of an original promiscuous horde ruled by mother right, Hobbes claimed that "in the condition of mere nature, where there are no matrimonial laws, it cannot be known who is the father, unless it be declared by the mother: and therefore the right of dominion over the child dependeth on her will, and is consequently hers" (131). The care of children in such a state falls out according to the whim of the primary caretaker. Hob-bes used this speculation about the origins of human society to de-fend his position that civil society necessitated an absolute monarch to control human instincts.

But whereas Hobbes used natural law to proclaim the innate depravity of human beings, the recognized authorities on natural law, Grotius and Pufendorf, ultimately denied that lawless behavior characterized man in the state of nature. Their appeals to a divine law that supersedes, at the same time that it dictates, natural law pre-served the belief that man originally and universally venerated the family. They believed human beings were endowed with a principle of sociability. Thus according to Grotius, "[A]mong the traits char-acteristic of man is an impelling desire for society, that is, for the so-cial life—not of any and every sort, but peaceful, and organized according to the measure of his intelligence, with those who are of his own kind. . . . This maintenance of the social order, . . . which is consonant with human intelligence, is the source of law properly so called" (*Prolegomena*, 11–12). As he goes on to argue, that innate sociability derives from man's rational awareness of relationship: "[S]acred history, besides enjoining rules of conduct, in no slight degree reinforces man's inclination towards sociableness by teaching that all men are sprung from the same first parents. . . . [A] blood-relationship has been established among us by nature; consequently it is wrong for a man to set a snare for a fellow-man" (14). Appropriately, Grotius describes the generation of civil law from natural law in terms that emphasize blood relation: "the mother of municipal law is that obligation which arises from mutual consent; and since this obligation derives its force from the law of nature, nature may be considered, so to say, the great-grandmother of municipal law" (15).[19] Feminizing legal history, Grotius manages to characterize human development in conventional, gendered terms as natural, civilized, pacifistic, and family-oriented without, however, challenging its patriarchal basis in law.[20]

The work of natural law theorists reveals a relative consensus according to which nature confirms sociability, and which, in making both concepts fit historically, redefines nature in turn. As in the prose fiction, the constructedness of the family is masked as an organic process. But the very terminological shifting of nature is also precisely what gives the family such flexible signifying power in eighteenth-century literature. It justifies both the institutional functions of the family and the existence of the institution in the first place. In making natural law synonymous with rational human behavior, Grotius and Pufendorf alike laid the theoretical groundwork for Locke's reading into the original state of humanity the rational characteristics of modern man. This in turn enabled him to contest the doctrine of a Hobbesian state of war, despite anthropological evidence from other contemporary cultures that appeared to support Hobbes. We can see the legacy of this reasoning in Hume's work, where, despite his radical skepticism in other matters, innate tendencies "such as benevolence and resentment, the love of life, and kindness to children," or the "natural appetite betwixt the sexes, which unites them together, and preserves their union, till a new tye takes place in their concern for their common offspring," help guarantee the social containment of "incommodious" desires (Hume, *Treatise*, 417, 486).

In its general outlines, then, seventeenth-century natural law reproduced the ancient controversy between Plato (who always felt that family, to some extent, impeded governance) and Aristotle (who thought that family constituted governance). For the most part, both sides were content with elaborating theories that did not so much identify the origins of the family as explain its modern function in society. In this they reflected the more immediate interests of their society in establishing some kind of coherence between private and public sociability. To the extent that Locke helps establish what might be called a "modern" study of the family by exalting its right to govern itself according to egalitarian principles, he bequeaths to that study a fundamental and persistent contradiction, one eventually internalized by prose fiction. Locke's model of government (within and without the family) was, arguably, as much devoted to reinvesting patriarchal authority in the now liberated subject's attitude toward domestic economy as releasing the individual from tyranny. Just as eighteenth-century prose fiction sublimated origins in order to claim generic novelty, Locke (and natural law in general) reconceived the origins of the family in order to substantiate a revolutionary claim about social history. Locke's modernity, therefore, emanates from "modernizing" the family, turning its conjugality into a politically self-reflexive act of disengagement from political versions of the family like Filmer's. Affect seems to replace authority but does not always prove less coercive.

Family or Household?

Arguments about the family by Locke and natural law theorists are consistently intended to protect the freedom of the individual only insofar as that individual participates in a society established on shared material values. Although these writers were interested only

very generally in national populations, their remarks tend to reinforce connections between the subject's personal identity, family
affiliations, and demographic tendencies in the state as a whole.
Locke's work, in fact, appeared at roughly the same time as the first
comprehensive national census and coincided with widespread efforts to demarcate family structure. In 1696, Gregory King published *Natural and Political Observations and Conclusions upon the
State and Condition of England,* his famous and, for the time, authoritative synopsis of numerical evidence based on returns from
the Marriage Duty Act of 1694 (which required a "hearth tax"). The
first official state census was taken, largely by overseers, poor-law
officials, and schoolmasters, and compiled by John Rickman in 1801
in order to update King's estimates and substantiate government policy. These two works are the chief texts on population size in the
century, but they frame a series of influential studies that attempted
to enumerate English citizenry and account for its distribution in
families and households, matching domestic structure and political
action in a fashion alien to Locke's philosophy. Some of these studies resulted directly from legislative activity such as the Marriage Duty Act or the even more significant Hardwicke Marriage Act of 1753,
which prohibited the solemnization of marriage without banns or license and transferred punitive enforcement from the Church courts
to the secular courts. As noted earlier, the Hardwicke Act marks an
important stage in the shift Jacques Donzelot sees from the policing
of families to policing through the family; it appears to mark a
change in conception as well from regarding matrimony (and
therefore family) as a private spiritual sacrament to a public event
inseparable from secular political activities. Ironically, the more private the family seems to become in the eighteenth century the more
it succumbs to state intervention. As in natural law, where the individual is constituted by his or her sociability, eighteenth-century
demographic studies defined family relations in terms of their adhe-
rence to prescribed standards of civic disposition. But if Locke employed family ideology to demystify the monarchy's patriarchal authority, the later studies in population were linked to a revived

paternalism that characterizes the ministries who worked with the Crown in the years following the Glorious Revolution.

In many instances, the studies of population in the period stemmed from concerns about the relation of national stability to familial (and hence demographic) order. Richard Price's *Essay on the Population of England from the Revolution to the Present Time* (1779; six editions to 1803) links the progress of the English family as a social institution to the incidence of revolution in modern European history. In 1774, Thomas Percival published *Further Observations on the State of Population in Manchester, and other Adjacent Places*, an addendum to his *Observations on the State of Population in Manchester* (1773), in which he claimed that families no longer bound the nation. Most of the works of a similar kind were, according to Richard Wall, "always collected with some other object in view, a common motive being a desire to use mean household size as a multiplier for calculating the total population of the kingdom" and then to employ the results to justify, criticize, or recommend changes in national policy toward population control (167).[21] A growth in population demonstrated the efficacy of state policy; a decline indicated failures within the government's domestic program. Rather than evincing a history in which the conjugal family progressively guarantees liberal rights, the intensifying interest in locating the core of the household reflects the degree to which kinship and the nuclear family were being reduced to signs in a largely political debate about state nationalism. In discovering what already existed in at least some (if not all) families, analysts seemed to discover something new, a profoundly useful semiotic by which to justify and cloak the nation's domestic policy. The "new" family offered a compelling means to internalize a system of government that would silently (and therefore more effectively) parallel the overt political maneuvers of an increasingly nationalistic and industrial state.

Although their ideological aims were nearly opposed, both of the most famous exponents of political arithmetic in the period, Thomas Malthus and Adam Smith, maintained that population control facilitated economic progress. Malthus developed his theories about

the tendency of population to increase faster than the means of subsistence as a corrective reaction against the optimism diffused by the
school of Rousseau, most notably in Godwin and Condorcet. His
deduction from the work of David Hume, Adam Smith, David Ricardo, and Richard Price that "population, when unchecked, increased in a geometrical ratio, and subsistence for man in an arith-
metical ratio" (73) led him to argue that "positive" or natural checks
to population existed in the form of disease, poverty, and war. At
the same time, he held that such threats served to heighten prosperity since families, driven by the "hope to rise, or fear to fall, in society," would be eager to sustain "animated exertion" in order to better their own condition, and thus "tend rather to promote, than impede the general purpose of providence" (128–29). Displacing fertility onto economic productivity, Malthus effectively harnessed biological imperatives and conventional family sentiments to a consumer ideology.[22]

Acceptance of Malthusian economics in the later-eighteenth century derived partly from the conjecture that such arithmetic principles absolved the rich and powerful of responsibility for the condition of the laboring and indigent classes. If they had chiefly themselves to blame for their own biological excess, the fate of the impoverished could not be attributed either to the dereliction of their
superiors or to corruption within the nation's institutions. The
mechanistic nature of Malthusian precepts discouraged active effort
for social improvement on the principle that increased comfort
would result in increased numbers and so induce the imbalances between population and subsistence that caused human misery. Challenging the powerful influence of family ideology, Malthus down-
plays how moral constraint (internal delimitations enacted by families that were based on affect, economic insight, and perceived duty
to one's offspring) also made populations somewhat self-regulating.
This omission stems in part from a greater interest in demographic
patterns than in the family's historical aspect. In the same way that,
as one historian has put it, anthropologists frequently fail to recognize that, in some senses, family originates marriage rather than the
reverse,[23] Malthus tends to assume that the family is a peripheral

rather than fundamental element of population. By externalizing and mechanizing the processes that control procreative behavior, Malthusian theory sought to regulate human causality as rigorously as the moral and philosophical discourse of the period, which tended to attribute control of sexual and affective conduct mostly to internal compulsions that extended from the individual out to the social good of the state. To enhance the disciplinary regime he wanted the family to serve, Malthus separated conjugal principles from the sentimental forms they were beginning to inhabit. His work may be seen as an attempt to resist the affective reinforcement of the nuclear family in liberal discourse and sentimental fiction, producing, in turn, a monolithic view of domestic government. His system of "checks" lessened the force of both biological determinism and the politics of consent (even in private sexual affairs) and subordinated them to the power of a national economic will.

For Adam Smith, population growth was an extension of humanity's innate desire for economic improvement and as such was a measure of progress. Without ignoring the real miseries caused by overcrowding or lapses between population and subsistence, Smith nevertheless argued that an increase in the number of laborers eventually corresponds to an increase in national productivity. In his view, nature has made provision for social well-being by the principle of the human constitution that prompts every man to better his condition: the individual aims only at his private gain but is "led by an invisible hand" to promote the public good; human institutions, by interfering with this principle in the name of public interest, defeat their own end; but, when all systems of preference or restraint are removed, "the obvious and simple system of natural liberty establishes itself of its own accord" (112).[24] This latter principle is characterized by the idea of the right of the individual to an unimpeded sphere for the exercise of his economic activity. The growth in a country's population is a measure of its growth in productive labor and hence its greater capability in the division of labor and its progressive contribution to the wealth of the nation. Like Malthus, Smith tends to reduce the function of the family to its economic role; in general, he neglects the complex connections between the internal laws of the family and the laws of economic production within the national state. But whereas Malthusian "checks" upon the family functioned in relatively overt ways, Smith's "natural liberty" achieved institutional efficacy through a concealed process, the "invisible hand" that induces the subject to pursue economic interests aligned with the nation's concerns. Where Malthus regards individual desire as a potential burden to the state, Smith makes it consonant with the political will of the nation. Individuals, as potential producers, are not only its "wealth" but also its will. Here Smith articulates the process of familiarization at work in the various social fictions produced in eighteenth-century literature. The state uses the idea of the family to support its own practices and, in the course of this dissemination, modifies the way the family identifies its purpose and domain. The family, by a similar though not homologous process, conveys various techniques of power to its members. The individual, in turn, affects the ideological and functional character of the family, which returns an image of its own altered practice to the state.

For King, Price, Malthus, Smith, and others, important knowledge about the family extended only to immediate political issues, despite their crucial interest in the legitimate reproductive behavior of the nation. The social history of the family, either in terms of its origins or its exact constitution, stirred little intellectual attention. Indeed, as Wall explains in "Mean Household Size," despite the interest in the political effects of family reproduction, the precise dimensions of the family "was a subject which in its own right aroused little interest in either the seventeenth or eighteenth centuries" (167). We find evidence of this in the continued failure throughout both centuries to define the family as separate from the cultural space it occupies: the household. Nothing fully explains "why so many writers of the seventeenth and eighteenth century found nothing exceptional in dividing populations into units described ambiguously as 'houses or families'" (163). Assuming that household size remained constant over time, the arithmeticians in general did not examine the sociological implications of demographic transformation. "Several writers commented on a change in social relations which, if true, must have had a very important effect on the size of the household"—Wall cites the practice of keeping unmarried servants under the farmer's roof—"only rarely, however, did political arithmeticians seek to trace the effect of such changes on the mean size of the household" (170).

The confusion over house and family suggests that demographers were more interested in the economic (as opposed to the sociological or anthropological) function of the family. The family became synonymous with the property to which it was attached; information about its existence was interesting only insofar as it reflected the larger concerns of the state. The demographic material is striking for its utter disinterest in the microhistory of the family. Moreover, the implicit assumption that, between King's 1695 "census" and the official census of 1801, household size did not change suggests that the rise of the modern domestic nuclear family as a fundamental social change in the period was not perceptible to observers ideally situated to make note of its increasing effect on English culture. Either the demographers did not look with eyes that could see such change or, motivated by different political or ideological aims, they did not regard what others saw as a significant shift in social values. Or, perhaps, there was little quantitative change to observe because that change, if there ever was one, had already taken place.

Conducting Families

To some extent, the microhistory ignored by the economists, demographers, and political arithmeticians appears in conduct literature, a term I use here rather broadly to include didactic and moral essays, sermons, epistolary collections, domestic guides, and treatises on manners. Locke's *Some Thoughts on Education* would be included in such a grouping, but that grouping would also contain texts that range from the end of the seventeenth century well into the nineteenth and that were as diverse as Mary Astell's *A Serious Proposal to the Ladies* (1692), William Fleetwood's *The Relative Duties of Parents and Children, Husbands and Wives, Masters and Servants* (1705), William Law's *A Serious Call to a Devout and Holy Life* (1729), Edward

Cother's *A Serious Proposal for Promoting Lawful and Honourable Marriage* (1750), Robert Dodsley's *The Oeconomy of Human Life* (1751), Sarah Pennington's *An Unfortunate Mother's Advice to Her Absent Daughter* (1761), Hester Chapone's *Letters on the Improvement of the Mind* (1773), Philip Dormer, Earl of Chesterfield's *Letters Written by the Late Right Honourable Philip Dormer, Earl of Chesterfield, to His Son, Philip Stanhope* (1774), Elizabeth Bonhote's *The Parental Monitor* (1788), the Countess Dowager of Carlisle's *Thoughts on the Form of Maxims Addressed to Young Ladies on their First Establishment in the World* (1789), Samuel Stennet's *Discourses on Domestic Duties* (1800), Elizabeth Hamilton's *Letters on the Elementary Principles of Education* (1803), and various instructional "companions" like those printed periodically in Philadelphia as *The Young Man's Own Book* or *The Young Lady's Own Book* (1832–1845). To the extent that these may be seen as comprising a fairly specific ideology, one concerned with organizing the range of responsible social actions within the domestic sphere, they may be regarded as indices of how eighteenth-century culture ideally viewed the form and function of the family. Apart from their discursive variety, these texts link household government to a multitude of competing social issues such as economy, law, ethics, holy life, education, and epistemology. They generally extol private life, but often only as a means to help administer a complexly fissured public sphere.

Both Mary Poovey and Nancy Armstrong have suggested that there is a remarkable degree of homogeneity in the behavioral literature, particularly among conduct books for and about women. According to them, and others as well, the didactic discourse of this period focused predominantly on reconceiving and politicizing the figure of the domestic woman. Armstrong in particular argues that "written representations of the self allowed the modern individual to become an economic and psychological reality" and that "the modern individual was first and foremost a woman" (*Desire and Domestic Fiction*, 8). She links "the history of British fiction to the empowering of the middle classes in England through the dissemination of a new female ideal" (9) and argues further that conduct material, along with prose fiction, determined much of this change in ideology.

"On the domestic front, perhaps even more so than in the courts and the market-place, the middle-class struggle for dominance was fought and won" (24). Poovey describes the "conversion" of the feminine ideal in more moderate terms that suggest a greater degree of historical continuity. Extrapolating from Puritan principles of female conduct, she points out that "one of their legacies, the elevated and spiritually significant position of the home, reinforced women's social importance when separation between the home and the workplace became the middle-class rule rather than the exception. So completely was their spiritual office fused with their superintendence of family integrity that, by the early decades of the eighteenth century, women could even take pride in sacrificing their sexual desires for this 'higher' cause" (8). As a result, a pervasive and relatively sophisticated material discourse arose, especially toward the end of the eighteenth century and on into the nineteenth century, for the purpose of popularizing, regulating, and maintaining normative behavior within the family.

It is difficult, however, despite their often deadening repetitiousness, to discern the compelling uniformity Poovey and Armstrong imply in the wider conduct literature of the eighteenth century. Like other discourses, this literature observes, with perhaps some greater regularity, a variety of shifts in purpose and effect. Neither simply a reflection of, nor a subordinate agent for, the political manipulations of the modern industrial state, written discourse about sexuality and family government served the purpose of modeling social expectations about the appropriate functions of the family, perhaps more extensively and more complexly than at any prior time in English history. Like the discourses governing penal institutions, psychiatric and medical practice, modern economics, linguistics, and natural history, particular forms of expressing sexuality or domesticity in the bourgeois home, as Foucault has noted, underwent a period of broad, though not always overt, surveillance and classification, producing a series of tactical measures that often worked at cross purposes (*History of Sexuality*, 2). On the one hand, the various discourses governing domestic behavior endorsed privatization of the family by encouraging households to become progressively insular and self-regulating; on the other hand, this very internalization of discourse guaranteed a measure of supervisory control that belied its affirmation of privacy. The more the nuclear family was encouraged to regard itself as "closed," the more it was exposed to public notice. In its supposedly greatest moment of retirement, the bourgeois household became a public monument to social and political order. This accounts for its particular effectiveness, or for the belief, at the very least, that individual families could be made to follow the political destinies of the state without obvious techniques of interference.

One of the symbolic cruxes of this long revolution in the discursive identity of the family was the domestic woman. Both Poovey and Armstrong argue that the burgeoning ideal of the private, modest, and economical lady of the house projected the precise ideological maneuvers underlying the changes in didactic instruction and middle-class influence. Armstrong notes that didactic writing about the family in the later-eighteenth century tended to extol a new kind of family environment, one chiefly presided over by a female authority. This figure's position in the middle-class home not only consolidated new ideals of bourgeois domesticity but also gave birth to modern conceptions of gender, rendering her the source of ideological value for a class in need of self-definition. Private and refined, the domestic woman nonetheless projected, or was supposed to project, the public concerns of society.

The process of change in representing the family that these scholars have articulated adds a complex dimension to the historical account I have been making. Yet, some of the discursive changes they describe did not necessarily arise from (or engender) changes in how the household operated but may instead have reflected concerns about the household's symbolic uses; nor were the changes exclusive or even dominant features of the domestic literature. Indeed, the tendency in the critical literature to stress the numerical superiority of conduct books about women is akin to the popular but false notion that female writers of fiction far outnumbered male writers. This assumption has, in turn, been used mainly to reverse a previous misperception that male writers made the greatest contributions either to the development of prose fiction or to the discourse on private behavior.[25] As I will go on to show, however, the conduct literature's authorial and ideological diversity, like the fiction's, renders any homogeneous account of domestic experience misleading. Indeed, the very vehicles that were supposed to shape uniform conduct were themselves contending for unique pedagogical status.

Many of the tracts on marriage, filial duty, and sexual behavior were apparently motivated by a perceived crisis in behavior, but they were often occupied not so much with redefining as with restoring moral order. That is, many conduct writers used the modern nuclear family to reframe conservative domestic and political issues. Fearing that the "latitude concerning *Women* . . . which our *Libertines* in this Age would have lawful" (7) and the consequent "neglect, and abuse of *Marriage*" and "decay of our Numbers" would result in the "dwindling away" of "civil society" (9), the anonymous writer of *Marriage Promoted* (1690) urged adoption of legislation "obliging all Men from *Twenty One Years of Age, to Marry*, or, in default, to pay a *Mulct* in proportion to their Fortunes" (30). In 1700 the complaint was still much the same. Alarmed by the daily "Rumours" of "so many *Skirmishes* and Domestick *Discords*, of such *Broils* and *Dissentions* in several *Families*, which are perfect Epitomies of a Civil War" (13), Castamore contended that the "Abominable Iniquity" (19) of "Conjugal Libertinism" (17) had become "so Epidemic an English Vice" (19) as to "*emasculate* the *Age*" (6) and induce "odious Civil Consequences" (17). These early remonstrances, clearly occasioned by Restoration "profligacy," typically aligned the sanctity of marriage and conjugality with the welfare of the state in terms both nationalistic and patriarchal. Both were concerned with the military vigor of England (by supplying an "increase of Hands to defend it") and with the rational preservation of estates (according to verifiable matrilineal descent). Here, clearly, the concern about family government originates in fears about the decay of masculinity; the libertine expression of sexuality, particularly outside the laws of marriage, exposes men to the enervating influence of prostitutes and adulteresses, of which libertine sexuality is the obverse. While the unspoken sentiment might be that a "proper wife" would correct and remasculate the errant male, force of change must originate in the men to reinstate their political identity and restore "civil society."

One crucial aspect of the domestic literature in the period was precisely this reconfiguring of masculine norms; not only was female conduct regarded as a symbol of modern civic value, as Armstrong argues, but male decorum proved to be no less a necessary and defining attribute of newly imagined forms of subjectivity. There is a shifting of male roles in these texts which implies that the man's function in the domestic sphere was to become an authoritative figure of silent, and sometimes even invisible, spectatorship. Indeed, it is no coincidence that Addison and Steele's *Spectator Papers*, one of the most influential eighteenth-century works on social voyeurism as well as civil behavior, praised female domestic industry with particular intensity at the same time that it verified male control of the terms by which household activity was to be managed.[26] This detached male position in the domestic sphere (not unlike Adam Smith's "invisible hand") helped explain the already established absence of the man in a conventional household setting; moreover, it imagined the husband or father as a particularly effective symbol of modern ideology, the figurehead of a system of principles that operated as a pervasive but indirect form of moral influence. By transforming male withdrawal from everyday family government into an ethical imperative rather than merely an economic convenience, it justified the man's split attachment to the public and private spheres.

While it seems inevitable that Restoration moralists would castigate an age in which libertine defiance of regular conjugal relations was tacitly accepted, later writers continued to be alarmed by the disintegration of marriage and family and the consequent effect on male and female roles in civil society. Using the pseudonym Philogamus, one pamphleteer wrote that "the sacred Rights of Marriage, were never so much prophaned, and trampled upon, as in these later Ages. One might find more Examples of Conjugal Fidelity, in both Sexes, among the *Hotentots* and *Savages*, than among Christians, even among those, who yet think themselves so" (5). Simultaneously demonizing and idealizing the savage other, Philogamus employs a conventional trope in the domestic conduct material that parallels the modern dissolution of family values with a return to barbarism. He blames, among several causes, "the Decay of Christian Piety" (15); "the almost universal Corruption of Morals" (15); the "wretched Way of educating our Youth: Particularly our young Ladies" (17); "unequal Matches" (30); "the too great Liberty allowed our Women, and the want of true Love in the young Couple" (37). In most of these causes the stress falls either on the decline from a prior state of health or on the adoption of new liberties that threaten stability. Both of these emphases, in turn, imply a national need to reestablish codes of behavior. As with Castamore, women are assigned equal blame (because of the liberty and "wretched education" afforded them) as the men; the implied solution, however, is not to liberalize their education but to constrain it in such a way as to limit women's freedom—that is, their capacity to represent cultural values in themselves. Accentuating female depravity or the need for educating "young Ladies" thus indicates not a conversion of them into symbols of modern subjectivity but a recognition of the complementary effects of female behavior on the conjugal norm that was the model of civic identity for most British subjects in the eighteenth century.

When the Marriage Act of 1753 passed into law and began addressing the kinds of issues that alarmed Philogamus, it did not entirely silence complaints about the modern decay of marriage or fears that conjugality no longer served as a potent symbol of civic identity. Many of the changes enacted were the result of expressed fears that clandestine marriages confused inheritance claims, multiplied bastardy, encouraged rash and therefore unhappy marriages, and, in the words of Henry Gally, caused "a Disgrace to any civiliz'd Nation" (29). More frequently, men were criticized for their lack of sexual discipline and economic responsibility while women were exalted as both economic and sexual ideals (or, at least, as the figures most likely to embrace a new doctrine of conjugal and domestic management). Seeking amendments to the "common and statute laws, respecting love, marriage, and adultery" (3), a 1789 pamphlet entitled *Letters on Love, Marriage, and Adultery* contended that "the abuse of parental authority, and of the laws respecting marriage, are the general causes of infidelity to the marriage vow" (97) and concluded that the equally general misery occasioned by "conjugal infidelity" was deserved, particularly by men, whose "common licentiousness . . . renders possession the grave of love. . . . *Our wanton licentiousness and tyranny should have all its infamy and all its misery*" (93–94). Such concerns about the contemporary dissolution of the family (as much as progressive impulses to redefine it) seem to have generated the need to provide an effective countermyth.

As late as the 1770's and 1780's then, writers were bewailing the failure of marriage as an institution in much the same terms as at the beginning of the century. What had come to be believed generally, if not universally, was that women must be mobilized to correct sexual and civil licentiousness, principally through their powers of household management. This granted women a symbolic economic power that only seemed to stand for a new and modern subjectivity but was largely just a rationalizing of previous behavioral norms. Whereas Lord Halifax bluntly argued in *Advice to a Daughter* (1688) that "for the better Oeconomy of the World, the Men, who were to be Lawgivers and Governors, had the larger Share of Reason bestowed on them," writers toward the end of the century, like Melmoth Editor, were claiming "that women fill up their appointed circle of action with greater regularity and dignity than men; the claim of preference cannot justly be decided in our favour. In the prudential and economical parts of life, I think it undeniable that they rise far above us" (48). The burden of economy (reflected in words like regularity, dignity, and prudence) shifts, albeit in a limited sense and perhaps only ostensibly, to the domestic woman, making her house the sign of her involvement in public affairs. As Editor goes on to observe, "[H]ow much the interest of society is concerned in the rectitude of [women's] understandings. That season of every man's life, which is most susceptible of the strongest impressions, is necessarily under female direction; as there are few instances, perhaps, in which that sex is not one of the secret springs, which regulates the

most important movements of private or public transactions" (49–
50). The wife's function, in both political and spiritual terms, is exalted so as to position her more resolutely in the domestic sphere assigned to her a priori. If she becomes a symbolic figure of modern
subjectivity, it is at the expense of her access to a modern, public
world. What she gains as a sign, she loses in practice. Although an
icon of modern subjectivity, she does not necessarily embody it herself. As James Fordyce suggests, the role of the wife is to confer
upon her husband the attributes of modern civility, not to obtain
them for herself: "The man not only protects and advises, but
communicates vigour and resolution to the woman. She in her turn
softens, refines, and polishes him; in her society he finds repose
from action and care; in her friendship, the ferment into which his
passions were wrought by the hurry and distraction of public life,
subsides and settles into a calm; and a thousand nameless graces and
decencies, that flow from her words and actions, form him for a
more mild and elegant deportment" (*Sermons to Young Women*,
283). The woman's discipline of passion, like the ordering of the
household, helps shape the man, the individual more directly engaged in business, whose "ferment" derives from the "hurry" of the
market place, at once the opposite, the complement, and the sus-
tainer of the household.

Increasingly, over the course of the century, this exaltation of the
woman's economic and civilizing capacity came to be regarded as
one of the chief adjuncts to national recovery. A plethora of conduct material appeared in the latter part of the century and on into
the nineteenth, extolling the power of a bourgeois household governed by a woman to signify a quasi-professional role in the state:
"The arts of housewifery should be regarded as *professional* to the
woman who intends to become a wife; and to select one for that station who is destitute of them, or disinclined to exercise them, however otherwise accomplished, is as absurd, as it would be to choose
for your lawyer, or physician, a man who excelled in every thing
rather than in law, or physic" (Editor, 118). The heightened fervor
with which women are encouraged to regard domestic responsibilities manifests the economic and political urgency of this profession-

alization. As Hester Chapone observes: "Economy is so important a part of a woman's character, so necessary to her own happiness, and so essential to her performing properly the duties of a wife and of a mother, that it ought to have the precedence of all other accomplishments, and take its rank next to the first duties of life. It is, moreover, an *art* as well as a *virtue*" (quoted in Editor, 348). The focus on the economy of the household, not incidentally, parallels one of the critical concerns of the national economy: how to create surplus value. As long as labor is made to seem an end in itself, or a matter of "character," "virtue," and "art" (whose reward is simply the "happiness" it confers on the wife), it remains categorically separate from the "business" that engages the husband and for which he expects capital reward. As capitalist modes of production intensify the need to profit by exploiting the differential gap between earnings and expenses, unpaid labor, in the form of household government, realizes a tidy profit not only for the husband engaged in "business" but also for those economies that engage the husband. For the woman the profits are frequently intangible: improvement of character, expression of virtue, the experience of art. For the man, economics is something he engages in; for the woman, economics is part of her character.

That many of the domestic treatises were written by and for women could certainly evince a groundswell of female self-determination, suggesting one of the means by which women participated in the fundamental social changes at work in the period. At the same time, however, it could also demonstrate the sophisticated practices by which women were made to participate in the glorification of their domestic condition. This would have served an urgent cultural purpose: the more that liberal political dogma obtained in eighteenth-century English culture, the more the unequal condition of the domestic woman needed to be ideologically enhanced. The seemingly empowering changes that accompanied the transformation of the woman's household identity might simply, then, have reworked the behavioral prescriptions associated with earlier versions of the domestic woman. If so, the delegation of such powers to wives encoded patriarchal ideals and represented the subtle ways in which British culture attempted to adapt democratic principles to existing, and often conservative, models of family economy. Many of the domestic treatises, in fact, express grave concern about the dwindling interest among women in maintaining the household, and they share with Thomas Gisborne the impression that:

Young women endowed with good understanding, but desirous of justifying the mental indolence which they have permitted themselves to indulge; or disappointed at not perceiving a way open by which they, like their brothers, may distinguish themselves and rise to eminence; are occasionally heard to declare their opinion, that the sphere in which Women are destined to move is so humble and so limited, as neither to require nor to reward assiduity; and under this impression, either do not discern, or will not be persuaded to consider, the real and deeply interesting effects which the conduct of their sex will always have on the happiness of society. (*Enquiry into the Duties of the Female Sex*, 10–11)

As notions of modern individual fulfillment came to be identified inescapably with professional, public, and intellectual accomplishment, the conduct material needed to glamorize the "deeply interesting effects" of women's household function on the "happiness of society" in order to make them "like their brothers."

Defending the education of a woman in areas outside of "managing her family," Eliza Haywood similarly argues in *The Female Spectator* that the knowledge of subjects like philosophy could only improve domestic efficiency:

[W]ould too imperious and too tenacious man be so just to the world as to be more careful of the education of those females to whom they are parents or guardians! Would they convince them in their infancy that dress and show are not the essentials of a fine lady, and that true beauty is seated in the mind; how soon should we see our sex retrieve the many virtues which false taste has buried in oblivion! Strange infatuation! To refuse us what would so much contribute to their own felicity! Would not themselves reap the benefit of our amendment? Should we not be more obedient daughters, more faithful wives, more tender lovers, more sincere friends, and more valuable in every other station of life? (57)

This passage looks back conservatively to a time of neoclassical and patriarchal family values ("which false taste has buried in oblivion") to validate what many men evidently feel is a dangerous innovation: the education of women in matters outside domestic affairs. Haywood's work suggests that the discourse about conduct, manners, and behavior often reveals the strange and unofficial ways in which ideology and practice interact. As she goes on to argue, the education of women serves to make them more proficient in correcting men's behavior and in demonstrating how culturally disadvantaged male authority is:

There is, doubtless, somewhat more to be expected by a man from that woman whom the ceremony of marriage has made part of himself. She is, or ought to be, if qualified for it, the repository of his dearest secrets, the moderator of his fiercer passions, the softener of his most anxious cares and the constantly cheerful and entertaining companion in his more unbended moments. We all groan under the curse entailed upon us for the transgression of Eve—"Thy desires shall be to thy husband, and he shall have rule over thee"—but we are not taught enough how to lighten this burden and render ourselves such as would make him ashamed to exert that authority he thinks he has a right to over us. (59)

Beginning conventionally enough by urging women to be the "softener" of men's cares, this passage concludes by encouraging female resistance to male tyranny. But it advances this position in such a way as to alleviate a fundamental contradiction for the male in a putatively democratic society that issues from a patriarchal state: how to govern ostensibly equal subjects. The woman appropriates the very dictates that the man ordinarily insists upon in order that she may circumvent the shameful tendency in him to "exert" his domestic rights.

Even more fully radical accounts of education establish female intellectual credentials by mirroring male capacities, rather than contrasting them. According to Catherine Macauley, similar rules for male and female education should obtain because "there is but one rule of right for all rational beings, consequently true virtue in one must be equally so in the other. . . . [W]e cannot justly lessen, in one sex or the other the means by which perfection . . . is acquired" (*Letters*, 21). In *A Vindication of the Rights of Woman*, Mary Wollstonecraft defends equal education not to distinguish but to equalize male and female conduct: "Let woman share the rights and she will emulate the virtues of man; for she must grow more perfect when emancipated, or justify the authority that chains such a weak being to her duty" (194). Whether toning their rhetoric in order to reach a broader audience or fearing the consequences of a specialized domestic role for women, these writers employed a masculine ideal to measure the imagined accomplishments of educated women that only reasserted women's subjection to male approval.

If the purpose of such strategies is to extract the ideal woman from economic and political contingencies, making the home seem a place that surpasses the flawed world of commerce in order to further install real women in the very processes that they are being excluded from, they also tend to muddy the relationship between public and private experience. The ideal of the private nuclear family, while preserved to some extent, also seems to dissolve readily into public ideology. The conduct material may be seen as a less exotic but more personal part of what Foucault has seen as the "web of discourses, special knowledges, analyses, and injunctions" that settled upon the internal functioning of sexuality and the family (*History of Sexuality*, 26). That is, the purported rise of the nuclear family in pre-industrial Britain may have generated a perceived need for authoritative advice about the family that could help regulate sexual and affective behavior without seeming to act on behalf of the state.

This complex redistribution of both male and female roles microcosmically reproduces the contradiction in eighteenth-century conduct literature between conservative and radical impulses and suggests the ways in which political concerns entered domestic rhetoric. A part of the continued generation of signs, this "new" domestic woman was (or might have been) made to experience household duties in such acutely defined ways as to thoroughly ground her influence outside the "proper sphere" in household matters. That is, even when women managed to escape the often deadening limitations of a home life, they were still deeply conditioned by the ideology of female domesticity, and therefore safely absorbed into social and economic activities apart from the home. The frequent emphasis on women's "moral management" or their "economic and psychological reality" could thus be a means, on many occasions, of covertly addressing a male conundrum about exercising authority without appearing authoritarian. Liberal depictions of conjugality may thus have increased general awareness about the difficult process of making domestic responsibility coincide with individual fulfillment, dispersing paradigms of modern subjectivity over a wide range of cultural symbols.

Like arguments that assume that matrilineal cultures necessarily empowered women, the rise in female conduct literature can too easily be seen simply as evidence of "progressive" change. Armstrong claims in *Desire and Domestic Fiction* that such a rise led to the withering away of conduct material aimed at males, which mutated into other forms of discourse, such as satire. But when Armstrong then explains the eventual disappearance or transmutation of female conduct literature she reasons that it occurs "not because the female ideal they represented passed out of vogue" but because "the ideal had passed into the domain of common sense" (63). Since this latter logic might just as easily apply to the male conduct material that supposedly vanished toward the end of the eighteenth century, the claim that eighteenth-century culture lost interest in male conduct may point as much to a saturation of male instructional material as to its disappearance. Indeed, works such as Samuel Crossman's *The Young Man's Calling* (1678), Josiah Woodward's *The Young Man's Monitor* (1706), and William Darrell's *The Gentleman Instructed* (1704) continued to be widely sold late into the eighteenth century (and frequently into the nineteenth), and must be considered, in reprinted form, as a continuing part of the literature that shaped (and reshaped) domestic conduct. Typical of these more popular texts, Richard Allestree's *The Whole Duty of Man* (1658), alluded to in *Pamela* (Part II) and *Joseph Andrews*, had been published in more than 130 editions by 1800. James Fordyce, in writing *Addresses to Young Men*, his companion piece to the already enormously successful *Sermons to Young Women*, somewhat wearily articulates this very problem in justifying his own volume: "I could add but little to the large stores of moral and religious instruction, with which Young Men disposed to use them were already furnished from a variety of quarters" (vii–viii).[27] In such a market, female instruction would provide exactly the right kind of opportunity in which an anxious middle class could inscribe its own hegemonic desires. The very availability of the subject would seem to substantiate the bourgeois need to reconceive it. By attaching middle-class values to a hitherto neglected figure of social consequence (or at least by willfully seeing it that way) the middle classes could expose an apparent rift in the older order. In filling that space they could then claim moral elevation over their superiors by simultaneously revealing the latter's inadequacies and seeming to provide necessary correctives.

The diminishment of male advice in a number of conduct books may imply, then, that the male "subject" had already been adequately established, that assumptions about male conduct had become so absorbed by the end of the century as not to necessitate an extensive amount of dramatic reordering. In other words, the man's conventional role may have been more immediately adaptable to the refigured conjugal relations that appear in eighteenth-century depictions of the family. He may also have perfectly well represented the modern subject as one who could negotiate the increasingly complicated transition between public and private life, able to operate effectively in one sphere while still manifesting his affinity with the other.

Conduct material specifically addressed to men and extolling their regulatory power in the home does not, however, simply disappear over the course of the century. Many of the books addressing female manners, for example, appeared as companion pieces. Thomas Gisborne's *An Enquiry into the Duties of the Female Sex*, James Fordyce's *Sermons to Young Women*, and Timothy Rogers's *The Character of a Good Woman* were paired with Gisborne's *An Enquiry into the Duties of Men*, Fordyce's *Addresses to Young Men*, and Rogers's *Early Religion: or, The Way for a Young Man to Remember His Creator*. Such paired works appeared regularly in the period, from Eliza Haywood's *The Wife* and *The Husband. In Answer to the Wife* to the twin series I cited earlier as *The Young Man's Own Book* and *The Young Lady's Own Book*, both of which were subtitled "A manual of intellectual improvement and moral development" (and reprinted numerous times up until 1845). Even a single work such as Robert Dodsley's *The Oeconomy of Human Life*, where a section on the conduct of "Man" precedes one on "Woman," frequently resorted to a fairly predictable categorical positioning of both sexes, defining the appropriate domestic obligations of each in relentlessly conjugal terms.[28] These examples suggest that male conduct literature exerted a complementary influence in classifying and (en)gendering "subjectivity." That male behavior was in some respects feminized (just as female conduct was occasionally masculinized) may be arguable; nonetheless, gender continued to be a matter of relative definition. Part of a sexual economy that constantly rearranged its components, refigurations of one sex both determined and resulted from reconceptions of the other.

Domestic literature that assigned central authority and cultural currency to the male head of the household continued to appear throughout the last half of the eighteenth century. From treatises such as Thomas Percival's *A Father's Instructions to His Children* (1775) and John Martin's *Public and Domestic Devotion United* (1779) to works such as John Berkenhout's *A Volume of Letters to His Son at the University* (1790) and Hester Lynch Thrale Piozzi's "Letter to a Gentleman newly Married" (179?), conduct books were as likely to confer "modern" subjectivity on the father or husband as vest it in the domestic woman. Martin, for example, argues that the male must compensate for the domestic woman's "deficiencies in understanding" (34). Similarly, Piozzi cautions her newly wedded correspondent that in assessing his wife he should "[s]eek not for happiness in singularity; and dread a refinement of wisdom as a deviation into folly" (144). In these works, the male head of the household acts as overseer and internal monitor of the family's moral and economic station, a mediating figure between public and domestic spheres who symbolizes the very passage of culture in and out of the family. His role is at once intimate and objective; like the vicar of Wakefield, though much less gullible in the private affairs of the home, he both participates in the everyday construction of domestic life and examines it as a detached observer.

While the need to correct dissolute men in effective management of households often provided a useful fiction, no less potent was the supervisory and spectatorial role of the domestic male. Indeed, the power to discern the latent and natural industry of a potential wife remains, according to many of the conduct books, with the man, who must develop the finest of skills in scrutinizing the object of his choice. The minuteness of this scrutiny could, at times, be remarkable. As late as 1830, William Cobbett argued, straightforwardly it would seem, that the prospective husband could judge the industriousness of his future wife by observing "the labours" of her teeth because "she cannot make her teeth abandon their character." As he goes on to observe:

[W]hen she does bite, she cannot well disguise what nature has taught her to do; and you may be assured, that if her jaws move in slow time, and if she rather squeeze than bite the food; if she so deal with it as to leave you in doubt as to whether she mean finally to admit or reject it; if she deal with it thus, set her down as being, in her very nature, incorrigibly lazy. Never mind the pieces of needlework, the tambouring, the maps of the world made by her needle. Get to see her at work upon a muttonchop, or a bit of bread and cheese; and if she deal quickly with these, you have a pretty good security for that activity, that stirring industry, without which a wife is a burden instead of being a help. (115–16)

The alibi of nature here repeatedly diminishes the sense that the industry of the domestic woman proceeds from any active political will to shape her own identity. The presumption is that, for the most part, women will seek to disguise their "natural" character from the interested man (through needlework, tambouring, and mapmaking); the man must, as a consequence, develop a sophisticated reading of women to ensure his "security." The truly industrious woman achieves her status only as the result of an instinct found below consciousness itself in the activity of molars, canines, and incisors "upon a muttonchop." The "new woman," shut out of even her embroidered "world," finds her reward only by way of the man's careful gaze and informed selection. Such instructions in surveillance highlight a no less complex shifting of the domestic male as both the object and the implement of household reform.

That male instruction, moreover, often mutated into other forms of discourse suggests that, if anything, conduct literature for men was becoming increasingly sophisticated and specialized. One such form, for instance, was husbandry, and in this area we can see that men continued to play a significant supervisory role in the maintenance of the household and its environs. In a frequently republished work titled *The Complete Family-Piece: and Country Gentleman and Farmer's Best Guide*, for example, the male home owner is encouraged to cultivate his grounds as he would cultivate the inner environment of his house so that the outer perspective of his property reflects its interior order. This is but one of many examples that might indicate the complex and diverse means—the "variety of quarters" that Fordyce cites—by which habits of conduct were communicated in the period. As in *The Vicar of Wakefield*, where the vicar's roles as "priest," "husbandman," and "father of a family" are distinguished (however ironically), the advice material spreads masculine norms over a number of discourses, making them seem even more organic. A farmer can become the middle term linking a man's function as spiritual scion to his activity as paternal guide. Much of this secondary literature suggests, in fact, that, contrary to modern claims that the husband played a diminished role in the daily supervision of the home, his domestic role was complex enough that it had to be divided among several kinds of texts.

It would seem, particularly from the late-eighteenth-century cult of "the man of sentiment," that male conduct was as much an object of analysis and advice as female conduct, and it is very difficult to determine which preceded the other and whether either antedated "actual" social changes. Sterne's heroes, Fielding's Joseph Andrews, Rousseau's Emile, Mackenzie's "Man of Feeling," Richardson's Grandison, Goldsmith's vicar, and lesser-known paragons like those in Sarah Scott's *The Man of Real Sensibility or the History of George Ellison* (1766), Charles Jenner's *The Placid Man; or, Memoirs of Sir Charles Beville* (1770) and Edward Kimber's *The Life and Adventures of James Ramble, Esq.* (1755), which sets out to prove that "[a] man may be a finished gentleman, and yet pursue a course of virtue," adumbrate a long forgotten catalogue of fictional characters who sought to translate principles of tender and economical subjectivity into conventional male behavior. *Sir Charles Grandison*, we may recall, had an enormous literary and ideological influence over the writers following Richardson. Blake's and Austen's admiring responses to it are only the most notorious proof that it was often regarded as "a living system of manners."[29]

Domestic Empiric

The impression one often receives from reading nonfictional appraisals of domestic conduct from the eighteenth century is that they were, in part, eulogizing the family. This suggests that eighteenth-century British culture was as much concerned with preserving a normative image of a fast-disappearing social configuration as with creating a new one. Echoing such concerns, the anonymous author of *Considerations on the Cause of the Present Stagnation of Matrimony* (1772) bemoans the fact that marriage in the late eighteenth century so consistently failed to provide the necessary social stability as to require state intervention: "the luxury and extravagance of the age is the bane of matrimony; and the disorder hath run to such an height of malignity, that there is the greatest reason to think it must prove fatal, unless some empiric in politics should strike out a method of inoculating frugality" (70–71). These laments imply that what Peter Laslett describes as "the world we have lost" (one of eighteenth-century family cohesion) feared that it had itself lost a world, a prior order of affective domestic relations whose natural constitution desperately needed to be restored.[30] According to the conceit used by the pamphleteer, the state has sickened and requires an "empiric." If this is the case, we might want to consider the domestic material in light of how it broke with or modified tradition and how it conserved it. The creation of the sentimentalized nuclear household was both a conscious tactical maneuver and a means of making the family seem healthy, whole, and alive to its inalienable potential. Learning to function within the essentially bourgeois household described in most of the domestic literature of the period was a process seemingly of discovering an innate and natural self.

In the various discourses about the family, eighteenth-century writers were not so much creating actual new modes of conduct as appearing to do so in order to adapt certain valued codes of behavior that were becoming increasingly difficult to maintain. In assessing domestic relations, they had at least three options: tracing the family's distinctness from alternative forms of power, treating the family as a supplement to other social behaviors, or affirming its primary function in controlling civil order. These three approaches are by no means mutually exclusive within a body of texts—in fact, they often appear paradoxically in a single author's works (as in Locke's case), suggesting a complex network of ideological intentions. They are all, however, aimed in different ways at adjusting the uses to which family ideals could be put. Rather than solely championing middle-class domestic virtues, they were providing ideological compensation for the very sacrifices that accompanied the political and economic modifications that enabled the self-fashioning of the middle class.

Jacques Donzelot suggests that this process of re-representing the family as under siege is a recurring leitmotif in anthropological and sociological studies of the family in Western culture. Though describing the modern era, he could just as easily be expressing the attitudes of concerned eighteenth-century observers when he declares: "It has become an essential ritual of our societies to scrutinize the countenance of the family at regular intervals in order to decipher our destiny, glimpsing in the death of the family an impending return to barbarism, the letting go of our reasons for living; or, indeed, in order to reassure ourselves at the sight of its inexhaustible capacity for survival" (4). If the English conduct writers of the eighteenth century feared the death of the family, it is possible they did so because they could only imagine it surviving in a conventional form. The death they feared, then, was the demise of the specific family paradigm each defended and hoped to advance in the face of modern decline. Yet they also wanted to regard their idea of family as a birth; in the process, they needed to eliminate competing ideas of the family in order to transfigure them. That is, they simultaneously observed the "death of the family" and "its inexhaustible capacity for survival."

In all these discourses the family was the disputed territory for an ideological project whose alleged purpose was to normalize domestic relations. It is crucial, therefore, to read such texts in conjunction, to see how domesticity was presented as a universal condition ruled by immutable laws and yet also adaptable to modern self-sufficiency. The struggle over the family's meaning signals both the elasticity of seemingly obsolete norms and the way in which eighteenth-century assessments of domestic relations attempted to coordinate contending social forces. Laying bare the family's paradoxical constitution in earlier representations of household relations, the behavioral materials had to naturalize a new set of relations that could appear distinctive, and thus socially effective, and yet seem entirely familiar. They needed, in other words, to disguise the very discord that created their demand in the first place.

2

From Family Romance to Domestic Scandal: "Female Arts" in *The Fair Jilt*

> All Things in Nature cheat, or else are cheated.
> —Aphra Behn, *The Younger Brother*

Subverting Romance

Perhaps no stories are more homeless in the period 1688–1798 than Aphra Behn's. Her prose fiction rarely figures as an origin in histories of the novel, not only because its generally short length belies novelistic amplitude, but also because its vexed association with the romance tradition apparently counteracts any claims of authenticity. Lacking the comprehensive illusion of fact and betraying everywhere their author's obsession with aristocratic culture, her "novellas" tend to be regarded more as uncertain precursors to Defoe and Richardson than as novels in their own right.[1] Behn's claims to having witnessed the events described in *Oroonoko* and *The Fair Jilt* certainly appear to be compromised by her inclusion of patently unrealistic elements such as the characters' elevated discourse, the idealization of exotic cultures, and the bizarre excesses of physical valor. Drawn to the exceptional, Behn tends to exclude the mundane, the familiar, the domestic routine of everyday life that is increasingly prominent in eighteenth-century prose. That is, her anti-realist tendencies seem to parallel the fiction's anti-domestic tone.

There are, however, enough verisimilar aspects to Behn's narratives to suggest that she played an instrumental part in the development of realism in the eighteenth century.[2] Collectively, Behn's stories exhibit properties that have been frequently associated with the genre: contemporaneity, detailed evocation of place, psychological insight, factuality, compact plotting, and a self-conscious first-person narrator. Her role in the "history of the novel," then, is puzzling. Somehow necessary to it, she remains separated from its supposedly monumental phase in the "realistic" works of Defoe, Richardson, Fielding, and Austen. Her ghostly presence in the history of eighteenth-century fiction may be attributed partly to the problematic status of her work: making claims of verisimilitude and eschewing romance Behn fails, according to a teleological definition of the novel's history, to register her commitment to those principles in the stories themselves.[3] Her failure to generate consistently realistic narratives mirrors her failure to acknowledge "the novel's" dominant tendency toward everyday domestic subjects.

That critics frequently discredit Behn's realism, however, may simply occur because she fails to confirm a prescriptive history of "the novel." Consigning Behn to the domain of romance finesses the difficulty of positioning her in the history of prose fiction by conveniently separating her from that history. Such an approach, however, assumes that "novel" and "romance" are essentially incompatible genres. And yet romance is as capable of categorical instability as any other form and could be used, as Behn uses it, to subvert the very distinctions on which the terms "romance" and "novel" seem to rely. Like the sociological materials examined in the previous chapter, Behn's work juggles "actual" and "ideal" structures of behavior.[4]

If empirical discourse, in the supposedly liminal moment when Behn and others groped toward realism, was replacing the language of aristocratic romance, we should then expect realistic aspects of the narrative to play a subversive role. But it is predominantly romance (usually in the form of scandal) that complicates Behn's fiction and subverts her own validations of empiricism. This paradox, whereby romantic invention demystifies authentic history, not only suggests the arbitrary dualism that conventionally delimits realism and romance, but implies that their individual epistemological functions are reversible. Because Behn frames her narratives as rigorously empirical tales that she can verify either by first-hand knowledge or through reliable sources, her romantic inventions challenge the boundaries imposed by the realistic story and the world view it encourages. Moreover, it is the romance element, uncharacteristically, that appears to have provided the destabilizing effect usually attributed to realism. Despite her claims about witnessing her story, romance conventions pervade Behn's fictions and express her discomfort with strict generic prescriptions.

Behn's divided narrative framework implies that romance was susceptible to the same dialectical transformation as empirical tales. Since realism is conventionally equated with everyday life and, by extension, domestic ideology (expressed in the late seventeenth century through didactic conduct books that used fictional vignettes of commonplace lives to exemplify social etiquette), Behn's use of romance may in fact be aimed at subverting the domestic implications of an empirical ideology. That is, her fiction already contains a critique of the realism it seems only to herald. It was situated at a point when specifically aristocratic and middle-class conduct books that largely preserved direct and usually untroubled expressions of patriarchal domesticity were losing persuasive force. And these were not yet complemented by the less class-specific conduct book of the eighteenth century, which generally masked its patriarchal concerns by shifting a good deal of the responsibility for making the household a representation of ideal social behavior (in both material and ideological ways) onto the domestic woman. As a result, Behn's fiction tended to reproduce a marginal social space in which women could at least imagine a condition that, while it did not necessarily free them from patriarchal structures, also did not operate on them with the kind of conceptual rigor that characterizes later articulations of domesticity.

Literary critics have frequently invalidated the narrative aspects that qualify Behn as a novelist (and presumably a realistic one) by condemning her fiction on the grounds of its insufficient management of morality, feminine propriety, uniform narrative structure, and realistic detail.[5] Criticized for not unequivocally supporting the ideals of domesticity, she can be that much more easily dismissed for her failures of form. Thus, in a surprisingly large number of scholarly analyses of Behn's work, moral principle as much as formal accomplishment dictates her success or failure as a novelist. Her narratives trouble so many critics, in varying ways, not only because they affront decorum or exploit romance when they should be strengthening realism but because in doing so they alienate the family.[6] Frequently depicting women who compete for the same liberties of conduct and language as men, seek to escape the rigid strictures of family government, or manipulate the proprieties of female conduct for their own devious ends, Behn uses romance and scandal to evoke female discontent with a culture directed by ineffective or incompatible codes of domestic behavior. Indeed, Behn's work may be viewed as a special case of the conflict between the values of the scandal chronicle and those of the conduct book. If we regard the scandal chronicle as sensationalized romance (distilling the latter's delicate passions and decorums into spectacle, and frequently illicit spectacle at that), Behn's deployment of feminocentric romance becomes the means by which she couples problems of gender with the formal demands of prose fiction. The family certainly acts as an institutional force in these tales, but its marginal status indicates both its sublimated function as an organizing element of narration and Behn's antipathy to domestic coercion. For Behn, domesticity is the supplement to other social mechanisms of power rather than the central repository of cultural values. Because the family serves a public function, Behn's exposure of family relations discloses the larger political, economic, and moral uses of domestic representation in contemporary European culture. By focusing primarily on Behn's most aggressive scandal chronicle, *The Fair Jilt*, this chapter examines how Restoration narrative typically modifies domestic ideology by subjecting it to internal and external deformations that expose its own tenuous unity.

"Tubs Full of Blessings, and Houses Full of Prosperity"

In most of Behn's short and long fictions domestic scenes are both primal and intensely public; they concentrate on perversions that emanate from within the family and extend outward, usually to the point of obliterating or minimizing household structure. *Love Letters Between a Nobleman and His Sister* describes the illicit and corrosive relationship between Sylvia and her brother-in-law Philander, and is based on newspaper accounts of the scandalous elopement of Lord Grey and his sister-in-law Lady Henrietta Berkeley. Similarly, *Oroonoko*, which Behn claimed was based on witnessed fact, documents the violent rupture of the protagonist's marriage and family within two racially opposed cultures. Its balanced two-part structure suggests parallels between the sexual enslavement of women within an African harem and slave treatment within a European plantocracy in the West Indies. *The Fair Jilt*, another factual fiction and perhaps the preeminent example of Behn's devastating critique of both anti-familial rage and conventional domestic morality, traces the effect of an unscrupulous woman's financial schemes on her family's fortune as she pursues a series of lurid sexual adventures.

Behn's complicated attitude toward family and narrative in these fictions derives in part from skepticism about the hortatory value of domestic instruction and the logic of monogamous marital standards. This unease with domestic ideology appears explicitly in her mock conduct books, the two parts of *The Ten Pleasures of Marriage* (subtitled respectively *The Delights and Contentments that are Masked Under the Bands of Matrimony* and *The Confession of the New Married Couple*), in which the narrator's irony reduces courtship, wedding, and domesticity to a series of derelict pleasures. That is, rather than establishing a consistent moral context for the fiction, Behn's didactic works engage in the same process of demystification. It is perhaps characteristic, then, that she preferred to write mock, rather than genuine, conduct books; by doing so, she preserves the duplicitous voice that has continued to vex so many of her critics. In these works, almost all the pleasures Behn scrutinizes, from the wedding itself to the purchase of household goods, contain hidden psychological and material costs that constantly defer the experience of fulfillment they supposedly generate. The tenth pleasure of marriage, for example, demonstrates that the husband's desire to raise children becomes an activity that "shall hasten your death" (134). Indeed, the text as a whole implies that the more one seeks to locate the "tubs full of blessings, and houses full of prosperity" (16) that the marriage ideal promulgates, the more such happiness recedes—if it was there at all. As the narrator observes: "What a thick shell this marriage nut hath, before one can come to the kernel of it" (21). From Behn's satirical perspective, disappointment becomes the formative ground from (and against) which an illusory and self-deceiving faith in the pleasures of marriage emerges. Although she focuses on the happy family—if so only because it is blind to its own deception—she uses such deluded figures to accentuate the larger number of discontented families surrounding them. Not only is the happy family illusory (because it fails to perceive its own abusive economy) but it is itself an exception in a culture generally consisting of failed marriages. The possibility of establishing behavioral norms is thus doubly un-done; either proper codes of conduct are revealed to be dangerously volatile or they fail utterly in influencing a majority of households.

The Ten Pleasures of Marriage is written as if it were addressing a young man contemplating marriage, but by the end it is clear that Behn is parodying misogynistic advice in books written essentially for men, such as Richard Braithwaite's *Ar't Asleep Husband?* (1640), William Gouge's *Of Domesticall Duties* (1622), Joseph Swetnam's *The Arraignment of Lewd, Idle, Froward, and Unconstant Women* (1615), and William Whately's *A Care-cloth: or, A Treatise of the Cumbers and Troubles of Marriage* (1624).[7] When Behn relates the disenchantment that a husband must feel when he discovers after marriage that his wife is "vomiting up the venom that she so long had harboured under her sweet hypocrisie" (135), the evident dis-taste she describes is as much for the male attitudes toward married women that conduct material inscribes as for the hapless female vic-tim of the marital codes of behavior that reduce her to such venom-ous hostility. Mocking the helpful tone of advice material, Behn ul-timately uses the form of the conduct book to deconstruct its own dubious epistemological assumptions about marital felicity.

Behn's feigned conduct books, then, where happy families fore-ground malfunctioning ones, enact nearly the opposite tactic she adopts in her fiction, although ultimately to the same end. In both cases, scandal becomes the defining feature of affective relations, but the prose narratives highlight problematic courtships, marriages, and families without accentuating successes elsewhere. In the fiction, romance replaces conduct books as the mode by which behavioral precepts are communicated and circulated; the resulting household distress, however, is the same. Behn's use of romance, therefore, reveals the same intricate structure of signification as the didactic works: she mocks the very social conventions that her invocation of romance simultaneously articulates. For Behn, romance provides a vehicle for exploring scandalous sexual fantasies and dilemmas at the same time that, like conduct literature, it submits characters to rigorous codes of behavior.

While *Oroonoko* is probably her most famous prose work, Behn's fiction more frequently imitates the scandal chronicle, though always in conjunction with narrative events that typify aristocratic romance. In scandal, Behn discovered an expressive medium for intensely felt but ambiguous responses to female "subjection" (in terms of both cultural subjugation and subject formation). The scandal chronicle offered up a romance subject, usually a woman, whose actions contravened moral and domestic proprieties and in so doing threatened both social order and romantic ideology. Such actions were not generally consciously revolutionary or ideological (at least the characters themselves show no such awareness—indeed most of them act out of principles of pure ego gratification), yet their literary treatment often raised ideological issues grounded in female identity and resistance. Operating within the formal and ideological prescriptions of romance, the scandalous heroine did not simply reveal the ideal deportment by which readers should conduct themselves but persistently expressed the coercion of a social system that demanded such rules. A figure of disruption, the scandalous heroine discloses and simultaneously complicates the regulatory link between the romance and conduct literature. Many of Behn's female protagonists are thus not unlike the feral populations in Hobbes's description of human behavior. That is, they constitute the very anarchic force that eighteenth-century conduct books would eventually deny; driven by polygamous desire, they seek to satisfy rampant appetites in a culture that tries to bind them to a strict conjugal ideal.

Unlike the picaresque, the scandal chronicle, rather than extemporizing on an accidental series of narrative events, tends to relate the destructive actions of the heroine to marriage, property, family order, sexual propriety, and stable gender relations. While it aggressively distances itself from the romance—by being considerably shorter, contemporaneous, and "factual"—the scandal chronicle extends the essential sexual mythography of the romance (one critic calls *The Fair Jilt* "amoral romanticism").[8] The scandalous heroine acquires an identity in opposition to a fixed set of cultural assumptions about female behavior, assumptions that tend to reinforce the family, aristocratic and bourgeois alike, as a necessary institution. As in the romances they imitated, seventeenth- and eighteenth-century scandal chronicles exploited the precarious nature of female conduct in that period: according to Mary Poovey, the proper lady, while continuing to manifest her sexual allure, must remain impervious to any improper acknowledgment of desire (18–26). Because the scandalous woman makes a spectacle of herself, she challenges those limitations on desire and dramatizes the fundamental contradiction of eighteenth-century propriety, revealing the mesmerizing attraction of what supposedly does not exist (female desire) only because it is ideologically repressed. As an exaggerated reaction to didactic literature, the scandal chronicle indicated that although conduct books increasingly extolled a woman of superior moral and domestic principles, they still felt compelled to grapple with the model of the uncontrollable carnal woman, as if it were simply a given rather than the product of cultural, pedagogical, and scientific myths about innate female character.

Romance, insofar as it transcribed aspects of female sexuality and conduct that were not customarily addressed in polite society, furnished the means for women writers to explore taboo subjects, even if it also presumed a strict code of manners. In Restoration narrative particularly, the inclusion and reworking of the romantic dilemmas associated with the heroic romance produced hybrid forms, such as the scandal chronicle, that were especially suited to depicting volatile social and domestic relations. Frequently, the romance elements in Restoration fiction were coupled with seemingly incompatible features from other forms of fiction as diverse as the picaresque, imaginary voyage, anti-romance, and didactic story.[9] But Behn's narratives intensify this hybridity; their multiformity often produces a female literary subject whose identity is indeterminate, who is as capable of delinquent as decorous behavior, and who owes her existence as much to criminal literature as to the romance or the conduct book.

Part of this eclecticism, Behn's narratorial presence in her writings—generally in the form of dramatic asides—accentuates the particular and often peculiar female authority with which she invests the written word, linking it frequently and sometimes urgently to the ontological status of her central female characters. The manner in which Behn incorporates established narrative forms communicates the heterogeneity of female sensibility that is ultimately her main point of reference.[10] It is through this generic shifting that Behn suggests the unpredictable volatility of her subject: a woman on the brink of definition. This narrative fusion, particularly as it uses romance to challenge cultural assumptions about gender and family, occurs in almost all of Behn's fiction. In her work romance generates a referential field that for all its reactionary pedigree implies a radical and explosive femininity that ultimately finds expression in the form of public spectacle, an undefinable excess that moves aggressively beyond the private domestic sphere.

Behn's literary work in general interrogates the sexual paradox of the seventeenth century, the double standard by which the libertine insisted on modesty, decency, and domestic regularity in a woman at the same time that he demanded proof of her sexuality. Such a standard predictably encouraged the creation of a narrative subject whose very nature must have been divided. The scandal chronicle, capitalizing on a kind of social schizophrenia, offers its readers a figure who is fundamentally duplicitous. In narratives such as *The Fair Jilt*, Behn depicts female sexual intransigence in ways that are meant to be alluring and morally instructive at the same time. They censure the woman for her immodest behavior but in doing so invariably discredit the male system of sexual conduct that partly determines feminocentric spectacle. Behn's recourse to a criminal heroine in *The Fair Jilt* simply intensifies this tendency by tying anti-domestic conduct specifically to deviant and illegal behavior. The extremely visible spectacle of a woman's unlawful activity highlights the ambivalent moral and domestic expectations of the public sphere within which she circulates, exposing the assumptions behind both the accepted myth of uncontrollable female carnality and the problematic misogyny of male advice literature.

"Masculine Strokes"

The contradictions that characterize the scandalous woman are intensified in Behn's case by several atypical aspects of her life: that she was herself apparently unconnected to family most of her life, that as a government spy for Charles II she played an unusually active role in political events both in England and on the Continent (though her advice on national affairs was inevitably ignored), and that she was routinely accused of scandalous behavior in matters sexual as well as literary. To some degree, her literary work reproduces the dynamic tensions that shaped her public, private, and authorial concerns, consistently setting Behn's actual experience against the lives of the fictional women she describes. Her prose narratives, in particular, generally place their heroines within contexts that simultaneously implicate them in and extricate them from the culture in which they are defined. Functioning as catalysts for male behavior in religious, political, or economic circumstances, they rarely participate directly in such affairs, despite the fact that their histories are usually told by a woman who is herself actively involved in those very events.

It is not surprising, then, that Behn's literary works record the complex and ambiguous process of female individuation with which she was only too familiar from her experiences not only as a spy but also as dramatist. Behn's plays were routinely criticized by male critics for being inappropriate vehicles for a woman writer, despite their general conformity to the content and intention of Restoration

drama (*The Rover* is no more titillating or ribald than typical plays
of the period like *The Country Wife*). William Wycherley's comments in his poem about Behn, "To the Sappho of the Age. Sup-
pos'd to Ly-In of a Love-Distemper, or a Play," are crudely framed
and are part of a conventional partisan attack based on political differences, but they summarize the general view that Behn's plays
were as deviant as her lifestyle was supposed to be:

> Thus, as your Beauty did, your Wit does now,
> The Womens Envy, Mens Diversion grow;
> Who, to be Clap'd, or Clap you, round you sit,
> And, tho' they Sweat for it, will croud your Pit;
> Since lately you Lay-In, (but as they say,)
> Because, you had been Clap'd another Way;
> But, if 'tis true, that you have need to Sweat,
> Get, (if you can) at your New Play, a Seat. (156)[11]

Wycherley's taunting comments, riddled as they are with broad sexual puns about wantonness, illegitimate childbirth, venereal disease,
and parallels between Behn's dramatic art and sexual licentiousness,
suggest the blunt acceptance of the logical contradictions of the
double standard and its pervasive linking of women's legitimate creativity to approved, and presumably marital, sexuality.[12] Behn's famous response to this kind of criticism accentuates the sexual distinctions by which literary work was judged in the seventeenth century. In the preface to her play *The Lucky Chance*, published one
year before the appearance of *The Fair Jilt*, Behn complains that
dramatic indecencies are never noticed when the writer is male, but
that her play "is not fit for the Ladys: As if (if it were as they falsly
give out) the Ladys were oblig'd to hear Indecencys only from their
Pens and Plays" (185). Consequently, she challenges unprejudiced
readers to study her comedies and "compare 'em with others of this
Age, and if they find one Word that can offend the chastest Ear, I
will submit to all their peevish Cavills; but Right or Wrong they
must be Criminal because a Woman's" (185). Objecting that the
"Masculine Strokes in me, must not be allow'd" (186), her caustic remarks at the conclusion of the preface exemplify the dual concern

for preserving decency and challenging sexual restrictions that underscores nearly everything she wrote:

I must want common Sense, and all the Degrees of good Manners, renouncing my Fame, all Modesty and Interest for a silly Sawcy fruitless Jest, to make Fools laugh, and Women blush, and wise Men asham'd. . . . All I ask, is the Privelege for my Masculine Part the Poet in me, (if any such you will allow me) to tread in those successful Paths my Predecessors have so long thriv'd in, to take those Measures that both the Ancient and Modern Writers have set me, and by which they have pleas'd the World so well: If I must not, because of my Sex, have this Freedom, but that you will usurp all to your selves; I lay down my Quill, and you shall hear no more of me. . . . I am not content to write for a Third day only. I value Fame as much as if I had been born a *Hero*; and if you rob me of that, I can retire from the ungrateful World, and scorn its fickle Favours. (187)

The dialectic here, as in much of Behn's work, volleys between professional assertions associated with the male domain of "Masculine Parts," or "Heroism," and traditional female characteristics like "chastity," "good Manners," and "Modesty." Behn's argument attacks a widely held view that women writers posed a threat on two levels. First, by influencing female audiences specifically (through the contiguity of gender) they encouraged vice in those particular listeners. They thus challenged the grounds upon which the male establishment maintained its proprietary control over what it regarded as the innate depravity of the opposite sex—"Right or Wrong they must be criminal because a Woman's." Catherine Gallagher's reference to Behn's authorial persona as "the heroine-victim of the market-place" is here manifested as the professional woman writer's criminal activity (8).[13] Second, by crossing vocational boundaries women writers deconstructed conventional gender differences. Stressing the "Masculine Strokes" of her pen, "the Masculine Part the poet in me," and her heroic valuation of "Fame," Behn endorses a principle of androgyny that not only elicited charges of indecency but also legitimized equality between the sexes, attacking the foundations on which domestic privacy and education were constructed.

These same issues shape the representation of gender and family in Behn's prose fiction, which likewise exposes the limits of contemporary sexual ideology. But if the plays were criticized for their moral content and caused Behn to defend them on ethical grounds, her defense of the prose narratives uses entirely different tactics. Rejecting the polemical defense of female bawdy by which she frequently justified her dramatic works, Behn usually vindicated her prose fiction on the grounds of "truthfulness." This suggests that matters of authenticity in relation to gender and prose fiction were more important than matters of propriety. A woman's identity lay not in her moral character so much as in her narrative credibility. It also suggests that Behn and her readers believed that veracity legitimated lewdness, demanding the kind of sexual forthrightness expressed in the scandal chronicle. This further implies that readers of fiction, in this period at least, were less likely than theatergoers to be considered morally at risk (a fact that may be attributed to drama's more public presentation). By being true, Behn's prose fiction could represent scandalous behavior more safely. Truth would seem to protect the author from accusations of endorsing conduct that would undermine conventional sexual roles and hence family order.

Historical veracity, then, becomes the measure of aesthetic value in Behn's fiction and is linked specifically to conduct that disrupts domestic ideology, even if it does not endorse that conduct. In *The Fair Jilt*, for example, Behn repeatedly affirms the factual content of the story and, to legitimize that claim, refers to her own biography as a means to graph intersecting lines of action from the sexual and marital intrigues of Miranda, the "fair jilt" of the story's title, onto the religious and political realities of contemporary Flanders and the author's own secret role there as emissary to Charles II. Early in the story proper she asserts, "I do not pretend here to entertain you with a feign'd Story, or any Thing piec'd together with romantick Accidents; but every Circumstance, to a Tittle, is Truth. To a great Part of the Main I myself was an Eye-witness; and what I did not see, I was confirm'd of by Actors in the Intrigue, Holy Men, of the Order of St. *Francis*" (74). Later discussing the movements of the hero, Prince Tarquin, she mentions that his arrival in Antwerp (the narrative setting) occurred "about the Time of my being sent thither by King *Charles*" (98). These factual asides are conventional gestures

in seventeenth-century narratives, serving to frame the act of reading fictionalized accounts of seemingly factual events; as has been
frequently noted, they justify the fictionalizing act itself and signify
the stricter distinctions being drawn at the time between factual and
fictional discourses.[14] But they serve the further purpose in Behn's
case of vouchsafing the word of a female author, one particularly
suited to tell such stories by virtue of her unique involvement in
contemporary political intrigues. As usual, the validity of that claim
is posed in terms of the apparent rejection of romance, which, as a
prototypical female discourse, was thought to damage narrative
authority (even in a story saturated with romantic features). Furthermore, claims to verisimilitude seem to authenticate the rather
alarming accomplishments of Behn's heroine—more than just mere
fancy, Behn's work documents genuine (that is, verifiable) female
behavior. Here Behn uses realism to substantiate the romantic excesses of the scandal chronicle, itself a strange composite of embel-
lishment and fact.

A figure consigned to the domestic sphere, where her polygamous and political energies become destructive, Miranda can have
an historical impact on her culture only through her shadowy effect
on prominent men. Her history, like the scandal chronicle, is both
factual and unsubstantiated, part of family history that only occasionally emerges from its private domain. Behn's prefatory dedication to *The Fair Jilt* alerts us, in an odd way, to the unrecorded impact of domestic women on political events, and the tendency of
that exclusion to make them devious participants in the affairs of
state. In the story proper, Behn depicts a woman destroying male
family honor, yet in presenting the work to her male patron, Henry
Neville Payne (a prominent Catholic, Tory, and Royalist sympa-
thizer), Behn writes a dedication that focuses on Prince Tarquin as if
Miranda were secondary. Emphasizing that the prince is an actual
historical figure known to Payne, Behn shifts attention away from
the catalytic figure of the heroine, concentrating instead on the political implications of Tarquin's claim to be "the last of the Race of
Roman Kings" (70). She parallels her patron's heroic support of the
Stuart cause, his "Imprisonment and Sufferings, through all the

Course of our late National Distractions" (70), with Tarquin's presumed nobility.[15] In doing so, she illustrates two historical versions
of the same family romance: that is, the attempts through the sheer
genealogical imperative to fuse the destiny of the state to royal biol-
ogy in both Rome and England. With the dedication, Behn apparently wants to equate England under Stuart governance with Roman
history, paralleling the lineages of kings and emperors and thereby
exalting Stuart legitimacy. Tarquin, however, may also symbolize
Stuart destinies since, despite his supposed pedigree, he has neither
power nor estate. Nor, as the only remaining representative of the
Roman kings, does he have a continuing family line by which to ensure his fame. Instead, his love for Miranda degrades the very source
of his "power," his noble heritage. Indeed, the alliance with Miranda
seriously damages Tarquin's credibility (particularly when he attempts to murder her sister). Although Tarquin is ambiguously extolled, this only further emphasizes Payne's eminence: if Tarquin's
ancestry elevates both men, then his weaknesses simply magnify the
integrity of the representative Stuart figure (in the person of Payne).
Nevertheless, publishing *The Fair Jilt* in 1688, Behn would have
been particularly sensitive to the impaired fortunes of the Stuart
family, and James II in particular. Despite the glorification of Payne,
the cynical view of family in Behn's narrative only suggests her pessimism about family ideology on a national and political level.

In the dedication, then, Behn virtually ignores the heroine and
the import of her actions on the political and social constitution of
Flanders in favor of an elegiac reference to the decline of masculine
systems of genealogical authority in Rome and England. Although a
constitutive part of the narrative and the referent of its title, she is
effaced from the critical paraphernalia attached to the story. Were it
not for the fact that the dedication also serves a prefatory function,
outlining the theme and purpose of the narrative, this would not
seem all that significant. The dedication, however, establishes the
ideological and aesthetic bases for literary judgment of the work itself—truth (in the form of narrative verisimilitude) and value (in the
guise of a "noble" subject who symbolically reinforces the Stuart
cause). The heroine's absence from this discussion suggests that the

"noble" aspects of the narrative—Tarquin and royalty—are not synonymous with its main subject, Miranda, the fair jilt. Though describing a work that delineates female domestic aggression and portrays men as helplessly vulnerable to feminine beauty and guile, the dedication serves the opposite purpose, extolling male power and virtue. Before she has begun, Behn effectively erases the critical element of the narrative—the heroine's duplicitous, mutable, unenclosed being. Behn thus excludes her heroine from any "history" that would appeal to a reader like Henry Payne. Lying outside larger cultural demarcations, Miranda apparently has no direct role to play (symbolic or otherwise) in either the conventional domestic sphere or a political arena dominated by transgenerational obsessions over genealogies, inheritances, birthrights, and destiny. She is seemingly "free" of historical context, and, therefore, of a "familiarizing" context, disinherited from a "world" that would place her firmly within its moral superstructure, and yet still capable of having a severe impact upon it. In the terms that this book uses, Miranda's story marginalizes family relations in order to estrange standard forms of conduct, yet it is framed by a supplementary address to a political figure of Roman Catholic descent, whose behavior represents an ideal marriage of private and public virtue.

"The Cause Why"

Possibly drafted as early as 1678 but frequently told as an oral tale before being published in complete form in 1688, *The Fair Jilt*, one of Behn's most popular scandal chronicles, may be best described as an account of female passion publicly at odds with normative cultural expectations. While it may seem to lack a rigorous organizing principle, there is, as in *Oroonoko*, a distinct symmetry to the two parts of *The Fair Jilt*: the first half describes how Miranda tries to seduce a priest named Henrick, despite his profound religious convictions; the second half concerns her seduction of and marriage to Prince Tarquin. The parts are thematically linked by Miranda's obsession with male figures whose aristocratic heritage embodies family authority: Henrick, a German prince who has taken holy orders in order to forget a romantic courtship destroyed by his elder brother, represents spiritual eminence; Tarquin, a man of regal appearance who claims to be the last of the line of Roman kings, symbolizes historical continuity. The structural mirroring of the story's two parts—typical of Behn's fiction—emphasizes the ideological equation between the marital (and familial) and the nonmarital (or anti-familial) actions within the tale. It also accentuates the correlation, rather than separation, of public and private experience. For Miranda, as for Behn, family signifies political alliance with other families of quality, and therefore comes to generate intensely public modes of display.

The "seductions" of Henrick and Tarquin suggest, in complementary ways, Miranda's general power over the highest order of men; they signal her desire to couple sexuality and domesticity with cultural power. As the narrator observes: "She lov'd nothing so much as to behold sighing Slaves at her Feet, of the greatest Quality" (77). Her mastery over them is comprehensive and is expressed consistently in the form of public show (the counterpart to domestic privacy in Behn's fiction). When Henrick, for example, rejects Miranda's passionate advances in the confessional, she accuses him of rape before witnesses gathered at the church and eventually has him condemned to death. A measure of Miranda's volatile nature, the suddenness with which her passion for Henrick turns into vindictive rage typifies not only the superficial content of her "love" but also the manipulability of sexual desire in Restoration culture. Henrick, the strict adherent to conjugal faithfulness (resorting to religious celibacy when marriage to the woman he loves becomes impossible), looks impotent and foolish in the face of such demonic possession. Similarly, after Tarquin falls passionately in love with and marries Miranda, he agrees to murder her sister, Alcidiana, because his wife wants control of the family fortune. In both instances, the victimized male participates in a lurid public defamation of his character. Henrick undergoes a prolonged imprisonment, trial, and judgment during which he refuses to defend himself because of the secrecy of the confessional and his own indifference to life, though he ultimately escapes punishment when Miranda finally recants.

Prince Tarquin, rather more dramatically, is charged with attempted murder but survives a poorly aimed blow of the executioner's axe and, though severely wounded, finds asylum at a Jesuit monastery where he is carried by a crowd of ecstatic onlookers. These conspicuous instances of Miranda's unremitting persecution of noteworthy men expose the misdirected but nonetheless powerful capacity in her to shape public events through private means.

The heroine's manipulation of public perception, the power she gains from this, and the way it reveals the complicity between private and public domains, surface at every point in the two parts of Behn's narrative. The story as a whole relies on spectacle—the failed execution of Tarquin, for example, is so remarkable that one spectator promptly dies of amazement and fear. But Miranda, in using spectacle to her advantage, dramatically reverses the assumption that women represent private experience, exposing the interdependence of public and private ideology. In one particularly morbid tableaux, Miranda is punished for instigating a murder attempt by being publicly displayed during her servant Van Brune's hanging. She is sentenced "to stand under the Gibbet, with a Rope about her Neck, the other End of which was to be fastned to the Gibbet where the Page was hanging; and to have an Inscription, in large Characters, upon her Back and Breast, of the Cause why; where she was to stand from ten in the Morning to twelve" (107–8). The rope joining Miranda to the hanged man symbolizes the causal and therefore identifying relationship between Miranda and her male victims. They only become definable characters through or by their attachment to Miranda. As "the Cause why" she turns them into subjects and makes herself visible, public, as both a linguistic and a sartorial icon. That she becomes the focus of a criminal spectacle, written almost directly on her body, exposes the actions of all the men who make it their "Business" to see Miranda by publicly displaying their illicit desire. The narrative repeatedly accentuates the duping of men as well as their willing surrender of political and moral authority to a woman who aggressively overthrows sexual and domestic order, as if the best expression of male desire were such submission.

As spectacle, Miranda's punishment in itself reveals a complex interplay of legal authority, criminal display, illicit entertainment, and family iconography. When Miranda is first charged with attempting to murder her sister, Tarquin leads Miranda to prison in pomp and circumstance, rejecting the judgment of the world upon Miranda's scandal, failing even to condemn his wife's crime. Typically, Miranda clothes an occasion that ought to mortify her in the dress of respectable spectacle:

But the whole City being over-joy'd that she should be punished, as an Author of all this Mischief, were generally bent against her, both Priests, Magistrates and People; the whole Force of the Stream running that Way, she found no more Favour than the meanest Criminal. The Prince therefore, when he saw 'twas impossible to rescue her from the Hands of Justice, suffer'd with Grief unspeakable, what he could not prevent, and led her himself to the Prison, follow'd by all his People, in as much State as if he had been going to his Marriage. (107)

A premonition of her triumphant conversion of punishment into self-promotion, this scene accentuates the elements that typify Miranda's place in society, literally in the marketplace. The city's "over-joy'd" response to Miranda's crimes reflects her powerful hold over each citizen. She figures (again quite literally) as a woman who brings to a near frenzy the anxieties of her culture—the need to witness the "unspeakable," indulge in crimes that subvert moral order, and yet see that moral order restored and affirmed in a punitive spectacle.

Behn emphasizes her heroine's irremediable power when Miranda goes to the public gate for her punishment and arrives in regal splendor, supported by her entire household:

The following *Friday* was the Day of Execution, and one need not tell of the Abundance of People, who were flocked together in the Market-Place: And all the Windows were taken down, and filled with Spectators, and the Tops of Houses; when at the Hour appointed, the fatal Beauty appear'd. She was dress'd in a black Velvet Gown, with a rich Row of Diamonds all down the fore Part of her Breast, and a great Knot of Diamonds at the Peak behind; and a Petticoat of flower'd Gold, very rich, and laced; with all Things else suitable. A Gentleman carry'd her great Velvet Cushion before her, on which her Prayer-Book, embroider'd, was laid; her Train was borne up by a Page, and the Prince led her, bare; followed by his Footmen, Pages, and other Officers of his House. (108)

In addition to making a spectacle of herself, Miranda here makes a spectacle of the penal situation and the family propriety it seeks to defend. The language of this passage—its lush enumeration of jewels, clothing, supernumeraries, and perhaps most brazenly a prayerbook on an embroidered velvet cushion—serves not only to convey the fair jilt's ability to transform punishment into household pageant but also to make the actual description of events shine with the same luster that surrounds her. The felon, treated romantically, seems to swell to the size of embodied myth before the dazzled eyes of the spectators. She becomes the appropriate commodity for the very marketplace they populate. Despite her moral condemnation of the heroine, the narrator seems to participate in Miranda's glorification, showing some of the vicarious gratification that occasionally punctuates contemporary accounts of criminal behavior. What the display celebrates most prominently, however, is the apparent indissolubility of marriage and family (Tarquin, after all, is determined to stand by his woman, surrounded by all the finery that marks the splendor of their household). The scandalous moment represented by the execution serves, then, to manifest what, according to late seventeenth-century standards, should have simply been either assumed or concealed: the abiding love of a husband for his wife, the fidelity of household servants, the financial circumstances of the family, and even the rivalry between sisters.

The execution of Van Brune typifies the narrative's treatment of the scandalous woman. Miranda suffers some public mortification for her crimes but survives largely unscathed, is occasionally glamorized (as in the above example), and, we are told at the end, finally becomes penitent. Throughout, the narrator alternates between deprecating her heroine's mercenary acts and relishing their utter bravura. When, however, the narrator casually remarks in the very last paragraph, "Since I began this Relation, I heard that Prince *Tarquin*, dy'd about three Quarters of a Year ago" (124), the reader may be inclined to meditate on the cause of death by recalling Miranda's criminal record—false accusation, perjury, falsification of evidence, extortion, and two conspiracies to murder. In this light, the irony of the narrative's concluding statement belies the talk of penitence and happiness. Miranda ends up a rich widow in full possession of her husband's prosperous estate. Like the morally ambiguous endings to several of Defoe's narratives, this conclusion seems to leave the sinful protagonist not only unpunished but ultimately rewarded. For all the demonstrable repugnance that Miranda's actions elicit (explicitly in the narrator, presumably in the reader), they express an alienated rage that subsumes two exemplary male figures. Delight and horror seem equally appropriate responses to a woman condemned for attempted murder and yet seemingly exonerated of her crimes through the very act of criminal and literary spectacle. We are left to speculate whether the narrator, without exactly condoning the actions of her heroine, sees in the ironic conclusion to Miranda's tale a tempting parable of female vindication. Escaping domestic invisibility, Miranda, for a time, successfully appropriates public power, is punished, but then returns, even more fully rewarded, to the privacy of home.

What Behn's narrative depicts, then, is pure Hobbesian ego. Miranda is spectacular in her self-absorbed use and abuse of social institutions that ideally are aimed at connecting the self with others—family, law, economy, religion, and politics. On the one hand, Miranda appears to represent an insatiable urge toward self-gratification; on the other hand, she seems to concentrate around her the socializing energies of a society bent on delimiting the range of her power. Exploiting those social tendencies, she uses marriage and family for entirely personal ends, thereby exposing how easily they serve and protect mercenary purposes. For Miranda, domesticity is an adjunct to political and economic relations rather than an end in itself. She is a sign of a radical identity that the courtesy material of the period could not effectively regulate, insofar as it had not yet adequately shifted emphasis from the carnal woman in need of domestic correction to the proper lady of the household in charge of domestic economy. Like the conduct materials of the late seventeenth century, Behn's protagonist manifests a slippage in the domestic ideology that simultaneously created, banished, and enabled the particular femme fatale that Miranda represents. A figure who helps define the social contract, even as presented in the more liberal articulations of Lockean doctrine, she also forces redefinitions of modern subjectivity that seek to act upon individuals (at least in public shows) by making their adoption of domestic ideology seem self-motivated.

"Galloping Nuns" and "an Uninclos'd House"

By seventeenth- and eighteenth-century standards, Miranda displays every vice that a proper woman should rigorously avoid. She destroys family, marries for mercenary ends, and is willfully unchaste; she regards sex as divorced from the creation of family, uses her sexuality to falsify reality, and acknowledges no kinship. This radical antagonism toward domestic ideology and Miranda's corresponding obsession with men of impeccable family credentials stem in part from her own problematic relation to pedigree. Behn uses the withdrawal of parental guidance not so much to emphasize its desirability as to signal a general cultural and institutional confusion about the proper domestic management of female desire. Miranda's story begins when she loses her parents at an early age, inheriting a vast estate divided between herself and her younger sister. The narrative is relatively silent about the heroine's early experiences of home, making few causal connections between Miranda's "unguarded" and "ungoverned" behavior and her familial origins. What we see instead is the reproduction and displacement of family structure and guardianship onto the nunnery Miranda enters after the death of her parents. That is, Behn clarifies the institutional character of domestic training by shifting the heroine's formative influences from her biological family to a substitute family organized around highly articulated public functions.

An unusually pliant religious institution, whose real purpose is to socialize and cultivate young women of distinction for marriage, Miranda's nunnery instructs women in the necessary "female arts" required in married life. Called "Galloping Nuns" because their vows of chastity are temporary, part of a waiting period before marriage, they signal the essentially ambiguous social status and uncertain use attributed to unmarried women in the period. Miranda puts herself into this "uninclos'd religious House" (76), and initially, it seems to replicate the family adequately, providing a stable moral environment. As an institution to regulate female behavior, however, it reveals a tendency to cater to, rather than manage, female will:

These Orders are taken up by the best Persons of the Town, young Maids of Fortune, who live together, not inclos'd, but in Palaces that will hold about fifteen hundred or two thousand of these *Filles Devotes*; where they have a regulated Government, under a sort of *Abbess*, or *Prioress*, or rather a *Governante*. They are oblig'd to a Method of Devotion, and are under a sort of Obedience. . . . Every one of these have a Confessor, who is to 'em a sort of Steward: For, you must know, they that go into these Places, have the Management of their own Fortunes, and what their Parents design 'em. Without the Advice of this Confessor, they act nothing, nor admit of a Lover that he shall not approve; at least, this Method ought to be taken, and is by almost all of 'em; tho' *Miranda* thought her Wit above it, as her Spirit was. (75)

The endlessly qualitative language here suggests the disingenuous nature of the nunnery. "A sort of *Abbess*, or *Prioress*, or rather a *Governante*" obliging the women to "a Method of Devotion" and "a sort of Obedience," and a "Confessor, who is to 'em a sort of Steward" schooling them in how and with whom to accept romantic advances, hardly constitute an appropriate governing body for a religious institution. The nunnery masks a house of sexual intrigue that at best encourages marriages of convenience. It advocates the behavior it ostensibly exists to control and rechannel into appropriate symbolic acts:

But as these Women are, as I said, of the best Quality, and live with the Reputation of being retir'd from the World a little more than ordinary, and because there is a sort of Difficulty to approach 'em, they are the People the most courted, and liable to the greatest Temptations; for as difficult as it seems to be, they receive Visits from all the Men of the best Quality, especially Strangers. All the Men of Wit and Conversation meet at the

Apartments of these fair *Filles Devotes*, where all Manner of Gallantries are perform'd, while all the Study of these Maids is to accomplish themselves for these noble Conversations. (75–76)

Relying heavily on the ironic misdirection of words like "reputation," "sort," "strangers," and "conversation," Behn reveals how the nunnery resembles a procurement service more than either a place of worship or an effective substitute home. As a kind of visual space of deranged domestic instruction, rendering what is customarily private strangely public, it is roughly equivalent to the conduct books of the late seventeenth century, replete with its own deviations, coercions, contradictions, and failures of purpose. Like them, it seeks to provide a moral dimension to the dispensation of women while preserving the erotic, aristocratic appeal of the romance heroine. On the one hand, it retains some of the formal household rigor traditionally associated with the convent; on the other hand, it tries to validate the economic, social, and political desirability connected to women of "quality," as if the sensibilities of the convent and court could somehow be collapsed.

Behn's oxymoronic "uninclos'd" nunnery implies not only its dubiousness as a moral institution but also the general difficulty of assigning an appropriate place to unmarried women. Here, repression constructs, rather than governs, sexual indiscretion and willfulness. The isolation of the nuns increases their availability, which in turn increases their susceptibility to corrupting influences. Indeed, society itself is revealed as sanctioning the prostitution of its noble daughters. The nunnery is thus Miranda's societal counterpart: like her, it nurtures illicit behavior under the guise of propriety. As a substitute family, a force of governance, it fails utterly, ultimately fostering a feminine practice it was devised to expunge: "So that to manage these Gallantries, there is no sort of Female Arts they are not practis'd in, no Intrigue they are ignorant of, and no Management of which they are not capable" (76). It is these "female arts," ostensibly of domestic management, that Miranda, in turn, uses to entrap and destroy her male victims. In Behn's nunnery, where "galloping nuns" scramble for available men, the domestic conduct book is rewritten as a "libro de amor" to negotiate the competing claims of cloistered virtue and courtly appeal.

The nunnery may be said, then, to produce Miranda, encouraging her to develop a view of the world based on sexual gratification. Not simply an individual rebelling against restrictive circumstance, but a figure who materializes the contradictions of her social environment, Miranda enacts only the institutionalized forces engendered in her by society. Behn uses the homology between the brothel (as a place of sexual initiation) and the nunnery (as a place of strict moral instruction) to suggest a similar correspondence between the sexual and ideological requisites of the patriarchal household. Accustomed to the attentions of all men, Miranda becomes a figure of polygamous excess, ridiculing the market-value arrangements within such pious institutions of marital guidance as the nunnery. In effect, she defines herself in opposition to the central values of courtship, marriage, and monogamy to which her society ostensibly adheres, questioning the very concept of domestic instruction in "female arts." Rather than demonstrating the superior "Quality" of the aristocracy, she expresses its excesses of luxury and corruption, becoming in the process a destabilizing figure that deforms the sexual contract. She inverts the image of the cloistered romance heroine in whose features the aristocracy would hope to discover its moral and domestic virtue.

Those who suffer most from Miranda's willful misapplication of her "female arts" are the very men for whom such arts are created:

She was naturally amorous, but extremely inconstant: She lov'd one for his Wit, another for his Face, and a third for his Mein; but above all, she admir'd Quality: Quality alone had the Power to attach her entirely; yet not to one Man, but that Virtue was still admir'd by her in all: Wherever she found that, she lov'd, or at least acted the Lover with such Art, that (deceiving well) she fail'd not to compleat her Conquest; and yet she never durst trust her fickle Humour with Marriage. She knew the Strength of her own Heart, and that it could not suffer itself to be confin'd to one Man, and wisely avoided those Inquietudes, and that Uneasiness of Life she was sure to find in that married State, which would, against her Nature, oblige her to the Embraces of one, whose Humour was, to love all the Young and the Gay. (77–78)

This passage, more than any other, reveals the contradictions in Miranda's obsession over masculine "Quality"—that is, men of good family and breeding. For her, quality is of purely superficial value, manifested in the carriage, gallantries, and ostentation of the individual. Miranda fails, in other words, to see that quality depends on a familial ideology to which she is fundamentally opposed; she values precisely what she seems constitutionally unable to realize fully for herself, since quality ideally signifies the maintenance of family reputation.

More important, however, the men passively submit to this surface evaluation as if they were equally confused about their status within a sexual economy. Until she meets Henrick, Miranda's ideal man is dispersed among many, and the multiplicity of her affairs is in itself an implicit critique of male ego and pretenses. Rather than figures of total presence, the men that Miranda courts and conquers are fragments of an unrealized ideal self. One she admires for his "wit," another for his "mein," another for his "face." Miranda may herself be degenerate, but the men surrounding her are no less irredeemable. Drawn to the convent for its promise of institutional models of domestic rectitude, they discover there an irresistible attraction to female ambition and carnality. As a cultural cypher, Miranda reveals the marital hypocrisy and sexual or romantic limitations in the conduct of her social class. Consequently, her promiscuous behavior is the product as much of male inadequacy as of personal desire. Superficial herself in many ways, she nonetheless exposes both the superficialities of her culture and its failure to provide integrated models of affective conduct.

How thoroughly Miranda dismisses the regulative force of family emerges in the way she reacts when Cornelia (one of her convent acquaintances) relates the details of Henrick's life. The story comprises a fairly long sentimental interlude about the perils associated with patriarchal family government, but Miranda concentrates only on the beginning and end where Cornelia extols Henrick's "quality" as a Prince of Germany. In its entirety, Cornelia's account traces a familial drama in which an older brother usurps Henrick's true love, exiles him from the family, strips him of his national identity, and, with the help of their mother, tries to murder him. When Henrick returns to find his "Mistress" compelled by her parents to marry the older brother, he initially blames her of inconstancy, but eventually they rediscover their passion (though virtue and their new family relation prevents them from consummating their love). Enraged by finding a "dreaded Rival in the same House with him, with an Authority equal to his own" (82), the brother secretly plots another murder, but Henrick, convinced by his father and his own conscience, retreats to a Franciscan monastery in Flanders where he discloses the history of the affair in letters to his father, his lover, and his brother. The young princess languishes "from the Moment of his Departure; and he had this to confirm his devout Life, to know she dy'd for him" (85).

A melodramatic story involving perverse family relations, internecine conflict, deceit, and betrayal, Cornelia's account highlights the consequences of confusing the political with the domestic household. Yet Miranda, trained by the nunnery to mix public and private motives, can see neither the passive virtue of Henrick's devotion to family nor the immorality of his brother's destruction of it, hearing only what impinges on her desire personally. At the conclusion, when Cornelia reiterates that Henrick was a prince before becoming a monk, Miranda's response, italicized for effect, reveals her particular interest in the story: *"What!* replied Miranda then, *is Father* Henrick *a Man of Quality?"* (85). Reducing Henrick's tragic tale to evidence of his quality, she ignores the complex domestic and national import of what he has suffered. That indifference to family drama reflects her Hobbesian drive; by refracting the lives of others through her own desire, she effectively undermines the ideological authority of the family. At the same time, her comic insensibility to the story reduces Henrick's pathetic tale to absurdity. His is a romance in miniature, whose purpose, like that of a conduct book, is to demonstrate the need for household integrity; however, because it is contained within and parallels Miranda's scandal chronicle, in which romantic sentiment is systematically stripped, Henrick's story, particularly because of his obedient retreat from the conflict with his brother and the ensuing death of his lover, makes even the principles of the heroic romance seem hollow. As in Behn's mock conduct books, human passion repeatedly obstructs and falsifies the systems of behavior according to which families are supposed to regulate themselves in both domestic and national affairs.

To a large extent, the jilt typifies various distortions of late-seventeenth-century social and sexual contracts, largely because she is linked to a narcissistic sexuality that obstructs the legitimate growth of the body politic. She signals forms of displacement that were regarded not only as false expenditures of sexuality within the nation's domestic economy but also as alarming evidence of perversion in the national character. Her success suggests that behavioral literature of the period did not effectively police such conduct. An anomaly, Miranda desecrates the principles that shape the patriarchal family—romantic love, domestic order, family honor, sexual propriety—only to disclose the weakness accompanying its various systems of control.

Resolving to Be Lucretia

Miranda's ability to deform sacred principles of sexual conduct appears most forcibly in her manipulation of alleged rape. Violation, one of the central symbolic actions of *The Fair Jilt*, becomes a sign not so much of patriarchy's brutal control of women as of its susceptibility to impassioned female discourse. In her relationship with Henrick, Miranda fabricates rape as a means to gratify her own desires, taking romance rhetoric to violent extremes, as if rape (or the accusation of it) were the inevitable obverse of romantic courtship. Such an inversion emphasizes the connections between sexual ideology and social order. This correlation is made emphatic, since the "rape" occurs at the narrative midpoint between the two accounts of Miranda's seductive power over Henrick and Tarquin; it substantiates the authority of the female "victim" and relates that authority to the narrative abilities of the teller. Miranda's false accusation constitutes one of the most negative expression of her radical energy, but because it strips official language and morality of their ability to regulate social behavior, such energy also challenges the adequacy of institutional limits on sexuality and power. In *The Fair Jilt*, where the male is criminally victimized, the manipulation of the threat of rape exemplifies female power over a range of aesthetic, discursive, and legal practices.

In Miranda's accusation, we see how a desire that is largely constituted by authoritarian dogma can, in extreme circumstances, bend those principles to challenge the ruling discourses of power. Her vanity provoked at failing to impassion the resistant Henrick under the pretense of religious confession, Miranda resorts to violent threats:

Behold her now deny'd, refus'd and defeated, with all her pleading Youth, Beauty, Tears, and Knees, imploring, as she lay, holding fast his *Scapular*, and embracing his Feet. What shall she do? She swells with Pride, Love, Indignation and Desire; her burning Heart is bursting with Despair, her Eyes grow fierce, and from Grief she rises to a Storm; and in her Agony of Passion, with Looks all disdainful, haughty, and full of Rage, she began to revile him, as the poorest of Animals; tells him his Soul was dwindled to the Meanness of his Habit, and his Vows of Poverty were suited to his degenerate Mind. "And (*said she*) since all my nobler Ways have fail'd me; and that, for a little Hypocritical Devotion, you resolve to lose the greatest Blessings of Life, and to sacrifice me to your Religious Pride and Vanity, I will either force you to abandon that dull Dissimulation, or you shall die, to prove your Sanctity real. Therefore answer me immediately, answer my Flame, my raging Fire, which your Eyes have kindled; or here, in this very Moment, I will ruin thee; and make no Scruple of revenging the Pains I suffer, by that which shall take away your Life and Honour." (92–93)

Miranda's exaggerated romance rhetoric, heightened by the narrator's shift into the present tense, threatens to undermine conventional truth altogether. She pits her sexual force against his passive resistance and "Hypocritical Devotion." Whereas her passion is real and "nobler," his "dull Dissimulation" is base and inhuman ("as the poorest Animal"). Her reaction here seems to advance beyond calculated seduction to frenzied conviction, validating the passion that informs her conduct as more authentic than the religious piety that guides Henrick. If Miranda's parodic excesses of romantic self-representation destabilize social norms, they also redefine sexual practices.

The stark opposition between Miranda's desire and Henrick's piety further accentuates the threat she poses to institutional forces like the Church. Accused of rape, Henrick is sentenced to be burned at the "Market-Place," partly because he refuses to betray the confidentiality of the confessional. The entire episode ultimately assumes political overtones when the clergymen defend Henrick while the young Cavaliers at court extol Miranda: "he had all the Gown-men on his Side, she had all the Hats and Feathers on her's; all the Men of Quality taking her Part, and all the Churchmen his" (97). As on other occasions Miranda's individual actions trigger larger social repercussions, expressed here in the fierce contention between political and religious factions.

Miranda's recourse to the very system of legal, moral, and political liability that dictates Henrick's conduct reveals how effectively she has learned to reverse relations of power. Repeating this pattern of inversion in her seduction of and marriage to Tarquin, she reveals its systemic application. Like the false rape, Miranda's temptation of Tarquin is figured as female violation, Tarquin believing that he has, in fact, seduced her. Miranda regards the whole affair as an intricately planned scheme in which she is "resolved to be the *Lucretia* that this young *Tarquin* should ravish" (99). Miranda's calculations challenge stereotypes of the distressed heroine of sentimental drama, and set her against social and literary ideals of femininity. Rape and seduction are, after all, the consistent crises with which romance heroines must contend. In Behn's version a fabricated "rape" induces a series of institutional repercussions for the accused male, binding him to a logic of accountability that the accusing woman has managed not only to elude but to manipulate. That sequence of events, in turn, prompts similar strategies for refiguring household politics in her strangely durable marriage to Tarquin.

Not yet consigned to a historical moment when the ideal of the domestic woman had become particularized, Miranda manages to deform the social contract implicit in courtship and marriage at the expense of men who are unreservedly committed to it. Their vulnerability derives, in turn, from the willpower, linguistic conviction, and apparent truthfulness of a desiring female subject. Miranda's verbal and psychological coherence is, however, based on falsehood; a disruptive figure, her actions tend to dismantle domesticity both from without and from within marriage. She represents the kind of agonistic energy that became increasingly sublimated in later-eighteenth-century accounts of womanhood and that put into sharp relief the equally constructed nature of domestic behavior. By the second half of the story, distinctions among such concepts as rape, seduction, courtship, marriage, and domestic responsibility evaporate entirely, as if coercion and duplicity were complements to marriage. Prohibitions against illicit heterosexual behavior become accepted attributes of legalized heterosexual conduct. Thus, the very conceptual force associated with the married woman, what traditionally gave the seventeenth-century woman a unified and meaningful identity, is defused by the ease with which the scandalous woman blurs rape, romance, and marriage.

Family Crimes

Miranda's incorrigibility suggests that she operates in a fluid moment when female domestic strictures were precariously balanced between two paradigms, one in which the woman was beginning to be a standard of household economy and vigilance and another in which she was a household subject who needed to be domesticated herself. Such a figure becomes inaccessible to the social systems— from the nunnery to marriage and the legal court—that were supposed to situate her properly in her community.

Tarquin's susceptibility to Miranda and gradual surrender of household government after their marriage, suggest the conceptual indeterminacy of the domestic male, disrupted by changes in the representations of domestic functions. Like the diminished patriarch in Locke's *Treatises on Government*, who must surrender some of his ideological force to accommodate more egalitarian principles of family rule, Tarquin strives to include an ambitious woman in his own ineffective systems of sexual governance. The men in Behn's narrative embody Behn's alarm over the failure of the Stuart monarchy to control the political imagery of domestic relations and maintain a strong hereditary power. Tarquin, sacrificing his own royal Roman lineage, dies without issue and leaves his estate to a woman who devours, rather than nurtures, her own family assets. The romantic male of the pre-settlement Stuart period appears to prompt the confusion about male and female domesticity and its relation to national policy that eventually triggered attempts in the eighteenth century to harness the image of family government. Tarquin's relationship with Miranda comes to embody, then, the shift in tactics discussed in Chapter 1, from making household order seem the husband's responsibility (usually through his absolutist command of wife and servants) to assigning domestic management to the woman (with the man occupied outside of the home). In Behn, however, we see the disruptive consequences of this kind of cultural shift in moral management.

Connected as Tarquin is to the Stuart monarchy through his association with Payne, and given that his near beheading may be construed as a symbolic recreation and correction of the execution of Charles I, Tarquin ultimately seems to license Miranda's behavior (Charles was similarly accused of allowing Queen Henrietta to influence him). In a sense, then, Miranda mirrors the romantic excesses, political scandal, and libertinism that came to be associated with the demise of the Stuart monarchy. Her expedient use of family operates doubly to expose the cynical manipulation of domestic ideology in European culture and the monarchy's own devaluation of its genealogical right to rule. Behn's narrative critique, then, serves a dual political and social function, condemning both the individual's resistance to communal norms and the community's complicity in individual acts of transgression.

Miranda's symbolic domination of Tarquin is measured by his ability to commit the most heinous crime of all: familial murder. His reactions to her various intrigues are always blindly devotional. In a sense he truly becomes hers only in the moment he enacts her most radical desire. Miranda, fully understanding this, dramatizes the total submission of his will by proclaiming her own irrational and unnatural motivations for killing her sister: "[S]he wept, and cry'd out, 'She could not live, unless *Alcidiana* died. This *Alcidiana* (*continued she*) who has been the Author of my Shame; who has expos'd me under a Gibbet, in the Publick Market-Place—Oh!—I am deaf to all Reason, blind to natural Affection. I renounce her, I hate her as my mortal Foe, my Stop to Glory, and the Finisher of my Days, e'er half my Race of Life be run'" (110). In convincing her husband to act contrary to his code of honor, Miranda emphasizes precisely those elements of her character that stigmatize her. "Deaf to all Reason" and "blind to natural Affection," she makes a calculated virtue of virtuelessness, irrationality, and uncontrolled passion. By plotting against the life of one of her own family members, by rejecting reason and nature, she attacks the foundations of civil society as they were most often understood in late-seventeenth-century Europe.

Centering entirely on family property, Miranda's attempt to murder Alcidiana emanates from the economic realities of the aristocratic household. As long as Miranda's sister remains unwed and therefore under her governance, Behn's heroine accepts, even encourages, Alcidiana's presence in the household. She is careful, of course, to impede any lasting relationship between Alcidiana and her lovers. But when Alcidiana threatens Miranda's outright control of the family estate (by claiming her portion of the inheritance when she marries or comes of age), Miranda rejects biological ties. The physical consequences of Miranda's attempted murders of Alcidiana are described with a shock and fascination that accentuate the horror of the crime: "[T]he Doctors said, she had taken Mercury. So that there was never so formidable a Sight as this fair young Creature; her Head and Body swoln, her Eyes starting out, her Face black, and all deformed" (105). She becomes, in effect, a symbol of her own sister's raging passion and greed, a cypher of familial violence.

On one level, *The Fair Jilt* is simply a story about familial crime; and to the extent that it shares certain features with criminal biographies, Behn's narrative demystifies the sexual and familial ideology of romance. The deviant personality is ultimately comprehended (that is, both understood and contained) within a homeostatic structure—the family—which both defines the difference of the deviant and seeks to reduce that difference to explicable form. In typical criminal biographies, the familial order by which the deviant acquires a specific identity in turn generates a system of causality operating within the culture as a whole.[16] The radical anarchy of violent family crime can be tolerated only as long as it reestablishes a governing system of social alliances. Thus it is that reasons, causal stories, and redemptions (a crude etiology of crime) are always sought in those criminal biographies rooted in familial transgressions. The criminal must be made to reveal an intelligible process because his or her act of murder challenges fundamental social beliefs. Analogically reproducing the stable coherence of civic and state organization, which in turn substantiated the benevolent universe organized by God, the family reconfirms the uniformity of existence by drawing a line from the singular to the social and then finally to the universal.

Miranda defiantly ruptures such lines of signification. Her story is disturbing because the moral consequences of her actions find no climactic arena in which to be exposed. Unlike other criminal narratives, there is no redeeming gallows ending to place the deviant's behavior within a context of moral transfiguration. Moreover, the conclusion of *The Fair Jilt* leaves unanswered questions having to do with the attribution of guilt and punishment, the meanings of actions and their relationship to identifiable ethical and psychological standards, and the understanding of personality rooted in Judeo-Christian dictates about lawful behavior. That is, after seeming to settle the matter of explainable personality—Miranda appears to go through a credible recantation that would place her in the conventional moral system of the criminal biography—the story reverts in the end to the gratification of Miranda's secular desires. If her unreasonable and unnatural motivation has its source in vanity, ambition, and greed, her punishment is neither commensurate with those antisocial instincts nor effective in governing them.

If, as with the standard criminal biographies of her day, Miranda's tale ought ultimately to position her within an orthodox behavioral regime, there is something in her that continually seeps beyond such bounds. Punishment and glorification seem nearly inseparable in Behn's narrative. Miranda's escape from lasting punishment may have to do with the privileges of her class, or with the intractable nature of truthfulness (since the story's events may indeed be true), but it nonetheless emphasizes the unboundedness of the heroine's personality. Behn's tale is filled with disparities that the heroine's behavior heightens: aristocrats who are not aristocrats, convents that are not convents, homes that are not homes, families that are not families, punishments that are not punishments. A product of and yet always somehow beyond acceptable social conduct, Miranda dramatizes the arbitrary limits of decorum. As much an account of female willfulness as a moral exemplum about feminine (or criminal) desire, Behn's narrative charts a complicated path through the sexual ideology of romance, the socializing tendencies of the criminal biography, and the libertinism of the scandal chronicle. In the process, it dismantles the generic conventions that would putatively distinguish these narrative types. This irresolution and the seeming lack of integration among the biographical, political, and aesthetic elements in Behn's fiction make it seem unlike conventional prose narratives; yet these qualities also give it the radical anti-romance attitude Michael McKeon traces in late-seventeenth- and eighteenth-century fiction (55–58).[17] The "problematic" nature of the text suggests that the difficulty of situating it in a history of the novel stems from its resistance to a teleological rendering of the novel's development in which works of prose fiction would naturally fall on either side of a great generic divide.

The prefatory dedication to Behn's narrative indicates that one of its primary analogues is the romance. But romance in *The Fair Jilt* quickly shifts into complementary, if seemingly incompatible, discourses (in addition to the scandal chronicle and criminal biography, it incorporates conduct literature, spy tale, and travelogue material). Although she frequently ridicules the formal and behavioral rigor of the romance, Behn nonetheless exploits its more iconoclastic potential. Her relatively complex deployment of the romance suggests that, as a genre, it is capable of effects not customarily associated with it, such as contemporaneous political observation, and involved psychological perceptions. The narrative consistently alternates transgressive and conservative impulses; to a large extent, it delivers radical, antisocial feelings in order to contain and thus ultimately regulate them. But, given that Miranda's energy remains, in some measure, uncontrollable, it also resists prescriptive norms that Behn herself ridiculed in her own mock conduct books. In the end, the scandalous heroine recedes ambiguously into the family estate, that familiar sign of social, political, and economic cohesion, now transformed into a marginal and dubious space. The unspeakable in Behn's narrative is what the heroine, already a suspicious character, does behind the closed doors of an estate emptied of all but the physical trappings of domestic patriarchalism. As in the mock conduct books, there is no functioning household to be seen in Behn's fictional landscape.

In creating an irredeemable figure like Miranda, whose discursive power is great enough to frustrate the social, political, and religious forces of a modern European city, Behn identifies some of the unconventional and adversarial motivations that may have prompted her to write in a culture that refused to accommodate her own social, political, and philosophical capacities, except in the most oblique ways. In *The Fair Jilt*, as in most of her other fiction, Behn demeans the conventional family of the conduct books in order to exaggerate the treacherous, though often vital, energy of those who reject domestic indoctrination, and then to emphasize the hazards of letting family and domesticity overdetermine an individual's character. Like many other popular late-seventeenth- and early-eighteenth-century narratives (such as Richard Head's *The English Rogue* [1665], John Dunton's *The Night Walker: or Evening Rambles in Search After Lewd Women* [1696], Mary dela Riviere Manley's *Secret Memoirs and Manners of several Persons of Quality, of Both Sexes from the New Atalantis* [1709], and Alexander Smith's *The History of the Lives and Robberies of the most Noted Highway-Men, Foot-Pads, House-Breakers, Shop-Lifts and Cheats of both Sexes in and about London and Westmin-*

ister [1713]), Behn's fiction capitalizes on cultural fantasies about deviant and criminal behaviors that distort family relations and expose ambivalent domestic expectations within the public sphere. *The Fair Jilt* reveals the cultural consequences of a late-seventeenth-century female subject who is uncharacteristically released from the social constraints provided by the family. By disfiguring the social contract, Miranda exposes the artificial limits to a domestic order within and against which she is defined.

3

Robinson Crusoe and the Orphaned Family

The Pleasure of a married State consists wholly in the Beauty of
the Union, the sharing Comforts, the doubling all Enjoyments; 'tis
the Settlement of Life; the Ship is always in a Storm till it finds this
safe Road, and here it comes to an Anchor: 'Tis the want of a taste
of Life makes Men despise that Part of it which Heaven at first
constituted to compleat the Happiness of his Creatures.

—Daniel Defoe, *Conjugal Lewdness*

Prodigal Fiction

This chapter argues that the same process that makes domesticity
strangely marginal in Behn's fiction shapes the progress of Defoe's
protagonists as they seek to reintegrate the symbolic force of kinship that they themselves have willfully made unfamiliar. Defoe's
prose fictions, all written in the form of autobiographical memoirs
and all beginning with an initial loss of or escape from the family,
present stark instances of domestic alienation—"the want of a taste
of Life." Unlike Behn's scandal narratives, Defoe's fiction signals
this condition not by the protagonist's heady subversion of family
but by an anxious separation from it. In *Robinson Crusoe*, for instance, the hero's adventures occur only because he rejects the secure life proposed by his parents; he obstinately (and guiltily) plays
the part of the prodigal son. Like the "Storm" that plagues the unmarried "Ship" in *Conjugal Lewdness*, Crusoe suffers both figurative
and real maritime disasters before he finally learns to domesticate
himself. Yet Defoe wrote his major fictional narratives at roughly
the same time (1719–1724) that he was producing treatises like the

two parts of *The Family Instructor* (1715; 1718), *Religious Courtship* (1722), *The Protestant Monastery* (1726), and *Conjugal Lewdness* (1727), which extol the values of the "closed domestic nuclear family" (see Stone, *The Family, Sex and Marriage*, 149–299). As Defoe notes in *Conjugal Lewdness*, "all that can be called happy in the Life of Man, is summ'd up in the state of Marriage" (96).[1] Nonetheless, though Defoe promoted conjugal ideals, he never created a narrative in which his protagonist unambiguously embraces domestic life. The absence or disruption of family in Defoe's stories is meant to isolate the protagonists in such a way as to accentuate the moral purpose to which the narrator puts them and to emphasize their distinctness from the domestic types that his plots seem intended to affirm. Defoe's conduct literature, conversely, though related to the moral project at work in the narratives, does not reproduce their didactic strategies. Though it often employs fictional stories and provides an ideological context for the imaginary works, its typical method continually contrasts instances of failed and successful domesticity.

In exploring these tactical differences, this chapter focuses on Crusoe's attempts to replace household relations with symbolic ones that duplicate his own desire to renew the social obligations of the individual. Similar to the intersecting discourses discussed in Chapter 1, the Crusoe saga reveals a complicity among imaginary constructs, fictional rhetoric, and conduct-book norms whose function is to diffuse the discursive and ideological tensions apparent in eighteenth-century household government. Where Behn's criminal heroine distorts normative behavior in order to fulfill personal desire, Defoe's hero desperately seeks to make his "strange and surprizing" life serve a normal pedagogical lesson.

For the most part, critics have contended that the adversarial family in Defoe's fiction manifests a common novelistic opposition between individual desire and social restraint.[2] However, while Defoe's narratives certainly seek to dramatize the efforts of an authentic self to resist ideological pressures, they also persistently deny the possibility of such evasion. In their distinct ways, early-eighteenth-century writers like Behn and Defoe already knew that a transcendental ideal (the authentic self) was unrepresentable, and they therefore wrote fictions in which distinguishing individual desire from ideological constraints was both tantalizing and futile. As Defoe's narratives suggest, emerging concepts of identity often pitted the individual against community, tradition, and social (particularly familial) responsibility while depending upon those traditional social structures individualism appeared to oppose.

Defoe used the nuclear family to set up normative models by which his characters differentiate themselves, but in doing so he inevitably reinscribed the domestic ideal his characters so persistently flee. For Defoe, the urge to define character required family background, but the desire to fantasize about the unbounded potential of the individual demanded a suppression of familial discourse (spouses and children are constantly shuffled offstage). Often compensated for by the substitution of displaced family members with characters who assume the role of parent, sibling, or child (Friday, for instance), this resistance to domesticity produces a complex double focus in the narratives. The continual abolishing, substituting, and resurrecting of family relations in Defoe's fiction (and in many eighteenth-century narratives generally) indicates a rejection of bourgeois family values at a time and in a literary form that paradoxically seems committed to establishing bourgeois ideology.

Because of this double posture, the visible absence of the family (what I have been calling its marginalization) is a constituting element in Defoe's narrative strategy. Even toward or about the most intimate social contacts in life, Defoe's protagonists are conspicuously mute. Typical of Defoe's procedure in this regard is Moll's observation about life with her first husband, Robin: "It concerns the Story in Hand very little to enter into the farther Particulars of the Family, or of my self, for the five Years that I liv'd with this Husband, only to observe that I had two Children by him, and that at the end of five Years he died" (*Moll Flanders*, pt. 1: 57). Though Defoe always begins the history of a character with a description, however minimal, of his or her family background, he advances the story by eliding the complex relations that sustain identity. To maintain the interest of the reader and continue the story, the fam-

ily circle had to be severed. Thus the first thing that must be con-
ceded about Defoe's narrative attitude to the family is that domestic
relations are thematically downplayed. They provide an initial reference point but do not have a sustained structural purpose. Even
the stories that most concern marriage and remarriage—*Moll Flanders, Colonel Jack,* and *Roxana*—tend to disregard the intense issues
of family government and kinship responsibilities. Thus a certain
phase of ideology, or the ideology that sought to rationalize the activities of a rising bourgeois class, is literarily maintained in Defoe's
fiction by ruptures and silence. This may be an odd thing to say of
Moll, who of literary heroines seems the most entangled in the
troubling mesh of daily existence, but the dramatic ellipses or dizzying summations of her story reveal how her life differs from conventional married life. The text addresses not what is familiar, the
quotidian exchange of power between husband and wife, parent and
child, or master and servant, but what lies beyond in the realm of
criminality, escape, adventure, and exploration. Though Defoe has
traditionally been valued for his explicitness, when we read his fiction we discover that much in fact is left undisclosed. As Roxana
says, "Secrets shou'd never be open'd, without evident Utility" (*Roxana,* pt. 2, 155).[3]

At the same time, given the promotion of bourgeois family relations in his didactic tracts, Defoe does not want to suggest that the
family is a negligible institution. Consequently, many of the critical
turning points in Defoe's fiction do finally center on family concerns: Crusoe's continuing insistence that all of his woes can be
traced back to his original disobedience of his father, Moll's recognition that she has committed incest with her brother, Jack's reconciliation with his first wife or his obsession with recovering his gen-
tlemanly status, Roxana's apocalyptic reunion with her daughter Susan. Implicitly, the family always seems to draw its wayward children back within its grasp.

In Freudian analysis it is, of course, possible to read the language
of the unconscious in the absence of certain words or in their transmutation to a different conscious vocabulary. This concealed text
tends to realign the social and sexual determinants embodied by the

family in the fantasies, games, and romantic fictions of the child. Persistent substitution reasserts the familial context from which the fiction of identity derives, forcing individuals to resume the social forms they previously denied. In Defoe's fiction the ideological patterning of the subject by the family is similarly repudiated and then restored through the apparently subversive and nondomestic action of adventure stories and criminal biographies. Extending this model, Pierre Macherey argues that the unspoken always compromises the overt declarations of the text: "Either all around or in its wake the explicit requires the implicit: for in order to say anything, there are other things which must not be said" (85). I regard the pervasive avoidance of detailed family background in late-seventeenth- and early eighteenth-century prose fiction as just this kind of significant omission. For Macherey the *"non dit"* represents in the literary text what Freud in his analysis of the human psyche called the unconscious, an unspoken or silenced language of the self.

Following Macherey's suggestion, we might reasonably question the purpose of Crusoe's relative silence concerning family relations. If we assume that in most instances Defoe's characters are curiously taciturn about kinship, how does the family reenter the economy of discourse in Defoe's fiction, and what does its absence signify? Part of the answer may lie simply in the fact that the adventures of a hero or heroine would be impeded by domestic obligations. But Defoe's indifference to family does not stem merely from his attempt to meet popular expectations over the content of adventure stories. Whether consciously or not, Defoe constructed narratives that insist on exploiting the vexed relation between self and other—that deal, in other words, with ethical and political issues not customarily undertaken in an adventure narrative. Often, the search for economic and social power becomes so threatened by enduring family obligations that Defoe suppresses domestic details; he seems to be more concerned with the efforts of the individual to seek some form of self-sustaining power. Yet this neglect, in turn, emphasizes the disparity between the individualist ethic and the bourgeois conception of family.

Apartments in the Tree

The function of this expendable family in Defoe's narratives has often been regarded as one facet of a larger issue of exchange: Crusoe's relations with his parents and Moll's marriages are couched in economic terms; that is, relations are the means to some sort of security, as in Moll's case, or a hindrance to escaping a fixed economic system, as in Crusoe's case. Each achieves financial security through alliances, but at the expense of stable, intimate relations with others. The same may be said of Roxana and Jack, for whom the prospective and affective are clearly at odds. If Defoe often regards family relations in utilitarian terms, it is partly because he sees the family unit (at least in the fiction) as unproductive and static. Thus Defoe's characteristic diminishment of family is, to some degree, consistent with the market attitudes his fiction intermittently extols. Defoe silences what he assumes operates readily as a given, but which may also conflict with the ideological designs of his economic myths.

This reservation about the family is apparent in the opening pages of *The Life and Strange Surprizing Adventures of Robinson Crusoe*, where Crusoe both honors and depreciates his genealogical history. As in Defoe's other narratives, *Robinson Crusoe* begins with a short and problematic synopsis of the narrator's family past:

I was born in the Year 1632, in the City of *York*, of a good Family, tho' not of that Country, my Father being a Foreigner of *Bremen*, who settled first at *Hull*: He got a good Estate by Merchandise, and leaving off his Trade, lived afterward at *York*, from whence he had married my Mother, whose Relations were named *Robinson*, a very good Family in that Country, and from whom I was called *Robinson Kreutznaer*; but by the usual Corruption of Words in *England*, we are now called, nay we call our selves, and write our Name *Crusoe*, and so my Companions always call'd me. (pt. 1, 8)

Crusoe treats his past warily, linking his origins to the instability of language itself. In one breath, he seems to establish and undermine his background, capturing in a few sentences the contrary impulses toward acceptance and denial that typify his view of kinship throughout the narrative. Crusoe's doubt about the linguistic permanence of his name reflects the bewilderment that all of Defoe's characters feel about their identity. Indeed, they are always asking themselves some form of the questions, "Who am I? From where have I come?"[4] When Crusoe raises the questions "what am I" and "whence are we" (pt. 1, 105), during the sickness that finally precipitates his spiritual awareness, he begins to attribute his actions to his neglect of origins, blaming himself for his disobedience to his father and his ignorance of God. Most of the book, however, traces Crusoe's efforts to displace origin; he cannot effectively recognize his spiritual, biological, and economic heredity until he has separated from it.

Like his uprooted family, Crusoe will be equally drawn to a settled and an unsettled life. Though a spokesman for stability in his later years, Crusoe's father, a German immigrant, unwittingly bequeaths to his sons a legacy of wandering. Contrary to his advice about the middle station and the joys of home, all of the sons reject the domestic life. The eldest joins "an English Regiment of Foot" and dies in the battle of Dunkirk. The second vanishes without a trace (pt. 1, 1). Following both his brothers' and, to some extent, his father's restless ways, Crusoe reverses the paternal path, leaving England by traveling from York back to Hull (pt. 1, 1, 6). The narrative line begins, then, with an unsettling of the family line, a doubling back that renders suspect the progressive linearity of both plot and ancestry. Hoping to strike out in his own direction, Crusoe falls instinctively into his father's footsteps. Both a repetition (the reinscription of paternal precedence) and an apparent revolt (the articulation of filial iconoclasm), this gesture reflects the self-dividing need of a mobile middle-class society. Always fascinated by those instincts in his characters which lead them to construct anti-familial histories, Defoe nonetheless revokes the very freedom such instincts seek out. Because it has to be "natural," moreover, the break from family cannot be ascribed directly to economic aspirations but instead must be the result of indefinable urges such as Crusoe's "rambling Thoughts," "wandring Inclination," and "secret overruling Decree" (pt. 1, 1, 2, 14). The impulse to narrate, like the impulse to flee, is, then, linked to the desire to witness one's own treacherous rewriting of the family past.

Defoe's own view of family history was often as ambiguous as that of his protagonists. Crusoe's insistence on making clear his family background—its fortune and vicissitudes, its rootlessness and lack of national identity—echoes issues Defoe raised in *The True Born Englishman*. Written in response to a xenophobic pamphlet by John Tutchin called *The Foreigners*, which discredits immigrants and attacks King William's Dutch allegiances, Defoe's poem derides national and ancestral bigotry. Blood claims are delusive because English origins can be traced back not to a splendid pedigree but to a debased heritage of barbarism:

> Thus from a Mixture of all Kinds began,
> That Het'rogeneous *Thing, An Englishman*:
> In eager Rapes, and furious Lust begot,
> Betwixt a Painted *Britain* and a *Scot*.
> Whose gend'ring Off-spring quickly learn'd to bow,
> And yoke their Heifers to the *Roman* Plough:
> From whence a Mongrel half-Bred Race there came,
> With neither Name nor Nation, Speech nor Fame.
> In whose hot Veins new Mixtures quickly ran,
> Infus'd betwixt a *Saxon* and a *Dane*.
> While their Rank Daughters, to their Parents just,
> Receiv'd all Nations with Promiscuous Lust.
> This Nauseous Brood directly did contain
> The well-extracted Blood of *Englishmen*. (42)

According to Defoe, those who cite an inviolate origin to justify their pretensions to power falsify history. Paternal legitimacy becomes the means by which a dominant class seeks to validate its principles of moral authority. The family name, a kind of totemic icon that magically conveys the origin, identity, property, and class of the bearer, symbolizes legitimacy. But as *The True Born Englishman* suggests, ancestry (which unites both linguistic and procreative transmission) divulges the limitations of traditional forms of kinship, revealing that heritage usually masks a corrupt history of ownership and power. Names can be unstable and, in a sense, untrue.

To some extent, Defoe's repeated gestures of denial toward the family offer a means of challenging myths of blood and property. Defoe's narratives are fables of, among other things, achieving property and status despite the restraints of opportunity and class; that is, they are ways of eliminating the problem of origins and rewarding characters who challenge orthodox social arrangements.[5] Crusoe validates himself by seeming to originate civilization at an entirely personal level. He retreats from the middle station sanctioned by his father to indulge his wandering inclination, perhaps because he cannot view his father's comfortable life as anything but a preconcerted history which, instead of giving him a satisfactory identity, presupposes a convenient character for him.[6] The passage of money from family member to family member cannot be a systematic part of meritocracy; indeed, that Defoe underscores breaks from the family in his fiction emphasizes the enviable capacity in the protagonists to create their own wealth. Crusoe wants to experience difference. He wants to remake a world in his own image, not have the world configure him as a type of social and economic respectability. He wants no inheritance except that which comes to him through the uninterested kindness or dutiful obligation of others. Apparently, the experience on the island, for all its physical, economic, and religious hardship, represents an occasion for Crusoe to fashion the world anew. From his desolate start on the island, Crusoe believes he is able to establish a degree of priority, of having done things for the first time, thus halting the evident anxiety he feels about living according to his father's prior vision of the world.[7]

Macherey calls *Robinson Crusoe* a "meditation on origins" (240). That Defoe begins this meditation with his genealogy is not surprising, since family often provides the context for an individual's initial sense of origin. Yet he also wants to eschew the dependence that kinship raises because he wants to imagine a state in which his hero can act as if he had no antecedents, either financial or genealogical. As Crusoe wrongly assumes about his island: "I firmly believed, that no humane Shape had ever set Foot upon that Place" (pt. 1, 112). This may account, in many respects, for the autobiographical form in which Defoe persistently cast his long fictional narratives because such presentation allows the narrator to reduce all external relations and objects to products stripped of their autonomy and made the subject of the storyteller's desire. But if Crusoe's flight from England represents an annulment of the family, an attempt to establish the autonomy of the self, then his island life, with its transfiguration of the raw natural world into the comfort of a bourgeois home and its partial replication of a system of capital, reasserts the impelling influence of kinship patterns.

Once on the island, most of Crusoe's actions are aimed at domestic comfort, at being, as Pat Rogers has pointed out, "Homo domesticus."[8] After the harrowing escape from the shipwreck he climbs a tree to rest for the night, calling this temporary shelter "my Lodging" and "my Apartment in the Tree" (pt. 1, 53, 54), a symbol of the harmony between the natural and the social that the narrative as a whole seeks to demonstrate. Subsequently, when he builds his fortress home he refers to it as lodgings, settlement, house, estate, residence, country seat, and plantation, as well as fortress, castle, and kingdom (pt. 1, 67–176 passim, 241; pt. 2, 50). He speaks of his "household Stuff and Habitation," of "managing my household Affairs" and of the need of "household Goods" to "furnish my House" (pt. 1, 79, 87, 92, 85). Crusoe reverses the cliché that Wemmick actualizes with his moated home in *Great Expectations*: the defensive fortress becomes a home. The cave he digs is alternately his kitchen and his cellar (pt. 1, 68, 69). Later, after building his second abode in the woods, he begins to differentiate the two homes, calling the initial one his "Sea-Coast-House" and the other his "Country-House" (pt. 1, 117). Through self-directed discourse Crusoe simply merges nature with the economic and domestic paradigms that have shaped him. Instead of imagining a new identity, Crusoe merely internalizes the familial constraints that he has seemed determined to flee.

The point of these designations is, of course, familiarity; Crusoe reacts almost immediately to a hostile and desolate environment as if he had only to transform it into an English estate in order to survive. As with his independent speaking voice, and the fiction that contains it, he makes estranged habits seem perfectly customary. He also acts, naturally enough, as if there were every reason to believe that he will have to deal with other human beings. He builds his fortress home to protect himself from attacking savages; he stays by the shore so as to be ready in the event a passing ship should come into hailing distance; he collects and hoards gold, which he admits is of no use to him; and he begins a journal shortly after landing. All these actions are practical, but in addition they raise the expectation of some kind of immediate social intervention, whether in the form of battle, deliverance, companionship, barter, or conversation (events that do not, in fact, occur until many years pass). It is as if he must believe that real human contact is imminent; otherwise, he is forced to confront his isolation and the demands it places on his notion of selfhood.

Determined to create his own world, or at least to remove himself from binding origins, Crusoe deserts his "Father's House" and rejects God, refusing to admit their priority. But when he finds himself in a situation that recreates a possibly unique and pure origin, Crusoe's functional acts—using material from the ship, writing a journal, fortifying himself against others, reading the Bible, creating a home—negate such pretexts and lead him to accept a prior history lodged in both God and man. Biblical history, family stories, and even his own autobiographical writing remind Crusoe that genealogy is an inescapable condition of narration itself.

Crusoe's central problem with the family, then, is that it is both a unit of self-sufficiency and a social group that relies on the dependency of its individuals. Crusoe obviously reflects the drive toward self-sufficiency in his labor on the island, but it must be noted that he attains it only through reduplication of the formal strategies of community; he can create surplus comfort for himself only through imitation of the social relations he has observed. If, as some critics have argued, Crusoe's attainment of wealth is a measure of his growing autonomy and self-development,[9] how can it be said that he has freed himself from the social processes (like exchange) that impede the "expression of self?" Crusoe is not an antithesis but a microcosm of society; his reliance on the ship, which provides him with much of the material that enables him to purchase a life on the island, shows more clearly than the real experience of Alexander Selkirk did that civilized comfort is not achieved ex nihilo. The objects Crusoe uses on the island manifest the social relations he has apparently exchanged to indulge his wanderlust.

In fact, in everything he does, Crusoe wants to replace, not eradicate, the domestic comfort represented by his father. Even before his isolation on the island, he seeks paternal surrogates. The master of the first ship gives Crusoe fatherly advice about a man's calling and reiterates the dire injunction of the real father: "he afterwards talk'd very gravely to me, exhorted me to go back to my Father, and not tempt Providence to my Ruine; told me I might see a visible Hand of Heaven against me, *And young Man*, said he, *depend upon it, if you do not go back, where-ever you go, you will meet with nothing but Disasters and Disappointments till your Father's Words are fulfilled upon you*" (pt. 1, 15). His second master, the ship owner who leads the only successful seafaring project of Crusoe's youth, adopts a similar paternal attitude, directing the young man in matters of commerce and teaching him mathematics, navigation, and sailoring with "disinterested Honesty" (pt. 1, 17). This unexpected concern also characterizes the Portuguese captain who saves Crusoe and Xury and whom Crusoe makes his "universal Heir" (pt. 1, 44). That these father substitutes repeatedly take the form of economic mentors as well suggests that Defoe implicitly regards the family as a social group that must continually transform itself, both imaginatively and economically. The exclusion of the original family provides the opportunity for this reinvention, even if the reimagined state simply duplicates prior models of domestic affiliation.

As a corollary to this pattern, Crusoe also adopts surrogate sons in black slave figures. Very much like Friday, the boy Xury appears, in fact, to be his precursor. As part of the world that threatens Crusoe during his captivity to the Sallee Moor, Xury is quickly assimilated into the white man's order by the simple threat of extinction at the hands of the father figure. Crusoe's power often stems from this near magical ability to induce filial gratitude without really deserving it, appropriating the arbitrary rule of the fathers that we see

in earlier didactic and political treatises such as Gouge's *Of Domesticall Duties* and Filmer's *Patriarcha*. Only when Xury offers to risk
his life by going ashore to reconnoiter the African coast does Crusoe
speak of loving the boy "ever after" (a promise rescinded when Crusoe sells him to the Portuguese captain). With Xury, Crusoe gains
both a servant and a son; indeed, Xury stands symbolically for affective values otherwise lacking in Crusoe's life, but because of his race
and status he remains peripheral to Crusoe's or Defoe's family ideal.
Crusoe thus exploits Lockean notions of relative independence when
he is the son, but combines Filmerian autocratic rigor and Hobbesian monarchism when he plays the father. Like the pro-revolution-
ary logic that Defoe inherited, the family principles Crusoe employs
function strategically to shore up both liberal rights and monarchical justifications, according to the shifting relations of power he establishes with others. Symbolic rather than real family relations are thus
more comfortable to the ideological purposes Defoe attaches to the
family.

Crusoe is therefore not prepared to recognize the general meaning of the paternal signs that surround him until physical danger induces his religious awakening. It is only after recovering from his
moral and physical sickness, when he finds the bibles that lead him
gradually to repentance and then faithful communion with God (pt.
1, 99–111), that Crusoe realizes his identity can be established solely
in relation to a larger moral and social context. He begins to define
himself not in terms of isolation but in relation to God. Only in this
way can he make a home for himself: "I had liv'd a dreadful Life,
perfectly destitute of the Knowledge and Fear of God. I had been
well instructed by Father and Mother; neither had they been wanting to me, in their early Endeavours, to infuse a religious Awe of
God into my Mind, a Sense of my Duty, and of what the Nature
and End of my Being requir'd of me" (pt. 1, 151). The links here between family and God as they determine character follow a causal
sequence that Defoe always found necessary. As in *The Family Instructor*, a well-governed family provides the instructional conversation that engenders a continuing sense of moral identity and proper
relation to God through sincere and pious language.[10] Without a due

sense of filial obligation, chaste speech, and thankfulness to God, an individual has no identity, no sense of "what the Nature and End of my Being requir'd of me." Paradoxically, Crusoe's personal sense of uniqueness corresponds to his awareness that his personality reflects his family background and his ultimate filiation to God. The paternal relation that he rejects when he abandons his father's house is partly recovered, though only on a symbolic level, with acquiescence to the Divine Father. The moral, libidinal, and acquisitive economies that Crusoe's experience on the island seems to dissolve are reconstituted in his union with the unadulterated Father who fulfills all his emotional, economic, and social needs.

Crusoe's struggle to avoid his father's rule takes the form, then, of an abstract paternal embrace. He is able to carry on his adventures in the physical absence of the real father, indulge his guilt for having committed an "original sin" (leaving his father's house), and spiritually atone for his remission without ever having to face the biological father again. He can both depend on and free himself from his origins. For all the real patriarch's ineffectiveness as a moral and practical presence, then, paternity in Crusoe's life turns out to be omnipresent. But unlike the prodigal son, to whom Crusoe constantly compares himself, Defoe's hero returns to the homeland a financially successful man and not until long after his father has died. He may pay in spiritual currency for his filial disobedience, but he avoids the material humbling that his biblical counterpart experiences in the presence of paternal authority. If Behn's scandal narratives embrace the family in order to reject it, Defoe's fiction rejects the family the better to embrace it. Its absence dramatizes and therefore increases the value of a return to home as long as returning preserves the transformative power of the prodigal self. The domestic sphere, already abandoned in its original form, is thus symbolically reabsorbed by an apparently autonomous masculine self in search of social and economic power. Like the earlier models of prose fiction or political power that Defoe seemed to reject (including his own didactic material), Crusoe's attitude toward the family recasts an older paradigm as if it could somehow both maintain traditional support from the past and occupy an utterly uncharted realm.

A Familiar Island

Once Crusoe restores the temporal father by devoting himself to a spiritual father, he turns much of his energy to adopting his own paternal rule. Having replaced the deserted father, Crusoe wants to be a father himself. Of course, the sexual abstinence that shapes his island experience makes this desire difficult to fulfill, and Crusoe must again resort to linguistic manipulation, to making life an allegory, in order to realign it with conventional family order. He busies himself with recreating a comfortable home life largely because he dreads confronting his homeless self. Such industry also explains Crusoe's peculiar lack of sexual anxiety, his obliviousness to the one component of home that he cannot adequately reproduce, female companionship.

In the absence of human reproduction, therefore, Crusoe turns various animals into family, making nature generate the kinship he needs to sustain his identity. As with the apartment in the trees, material and affective relations are naturalized, while still revealing the power of the bourgeois subject to shape nature himself. When the domestic cats that escape from the ship multiply with the wild cats and become a nuisance, he refers to the "Increase of my Family" (pt. 1, 117–18). A lamed kid goat he discovers becomes "one of my Domesticks" (pt. 1, 129) which, because of an emotional attachment, he cannot kill. At one point, he even treats his pets as comic versions of the royal family:

It would have made a Stoick smile to have seen, me and my little Family sit down to Dinner; there was my Majesty the Prince and Lord of the whole Island [his dog]; I had the Lives of all my Subjects at my absolute Command. I could hang, draw, give Liberty, and take it away, and no Rebels among all my Subjects.

Then to see how like a King I din'd too all alone, attended by my Servants, *Poll* [the parrot], as if he had been my Favourite, was the only Person permitted to talk to me. My Dog who was now grown very old and crazy, and had found no Species to multiply his Kind upon, sat always at my Right Hand, and two Cats, one on one Side the Table, and one on the other, expecting now and then a Bit from my Hand, as a Mark of special Favour. (pt. 1, 171)

This diversion is especially revealing for how it conflates family and imperial rule; it may, in fact be a parody of Stuart delusions about the ideal state. Remarkably, however, the scene anticipates fairly exactly Crusoe's attitude toward his future human subjects. As we shall see, blind filial obedience, affection, and willingness to die for the father (specifically, Crusoe) become the forms of human alliance that Crusoe most trusts. By transforming liabilities into economic or political advantages, Crusoe familiarizes an alien landscape through personal filiation in which he is either the powerful father or the indulged son, roles he could not play satisfyingly in his own father's house.[11] More important, the fantasies about reproducing one's power through parthenogenetic means allow the male subject to circumvent biological necessities.

One of the central paradoxes of the narrative, in which individualism and patriarchy achieve an uneasy alliance, mostly at the expense of "female presence," this contradiction is the latent subject in much of Defoe's nonfictional discourse about family government. When Defoe responded to the political repercussions of the trial of Henry Sacheverell, a High Church Tory divine tried by the Whig government for delivering an antirevolution sermon on the anniversary of the 1688 Revolution, he used the opportunity to align Tory High Church policy with political cross-dressing. At the time, Defoe was working for a moderate Tory government led by Robert Harley but controlled by a largely Whig ministry. On May 9, 1710, he wrote:

[T]hey tell us a strange turn has been given to Affairs, in this Nation of UPS and DOWNS, and particularly by a Transmutation of Customs, as they affect the Sexes, *Viz.* The Women lay aside their Tea and Chocolate, leave off Visiting after Dinner, and forming themselves into Caball, turn Privy-Counsellors, and settle the State: The Men leave off Smoaking Tobacco, learn plain Work, and to knit Knots, play at push Pin, *Anglice Picket*; and leave the more Weighty Affairs of the Nation, to the newly assuming *Sex*, whose Business it is, they say, (under a Petticoat Government, *as they call it*) more now than usual. (*Defoe's Review*, Book 17, vol 7: 69)

Defoe's association of conservative, patriarchal, and clerical authority with a "petticoat government" suggests his antipathy toward tyrannical authority and women's political aspirations, both of which he regards as counterparts: "Tyranny in Government, and Non-Resistance in Subjects, are Doctrines more Natural, more taking, and more suitable to the Women, than the Men—And this is manifest by several Considerations, (*Viz.*) *First*, That they are most apt to Tyrannize themselves; and, *Secondly*, Feel less of the Mischiefs of Tyranny when it falls, than the Men" (71). According to Defoe, political women and reactionary religious government, both pernicious to a healthy civil state, share the same predisposition toward emotion, influence, and dogmatism: "Invasion of the Politicians Province, is an eminent Demonstration of the Sympathetick Influence of the Clergy upon the Sex, and the near Affinity between the Gown, and the Petticoat" (71). The burlesque excoriation of women here serves to demean political opponents, as Defoe makes clear when he draws "an undoubted exact Connection, between the Female Counsels we are speaking of, and the *Effeminate Counsellors* they would impose upon us" (71). Political women are unnatural because they naturally adopt postures that undermine civil government (itself supposedly of natural origins). They are doubly cursed: by being instinctively tyrannical as governors and overly passive as subjects they become incapable of either government or rebellion.

Yet since Defoe's attack on political forms of patriarchy accentuates their emasculated condition, his "revolutionary" rhetoric (now the property of the established government) endorses a distinct masculine authority reminiscent of the patriarchal hermeticism he denigrates (though his notions of female tyranny are made even more complicated by Queen Anne's management of the throne, which Defoe largely admired). He also does not condemn female government within the family: "I am not making Comparisons, nor speaking of Family Tyranny; I do not know, but some Female Government there, might do us good; but I speak of the Propensities of Nature, and the Temper of the Sexes" (71). What concerns him about the reversed political relations he describes through an inversion of gender, his fear that under such government "Trade Sinks, and General Commerce, feels the mighty Convulsion" (70), is that the innovative ascendance of female politics will make traditional Tory policy seem compelling. The consequences for England would be both political and domestic; Defoe imagines that feminizing politics would corrupt family life by, in turn, politicizing the feminine. The prostitutes of government would then invade the nucleus of the family, ruining the natural domestic character of wives: "[I]t has been matter of Family-Jealousie, as well as State Jealousie, that such and such great Men, and Great Magistrates . . . are unusually Visited by Women and strange She Faces, from the other End of the Town. . . . This I doubt will in time, oblige them all to bring their Wives into the Secret too" (70). Distinguishing female government in the family from female government in politics (and indeed endorsing the former), Defoe refuses nonetheless to allow domestic ideology entrance into the political.

Defoe's own conduct books, conversely, justify patriarchal governance within the family just as they inevitably express energetic resistance to arbitrary authority. The younger son in part 1 of *The Family Instructor*, presumably not influenced by the lure of primogeniture, urges the father to behave in a reformed fashion that would return parental authority and moral rigor to the household. The defiant elder son, representing a traditional attitude based on feudal notions, challenges patriarchal right despite the fact that it ultimately reinforces his own status as the oldest male progeny. He is ultimately chastised by the father for disagreeing in principle, and without reasonable justification, with paternal rule:

I might with much more Justice insist upon *my undoubted Right to govern my own Family*, without giving an Account to my Children *of what I do*; also in a Case so plain as this, *methinks*, they need not seek for a Reason for such an Order, *but* since they pretend Ignorance, *let them read* the Commands of God . . . Liberty *to do Evil* is an abandon'd *Slavery*, the worst of *Bondage*, and Confinement *from doing Evil*, is the only *true Liberty*. . . . [I]f you will not submit to *my Government*, you must quit *my Dominions* . . . for unless you will submit to regulate your Life after a different manner than you have done, and to receive Advice from your Father for your Conduct; *flatter not yourself* with your Father's Affection, *I'll love* none that *hate God*, nor shelter none of his Rebels. (124–25)

Mixing Old Testament rhetoric, biblical proof, and political metaphor, the father here suspends affective obligation and rational or "enlightened" explanation in order to maintain his "government." Similarly, one of the wives in part 3, having fled a husband she considers tyrannical and plotted to poison him until her conscience repels her, believes that she can control her own domestic fate. But as her husband notes to his wife's female confederate, her power is only a sign of his indecision: "[D]o you know, Madam, that I have Authority [as a Justice of the Peace] to command my Wife out of your Hands, and that you have no Authority to detain her? . . . If it were not in respect to my Wife, I should try it, Madam; I have other Power, I assure you, than my own. . . . [I]f she would have been pleased to let me speak with her, I should have treated her very kindly. But since she is prevailed upon to be so unkind, I will offer her no Violence, though I have Power to do it, as you see" (quoted in Curtis, *The Versatile Defoe*, 441–42). As is so often the case in eighteenth-century literature (and society, for that matter), the limits of affective and supposedly reasonable parental or conjugal relations appear when family crises emerge and legal action becomes possible. Affect actually, or potentially, dissipates in the presence of pragmatic considerations having to do with power and finances. While the husband indulges his affection for his wife and egalitarian respect for her dignity, his "kindness" is the complement of his "power," which he merely chooses to suspend.

In *The Family Instructor* father and husband extort obedience simply by threatening to exert their authority; conversely, neither son nor wife is capable of achieving liberty without the conscious suspension of power by the patriarchal figure. Both the younger son and the reformed wife realize what the older son can never grasp, that they must learn themselves to want and see the necessity of paternal rule. Thus, the wife finally accepts that "she had broke over all the Obligations and Bounds of her conjugal Relation, as a Consequence of her Rebellion against God; and as soon as ever she was struck with a Sense of her Sin against God, it carried her immediately back into the Course of her relative Duty" (quoted in Curtis, *The Versatile Defoe*, 448). Like Locke, Defoe hoped to make paternalism an active moral and political force that worked not arbitrarily upon subjects but responded to the desires of the subject. Instead of working externally upon the individual, patriarchal authority comes to work internally to produce "relative duty." Defoe's Revolution sympathies thus put him in the ambiguous position of defending the monarchy's conservative structures of power in order to guarantee liberal principles of government. The accumulated crises about family succession that characterize the period in which he wrote made household relations a volatile subject not only in Defoe's fiction but in his political and domestic advice as well.

Both the journalism and the conduct material reveal Defoe's troubles in reconciling political order and household government (particularly of a female kind). Establishing normative behavior becomes increasingly difficult as relations of power and gender shift. While "female government" offered a revolutionary means of reimagining political activity, for Defoe it also projected a fearful and unnatural system of sexual relationships. The fantasy of a solitary domestic survivalist exiled twenty-eight years on a deserted island apparently enabled him to circumvent the problem by downplaying gender and marginalizing the biological considerations that were haunting his own sentiments about the structure of English government. Like Behn, though with entirely different ideological motives, Defoe evaded in his fiction the political ramifications of depicting conventional domestic precepts at a time when ideal household policy and the Stuart monarchy's family affairs were often at variance. By isolating his characters from a normative domestic sphere, Defoe managed to highlight the value of the absent structures of daily household relations while extricating his stories from the ideological pitfalls that might attend the representation of everyday conjugal practice.

Crusoe's adoption of a patriarchal attitude toward his animal "Family" and then toward the later residents of the island, especially Friday, thus finesses the enigma of the womanless island state by collapsing sexual and domestic needs. Defoe criticism has mostly concentrated on the egocentric aspect of Crusoe's conversion of Friday, seeing in the relationship between the two a model of Hegel's master/slave dialectic. Crusoe names, clothes, and employs

Friday; he is especially eager to teach Friday the skills he himself has acquired on the island because he needs good cheap labor. We might note, however, that Crusoe is equally in need of conversation. As he admits: "I was greatly delighted with him, and made it my Business to teach him every Thing, that was proper to make him useful, handy, and helpful; but especially to make him speak, and understand me when I spake" (pt. 1, 244). That Crusoe finds Friday more than a mere servant is suggested by his complacency toward life on the island once he has trained his captured savage. Friday seems to answer almost all his desires: "I began to say to my self, that could I but have been safe from more Savages, I cared not, if I was never to remove from the place while I lived" (pt. 1, 244). Crusoe calls his first year with Friday the "pleasantest" year of his island life and soon regards the cannibal with paternal fondness: "his very Affections were ty'd to me, like those of a Child to a Father" (pt. 1, 247, 242).

To achieve domestic felicity Crusoe familiarizes Friday, transforming what initially represents total otherness—pagan black cannibalism—into an extension of himself, formulating the son from the father.[12] When Crusoe saves Friday, the latter is made at once obliging servant and son by the laws of gratitude.[13] Having escaped from the cannibals, Friday runs instinctively toward Crusoe's home fortress. Crusoe takes this as a special sign that Friday belongs to him (pt. 1, 234) and interposes himself literally between Friday and the antagonistic black community, appearing as god, savior, and father figure and thereby incorporating the alien savage within the comforting economy of the European bourgeois family.

The notorious exchange between Crusoe and Friday on the nature of God exemplifies this process of familiarization, bringing together several of Defoe's central preoccupations: religious instruction, the treatment of slaves, filial duty, and paganism. Crusoe carefully teaches Friday European religious values in a series of discussions that echo several pamphlets and portions of longer works written by Defoe on the dissemination of Christianity. Like the paraliterary material, these debates between Crusoe and Friday center on European conceptions of God as father. Friday mistakes Crusoe's question about the savage's origin for a question about paternity: "I ask'd him one Time who made him? The poor Creature did not understand me at all, but thought I had ask'd him who was his Father" (pt. 2, 1). Crusoe clears up this misunderstanding by asking him who made the natural world, at which point Friday tells his master about Benamuckee "that liv'd beyond all" that "made all Things" and to whom "the People who die in his Country went" (pt. 2, 1). At issue again is the problem of origin. Crusoe can displace Friday's belief in Benamuckee by affirming God's larger sphere of influence, greater creative power, and further distance from humanity. Curiously, it is this last attribute that Friday finds most convincing: "he told me one Day, that if our God could hear us up beyond the Sun, he must needs be a greater God than their *Benamuckee*, who liv'd but a little way off, and yet could not hear, till they went up to the great Mountains where he dwelt, to speak to him" (pt. 2, 2). The success of the argument depends on the mutability of Crusoe's concept of fatherhood. Crusoe argues that his Protestant god surpasses Benamuckee because he transcends the empirical world (and hence cannot be disproved) while still being accessible through direct prayer (Friday's god can only be addressed by way of the pagan priesthood). Thus the original paternal source is at once more removed and yet more available. Crusoe wants to convey to Friday the greater sense (as he sees it) of the Christian concept of origin, and its greater subtlety in establishing an uncompromised standard of truth.

This system of order also applies to Crusoe's immediate relations to his "family." In teaching Friday civilized manners and Christian morals, Crusoe wants to establish more than a working relationship. He also wants to reduce the threat of others by redefining them according to socially comforting terms. The catechistical dialogue between Crusoe and Friday on the nature of God and the devil conforms to a pattern of moral debate that Defoe constantly used in his didactic tracts on marriage and family. The interviews, particularly between parents and children, involve the same reversals of innocence and experience, where the authority of the teacher is undermined by the subtle naiveté of the questioner. In the first part of *The*

Family Instructor, for instance, the youngest son feels betrayed by
the neglect in his moral education. He blames his parents for not
providing sufficient religious instruction, for not holding family
prayers, and for not ensuring that the children obey the dictates of
the parents. The boy's innate religious sense causes the parents to
reassess their own piety and reconsider how they have raised their
family. Similarly, when Crusoe tries to explain how the devil operates in Christian doctrine he cannot clear up Friday's perplexity as
to why God, who is omnipotent, would allow the devil to exist at
all. Crusoe finds that in attempting to instruct Friday he also teaches
himself the very doctrine he is trying to authorize.[14] Thus the relationship with Friday proves enriching not only in terms of economic production but also as it relates to Crusoe's intellectual and
moral growth.

   Crusoe's attitude toward Friday is, nonetheless, one in which
power shapes affect. It does seem to equate filial duty with servitude;
to be a son is to be a slave. Nor does Crusoe seem to acknowledge
the illuminating contrast between his failure as a son and Friday's
obedience to both him and Friday's natural father. In fact, though
Friday has been carefully instructed in Christian morality, much of
which involves the duty of son to father, he is bound to follow Crusoe even if it requires abandoning his natural father (no mention is
ever made of the mother). And though Friday wants to go with
Crusoe, it is surprising that he mentions no concern for what will
happen to his father when the old man returns to the island with
the Portuguese castaways to face the remaining mutineers. Crusoe
treats Friday at this juncture with a peremptory license that seems at
odds with his moral stance. His assumed paternal right exceeds what
he has earlier affirmed to be the right of the natural father, presumably because the natural father in this case is a "savage." The
relevance of the theme of filial duty is abruptly replaced by concerns
that center on racial supremacy.

   We see, then, that Defoe's competing interests in relation to Friday—filial obedience, natural gratitude, religious instruction, slave
labor, and white Christian domination—are not easily synthesized.
This ambiguous treatment of Friday, the use of him as both child

and servant, can occur because Crusoe gratifies his paternal desires in the absence of the mother and wife. Friday can be treated with diffidence in moments of convenience because, though very much like a son, he has no genetic connection to Crusoe, who assumes the privileges that family confers upon the patriarch without also accepting the biological complications. To locate himself in and demonstrate his power over a world that seems always to subordinate him, Crusoe fabricates a family that reflects his authority but can never then challenge his claim to that authority. Defoe feels compelled, in other words, to downplay the conventional family in order to create a surrogate model of domestic relations that, while retaining the persuasiveness of a traditional patriarchal system, more effectively reproduces the exchangeability of human affect that Defoe is attracted to but cannot, in seeming conscience, condone.

The most striking example of this conflict between power and affect is Defoe's treatment of Crusoe's desire. While critics have often noted the absence of overt sexuality in Crusoe's story and have speculated on how it is reinscribed in the text—through the multiplying cats, the spilling of seed, Friday's companionship—it is perhaps easier to show how Crusoe's passion appears in his urge to create a purely symbolic family. Thus, he responds to his domestic exile by transforming his pets, his domiciles, and the later human inhabitants of the island through language that invests the external world with familial significance, as if the world had magically substituted for the loss of sexual need.[15]

Indeed, we are led to believe that the satisfaction Crusoe gains from fulfilling his survival needs and overcompensating for his initial lack of domestic comfort, power, and control supplants whatever libidinous urges he may ordinarily have felt. After setting his house in order he explains:

I was remov'd from all the Wickedness of the World here. I had neither the *Lust of the Flesh, the Lust of the Eye, or the Pride of Life.* I had nothing to covet; for I had all that I was now capable of enjoying: I was Lord of the whole Manor; or if I pleas'd, I might call my self King, or Emperor over the whole Country which I had Possession of. There were no Rivals. I had no Competitor, none to dispute Sovereignty or Command with me. . . . In a Word, the Nature and Experience of Things dictated to me upon just Reflection, That all the good Things of this World, are no farther good to us, than they are for our Use; and whatever we may heap up indeed to give others, we enjoy just as much as we can use, and no more. The most covetous griping Miser in the World would have been cur'd of the Vice of Covetousness, if he had been in my Case; for I possess'd infinitely more than I knew what to do with. I had no room for Desire, except it was of Things which I had not, and they were but Trifles, though indeed of great Use to me. (pt. 1, 148-49)

His claim that desire is suppressed when one achieves the limit of potential satisfaction that impoverished circumstances allow simply exposes the rationalizations to which his situation has driven him. And his argument that covetousness would be satisfied in a state without comparative levels of ownership does not make much sense since possession has no real significance in the absence of competition. Thus the paternal terms by which he measures life on the island—being lord of the manor or king of the land—are empty of meaning, and the desire he claims he does not feel while on the island reasserts itself in the metaphoric language that he uses. Here, Crusoe seems to be hiding the fact that his lack of desire is not an absence of desire but a willed drive not to be conscious of desire. This dispassion characterizes all of Defoe's characters, who seem to affirm their author's contention in *Conjugal Lewdness* that passion must be closely regulated by reason. What we see in Defoe's fictional narratives is a suppression of desire in the self within texts that exploit the desire to assert the self.

Crusoe's apparent lack of passion seems, as he has earlier asserted, to be a response to his isolation from the contingencies of a social world in which desire stems from systems of ownership and exchange:

[B]y a constant Study, and serious Application of the Word of God, and by the Assistance of his Grace, I gain'd a different Knowledge from what I had before. I entertain'd different Notions of Things. I look'd now upon the World as a Thing remote, which I had nothing to do with, no Expectation from, and indeed no Desires about: In a Word, I had nothing indeed to do with it, nor was ever like to have; so I thought it look'd as we may perhaps look upon it hereafter, *viz.* as a Place I had liv'd in, but was come out of it; and well might I say, as Father *Abraham* to *Dives, Between me and thee is a great Gulph fix'd.* (pt. 1, 148)

Application to the word of God suggests to him the possibility of an existence disassociated from conventional social habits. But Crusoe's religious devotion reasserts the equation between identity and social coercion because it reintroduces the family metaphor that eventually forces him to regard his life in terms of transmission, intercourse, and legacy. His knowledge is not so changed; as it turns out, he must and will propagate a family on his island.

The Unassimilated Wife

As we have seen, Crusoe finds the means to regain parental guidance and adopt children without endangering his own will to power by a sheer act of imagination. The one member of the nuclear family that he cannot assimilate, the wife, remains unintegrated because the world he occupies and the way he views that world are pathologically masculine. The great absence in Defoe's text—woman—is not merely the consequence of a plot that strands a man on a deserted island; it is the result also of a powerful rhetorical exclusion of women and the heterosexual desires associated with them. Crusoe's obliviousness to desire, more often related in economic than sexual terms, and his overwhelming satisfaction with Friday's companionship, indicate that the customary functions served by a wife are in *Robinson Crusoe* appropriated for a relentless male ordering of language, economy, and sex. Thus, if Friday acts as son and slave, he also performs many of the duties of a wife, assuming the responsibilities that were earlier associated with Crusoe's own domestic housekeeping. In many respects he is as providentially sent to Crusoe as Eve is to Adam. And we might recall that Friday makes his master so happy with his conversation, affection, and obedience that Crusoe would choose to remain on the island forever were it not for the threat of further attack from cannibals. On a practical level, these actions stem merely from necessity; on a symbolic level they indicate the essential function that activities traditionally allocated to women serve in the survivalist myth. As an exclusively male fantasy, Crusoe's adventures reveal a powerful striving for parthenogenetic and phallocentric reproduction; yet the forms that Crusoe's desire assumes reassert to some extent the formative influence of the conjugal model.

Defoe faced a difficult task in trying to wed his view of married life as depicted in *The Family Instructor* or *Conjugal Lewdness* with his desire to construct a narrative of self-actualization. In *Robinson Crusoe* matrimony provides no significant thematic, narrative, or even metaphoric coherence. Crusoe's parents do not provide an entirely ideal model for the kind of family envisioned in the didactic works, the father being unable to convince any of his sons to follow the bourgeois example he sets. "The upper Station of *Low Life*" (pt. 1, 2) is too static a model for Crusoe to embrace. The mother, a nominal figure at best, refuses to petition her husband on behalf of her son. Her unreceptiveness is reflected in Crusoe's dismissive remark that he waited to speak to her until she was "a little pleasanter than ordinary" (pt. 1, 5). When Crusoe describes his own marriage and family life at the conclusion, he dispatches his wife and children in two blunt sentences: "I marry'd, and that not either to my Disadvantage or Dissatisfaction, and had three Children, two Sons and one Daughter: But my Wife dying, and my Nephew coming Home with good Success from a Voyage to *Spain*, my Inclination to go Abroad, and his Importunity prevailed and engag'd me to go in his Ship, as a private Trader to the *East Indies*" (pt. 2, 105). The domestic alliance is expressed in double negatives ("not either to my Disadvantage or Dissatisfaction"); the effect seems to be one of calculation and indifference. Moreover, in the same sentence describing his wife's death, Crusoe also declares his intention of continuing his adventures. The cause and effect is starkly articulated here. Domestic obligations impede the adventure and hence the advancement of plot, and yet the kind of narrative that Defoe wants to endorse should affirm family responsibility. And because of this indeterminacy, the ending of *Robinson Crusoe* swerves away from the domestic resolution with which Richardson, Fielding, Austen, and later English writers frequently concluded their work.

That Defoe was aware of this marital gap is evinced by his emphasis on the nuclear family in the sequel. The figure of the wife inevitably structures Crusoe's behavior, becoming, by the time Defoe wrote *The Farther Adventures of Robinson Crusoe*, the overt locus of value in the developing history of the island. While *Robinson Crusoe* slights matrimonial issues, *Farther Adventures* emphasizes the relevance of conjugal relations to civil government.[16] One might even claim that much of the sequel to Crusoe's adventures is a paean to family life. To begin with, the summary of his married life changes dramatically. If the first description of marriage lacks feeling, the sequel's version is intensely sentimentalized. Though still obstructing his "native Propensity for rambling" (pt. 2, 111), the goodness, integrity, and usefulness of his wife make her a paragon. Noticing his obsession with returning to his island, she offers to accompany him in his travels though she believes it to be a "preposterous Thing" (pt. 2, 114). The basis of her argument is all the more surprising for the way in which it anticipates her death: "[S]he found nothing hindred my going, but my being engag'd to a Wife and Children. She told me that it was true she could not think of parting with me; but as she was assur'd, that if she was dead, it would be the first Thing I would do: So, as it seem'd to her, that the Thing was determin'd above, she would not be the only Obstruction" (pt. 2, 114). Further on she makes the link to fate even clearer: "I won't leave you; for if it be of Heaven, you must do it. There is no resisting it; and if Heaven makes it your Duty to go, he will also make it mine to go with you, or otherwise dispose of me, that I may not obstruct it" (pt. 2, 114–15). There are deep implications in this exchange between husband and wife that Defoe may or may not have been interested in, but I think it would be difficult for many readers not to see a curious self-sacrificing, even suicidal, impulse on the wife's part, and a hint of sinister desire in Crusoe. Not merely an occasion for Defoe to preach about obedience in a wife, this sequence accentuates the ideological conflict in Defoe's fiction between domestic harmony and novelty (in all senses of the word).

In his sequel Defoe makes the process of diminishment even more emphatic by initially emphasizing the capacity of domesticity to contain Crusoe's desire for mobility. Thus, convinced by his wife's remarks to resist his traveling urge at the beginning of the renewed story of his life, Crusoe begins to recognize his obligations to his family:

This affectionate Behaviour of my Wife's brought me a little out of the Vapours, and I began to consider what I was doing; I corrected my wandring Fancy, and began to argue with my self sedately, what Business I had after threescore Years, and after such a Life of tedious Sufferings and Disasters, and closed in so happy and easy a Manner, I say, what Business had I to rush into new Hazards, and put my self upon Adventures, fit only for Youth and Poverty to run into.

With those Thoughts, I considered my new Engagement, that I had a Wife, one Child born, and my Wife then great with Child of another; that I had all the World could give me, and had no Need to seek Hazards for Gain. (pt. 2, 115)

Acting upon this resolve, he purchases a farm in Bedford removed from "Things relating to the remote Part of the World" where through industry he becomes a country gentleman in less than a year, achieving the station that his father had originally intended for him: "Now I thought indeed, that I enjoy'd the middle State of Life, that my Father so earnestly recommended to me, and liv'd a kind of heavenly Life" (pt. 2, 116). What would perhaps have been the conventional ending to his story in a later work becomes the beginning of the sequel to his adventures. The pattern of *Robinson Crusoe* is recapitulated: in the sequel his own family provides the framework of bourgeois security that his father's family had represented in the original; his wife replaces his father as spokesperson of bourgeois domesticity. But unlike the first adventures, the *Farther Adventures* begins with Crusoe actually enjoying the middle station. Absent is the outright rejection of bourgeois life; the slightly maturer man accepts the domestic conditions expected of him and is able to integrate himself into the social fabric and maintain a sexual and social relationship. Though to some extent Crusoe still separates himself from the world, creating an autonomous environment on his farm that duplicates the isolation and self-sufficiency of his island life, he is much more committed to family life than he was as a youth:

"What I planted, was for my self, and what I improved, was for my Family" (pt. 2, 116). Thus in the sequel the family context is given greater validation; the heroic actions of the wife signify much greater domestic value than the professions of Crusoe's gout-ridden and complacent father in the original.

Nonetheless, when Crusoe's wife dies, narrative is unleashed. The exigencies of plot and fate are neatly wedded. In contrast to the description in *Robinson Crusoe*, Crusoe's account of her death in *Farther Adventures* records his staggering grief, though, as with the initial description, it still announces the return of his wandering inclination. If anything, although he evinces much more regret, the death seems a mere pretext for the farther adventures. Where before, her death had seemed an incidental affair, it now appears to be a willed event that in some ways determines the continuance of plot:

But in the Middle of all this Felicity, one Blow from unforeseen Providence unhing'd me at once; and not only made a Breach upon me inevitable and incurable, but drove me, by its Consequences, into a deep Relapse into the wandring Disposition, which, as I may say, being born in my very Blood, soon recover'd its hold of me, and like the Returns of a violent Distemper, came on with an irresistible Force upon me; so that nothing could make any more Impression upon me. This Blow was the Loss of my Wife. (pt. 2, 116–17)

Rhetorically, this passage heightens suspense by postponing revelation of the first long sentence's substantive ("one Blow") until the simple direct and explanatory second sentence ("This Blow was the Loss of my Wife"). Occupying the intervening space is a relatively complex explanation of Crusoe's psychological constitution that employs a variety of conjunctions linking together a long sequence of modifying phrases. Both in terms of subject and technique, the delaying psychodrama nearly supplants the main emphasis of the paragraph: the wife's death. It takes an uncharacteristic simple declarative sentence to restate the tragedy and satisfy the reader's curiosity about the "Blow" to Crusoe's fortunes. Perhaps this suspension increases the effect of the death sentence, but it also seems to foreground the consequences rather than the event itself. The discussion of Crusoe's reaction to the "Blow" does in fact have a distinctly richer adjectival modification than the bald statement of the wife's loss.

I do not mean to suggest that Crusoe is callous about his wife's death. Indeed, he reveals strong feelings for her in the following paragraph, where for perhaps the only time in his life Crusoe acknowledges the importance of an interpersonal relation to his psychological makeup:

> It is not my Business here to write an Elegy upon my Wife, give a Character of her particular Virtues, and make my Court to the Sex by the Flattery of a Funeral Sermon. She was, in a few Words, the Stay of all my Affairs, the Center of all my Enterprizes, the Engine, that by her Prudence reduc'd me to that happy Compass I was in, from the most extravagant and ruinous Project that fluttered in my Head, as above; and did more to guide my rambling Genius, than a Mother's Tears, a Father's Instructions, a Friend's Counsel, or all my own reasoning Powers could do. I was happy in listening to her Tears, and in being mov'd by her Entreaties, and to the last Degree desolate and dislocated in the World by the Loss of her. (pt. 2, 117)

The wife transcends the roles of parent, friend, and even self in influencing Crusoe. She seems to be the embodiment of all conventional family values, producing children, acting as perfect companion, offering sage advice, and yet subordinating herself entirely to her husband's desires. She is linked, above all other things, to the happiest period of Crusoe's life. The only other character for whom Crusoe feels and declares nearly the same emotion is Friday. Intended to rectify the dispassionate appraisal of family life at the end of *Robinson Crusoe*, this portrait provides the reader with a model of the marital relationship that Defoe endorsed in his didactic works. It is, in fact, the only depiction of a wife in all of Defoe's major fictional narratives that seems to follow his own conjugal injunctions in the conduct literature (and even then, he implies, it would be more pertinent in a funeral sermon or elegy, conventional forms of exemplary conduct, than in the narrative he is currently relating).

But for all her vital impact on Crusoe's life, the function that the unnamed wife performs in the resolution of the plot is slight indeed, even in the sequel. Crusoe says that her death causes him to feel alienated in the world, driving him once more to sea: "When she was gone, the World look'd aukwardly round me; I was as much a Stranger in it, in my Thoughts, as I was in the Brasils, when I went first on Shore there; and as much alone, except as to the Assistance of Servants, as I was in my Island . . . my Sage Counsellor was gone, I was like a Ship without a Pilot" (pt. 2, 117–18). With her passing, domestic comforts lose their appeal and are equated with near sensory deprivation: "all the pleasant innocent Amusements of my Farm, and my Garden, my Cattle, and my Family, which before entirely possesst me, were nothing to me, had no Relish, and were like Musick to one that has no Ear, or Food to one that has no Taste" (pt. 2, 118). He thus promptly arranges for the care and education of his children without worrying too much about his family responsibilities, though his "ancient good Friend the Widow" tries to dissuade him from leaving (pt. 2, 121). The "want of a taste of Life" that Crusoe experiences after his wife's death, while reactivating his desire to roam, never again provides a structural or thematic principle of the plot, even though it motivates the adventures that constitute that plot. In an odd way, then, Crusoe's wife seems to be both necessary and irrelevant to the developing narrative, a haunting presence that never rematerializes. She represents all the points of crisis in Defoe's narratives where the dislocated family challenges—if only in a fatal form—the individualistic triumphs of his solitary protagonists.

Farther Adventures in Domesticity

The sentimentalized portrait of the wife at the beginning of *Farther Adventures* signals a fundamental change in Crusoe's attitude to family and ultimately in Defoe's symbolic purposes regarding the island. Unlike *Robinson Crusoe*, in which the island represents a bachelor's illusion of independence, in the *Farther Adventures* what finally sanctifies the island is matrimonial, and, hence, civic order. Defoe seems to have been at pains to redress the obvious omissions of sexual union in the first installment of the story. When Crusoe arrives on his island after an absence of nine years, he and the

French priest accompanying him are shocked by what they call the "Adultery" of the colonizers, who live with women they have not properly married. The two men decide to perform the requisite ceremony ex post facto because to do otherwise challenges the legality of the entire colonial venture. According to the French priest,

[T]he Essence of the Sacrament of Matrimony (so he call'd it, being a *Roman*) consists not only in the mutual Consent of the Parties to take one another, *as Man and Wife*, but in the formal and legal Obligation, that there is in the Contract, to compel the Man and Woman at all Times, to own and acknowledge each other, obliging the Men to abstain from all other Women, to engage in no other Contract while these subsist; and on all Occasions, as Ability allows, to provide honestly for them and their Children, and to oblige the Women to the same, or like Conditions, *mutatis mutandis*, on their Side. . . . [T]hese Men may, when they please, or when Occasion presents, abandon these Women, disown their Children, leave them to perish, and take other Women, and marry them whilst these are living. . . . How, Sir, is God honour'd in this unlawful Liberty? And how shall a Blessing succeed your Endeavours in this Place? *However good in themselves*, and *however sincere in your Design*, while these Men, who at present are your Subjects, under your absolute Government and Dominion, are allow'd by you to live in open Adultery? (pt. 3, 20)

This passage articulates many of Defoe's own thoughts on matrimony, but more important, it links contractual obligation in the conjugal household to the success of the social unit and in turn to the lawful liberty that God represents.[17] Here, Defoe states his personal attitude, voiced, oddly enough, by a Roman Catholic spokesman, toward contemporary marital conditions in England—to him, culture and monogamy are synonymous.

The effectiveness of Crusoe's "Government" depends therefore upon his ability to install a proper system of sexual alliance. Considerable attention, perhaps one fifth of *Farther Adventures*, is dedicated to the problem of matrimony. An extended dialogue between the reprobate Will Atkins and his wife occupies much of this space. The dialogue mostly illustrates the opinion that wife and husband should agree on religious matters (a matter similarly explored by Defoe in *Religious Courtship*, where the widowed daughter describes how she resisted her husband's attempts to convert her to the Catholic faith). The exchange also demonstrates the influence of a virtuous wife. Atkins, one of the original mutineers, and a continued troublemaker in Crusoe's absence, is redeemed by his wife, one of the captured cannibals. Through Atkins she learns about Christianity and begins to fear that he will be punished for his intransigence. As a consequence, Atkins repents his former sins and undertakes their mutual religious training in a series of conversations much like those between father and son at the beginning of *The Family Instructor*, or between Crusoe and Friday on the subject of Christianity.

What makes the exchange between Atkins and his wife crucial is that it illuminates Crusoe's own crisis of faith. The wife's naiveté forces Atkins to question his own moral behavior and leads him to confront his filial disobedience, which he describes as a form of patricide: "I murder'd my poor Father . . . I did not cut his Throat, but I cut the Thread of all his Comforts, and shorten'd his Days" (pt. 3, 43). This confession in turn causes Crusoe to perceive his rejection of his "Father's House" as a parallel instance of patricide: "Atkins, every Shore, every Hill, nay, I may say, every Tree in this Island is witness to the Anguish of my Soul, for my Ingratitude and base Usage of a good tender Father; a Father much like yours, by your Description; and I murder'd my Father as well as you, *Will Atkins*, but I think, for all that, my Repentance is short of yours too by a great deal" (pt. 3, 44). Rather than the site of a pure beginning, the island has become the repository of all of Crusoe's preemptive guilt.

Unlike Atkins, Crusoe cannot or refuses to atone for his guilt by remarrying. For all his moral approbation of marriage he himself cannot find satisfaction within the nuclear family. Consequently, his moral professions about matrimony become increasingly hypocritical, and he becomes farther distanced from his own island. If we read the Crusoe saga only through the protagonist's eyes (a compelling option given its autobiographical form), we encounter what Carol Kay rightly describes as "post-Hobbesian political philosophy," in which "family life may be an important influence and training ground for social life, but fundamental rights and duties cannot be derived from parental authority" (77). Crusoe's chastening experience with Atkins, however, reveals a second model that undermines his solitary and embattled conclusions about life. When he discovers through Atkins that the savages maintain more rigid marital codes than he automatically assumed, Crusoe is confounded. Having believed that Atkins would fail in using political, legal, and economic justifications to explain Christian matrimony to his native wife, Crusoe reveals his instinctive acceptance of sexual promiscuity in a state of nature as assumed by Hobbes, and later Hume: "You talk like a Civilian, *Will*; could you make her understand what you meant by Inheritance and Families? they know no such Thing among the Savages, but marry any how, without regard to Relation, Consanguinity, or Family; Brother and Sister, nay, as I have been told, even the Father and Daughter, and the Son and the Mother" (pt. 3, 46). Here, the relation between culture and sexual economy is manifestly clear, almost too easily assimilated into Lévi-Strauss's argument that "the incest prohibition is at once on the threshold of culture, in culture, and in one sense . . . culture itself" (12). For Crusoe the legally minded "Civilian" accepts the incest prohibition, but the "Savage," unschooled by culture, cannot associate sexual behavior with economic and moral principle. In this instance, Crusoe plays the part of ironic dupe and Defoe uses him to either demystify conventional notions of "natural man" and/or naturalize the norms of civilized culture.

Atkins's reply reveals that Crusoe is indeed "misinform'd": "my Wife assures me of the contrary, and that they abhor it; perhaps, for any farther Relations they may not be so exact as we are; but she tells me they never touch one another in the near Relations you speak of" (pt. 3, 46). Crusoe's attitude to family is, as usual, self-serving. He does not see that his own "patricide" should be considered on the same level as the incest he views with such disapproval.[18] On the one hand, because he eventually profits from his island exile, he can justify his resistance to patriarchal guidance, however guilty it makes him feel; yet, on the other hand, he judges the sexual conduct of others according to their economic contribution to patriarchal family structures. Unable to integrate sexuality in his personal life (to deal, that is, with the other—the woman he has so rigorously exiled from his discourse), he characteristically commands it in others. That the supposed savages manifest strong familial sentiments merely accentuates Crusoe's weaker dedication to matrimonial and parental obligations.

Atkins's discussion of marriage with his wife suggests, oddly enough, that Crusoe is the most ill-equipped person on the island to participate in social arrangements. Though he never questions orthodox domestic relations, since for him the family buttresses civil government (hence his affirmation of the incest taboo), he does violate the conjugal ideal through his unwillingness to guide his own life by the moral and social values he espouses. Even his idyllic marriage succeeds only through the repression of his individualist drive toward adventure and wandering. In terms of ethics, then, Crusoe avows the obligations of kinship; as a force of narrative energy he undermines them. If the marital dialogue leads Atkins to seek forgiveness from God, knowledge of Christ, and atonement for filial disobedience, it pushes Crusoe farther out to sea. For Crusoe the meaning is clear: Atkins's remorse is more sincere, his commitment to family more lasting, and his filial penitence more exacting. Atkins's moral change and the general symbolic function of the island community point to the empowering myth of family and the practical importance of a system of kinship in Defoe's moral and political thought. Crusoe's subsequent retreat from the island, however, accentuates the limits of his narrative usefulness as a character who could reconcile Defoe's ethical intentions and aesthetic designs.

Despite all of the attention to family details throughout the first half of the *Farther Adventures*, Crusoe himself seems strangely detached from them. There is no vindication of the wife's opinion that her husband's desire was madness, no validation of the life she and his father had affirmed. In Defoe's sequel Crusoe adopts a paternal attitude toward his settlers. But though he constantly refers to them as his "Family," he never associates the moral conduct he is supervising on the island with his own personal experiences in any lasting way. The colonizers have appropriated the island, and its future lies with them. Crusoe maintains a supererogatory role in its "Government," but for all intents and purposes he withdraws, having himself become the obsolete father:

I was possest with a wandring Spirit, scorn'd all Advantages, I pleased my self with being the Patron of those People I had placed there, and doing for them in a kind of haughty majestick Way, like an old Patriarchal Monarch; providing for them, as if I had been Father of the whole Family, as well as of the Plantation: But I never so much as pretended to plant in the Name of any Government or Nation, or to acknowledge any Prince, or to call my People Subjects to any one Nation more than another; nay, I never so much as gave the Place a Name; but left it as I found it, belonging to no Man; and the People under no Discipline or Government but my own; who, tho' I had Influence over them as Father and Benefactor, had no Authority or Power, to Act or Command one way or other, farther than voluntary Consent mov'd them to comply. (pt. 3, 80)

The claim to patriarchal command in this passage stresses the links between a father's responsibility and a ruler's obligations. Crusoe berates himself for not being good at either. He fails to care for his "Family" because he cannot put his own self-interest aside; once again his "wandring Spirit," the now familiar emblem of his cultural discontent, divorces him from the social contacts that verify his self-definition and will to power. At this point, only halfway through his farther adventures, Crusoe abandons the island, leaving it un-named, unowned, and ungoverned. In this way he preserves it, at least in his memory, as the site of an uncompromised beginning, the place where he could banish his past and create a new personal history. Ironically, what Crusoe fails to see is that in the condition he leaves it, on the verge of economic, moral, and political fruition, the island can only stand as a reminder of his social commitments.

The break between the island episode in the first half of the *Farther Adventures* and the continuation of the adventure narrative in the concluding half is startling, dramatically signifying the separation of Crusoe from his earlier attachments. In effect, it recapitulates the entire problem of domestic and individual conflict. Neither wife and family nor island community reassert themselves cognitively once Crusoe renews his adventures. By the time he leaves the island, all of the colonizers (his surrogate children) have been legitimately married, and from then on he gives them no substantial thought.

Even Friday, offspring of his island exile, is sacrificed to the exigencies of plot, dying when Crusoe's ship is attacked as it finally departs the island. But for a token gesture of support (sending supplies and additional recruits) and various claims that he has "done with" the island, Crusoe never mentions it again. We learn, in passing, that the island languishes, the settlers renew their bickering, and the economy fails. Crusoe is no longer interested. What has seemed a crucial moral component, a theoretical organizing force in his life and the life of the island, simply evaporates.

The remaining portion of the *Farther Adventures,* which reads more like a treatise on trading and idolatry than a story about its central protagonist, chronicles Crusoe's obsessive wandering until he finally returns to England. The momentum of his journey has carried him full circle, but he does not recognize the end. He reaches home, but home means nothing to him. He mentions no reunion with his family. And there is no indication that, having indulged his obsession with roaming, he is ready to embrace the middle station of life. There is merely cessation without any corresponding sense of purpose, and Crusoe ends his account without coming to grips with its significance. He speaks only of "preparing for a longer Journey than all these" (pt. 3, 220), an allegorical reflection on death that views the gravest end of all as yet another opportunity to travel. Crusoe can never reconcile his inner drive with the moral and narrative imperatives that always lead him back to the family. His failure to obey his father, learn from his wife, or care for his family does not, then, signify a rejection of bourgeois domesticity or the irrelevance of family life in Defoe's fiction, but rather the unsuccessful attempt to incorporate individualism within traditional patterns of social behavior.

Scattered Progeny

Though never explicitly revealed as a principal organizing element, family structure allows Defoe's characters to voice their existential doubts. In the end, the only place from which they can address their autobiographies is from within the social arrangement they seem to have been neglecting. With the exception of Crusoe, all of Defoe's characters conclude their stories by referring to their family situation. Captain Singleton, after years of wandering and plundering, abruptly settles in England, adopts his Quaker companion, William, as a "Brother," takes measures to keep his identity secret from the public, and eventually marries William's sister ("my faithful Protectress"), who has been guarding his illegal wealth (335). When Moll ends her fortunes and misfortunes, she settles all the necessary arrangements with her son in Virginia, telling him at last that she is married, and then returns to England where she and her husband "resolve to spend the Remainder of our Years in sincere Penitence, for the wicked Lives we have lived" (pt. 2, 175). Colonel Jacque writes his memoirs while exiled in Mexico, where his desire to go home and his "Absence from my Family" embitters what is otherwise a "favorably circumstanced" condition (pt. 2, 154); in the final paragraph he adds that after writing the memoirs he was able to return to London, put his Virginia affairs in order, and recall his wife (who had previously arranged for an extenuating pardon from the king [pt. 2, 156]).

The two narratives that do not conform to this pattern are Defoe's first and last experiments in extended prose fiction. As we have seen, *Robinson Crusoe* eludes the family closure it seems sporadically to promise. Roxana's case is different; of all Defoe's narrative endings, hers has generated the most attention, not only because it seems to reject the concluding family security promised in the other narratives, but because it also hinges on whether the protagonist has murdered one of her own children. Roxana may be seriously alienated from the family circle at the end of her account—she neither clearly states the condition of her life after the putative murder of her daughter Susan nor describes her relations with her Dutch husband (aside from a brief account of moving to Holland to live in high style). She nonetheless concludes her history by alluding to another daughter who "was the very Counterpart of myself" (pt. 2, 159), referring to the aftermath of Susan's disappearance and the effect of it on her relations with her servant, Amy, and, perhaps most important, clarifying the link between what happened to Susan and the calamities that befall her later: "the Blast of Heaven seem'd to follow the Injury done the poor Girl, by us both; and I was brought so low again, that my Repentance seem'd to be only the Consequence of my Misery, as my Misery was of my Crime" (pt. 2, 160). Here we have a stark instance of the direct succession of event and consequence that *Robinson Crusoe* evades. That cause and effect derive entirely from family affairs intimates the binding force that domestic relations would have in later-eighteenth-century prose fiction and suggests the degree to which Defoe was moving toward a more intense synthesis of family and narrative relations in his last mature work of fiction.

Roxana's attitude to her "Family of Children" heightens the narrative's familial determinism, and it reflects Defoe's shift in narrative strategy. Like Moll, she scatters progeny in many places. But unlike Moll, who feels little compunction about this abandonment, she is struck with remorse and, at least initially, only gives up her children in the face of a convincing necessity. Because her "Fool Husband" has squandered their fortune, she lacks the means to support the children when he abandons her, and so she leaves them with her husband's relations or to the care of the parish (pt. 1, 1–25). Elsewhere, Defoe argued that such a condition would palliate the crime— that it was better to surrender children to the state or to others capable of tending them than to let them starve.[19] Throughout her memoirs, Roxana expresses concern for her children, and as one critic has said, Susan comes to represent all the children who have been neglected in Defoe's fiction, demanding the attention that has been denied them all along (Zimmerman, *Defoe and the Novel*, 43, 163). The story's unresolved relations intensify the anxieties associated with family reunion and narrative closure, coupling them as if they were permanently, and yet undesirably, aligned.

The protagonist's inevitable return to some kind of family affiliation at the end of *Roxana* both renews and disrupts the plot's origins, suggesting at once an affirmation and repudiation of the narrative's moral subscript. Susan asserts her claim to Roxana's maternal attention, but by doing so she threatens to expose her mother's carefully constructed public persona. Because Susan knows about Roxana's scandalous past (having worked as a minor servant for her mother when neither knew of their biological relation), she has it in her power to demystify all of Roxana's final pretensions to respectability. Roxana realizes that it will only be a matter of time before Susan links the courtesan she worked for to the mother she now seeks to embrace. In the face of this contradiction between Roxana's biological accountability and her irrepressible drive to manufacture her own unrestrained identity, the narrative abruptly closes. Defoe evades the complexities of Roxana's dilemma by having Roxana's servant, Amy, murkily dispose of the daughter. The servant now appears to be an autonomous agent somehow acting out her mistress's unconscious desire to be rid of Susan without ascribing any responsibility to Roxana (who can claim after the event that she never desired it). The seemingly ineluctable progress of Roxana's story toward familial determinism in this concluding section dissipates into a fragmented and incomplete account of further fortunes and misfortunes: "Here, after some few Years of Flourishing and outwardly happy Circumstances, I fell into a dreadful Course of Calamities, and *Amy* also" (pt. 2, 160). Though Roxana admits that these calamities "seem'd" to follow "the Injury done the poor Girl," her final synopsis is striking for its stubborn avoidance of completing the eschatological moment with a firm directive to the reader.

To preserve class aspirations Roxana must violently repudiate family; to ensure narrative closure she must embrace it. To clasp one's progeny, however, involves costly psychic and economic expenditure:

[T]here was a secret Horror upon my Mind, and I was ready to sink when I came close to her, to salute her; yet it was a secret inconceivable Pleasure to me when I kiss'd her, to know that I kiss'd my own Child, my own Flesh and Blood, born of my Body. . . . No pen can describe, no Words can express, *I say*, the strange Impression which this thing made upon my Spirits; I felt something shoot thro' my Blood; my Heart flutter'd; my Head flash'd and was dizzy, and all within me, *as I thought*, turn'd about." (pt. 2, 96)

Here, confined in a ship's cabin that physically reproduces her claustrophobic fear of interpersonal relations as well as her unstable emotional condition, Roxana attempts to voice her psychosomatic response to her daughter's unexpected appearance. Despite their intensity, however, both the pleasures and horrors of family are unutterable; they are "inconceivable" and "secret," beyond narrative itself: "No pen can describe, no Words can express." Recorded instinctively and uncontrollably on the "dizzy" maternal body, Roxana's "Excess of Passion" for her own flesh and blood, like the name Susan itself, links both mother and daughter as one body trapped in its own embrace, its own inscription, and its own divided condition. To conceal her "Disorder," Roxana is forced to use "all manner of Violence with myself" because no means are given her to "retreat" (pt. 2, 96–97). As with most of Defoe's characters, what Roxana cannot disclose is what the text as a whole both requires and evades: the family determinism that would guarantee the protagonist's wholeness, biological continuance, and narrative credibility but that would, conversely, obstruct her desire for autonomous emotional, economic, and narrative control. Even at anchor, Roxana's "Ship," whether metaphorical or real, is, to quote again from this chapter's epigraph, "always in a Storm."

Roxana's participation in her daughter's ostensible murder thematically unites many of the family issues raised in earlier parts of the book but does not resolve them. Susan's death is not even verified in the text. While this omission may be the result of Defoe's carelessness, a sign that he had to rush or was unable to finish the narrative, an indication that a sequel was being planned, a revelation of Roxana's mental and therefore linguistic instability, or evidence that Defoe could not decide between accentuating his heroine's sinfulness and glorifying her seductive character, it nonetheless signals the complex deployment of consanguinity in Defoe's fiction.[20] Defoe's particular narrative strategy, the marginalization of relations, serves, in effect, to retain the symbolic structure of family while diminishing the specific material and political effects of domesticity. It accentuates how Roxana (as both character and text) uses the unspoken to shape a narrative practice in which family paradigms function secretly to moderate the radical impulses of the autobiographical subject.

Defoe's reluctance to resolve his protagonist's history at the end of *Robinson Crusoe* or *Roxana* reveals a skepticism about the likelihood of a person's finding satisfaction within family structures and a reticence to see life culminating naturally with a return to the originary structure of social interaction. The enormous distance that Crusoe puts between himself and his family—the entire width of the Atlantic—is the complement to Roxana's attitude toward family, in which the closest imaginable proximity between parent and child is coupled with oceans of emotional reserve. However, the only vocabulary available to Defoe in his scrutiny of individual autonomy resurrects the formative role of kinship. His fiction internalizes the conflict between self-seeking individualism and cultural dependency. Simply put, depictions of selfhood in Defoe's narratives, as in many early-eighteenth-century fictions, follow a pattern in which transgression becomes compliance. The self comes into conflict with laws that regulate behavior within the community. It then appears to surpass or subsume them. But ultimately, the self is sustained by those conventions even in their absence. The transcendental selfhood that Defoe's narratives presume is a literary fiction. Rather than the trace of an essential identity or recoverable origin, it reflects the writer's ideological need to prove the power of the self. Thus the language of the self in Defoe's fiction tends to dissolve rather than constitute the subject. Because an individual can only speak through a language acquired in childhood, the terms of self-expression are available only through the constructs of family and community. Defoe's narratives, in attempting to extricate the self from these boundaries, eventually prove that myths of self-essence depend on social transactions as much as fictional selves depend on linguistic transactions.

Thus Defoe's refusal to domesticate the text, whether the consequence of a generic disposition toward sheer adventure or the result of political, psychological, or philosophical refusal of bourgeois family doctrine, destabilizes narrative in a way that often makes it difficult for the modern reader to respond in conventional ways. Filled with what appear to be random incidents that lead to even more random endings, Defoe's narratives generate excitement by refusing

to settle down or, at the least, show displeasure at having to conclude. His fiction ends with some manifestation of the conjugal ideal
that he strenuously defended in his didactic work; but while mark-
ing the physical limits of the text, Defoe's conclusions invariably reveal the insufficiency of marriage and offspring to sum up the complexity and variety of a character's life history.

In Defoe's narratives, family appears as an alternating force, at
once a vital ethical source and a relatively displaced element in the
dynamics of self-affirmation. While storytelling usually begins and
ends in the family, Defoe's narrators perpetually seek to suppress,
evade, or ignore this fact, moving inexorably toward endings that
seem inconclusive, accidental, and often implausible. Yet the linger-
ing structure of family relations retains its power even in his radical
departures from domestic narrative. This irresolution, in turn, complicates Defoe's concerns about eighteenth-century paradigms of the
self: whether the individual possessed innate virtues, whether the
mind was a tabula rasa upon which social features were imposed,
whether the self controlled or was controlled by events, whether
human beings were in the hands of an angry, benevolent, or indif-
ferent God, and so on. A number of these problems are resolved in
Defoe's fiction by an intentional displacement of contradictions
onto metaphoric constructs which, because they do not truly replicate the family, do not then maintain the restrictive conditions of
kinship. By delimiting family while preserving its semiotic force,
Defoe reimagines domestic relations in such a way as to transform
them into novel forms of power without endangering the self-
sufficient masculinity of conventional models of government (even
those problematically related to the Stuart monarchy's legacy). And
yet, if he suspected, while writing *Roxana*, that fictional plots were
increasingly being wedded to definitive household norms, the attenuated moral assessment of his last major fictional heroine would
certify Defoe's reluctance in imaginary discourse to match individual desire (especially a woman's) and liberalized patriarchal ideology.

4

The Anxiety of Affluence: *Pamela: or, Virtue Rewarded*

Richardson peopled his scenes with beings who scarcely resemble human creatures. When we contemplate his finished pictures adorned with the most graceful drapery, we are nevertheless interested in the detail and opening of the characters; we find them made up of mortal passions, and are affected by those delicate shades and tints which suddenly give a glimpse of the heart, and tie the whole family on earth together.

—Mary Wollstonecraft

A Uniform Woman

The previous two chapters focused on narrative acts involving what I have been calling "marginalization," *The Fair Jilt*'s deformation of family behavior and *Robinson Crusoe*'s sublimation of domestic relations. Both trace deviations from household norms that are themselves barely adumbrated in the texts, hinting that such details are better reserved for conduct books. In fact, even in the paraliterary material of the two authors, behavioral principles are frequently lacking in uniformity. They suggest that norms are themselves never what they claim, that they are produced by contradictory and even evasive definition, and that they expose rifts precisely where British culture wants to be most harmonious, advising families how to act. The work of these writers was, in part, a product of a political climate in which the alignment of domestic practice and national ideology was complicated by events leading to the genealogical compromises of the Revolution settlement; their fiction thus employs a strategy of disassociation for accommodating that apparent rift in the social and political realms.

In contrast, this chapter and the next investigate a complementary narrative tactic that I call "legitimation," in which assessing normative domestic behavior becomes the text's central occupying force. Taken together, these two chapters plot separate variations in which an eponymous heroine grapples with the problem of merging proper conduct and household government. In Samuel Richardson's *Pamela* (Parts I and II), the woman is herself the repository of domestic values that she must impose on an unruly masculine domain, without, however, seeming to be an imposition. In Eliza Haywood's *Miss Betsy Thoughtless*, in contrast, the female character is unruly and must adapt to a patriarchal society that insists on propriety but finds it difficult to enforce. Richardson's extraordinary success with *Pamela* implies that it suited a fairly large audience in need of some dogmatic celebration of domestic virtue, whereas the widespread appeal of Haywood's work suggests that, only a decade later, successful application of Richardsonian propriety was being modified for less-peerless figures, perhaps drawing a distinction between idealization and practice. The relatively stable political conditions around the mid-century helped foster such narrative strategies in which domestic ideology was more easily assimilated to existing structures of government.

In seeking to explain the contemporary popularity of *Pamela*—its power as a cultural myth in the eighteenth century—critics often point out that as a master printer, devout Protestant, strict family authoritarian, and political conservative, Richardson, and by extension his art, perfectly embodied a bourgeois class that was consolidating its power, challenging aristocratic institutions of control, and transforming cultural as well as economic means of production. Terry Eagleton, for example, argues that Richardson participated in a revolutionary practice that involved "a fierce conflict over signs and meanings." The narratives "are an agent, rather than mere account, of the English bourgeoisie's attempt to wrest a degree of ideological hegemony from the aristocracy in the decades which follow the political settlement of 1688" (4). Richardson's stories certainly dramatize revolutionary conflicts over status and gender. But while Pamela's story records a struggle for personal and social freedoms, it also stresses anxieties that seem to accompany radical change, finally seeking to obliterate many of the liberating consequences it produces.

We have seen that *The Fair Jilt* and *Robinson Crusoe* allow the principal characters to react to the uncertainty of their environment in ways that are as immediate and disruptive as the religious, political, and economic circumstances that occasion their restless denials of family. In Richardson, and in the two parts of *Pamela: or, Virtue Rewarded* in particular, we find, conversely, celebrations of the protagonist's determination to impose coherence on a single, usually sexual crisis, through the unrelenting management of family principles. Richardson makes his heroine's reward so onerous that it becomes simply another part of the domestic woman's burden. All of her household efforts, in fact, serve to consolidate social relations even when they seem to Mr. B. and his class a sign of her "insolence." That is, to make his heroine's career "uniform" (one of Pamela's favorite words), Richardson retracts those distinctions (in virtue, penmanship, and class) that enable the heroine's entry into a potentially stable and powerful society ruled by strict codes of domestic conduct. What appears revolutionary must eventually be revealed as simply the desire to restore and memorialize conventional principles of behavior. A model of narrative incorporation, Richardson's story, like his heroine, constantly strives to "tie the whole family on earth together" without, however, threatening the precise demarcations of class.[1]

Family Letters

Like Defoe, Richardson gravitated to both storytelling and conduct literature, turning to long prose fictions only after incorporating trial narratives in his treatises on domestic behavior. His first published work, *The Apprentice's Vade Mecum*, was an instructional manual originally sent as a letter to his nephew, Thomas Verren

Richardson, who was apprenticed to Richardson in 1732. Revised and published as a pamphlet in 1733, it addressed the problems that arise when one family member enters the employment of another. Its thesis, also central to the ensuing fiction, is that contemporary "Depravity" has weakened family bonds and therefore social cohesion (v). According to Richardson, apprentices, like servants, ideally extend the social boundaries of family, and yet, as the "Source, that the most useful Members of the Commonwealth are derived; on whose Industry and Labour the Welfare of the Whole almost intirely depends," they also adopt the principles of those "Families into which they are transplanted for a Series of Years the most important and most critical of their whole Lives" (vii). In a circular exchange that characterizes Richardson's view of the household as a permeable yet rigorous system of mutual dependencies, the outsider both provides and receives ideological subsistence. The family, in the service of the state, rejects those who cannot participate in its self-perpetuating economy. Sounding like Crusoe, Richardson argues that "the Sea is a much better choice" for those young men who "cannot comport to the Rules of an orderly Family" (ix, 51).

The *Vade Mecum* set the stage for *Familiar Letters*, a much more ambitious didactic work that, according to Richardson, provided the inspiration for the first of his prose fictions, *Pamela: or, Virtue Rewarded*.[2] Like the *Vade Mecum*, *Familiar Letters* was an instruction manual, in this case on how to compose personal letters. It shows, however, a greater concern for exemplary actions and invents a wider range of dramatic situations, all having to do with the minute particulars of family life as they might be transcribed in epistolary form: "A Father to a Son, to dissuade him from the Vice of drinking to Excess" (Letter 36); "A Father to a Daughter, against a frothy French Lover" (Letter 70); "A Mother to her high-spirited Daughter, who lives on uneasy Terms with her Husband" (Letter 146); "A Gentleman to his Lady, whose Over-niceness in her House, and uneasy Temper with her Servants, makes their Lives uncomfortable" (Letter 167). Unlike the *Vade Mecum*, then, *Familiar Letters* illustrates its views on obedience, marriage, household management, family behavior, and chastity by using fictional examples that reproduce "factual" situations, much as Defoe's *Family Instructor* mixes invention and instruction. In it we see the transition from tutelary to substantially "literary" discourse.

The didactic intent, epistolary format, and domestic focus of these preliminary instructional texts obviously became the ideological basis for the fiction. Richardson's awareness of the close relation between pedagogical, epistolary, and narrative aims is reflected in the complete title to the first two volumes, *Pamela: or, Virtue Rewarded. In a Series of Familiar Letters from a Beautiful Young Damsel, To her Parents*. Describing his work as "a series of Familiar Letters," he acknowledged the influence played by *Familiar Letters* in his fictional prose. The form itself, the "familiar letter," allowed Richardson to maintain the instructional mode of the didactic literature, the pretense that what he was writing was real, and the exemplary force of his stories, without appearing overtly doctrinaire. Each successive stage of his writing, then, seems to make domestic ideology increasingly embedded in social practice rather than simply a set of prescriptions applied to it. Richardson himself felt the need toward the end of his career to re-present the moral precepts of his fiction in a single-volume collection distilled from *Pamela, Clarissa,* and *Sir Charles Grandison.*[3] Compressing the fiction into a final conduct book, he could show that all of his prose fiction developed an organic vision of the world in which cause and effect so circled one another as to make ideology and practice synonymous.

Richardson's use of edited letters, then, while paralleling Defoe's autobiographical method in reproducing the truthfulness of fact and immediacy of voice, also multiplies its public function. His epistolary method, what Richardson called "writing to the moment," relies on a narrative model of relation, immediacy, and imminent conflict.[4] Private thought is made visible in the shared and often appropriated texts between two or more familiar correspondents, thus giving the fiction a dialogic resonance largely absent in earlier prose narratives. Furthermore, unlike Behn and Defoe, he locates the complication and resolution of ideological differences within the conjugal family, or at least within the promise of that ideal. Whereas Defoe's and Behn's concerns tend to make their fiction diffuse,

Richardson confines experience to a relatively small number of events, which in effect merely repeat a single action based on sexual antagonism, class conflict, and family alliance. Locale is similarly restricted to domestic enclosures—indeed, there is little going abroad in Richardson's world. Where Defoe and Behn marginalize familial roles, Richardson makes them the conscious motive of fictional activity. His fictions confront the problem of family intensively, isolating it from larger social experiences and making it the source of a compelling mythic drama. Similarly, his articulation of the self depends entirely on the epistolary communication of the subject with a close relation, either a family member or a childhood friend linked to an earlier period of family harmony. That is, Richardson's approach to narrative form—the reading of a private family correspondence by others—ideally suits the private conjugal relations that his fiction attempts to validate at a more public level. Domesticity becomes invested with an enhanced moral and political significance that engenders, at least within the fictively imagined family, a symbolic duplication of social mechanisms of power like class and gender. A private correspondence, then, particularly one between parent and child, one that figuratively traces the family circle across a treacherous public space, where letters can be misdirected, intercepted, mutilated, and misread, is for Richardson perhaps the most potent symbolic document of a civil society.

The semantic relevance of the phrase "familiar letter" to both what is domestic (of the family) and what is customary or well known emphasizes Richardson's interest in depicting universal conditions through the particular and the domestic. In Richardson the text itself, both as individual and collected letters, plays an active role in the drama, bringing to a crisis sexual and economic differences between male and female characters. An instrumental part of the ongoing action, it unites form and event in a dynamic textual exchange largely absent in Defoe (where characters never have their biographies read and responded to by other characters). Richardson always constitutes the subject by inserting her into a dialogic relationship, one that magnifies particularized domestic events. The letters describing incidents of sexual and social harassment simultaneously unfold the changes that are wrought in the characters by those very experiences. Unlike Behn or Defoe, we are not reminded of the retrospective nature of fiction (though it is, admittedly, present in the implicit act of collecting and editing the correspondence).

Even in terms of audience, Richardson is subtly aware of the ontological relevance of "familiar letters," for the implicit readers in *Pamela* accentuate the problem of family, authority, and self, which the narrative considers as a whole. Pamela's letters in Part I pass through several presumed readings before the "actual" reader encounters them. Large portions of them are first read by Pamela's parents; her history is, consequently, supposed to be scrutinized by her family, her closest contacts with reality, before the text is submitted to a larger social inspection. In the end, the letters are collected as a whole, and then again presented to the parents. Indeed, throughout most of the narrative, the intended audience is always one or both of the parents. They may not always be the initial readers, however, since Mr. B. or sometimes Mrs. Jewkes occasionally intercepts letters and portions of the journal, but they are consistently addressed as the readers of the text. To some extent, then, we occupy both their familial space and that of usurping readers like Mr. B., Mrs. Jewkes, or eventually sympathetic outside readers like Lady Davers. In Part II the number of intended readers is increased to include a young female acquaintance, Polly Darnford, and members of Pamela's new family—particularly her husband, Mr. B., who now legitimately receives her correspondence, and Lady Davers, the principal recipient of most of the letters. As in Part I, these readers, in turn, share the letters with their own immediate community. Presumably, we are intended to be as enlightened by Pamela's private correspondence as these aggregate readers are. As Pamela declares to her parents: "this shall be my own Rule—Every one who acts justly and honestly, I will look upon as my Relation, whether he be so or not" (II, 3: 24).[5]

Only after these intersected readings do the letters pass into the public domain, organized and edited by the editor, who functions as yet a further screen. Ironically, then, Richardson's narratives, which appear initially to consist of private reflections, have embedded within them a complex community of specifiable readers who, either actually or implicitly, make rereading one of the book's recurrent and self-reflexive tropes. Pamela's development depends, therefore, on a series of household events, which become part of a larger public discourse (to which we are at last privy) only after the letters representing those events are interrogated within the family. In Part I, Pamela's most personal concerns—her function as a servant, the political nature of sexual relations, the coupling of desire and dread, the anxieties of sexual "intercourse," and the intimate details of early marriage—must pass through the internal censure of a daughter's correspondence with a mother and father, and, by accident, be subjected to a more alarming inspection by Mr. B. She is, in effect, translating the confusing signals of her experiences as both servant and "mistress" in Mr. B.'s household into the transparent language of moral and social values upheld by her family and, ideally, by her society (her letters mirror the popular epistolary method of a huge number of eighteenth-century conduct books). Part II similarly concentrates on domestic observations—about household management, trying encounters with Mr. B.'s relatives, adoption, the bearing and education of children, fears that Mr. B. has committed adultery. These letters must, in turn, sustain public surveillance not only so they can serve, like a conduct book, as an educational instrument but also so they can be validated as useful philosophy for the higher class Pamela has entered.[6]

In other ways, too, the act of reading "familiar" letters in *Pamela* symbolically enacts a ritual of family and class incorporation. Reading private letters presupposes, though it does not always actually reflect, a legitimate social alliance. Indeed, until they marry, few letters pass between Pamela and Mr. B. In order to examine the full "Text," Mr. B. must become an official member of the family; despite class differences, he must declare his acceptance of the conjugal model that Pamela's parents so clearly endorse before he can have complete and authorized access to his wife's "Writings" (I, 202). As long as the male remains a disruptive force—seducer, voyeur, rapist, "black-hearted Wretch" (I, 86)—he disrupts family communication, for Richardson the core of the social contract. When he joins the family in the role of suitor or husband he reestablishes the discursive lines and privileges he has interrupted. Narrative suspense stems from his transgression of family roles and class relations. Narrative resolution occurs because plot, and with it reunited family relations, becomes solidified once again—the letters finally reach their intended address.

The letter, as a symbol of personal identity, is, furthermore, both a sign of separation and an emblem of reciprocity. It is a link to the family and a reminder that Pamela can develop only in the absence of comforting social connections. When the narrative begins she is already installed in the aristocrat's household. Pamela's withdrawal from her family-of-origin at the beginning of her text, unlike Crusoe's, springs from the economic insufficiency of the family; she does not choose to be away from home and is not driven abroad by feelings of exile, rejection, or perverse desire. She is already established as a figure who seeks to incorporate family, not, like Miranda or Crusoe, to disrupt it. In this sense, she is the symbolic reverse of Defoe's and Behn's characters, a self, separated from family, who yearns to consolidate several biological, generational, and class affinities.

The paternal home, for all its primary value, is not the ultimate measure of Pamela's writing. In Richardson, heroines, like good prose, must always seek a higher register. Thus, when Pamela imagines going home, she describes it in terms of the cessation of language, when her "Writing time will soon be over" (I, 47). Interestingly, as the only place she never revisits, her parents' home disappears in the post-marriage fantasy of inclusion when Mr. B. asks Mr. and Mrs. Andrews to run his Kentish estate. If the daughter is to be uplifted, her mother and father's place, both literally and figuratively, must also be raised in degree. The paternal lower-class home remains unrepresented, despite its crucial symbolic function. Eventually, it has to absent itself or lurk in the genteel discourse of others (as it does in Pamela's learned writing).

The original home in *Pamela* represents the dangers of early narrative closure because it would effectively eliminate the tension between eliminating class boundaries and preserving them.[7] The story continues because Pamela's efforts to return home are constantly frustrated. The Andrewses are poor and cannot easily retrieve their daughter; the countryside is too treacherous for Pamela to attempt it alone; Mr. B. thwarts Lady Davers's offer to take her on; Pamela must finish "flowering" her master's waistcoat; she is abducted on the road back to her home; her shoes are taken away; the walls around the Lincolnshire estate prevent her from making her escape. A sequence of obstructions, sustained by social practice and her own submerged desire, conspires to separate the heroine from the source of her identity and ethical conformation. For all its affirmation of the parental home, the covert effect of Richardson's narrative is to applaud homelessness and confirm the desire to escape class affiliations without damaging the positive mythology of family. Richardson implies that personal identity emerges when one experiences alienation from the very social and material environment that creates it.[8]

The "familiar letter" is the appropriate vehicle for this double focus since it expresses the desire to be linguistically connected to the family while at the same time representing and preserving the writer's necessary distance from the family. Because she cannot go home, because the plot repeatedly prevents a reunion with her parents, the return to the biologic family Pamela so strongly desires appears to be false, one that must finally be rejected. Yet the ending of Pamela's history so duplicates the original ideals of home that it eventually affirms the rejected telos. The narrative must return to family, but it must not be exactly the same family. As Edward Said explains, this treacherous preservation of an origin conditions all storytelling; narrative tends to move away from its beginnings in order to return to them in a disguised form (66). For Pamela's text to exist, she must be in a position to write to her distanced family. Her sense of personal identity is inextricably linked to this discourse, but the discourse itself, while conceding the relation between the writing consciousness and parental instruction, emanates from the disjunction between them. The more letters Pamela writes, the more she demonstrates that narrative continually springs from the dynamic relation between displaced and replaced families. Pamela's absence from home enables the reproduction in language of family relations, making visible the process by which the artificial requirements of domestic conduct and its literature are made natural. She dramatizes, in other words, what similarly repetitive conduct books fail to render believably heroic, the ideological work required to validate the commonplace.

Useful Generations

If in terms of form, the "familiar letter" serves the purpose of maintaining the ideal of home while at the same time symbolizing a deviation from that ideal, the content of the letters themselves in *Pamela* represents a confrontation between two competing familial models. Like *Clarissa*, *Pamela* follows a plot trajectory that balances the lives of the principal actors. But whereas Clarissa and Lovelace move in proportionally opposite directions, she toward otherworldly transcendence, he toward an ignominious fall into the underworld, Pamela's and Mr. B.'s paths intersect in and then extend into the existing world of marriage contracts, family alliance, and estate management. Indeed, Pamela comes to see her whole life justified by family continuance: "All that I value myself upon, is, that God has raised me to a Condition to be useful in my Generation" (I, 407). The pun on "generation" here signifies not only her sense of belonging to a specific cultural moment and her awareness of how she can regenerate others but also her involvement in the transmission of kin—that is, her participation in history itself. As the editor remarks, "She made her beloved Spouse happy in a numerous and hopeful Progeny" (I, 409). If through isolation Crusoe achieves an autonomy mediated by archetypal models of family, Pamela's sense of identity derives entirely from a resolute adoption of those models.

Pamela stands in a mediating relation between two families, trying to construct for herself from these two different models a hybrid knowledge of class, sexuality, and family government that will exonerate her biological family, justify her dramatic change in status, and diminish the arbitrary power of the aristocracy that assimilates her, without sacrificing its benefits. Her mediation becomes the means by which social distinctions seem to be collapsed even as they are physically maintained. Only her verbal facility will allow the class consolidation the narrative demands.

For Pamela there is only one mode of verbal self-representation: domestic vigilance. In every action and in every word she must manifest an allegiance to family and class. As she repeatedly asserts, her will really belongs to her parents: "While I've a Father and Mother, I am not my own Mistress" (I, 132). In the contest between her and Mr. B. she does not relinquish her "family" will until his co-incides with hers. It is only after marriage that she can say, para-doxically, that her one possession, her will, really belongs to him. The "virtue" and "honesty" she learns from her parents and that preserve her in difficult circumstances are the conventional terms by which she is associated with a particular social, sexual, and familial domain. Pamela's virtue is, therefore, not only the subject of the let-ters as a whole; it is also an affirmation of her parents' existence ("the Loss of our dear Child's Virtue, would be a Grief that we could not bear, and would bring our grey Hairs to the Grave at once" [I, 27]). Part of a language construed by the parents to protect their daughter, her "Child's Virtue" can only be verified through a process of persecution (much as Griselda's or Job's rectitude must be proven by familial disasters): "O my Child! Temptations are sore things; but yet without them, we know not our selves, nor what we are able to do" (I, 38). When Pamela's parents urge her to remember her "self," they are actually asking her to remember her obligations to the family.[9] Her virtue will be their distinction. It resituates Pam-ela within the dynamics of family hegemony, genealogical purity, and class esteem. Pamela's virtue may serve as a symbol of her autonomy in relation to Mr. B., but as a social or cultural signifier it stands for something considerably less liberating, the parents' need to see their daughter always as "uncontaminated" (II, 3: 46).

The language that articulates Pamela's identity invokes, then, a complex meshing of both physical and cultural categories. The re-curring terms of the narrative's discourse—virtue, honesty, honor, will, innocence—are, at least for Pamela, part of a naturalizing rhetoric that reduces the body to a pure figure. Since the central crisis of the text involves the heroine's defense of her chastity, all language within it contributes to the pristine equation between figuration (language) and the figure itself (the body). As the narrative's subtitle (*Virtue Rewarded*) suggests, the heroine's name and virtue are consonant. This virtue, however, accentuates the interaction between individual identity and social manifestations of identity while seeming to glorify the heroine alone. Though the title erases Pamela's family name, the word "virtue" effectually rewrites it.[10]

To assert her identity, Pamela must conform to a universal standard bred in the family; her distinction comes from an apotheosized sameness. Yet one can also discern a hidden skepticism in this universalist faith, a recognition that language forces the self into assertions that run counter to individual identity. The moment Pamela uses language she betrays her claim to lucidity. Just as the function of maidenly chastity is to preserve the patriarchal myth of blood and to sustain a system of exchange in which women are reduced to property, the problems Pamela faces when she seeks to write about her self, her body, and her identity suggest that purity of expression, like chastity itself, is conditioned or defined by those things it refuses to recognize: impurity, corruption, temptation, and property.[11] To be aware of one's virtue, and furthermore to be rewarded for it— to be able to speak it—is to know what is not virtuous and be insensibly corrupted by that knowledge.

This is precisely the problem that sets Richardson's narrative into motion. *Pamela* begins with the heroine in a state of psychic ambivalence, her virtue under attack. Separated from her biological family, she has learned from her mistress to act in ways that conflict with her upbringing, that give her, as she says, "Qualifications above my degree" (I, 25). These include dancing, piano, needlework, reading, and most important, writing in a "genteel Manner." In effect, Pamela learns that her identity derives from two clear and opposed sources of behavior, one that teaches the value of industry, "honesty," and "virtue," the other that lays the groundwork for her aristocratic achievements—grace, learning, honor, and philanthropy. Long before Mr. B. aggravates the confusion she feels about her identity, Pamela experiences the wistful feeling of not belonging entirely to either social sphere for which she has been trained: "Much I fear'd, that as I was taken by her Goodness to wait upon her Person, I should be quite destitute again, and forc'd to return to you and my poor Mother, who have so much to do to maintain yourselves; and, as my Lady's Goodness had put me to write and cast Accompts, and made me a little expert at my Needle, and other Qualifications above my Degree, it would have been no easy Matter to find a Place that your poor Pamela was fit for" (I, 25). Though a servant, Pamela acts as a substitute child for Lady B. and is educated as a woman of quality. Because her language, duties, knowledge, and taste alienate her from her original condition yet do not make her entirely at home in her new situation, she can be treated by Mr. B. with a strange familiarity in which she is neither entirely a servant nor a potential lover and wife. Pamela's ambiguity here is not unlike the eighteenth-century conduct book's difficulty in trying to negotiate, on one hand, the supposedly absolute virtues of domestic life and, on the other hand, powerful distinctions in class context and behavior.

Pamela's energies at establishing a sense of identity in conditions that separate her from both the nurturance of her original family and the comfort of a surrogate home take the form of striving for linguistic parity and purity.[12] In order to combat her disordered sense of self, Pamela seeks in language and role-playing a means to establish certainty in the uncertain domestic landscape. The verbal nature of the conflict between Pamela and Mr. B. has often been examined, but rarely in terms of the relation of their linguistic confrontations to the government of the family. The verbal encounters between the two figures underscore the fact that their conflict is one contained by the ancestral house, the archetypal image of socialized conceptions of identity. There is, in fact, a symbolic pattern whereby Pamela's "conversations" with her master move her steadily closer from more public spaces (the summerhouse) to the intimate sites of the family home (the back parlor, the mother's bedroom and closet) and increasingly toward the male center of sexual and linguistic authority (the master's bedroom closet, which is, appropriately, a

library).[13] Her struggle to express an inviolable self, and his to challenge referential or transparent discourse, an exchange that several recent critics have shown at work in *Clarissa*, takes the form in *Pamela*
of a drama in which the key adversaries quarrel about family matters
in claustrophobic family spaces.[14]

As Mr. B.'s addresses to her imply, Pamela's susceptibility to his
"Plot" arises out of confusion over her role in her second family, literally what her name signifies. To Mr. B. she becomes a multitude
of things: Girl, Maid, little Fool, Hussy, artful young Baggage, subtle artful Gypsey, Equivocator, pretty Innocent and Artless, Bold-
face, Insolent, Sawcebox, Woman, Hypocrite, Angel of Light, Creature, Witch, Statue, Fool, Slut, Preacher, Wench, pretty Daughter,
Servant, little Villain, Child. The verbal energy and lexical range of
Mr. B.'s naming signals his own aggravated sense of her unclassifi-
able nature and the threat that such opacity poses to his belief in
class identity and household security. Her categorical instability actually mirrors his failure to situate her properly in his own household.

What bothers Pamela most about Mr. B.'s attacks on her chastity
is his confounding of language and status. Mr. B. claims that he can
make Pamela into a lady, and this suggests that he, a conventional
male aristocrat, believes that the boundaries of status are easily dis-
solved through influence, prestige, and money. While she strenuously resists such attempts to erase categories, to forget one's place,
Mr. B. advocates a fluid model of social intercourse as long as it
serves his immediate sexual purposes. During the first lubricious attack in the Summer-house she defends her improper speech to her
"superior" by virtue of his self-debasement and proportionate misuse
of language to her: "Well may I forget that I am your Servant, when
you forget what belongs to a Master. . . . You have taught me to
forget myself, and what belongs to me, and have lessen'd the Distance that Fortune has made between us, by demeaning yourself, to
be so free to a poor Servant" (I, 35). Mr. B.'s linguistic distortions
even force her to reappraise the customary language of domestic
conduct: "So I had better be thought artful and subtle, than be so, in
his Sense; and as light as he makes of the Words Virtue and Inno-

cence in me, he would have made a less angry Construction, had I less deserved that he should do so; for then, may be, my Crime would have been my Virtue with him" (I, 40). The complicated syntax and careful deployment of words in this sentence belie Pamela's assurances of untutored innocence and suggest that she already envisions the sexual battle between them as a control of language itself. Marked by paradoxical and conditional constructions, this passage shows how she perceives language as a symbolic system in which key functional words like "virtue" and "innocence," which in themselves signify states of purity, must struggle for their right designation. Pamela is all along aware of discrete social and discursive roles, and she wants to keep them hermetically sealed despite her fluid identity in the B. household.

This dilemma is nowhere more apparent than in the scene where Mrs. Jervis convinces Pamela to appear before Mr. B. dressed in her country clothes. When he pretends not to know who she really is, calling her Pamela's younger sister and taking freedoms with her, she emphatically lays claim to an essential self beneath the clothes: "O Sir, said I, I am Pamela, indeed I am: Indeed I am Pamela, her own self!" (I, 61). Pamela's modest dress, which Mr. B. sees as an example of disguise, hypocrisy, and duplicity, is, on the contrary, one more of Pamela's attempts to maintain strict generic lucidity. Pamela's change of costume reflects her desire to dress specifically according to status: "don't impute Disguise and Hypocrisy to me, above all things; for I hate them both, mean as I am. I have put on no Disguise. . . . I mean one of the honestest things in the World. I have been in Disguise ever since my good Lady, your Mother, took me from my poor Parents . . . so [I] have bought what will be more suitable to my Degree" (I, 62). To return home she feels obliged to dress in a way that corresponds to her parents' social and economic condition, strongly identifying her role in the family with her real self, and her place in Lady B.'s service as a period of disguise. When her intentions are misconstrued by Mr. B. she turns to a declamatory language, one she hopes expresses inner reality—"Indeed I am Pamela, her own self." Her language throughout (pitting honesty against hypocrisy) expresses her commitment to a referential ideal.[15]

Pamela's hermeneutic progress depends on her ability to measure word against act, and she gradually comes to understand exactly how Mr. B. manipulates the disjunction between signifier and signified: "For he professed Honour all the Time with his Mouth, while his Actions did not correspond" (I, 181). Her whole verbal struggle in the text amounts to no more than saying "I am Pamela," to consecrating the promise of the title and making her virtue correspond to her name. But through the treacherous dialogue with Mr. B. she learns how very difficult and how fraught with social, sexual, and political ramifications this direct statement is.[16] The letters help her resolve the problem and are one of the aspects of Pamela's life that Mr. B. both admires and fears: "That Girl is always scribbling" (I, 37). The sheer bulk of her writing, while it demonstrates Pamela's indefatigable will, also manifests the enormous verbal effort of self-definition.

One of the most overt indications of the problematic relation between public discourse and private truth, the position of the letters in relation to Pamela's body, serves to delimit and dilate this notion of the privileged and ultimately private self. Stitched into her clothes ("in my Under-coat, next my Linen" where "they grow large" [I, 120]), they are associated with her body. A number of critics have noted the symbolic function of the letters, concentrating on the sexual and material significance of their growth around her belly. They prefigure Pamela's future children (five of them by the end of Part II), tying the domestic woman's production of text, her art and imagination, to the maternal production of life and the continuance of genealogy. But since the letters are written to and for her parents, they also generate and preserve the values of the fallen bourgeois family that has largely produced her. She is giving birth to herself. She is both the creator (or recreator) and the transmitter of the familial ideology of a class (displaced gentry) that, in order to survive, must be grafted onto the aristocracy. Pamela's text makes her hotly defended self-expression the means by which her identity coincides with the prescribed and unindividuated roles of daughter, wife, and mother—a typical strategy of even the most radical of the eighteenth-century conduct books. Her very word is the word of others, and it inscribes a decidedly modern subject, an individual who is not simply acted upon by ideology but who actively and anxiously promotes it.

The rhetoric that emerges from Pamela and her master's confrontations centers on the female body as well as on how the female body is to be used in the family and how a daughter's status changes in the movement from one family to another.[17] Since the familiar letters are repeatedly designated in various ways as the very essence of her character, Mr. B. feels he must disrupt her writing in order to "situate" her in his own family. He makes her doubt or forget her "self" by separating her from the knowledge that she comes from a particular family with a particular set of verbal and moral values. He intercepts the letters to her family, partly to uncover secret affirmations of the attraction he hopes she feels for him, partly to ensure that she does not take liberties with the private affairs of his family, and partly because he suspects that her letter-writing nurtures her belief in an inviolable self inextricably linked to premarital chastity. When Mr. B.'s initial attempts at seduction and rape fail, he abducts Pamela to Lincolnshire, hoping to interrupt her self-affirming communication with her parents. He knows that when Pamela forgets her background she forgets herself. Pamela tries to continue writing to her parents by composing a journal account of her "Bondage," "Restraint," "Confinement," "Despair," and "Imprisonment," but she is fully aware that she has come perilously close to losing touch with her inner faith in herself because she has lost outer contact with the family. Her forty days of confinement are particularly difficult because she feels suspended between two domestic worlds that had previously engendered an identity for her. Though she continues to write, she despairs when her parental audience is gone: "Let me write and bewail my miserable hard Fate, tho' I have no Hope that what I write will be convey'd to your Hands!—I have now nothing to do but write, and weep, and fear, and pray; and yet, What can I pray for, when God Almighty, for my Sins to be sure, vouchsafes not to hear my Prayers" (I, 94). Mr. B.'s oppression works on Pamela because, without the knowledge that her parents are participating in her story, she no longer feels linked to the sources of her self-definition. It is this verbal as well as physical isolation from a nurturing dialogue that finally precipitates her moral catastrophe. When her last ally with the outside world, Parson Williams, is arrested (and can therefore no longer carry her or her journal back to Mr. and Mrs. Andrews), Pamela resorts to her desperate "plot" to escape. This too fails, and in a moment of deep anguish by the wall encircling "this wicked house," she moves toward a pond where she hopes to gain her freedom finally by drowning herself (I, 152).

For Pamela, this is the pivotal moment of her moral development; divided from her parental contact, which has already been attenuated to words on a page—language in the absence of a listener— she almost disregards her professed belief that "all that happens is for Our Good" (I, 32). Appropriately, she finally resists the temptation to commit suicide, to erase the "self" that has caused her so much pain, because her body (injured from attempting to scale the wall) prevents her from enacting her will: "my weakness of Body made me move so slowly, that it gave Time for a little Reflection, a Ray of Grace, to dart in upon my benighted Mind" (I, 151). With reflection comes repentance; her body, the matrix of the narrative's familial and linguistic disputes, leads her back to her duty to her family and her faith in God's ways: "wilt thou suffer in one Moment all the good Lessons of thy poor honest Parents, and the Benefit of their Example, (who have persisted in doing their Duty with resignation to the Divine Will, amidst the extremest Degrees of Disappointment, Poverty and Distress, and the Persecutions of an ingrateful World, and merciless Creditors) to be thrown away upon thee" (I, 153). Comparing her condition to her parents' circumstances and fortified by regenerated beliefs, she turns again to face the burden of repulsing Mr. B.'s sexual, psychological, and verbal assaults. She is enabled to do so because she has, almost literally, internalized the family in the shape of her own body.

At a crucial moment in the Lincolnshire sequence, when Mr. B. finally arrives to essay his servant one last time, Pamela prevents him from stripping her to find the hidden journal, which is lodged in the stays around her waist, by delivering it to him. At this point, the relations of power between servant and "Master" are dramatically inverted; reading his own words as transcribed by Pamela, Mr. B. becomes estranged from them, seeing reflected in the text—a "body" of discourse he has strenuously sought to dominate—the evidence of his own failure to behave in strict accordance to the values of his sex, class, and family. In Richardson, drama no longer centers on how the individual strives to acquire or resist appropriate principles of conduct but rather on how she endeavors to exemplify them for others in such a way that she never appears to be the source of domestic ideology. For all its intense scrutiny of Pamela's language and conduct, Richardson's narrative turns insistently away from ego and toward the servant's role as ideological vehicle. It exalts her character by making her the means by which others recover the family values that their own backgrounds once guaranteed. Like the conduct material it reworks, Pamela's "vade mecum" glamorizes domestic behavior not by inventing new codes of conduct but by reestablishing forgotten ones.

Unblemished Virtue and the Noble Estate

It becomes evident halfway through Part I, at the moment when Pamela surrenders her journal to Mr. B., that the figure of radical change is not the servant, Pamela, but the master. Her familiar letters are transformed, in effect, into a means of forcing the aristocrat to regard his own actions as morally deficient. As much as they describe the ways in which Pamela grapples with her own estranged circumstances, they also record the process that both displaces and converts Mr. B. in his own house. Though Richardson's work appears to be more obviously about the heroine's exile (from her home, her class, and her sexual identity), it also dramatizes Mr. B.'s transition from villain to hero, aristocratic rake to aristocratic gentleman, and family predator to family ideologue.

Lady B.'s treatment of Pamela as both servant and daughter has a dramatic effect on the new "Master" of the Bedfordshire house. As Pamela is gradually raised by her experience there, Mr. B.'s command of himself and his family diminishes. The more she approximates a genteel feminine ideal, the more he feels confused about her (and therefore his) role in the household. If she feels anxiety about being raised out of herself into an upper-class family, Mr. B.'s anxiety stems from fears that he will lose power within the family through the "witchcraft" of "this artful young Baggage." At several points he complains that she has exposed him and his relations, upset the smooth running of the house, and influenced the other members of the "Family" against him.[18] Motivated as much by family pride and class presumption as by libertine impulses, he consequently seeks power over his servant by making his desire a matter of class imperative. As Pamela says to him, "it seems your Greatness wants to be justified by my Lowness" (I, 75). We shall see, of course, that the reverse is true: Pamela's moral greatness is justified by Mr. B.'s low behavior. Her "unblemished Virtue" intact, she will both exonerate herself and reverse his estimation of himself, reconnecting him to a familial ideal originally preserved by his mother.

The opening of the narrative presents the male protagonist in an apparently lawless state, released from the compelling authority of the parents. The mother has just died. The father, having died years earlier, does not even seem to exist in memory; he is rarely, if ever mentioned and only incidentally affects the ethical attitude of his children. Unlike Pamela, whose first utterances convey her continuing involvement in and correspondence with the family, Mr. B. seems to have no will but his own and all the prerogatives of the master. The heroine's story, the history of the domestic woman, is thus triggered by the male antagonist's domestic confusion. Like the conduct books of the 1740's, which were effective precisely because they generally shifted the burden of domestic reform and moral management onto the mistress of the house, Richardson's narrative employs its heroine to correct the ideological vagaries of the aristocratic male. Pamela's purpose is to demonstrate through her own convictions about lineage and estate that her "Master" is obliged to honor Lady B. and, as a consequence, the moral legacy of his family and his class.[19]

In the first scene of the work, Lady B. urges her son to maintain household continuity. On her deathbed, she not only extols Pamela but also indirectly urges Mr. B. to adopt her into the family: "when it came to my Turn to be recommended, for I was sobbing and crying at her Pillow, she could only say, My dear Son!—and so broke off a little, and then recovering—Remember my poor Pamela!" (I, 25). On a literal level, she is simply telling her son to take care of Pamela, to keep her employed at B. Hall as a privileged servant, but she is also implying that her son requires wary observation. The phrase "Remember my poor Pamela" reinforces the tenuous and symbolically charged social condition prompted by Lady B.'s impending death: by accentuating the relation between the servant and the mistress through the possessive "my," the phrase invests Pamela with the authority of the mother (in remembering Pamela, Mr. B. will remember his mother) and emphasizes the problematic nature of ownership among mistress, master, and servant (to whom and in what capacities are Pamela's services owed?). Lady B. wants Pamela to represent a continuing maternal influence in the house, to be a reminder to Mr. B. of his biological and historical condition, but she also acknowledges his inconstancy. As he reports in Part II, his mother recognizes the ideological force of Pamela's relation to her son: "'You are a young gentleman, and I am sorry to say, not better than I wish you to be—Though I hope my Pamela would not be in danger from her master, who owes to all his servants protection, as much as the king does to his subjects. Yet I don't know how to wish her to stay with you, for your own reputation's sake, my dear son;—for the world will censure as it lists.—Would to God!' said she, 'the dear girl had the small-pox in a mortifying manner'" (II, 3: 116). Mr. B.'s interest in Pamela thus entails a sexual attraction or class bias but also is part of a complex family drama in which class, gender, aesthetics, pride, and governance converge. Her insistence that any "merit" she can "boast of" is "owing principally, if it deserves commendation, to my late excellent lady" (II, 3: 36) reinforces this merging of female servant and aristocratic mother.

Mr. B. has difficulty following his mother's deathbed injunctions. Having been urged to remember "poor Pamela," he promises to show special kindness to the young girl, but the particularity of his attention already reveals compulsive desires: "my Master said, I will take care of you all, my Lasses; and for you, Pamela, (and took me by the Hand; yes, he took me by the Hand before them all) for my dear Mother's sake, I will be a Friend to you, and you shall take care of my Linen" (I, 25). The reader will have already deciphered, long before Pamela does from broad hints by her parents, the sexual intent of Mr. B.'s words and actions. The singling out of Pamela from the other "lasses," the retrieval of her hand, and the euphemistic inference of "Friend" and "linen," both of which imply a different kind of intimacy than Lady B. had intended, point to the dual motivations on Mr. B.'s part to accommodate his mother's entreaty and indulge his own inclinations. Making a point of caring for Pamela in the name of the deceased mother, he manages to collapse maternal and libertine ideologies, willfully misapplying parental law to make a convenient equation between domestic and sexual authority.

Mr. B.'s obsession, nurtured in the past by the mother's unconventional treatment of a servant girl as a substitute daughter, derives, it would appear, from a latent desire to appropriate the mother's power. As he later admits in Part II, Mr. B. regards Pamela from the beginning as a token in his ritualistic combat with Lady B.: "Go on, my dear Mother, improving as fast as you will: I'll engage to pull down in Three Hours what you'll be building up in as many Years, in spite of all the Lessons you can teach her" (II, 3: 189). Here, Mr. B.'s libertinism is both an attempt to obstruct the affective bonding between Pamela and Lady B. and a rather more charged reaction to a matriarchal rule that threatens to cross sacred class boundaries and transform domestic space.

Pamela's fluctuating social status, her ability to disrupt the organization of roles within the family, and her resemblance to the aristocratic mother are all signaled by her sartorial transformations. When Lady B. clothes Pamela in a costume suitable to her raised stature from ordinary domestic to favored personal maid, their relationship modulates into a deeper affinity based on the affection of a mother for a daughter. That the mother's clothing becomes Pamela so well only intensifies Mr. B.'s resentment and admiration, and, in a perverse replication of desire, he himself later dresses her in those clothes: "a Suit of my old Lady's Cloaths, and half a dozen of her

Shifts, and Six fine Handkerchiefs, and Three of her Cambrick Aprons, and Four Hollands ones: The Cloaths are fine Silks, and too rich and too good for me" (I, 30). Even more evocatively, as Pamela notes, Mr. B. gives her stockings and silk shoes that fit her feet perfectly, "for my old Lady had a very little Foot" (I, 31). The luxurious enumeration and fortuitous matching of petite sizes (Pamela can literally stand in Lady B.'s shoes) accentuate the close ties between the two women. A premonition of the later moment in which Pamela, having married Mr. B., assumes the belongings of the dead mother, these ritual acts of gift-giving preserve the chain between mother and servant/daughter. Having received presents of clothing from the mother, Pamela appears in the guise of a sibling rival to Mr. B.; when she receives from him the clothing that the mother herself had worn, Pamela then appears to Mr. B. as a maternal substitute and class equal.[20]

The conflict between Mr. B. and Pamela, then, inheres not only in the distinctions between classes but also in the competition for the mother's attention. In Part II, Mr. B. speaks in fact of a very early sense of jealousy and revenge he feels for the servant child.[21] Their initial disharmony, which Richardson discloses only when Mr. B. is called upon to explain his motives for attacking Pamela, stems from a complex psychological displacement of household relations, which inverts the customary pattern of the child's seeking to replace the real family with an exalted one. In this instance, Lady B. wants to install the virtuous servant in the place of the absent, and to some extent inferior, offspring of the natural family. While Pamela is thus enabled in a morally feasible way to benefit from the replacement of her natural family, she also disrupts the aristocratic family in such a way as to emphasize its already disabled state.

The complex alignment of affective relations in the B. household—between Lady B. and Pamela, Pamela and Mr. B., Mr. B. and his mother and sister, Lady Davers and Pamela, Pamela and the other servants, and, of course, Mr. B. and Pamela—illustrates the close connections in the text between family structure, narrative pattern, and class relations. Pamela's domestic roles shift easily in the B. household because others readily adopt her—Mrs. Jervis becomes a mother; Jonathan and Mr. Longwood treat her as a daughter; even the originally hostile Lady Davers eventually treasures her sisterly relation to Pamela. For Mr. B., however, the inconsistency between maternal law and class rule is intolerable. The psycho-sexual intricacies in the domestic environment merge with class relations, but the fit between them, unlike that between Lady B.'s shoes and Pamela's feet, is not exact.

Pamela constantly turns on (and swerves from) this problematic relation between family value and class assumption, influential mothers and receptive servants. Before accepting Pamela, Mr. B. struggles against his admiration for her, disturbed that a servant can play the part of a lady better than members of his own class. Mr. B.'s psychology manifests the secret task of the narrative: to describe the radical ascension of the lower-class heroine, and perhaps even more important, the moral decline of the aristocracy. Though contemporary readers of *Pamela* either censured its deracination of class or celebrated its egalitarian purpose, the plot really addresses the failure of the upper class to meet its own ethical standards. On the surface, Pamela appears to urge a lower class to seek elevation; but beneath the dramatic disguises and verbal role-playing she rejects such impulses. As she insists in Part II, "it is my absolute Opinion, that Degrees in general should be kept up; altho' I must always deem the present Case an happy Exception to the Rule" (II, 3: 325). Like the folkloric fantasies it most resembles—Beauty and the Beast, Cinderella, and Griselda—Richardson's narrative undermines its own revolutionary tendencies by exalting the uniqueness of the subaltern figure rather than removing social obstructions that separate her from her apotheosis into a "noble Estate."[22]

Much of the story's subversive potential is thus defused by the heroine's exemplary status. *Pamela* constantly reminds us that Pamela the character is a special case, not likely to be duplicated. Typically, Richardson reiterates Pamela's story more than once to emphasize its unusual ideological implications. As Mr. B., defending his marriage, explains:

If, I say, my dear Friends, such a Girl can be found, thus beautifully attractive in *every one's* Eye, and not partially so only in a young Gentleman's *own*; and after that, (what good Persons would infinitely prefer to Beauty), thus piously principled, thus genteely educated and accomplished, thus brilliantly witty, thus prudent, modest, generous, undesigning; and having been thus tempted, thus try'd, by the Man she hated not, pursued, (not intriguingly pursuing) be thus inflexibly virtuous, and Proof against Temptation; Let her reform her Libertine, and let him marry her: And were he of princely Extraction, I dare answer for it, that no *two* Princes in *one* Age, take the World through, would be in Danger. (II, 3: 329)

Mr. B. demands that the entire narrative be reproduced in whole in order to justify other such transgressions of class, and his explanation reveals the calculated effort to rationalize (perhaps even rewrite) his life as a document of moral domestic enlightenment. Similarly, a repeated paradox of the narrative is that Pamela herself—the exemplar of modesty—must report her exceptional and exemplary status. When Mr. B., for example, commends his "Admirable Pamela" for sentiments "superior to those of all thy Sex" and concedes, "I might have addressed a hundred fine Ladies; but never, surely could have had Reason to admire one as I do you," she quickly disavows credit for herself:

As, my dear Father and Mother, I repeat these generous Sayings, only as they are the Effect of my Master's Goodness, and am far from presuming to think I deserve one of them; so I hope you will not attribute it to my Vanity; for, I do assure you, I think I ought rather to be more *humble*, as I am more *oblig'd*: For it must be always a Sign of a poor Condition to receive Obligations one cannot repay; as it is of a rich Mind, when it can confer them, without expecting or *needing* a Return. It is, on the one side, the State of the Human Creature compar'd, on the other, to the Creator. (I, 233)

Not only a sign of modesty, the praise Pamela reports encapsulates her social function as a self-denying cipher whose value depends on her "effects." She does not, then, represent a disaffected class; she is, rather, a catalyst to make the aristocracy witness its own depravity, strive to deify itself, and restore a social hierarchy that mirrors the divine chain of being. Like Richardson's apprentice in the *Vade Mecum*, she is the symbolic figure "on whose Industry and Labour the Welfare of the Whole almost intirely depends," but she can only acquire that potential by mirroring the stated values of the family into which she enters.

Richardson ultimately applauds the professed merits of aristocratic ideology and uses his heroine to justify a necessity that he never openly states: to ennoble landed wealth. *Pamela* is thus conditioned by a narrative principle in which the two antagonists move reciprocally toward aristocratic stability and class solidification. The heroine must learn to recognize her love for the aristocrat despite his depraved behavior and then prove (again and again) that she is worthy of her elevation; the aristocrat must learn to abhor his frivolous neglect of plutocratic ideals and come to regard his moral obligations—noblesse oblige, honor, charity, and restraint—as binding responsibilities. "Let us talk of nothing henceforth but Equality," Mr. B. says to Pamela after their marriage, "for if you will set the Riches of your Mind, and your unblemished Virtue, against my Fortune, (which is but an accidental Good, as I may call it, and all I have to boast of) the Condescension will be yours; and I shall not think I can possibly deserve you, till, after your sweet Example, my future Life shall become nearly as blameless as yours" (I, 294). Pamela is useful to Mr. B.'s class only if she rises above her own, but she can only rise above it by imitating elite conduct; this, in turn, suggests that the upper-class woman's labor, etiquette, and morality are ideally translatable into lower-class terms and hence have no distinction in themselves.

Mr. B.'s repetition of the gesture that begins the original seduction, bestowing his mother's possessions on Pamela, signals this pattern; but the gifts, now legally tendered through wedlock, include valuables that reflect the enhanced nature of their marriage: "He was pleased afterwards to lead me up Stairs, and gave me Possession of my Lady's Dressing-room and Cabinet, and her fine Repeating-watch and Equipage; and in short of a complete Set of Diamonds, that were his good Mother's; as also of the two Pair of Diamond Earrings, the two Diamond Rings, and Diamond Necklace. . . . He presented me also with her Ladyship's Books, Pictures, Linnen, Laces, etc. that were in her Apartments, and bid me call those Apartments mine" (I, 385). Here, possession and possessions, spatial appropriation, and material gain coalesce in a fantasy of social, moral, and economic solidification. Pamela finally merges into Mr. B.'s class not because she brings new ways of imagining it but because, like Lady B.'s wardrobe, it becomes her, and she becomes it. Consequently, she verifies Richardson's presupposition that the servant's radical "exaltation" also cautions aristocratic women about their necessary domestic subordination. The "middle sort" that Pamela represents, situated between her laboring father's family and her master's landed family, is not an autonomous class but the social conscience of the aristocracy.

Pamela's resemblance to a mother from whom the aristocratic family has estranged itself thus serves two crucial purposes. First, it links Pamela to a different family, a different status, and a different moral and economic system by allying her to a figure who both marks the servant's difference and her underlying structural sameness to the class of women she approximates. It thus balances Pamela's rise in stature with an equivalent demotion of the very gendered position—the lady of the house—that confirms and validates the servant's leap in status, the "place" or "condition" in which she finally finds herself. Second, in the master's case, the mother represents class obligations that he has failed to meet; embodied in and textualized by a servant, they embarrass him into recalling his "position" in the world.

Mr. B. knows that he and Pamela have been engaged in an arduous struggle for power over what home signifies, and what sexual, political, and social roles are to be established in it. For Mr. B., the route to this ideological command lies in the sexual act, or more precisely in the mere threat of sexual action. That he uses sexuality as a focus of contention is predictable since, for him, the determining factor in marriage is biological, the production of children being, as he puts it, "the end of the Institution" (I, 312). Before his conversion, Mr. B. regards sexual relations outside of marriage as a means to counter the domestic ideal represented by Pamela and his mother. Ironically, he wants to subvert what he sees as a female sexual ideology but which, in fact, is the product of patriarchal codes of conduct. By undermining family harmony, the libertine unwittingly sabotages the patriarchal system of exchange by which his power is generated. Mr. B. also fails to see that his potency depends entirely on an arbitrary use of physical enforcement and that the more he threatens to use it the less he is able to maintain it. Without a collateral dominance of language, his power remains arbitrary and, consequently, vulnerable to verbal resistance. At the moment when he states "now you are in my power," all he has proven is that he controls Pamela's physical movement; by the next day, when he reads Pamela's journal, he realizes that instead of truly exercising power over her he has lost his own authority. No longer able to sustain his faith in verbal persuasion, he abandons his "plot" and allows Pamela to return home.

With the recognition of verbal castration comes self-disgust. Mr. B. can no longer even take pleasure in the fiction that he has been engaged in a textual/sexual game over which he has ultimate control. Before he reads the latter part of Pamela's journal, he tends to refer condescendingly to her storytelling as literary convention: "There is such a pretty Air of Romance, as you relate them, in your Plots, and my Plots, that I shall be better directed in what manner to wind up the Catastrophe of the pretty Novel" (I, 201). To feel self-assured, he must entirely master her discourse, turning it into fiction rather than honoring it as fact. But Pamela's journal unleashes a discourse that overwhelms him and exercises its power over his sexual behavior. Pamela's domestic morality, engendered not only by her parents but by his mother as well (who, as her parents admit, "gave you Learning"), compels Mr. B. to reject his romance fantasy. The extensive and intense family correspondence alters him suddenly and completely as he surrenders to the language he has so vigorously been subverting. Her "pretty Novel" thus rises into the much more serious and, for Richardson, transformative language of the conduct book. That is, Pamela's letters duplicate Richardson's own need to regard fiction as a socially productive discourse.

Mr. B.'s transformation is not, therefore, necessarily a matter of technical clumsiness, as has often been argued;[23] indeed, it can be justified as the ineluctable effect of Pamela's "Itch of Scribbling" (I, 37; II, 3: 54). In a book that so persistently constructs itself on imputed acts of reading, it comes as no surprise that the narrative's crucial reversal results from an extended and ritualized act of reading. After all, *Pamela* is, among other things, a conversion narrative, both for its heroine and for the "amphibious" Mr. B., whose role-playing (villain, hero, rake, and husband) matches that of Pamela, the servant turned mistress. In both cases conversion leads as much to social as to spiritual restitution: Pamela eventually discovers her love for her would-be ravisher; Mr. B., having first fallen ill, renounces his libertinism for the moral rectitude of husband and father. For Mr. B., conversion is the product of conversation, both in the interviews with Pamela and in the reading of her family text. He is led to see himself in quite a different light once he sees his actions reflected through Pamela's script.

Reading Pamela's words, Mr. B. confronts a text that disorients his cultural and psychological assumptions, challenges the coherence of his class values, perceptions, and knowledge, and brings to a crisis his relation to language. He experiences both anxiety and desire as he reads, in particular, the section of the journal that recounts Pamela's contemplation of suicide beside the pond (her own moment of conversion). As he walks by the water reading the journal aloud to Pamela, he visits the exact locations where the described action occurs. He thus tries to materialize Pamela's "history" by uniting the written subject with the living subject. Projecting himself into the heroine's experience, he sees his own actions profoundly altered; she forces him to recognize the competing ideological forces within him—the destructive ideology of the rake confronting the conservative ideology of the aristocratic defender of family. But Mr. B. is not yet prepared to face the consequences of what he has read, because understanding Pamela's text requires his self-condemnation: "'Your Papers shall be faithfully return'd you, and I have paid so dear for my Curiosity in the Affection they have riveted upon me for you, that you would look upon yourself amply reveng'd, if you knew what they have cost me'" (I, 214). By witnessing his baseness and Pamela's virtue, Mr. B. acknowledges his misconduct toward her and toward his mother and the family ideals she hoped to inspire.

Mr. B.'s shock of recognition upon reading Pamela's words and reconceiving himself, are a sign, in fact, of his relative effacement in the critical sections of the text when Pamela experiences some of her most severe tribulations at the hands of female surrogates for his violent authority (such as Mrs. Jewkes and Lady Davers). This effacement serves to obscure the genuine problem Richardson had in unifying his didactic intentions and his narrative technique. Because he is so often absent, as both a letter writer and a figure of action, Mr. B. appears to have no decided narrative purpose, sometimes participating in the glamor of the romance while at other times objectifying the evils of family mismanagement. As I have been arguing, however, his self-disgust is an essential part of Richardson's moral conception. For revelation to occur, Mr. B. must genuinely transgress the ideals of the romance hero; at the same time, he is still destined to reconstitute the domestic order that his libertine activity has upset. His divided nature (which Richardson will figure separately in the guise of Lovelace and Belford when he writes *Clarissa*) dramatizes the very effect that domestic conduct books celebrated as a crucial result of moral management: because the libertine devalues himself in the act of devaluing the marriage ideal, he must by the force of cultural logic become a strict adherer to the conjugal model in order to liberate his true social identity.[24]

Searching the Herald's Office

For all Pamela's success at converting Mr. B. and convincing his family and friends of her superior values, class relations remain fairly static throughout her narrative. Once the aristocratic family admits Pamela as an exception—a well-fashioned commoner—and regards her as a bettering influence, it again closes ranks (in Part II, for example, Pamela's parents are almost entirely excluded from the action). Conversely, Pamela, though an agent of transformation, remains essentially the same. Richardson details the intensification, not the growth, of her belief in virtue and family integrity and plots the progress of her maturity from naive servant girl to sophisticated member of the privileged classes without requiring her to change her personality or moral convictions. While he traces Pamela's

dawning recognition of love for her persecutor, her growing attraction to Mr. B., often cited by critics as a change of character, is
nonetheless a static event, contingent upon Mr. B.'s more dramatic
change of heart.[25] Only when Mr. B. shows signs of amendment
does Pamela concede her latent attraction to him (an alteration
Richardson cautiously foreshadows).[26] Because Richardson intends
her to be a paragon, the "exemplar" of her sex, there can be little actual revolution in or revelation of personality. What seems most
important about her role in the narrative is the degree to which she
can remain essentially the same while reacting to significant external
changes in her condition, and engender not so much a moral change
as a moral homecoming in her "superiors."[27]

This uniformity in social relations typically extends to Pamela's
supervision of family. Whether as daughter, servant, wife, or
mother, she understands more than anyone else the need for clearly
defined roles in governing a household. At the conclusion of Part I,
the editor comments on this managerial talent: "From the Oeconomy she purposes to observe in her Elevation, let even Ladies of
Condition learn, that there are Family Employments in which they
may, and ought to, make themselves useful, and give good Examples
to their Inferiors, as well as Equals. And that their Duty to God,
Charity to the Poor and Sick, and the different Branches of Household Management, ought to take up the most considerable Portions
of their Time" (I, 411). Part II then simply fulfills this promise of
domestic rigor. As a whole, *Pamela* (Parts I and II) constitutes perhaps the most protracted and explicit fictional account in eighteenth-century English literature of what Pamela herself intermittently calls "family management," "family order," "domestic services," and "economy" (I, 135, 136, 205, 253, 256). Pamela's attentions
in the sequel turn exclusively to matters of domestic administration:
the appropriate accommodation of her parents on the Kentish estate
bequeathed to them by Mr. B., her practical and spiritual management of her own household staff, justifying her marriage to Mr. B.'s
relatives, directing and documenting her children's rearing, and perhaps most important, recounting the effect of her husband's apparent adultery in a mock trial judged by Mr. B. himself. Part of a long

process of incorporation, these actions serve to make the dominant metaphor of her personal and social being, the aristocratic house, a model of systematic organic relations that consolidates heredity, faith, economy, and law.

Each of Pamela's household duties facilitates rational systems of conduct aimed at preserving what one observer, using a crucial analogy, regards as the mechanical operations of the home: "I never saw such a Family of Love . . . it is an Heaven of a House: And being wound up thus constantly once a Week, like a good Eight-day Clock, no Piece of Machinery, that ever was made, is so regular and uniform, as this Family is" (II, 4: 76–77). The clock denotes both the ideal family circle and the enlightenment vision of spiritual, affective, and material domains in perfect self-renewing balance. Even the allusion to the "Family of Love"—a radical, dissenting group of the sixteenth and seventeenth centuries who modeled personal, economic, governmental, and religious obligations on a universal family—expands Pamela's mission to include historical and political concerns.[28] The domestic angel participates in a social revolution by turning clock-maker, at once the integral agent of highly monitored motions and the almost invisible factotum in an enormous automated structure. As Pamela emphasizes early in Part II, discussing the most mystified aspect of her relationship to Mr. B., "I am poor, as I have often said, in everything but Will—and that is *wholly* his" (II, 3: 5). Like her vaunted modesty, her will is both her heroic distinction and negation of identity. It is part of what she elsewhere acknowledges as her "self-denying Ordinances" (II, 3: 242). Throughout her long correspondence she may only report, in the narrative's fundamental gesture of recapitulation, what others celebrate about her. It is for those watching her to relate the otherworldly status that glamorizes her domestic role. As the observer enthralled by the mechanics of her home notes: "how can one avoid thinking of Inspiration in this Case; or that she was dropp'd down, when the creating MIND was forming Angels . . . to be received into bodily Organs, and to live among Men and Women, in order to shew what the first of the Species was designed to be" (II, 4: 77). The domestic woman is made such an amalgam of manual labor, upper management, and spiritual guide as to make her unpaid function in the economy the apotheosis of willed will-lessness, the angel in the machine.

Pamela belongs, then, to a long line of heroines who patiently await their secular assumption by steadfastly maintaining their domestic role, holding to their values with such tenacious logic that they end up signaling the value of others. As Pamela says to Mr. B. about the opportunity to do good that he has granted her: "Then shall I not stand a single Mark of God's Goodness to a poor worthless Creature, that in herself is of so poor Account in the Scale of Beings, a mere Cypher on the wrong Side of a Figure; but shall be placed on the right Side; and, tho' nothing worth in myself, shall give Signification by my Place, and multiply the Blessings I owe to God's Goodness, who has distinguish'd me by so fair a Lot!" (I, 303). By her own "Account," the man is whole, a "Figure" or number. The woman is a "Cypher" (or zero, according to eighteenth-century usage); she is nothing in the "Scale of Beings" and always confers value without having or gaining it. When the man is good—on the correct side, as Mr. B. is in marriage—the woman is on the "right" side of "Signification," multiplying the numerical value of his "Figure." When the man is immoral, as Mr. B. is during his attempted rapes of Pamela, she stands on the left and serves no purpose. The coupling of mathematical and spiritual terminology here thus distances Pamela from participating in her own destiny. Her development as a human being is less important than her placement on the "right" side of a matrimonial, social, and religious equation, a cypher that always stands for (and beside) something else. She is altered very little, but the conditions about her change "significantly" according to how she is situated and how, though "worthless" herself, she gives value to the male "Figure." But Pamela is also punning on the notion of multiplication here; the good she adds—the ability to multiply—is the power of reproduction. Her children provide a surplus in the domestic equation. Once more her value can only be measured in terms of empty "Signification." Indeed, Part II completes the cipher metaphor in Part I by repeatedly, even obsessively, remarking Pamela's maternalized body.

Two patterns, then, obtain in Richardson's account of Pamela's domestic experiences, or what Mr. B. calls her *"good Works"* (II, 3: 93). First, she must have a consistent and irreducible identity and yet experience this solidity of character as something that needs constant defense, a trial, perpetual reminders that she herself possesses no inherent value. Second, she must still allow for change, even appear to change herself, in order to adapt adequately to the new status she has acquired and have an impact on those born into it. That is, to be morally suitable for her role as the ideal domestic woman—the servant turned mistress—Pamela must demonstrate an inflexible, if invisible, will; however, to be sufficiently attractive as a model for others to imitate she must also show that hers is a dynamic condition, full of drama and scope.

When Mr. B., therefore, "persuades" her to appear at a masquerade, the single event in Part II that reproduces the turmoil of her premarital narration because it precipitates Mr. B.'s near affair with the Countess Dowager of ———, he introduces a symbolic event that aligns the two patterns of Pamela's domestic experience. The masquerade, the near adultery it causes, and the mock trial by which Pamela and Mr. B. restore their marriage pivot on the very issue of function, as opposed to role-playing, that is raised by Pamela's self-estimation as a cipher. In many ways, the interrelated events connected to the masquerade epitomize the entire narrative's task of making the conservation of older codes of domestic conduct seem urgent, dramatic, and visionary. They signal not only Pamela's changelessness, but also the dynamic energy required to sustain that immutability.

Pamela's costume signals the contradictions embedded in masquerade culture. Despite her visible pregnancy, she dresses as a "prim Quaker" at her husband's suggestion, paradoxically matching the very role she inhabits in domestic life. Her physical state thus accentuates the domestic and moral pressures that the carnivalesque atmosphere cannot dispel. The masquerade is certainly the place and provocation of anti-familial conduct, a saturnalian realm that Mr. B. easily occupies and Pamela resists (he meets a "nun" there—really the Countess Dowager—who becomes the quasi-adulterous obsession that endangers his marriage to Pamela). But Richardson makes Pamela, the figure of orthodox moral rectitude, the outsider in a mock society that appears to be unconventional but is, in fact, as rigidly conformist as the society it parodies. The irony of the masquerade scene, perhaps of all such scenes, is that those who are best suited to the categorical instability of the masquerade are those who cling to its anonymity and protection of "free" speech.[29] When Pamela, failing to observe masquerade decorum, commences a "general satire on the assemblée," she unmasks its own pretense—that it transgresses ordinary cultural habits. Instead, Pamela implies, it is a projection of them, a site of social disorder that merely reproduces social custom.[30]

Pamela is not so naive, however, as to continue believing that the social self can be wholly transparent. Role-playing is required throughout Parts I and II, and Pamela, despite her referential scruples, does not simply reject it; rather, she makes it a rigorous act of accountability. As she complains to Lady Davers: "If your Ladyship will not allow for me, and keep in View the poor *Pamela Andrews* in all I write, but will have Mrs. *B.* in your Eye, what will become of me?" (II, 3: 48). A new role, therefore, is desirable only as long as it preserves in memory the prior role(s) it extends. That is, each new role, rather than erasing prior identity, combines with other roles to compose a successive and iterable line of signification, a legal fiction. Pamela dislikes the masquerade not only because it masks truth and encourages indiscretion but because its disguises are not credibly enacted. It is bad theater and worse narrative: "I had imagin'd," she explains, "that all that was tolerable in a Masquerade, was the acting up to the Characters each Person assum'd" (II, 4: 115). Better histrionics can be found in the home, where roles are complexly combined and maintained, part of a rational delineation of character akin to Locke's ideal process of association. When Mr. B. dresses for the masquerade as Don Juan, he readopts the guise of seducer from his early experiences with Pamela, almost commits adultery as a result, a near catastrophe he later regards as a betrayal of his natural character. By reverting, he threatens to inhibit the next evolving stage of their relationship: family life. His decision to take his wife and unborn child to the masquerade subjects them to the incoherences and illegitimacies of an external social world from which his creation of family is supposed to protect them. In refusing to make their mutual interests proceed forward (adding incrementally to their domestic happiness) he risks losing the momentum that they have established.

When Pamela observes Mr. B.'s flirtation with the "nun" extend into their daily routine, she realizes that she must counter-act the effects of the masquerade with a performance of her own—the mock trial—in the theater of their London home. She decides that Mr. B. needs a dramatic reminder of his error, but she casts herself, rather than him, as the criminal. Making home the very counterpart of the masquerade, yet akin to it as a theatrical space, she arranges three of the family's chairs in imitation of a bar from which she pleads her case. Acting the part of the accused, she feels compelled to exonerate herself for her behavior (she has, apparently, failed to mask her discontent over his apparent infidelity); in doing so she manages to modify his domestic behavior without appropriating household law to herself. She can preserve his patriarchal authority and at the same time voice her own grievances. If the masquerade disrupts domestic order, the trial reestablishes the home's primary function as a systematic corrective, a legal domain in which the husband's power is not challenged but multiplied, and rendered more binding. She masks her superior domestic judgment as behavior that the patriarch must judge, revolutionizing domestic authority by ostensibly disavowing it: "You are the Judge, Sir; it is I that am to be try'd. Yet I will not say I am a Criminal. I know I am not. But that must be proved, Sir, you know" (II, 4: 202). She plays a role, but typically casts herself in a subordinate position. Mr. B. prefers to regard the scene as a "mutual trial," but the system of judgment Pamela creates allows him to preserve his authority through a determined displacement of responsibility: neither figure is guilty, but the woman must still prove her innocence. The master, conversely, has to be made to seem self-regulated and properly judgmental.

The masquerade and the domestic trial in Richardson's narrative provide complementary perspectives on social role-playing. In the masquerade, society is judged by appearances; it uses play ostensibly to resist domestic ideology. In Pamela's trial, the family is judged not as they appear but as they are (within the acknowledged limits of the social construction of behavior). The heroine's domestic conduct here is linked to the rigorous ideological imperatives of a legal system that, like the conduct book, insists on accountable behavior. If Pamela represents a new political subject, signifying a new conception of modern subjectivity, her new status is strangely upstaged; the new subjectivity she embodies is one that seeks self-abnegation. Paradoxically, her domestic performance, like the cipher metaphor, focuses on her as a figure while nonetheless making her disappear, making her seem different than she is only to reveal her as perpetually unchanged.

Reflected Glory

Marriage is for Pamela, then, a series of intensified domestic tribulations that serve to reinforce the presiding stillness of her home. Most of Part II focuses on Pamela's maternal "concernments": her fear of childbirth, her dread of midwives, her determination (thwarted by Mr. B.) to breast-feed her children, her distress about smallpox, her apprehension that she will lose her children if she and her husband separate, her meditations (at Mr. B.'s urging) on Locke's *Thoughts on Education*, and her collection of moral lessons and nursery tales.[31] If Part I underscores her disruptive role as household servant, Part II dwells on her duties as a married woman, implying a complementary structural relationship between the two. All of these subsequent acts, moreover, are ultimately aimed at justifying Mr. B.'s marriage to his family and friends. Pamela, then, must reenact the drama of assimilation and regeneration endlessly. What looks like security ends up being a cause for perpetual anxiety and vigilance. As Lady Davers warns her: "you cannot but think, that we, his Relations are a little watchful over your Conduct, and have our Eyes upon you, to observe what Use you are likely to make of the Power you have over your Man, with respect to your own Relations" (II, 3: 53).

In Part II, then, Pamela must continually reveal the fact that her rise in status occurs proportionally to her negation of her original background and status, to the point in the sequel where she prevents her maid, Polly Barlow—who hopes to be seduced and married by the nephew of Lady Davers—from imitating her own history. In her letters and in her travels with Countess C. and Lady Davers, Pamela publicly reveals her qualifications, and only through this kind of domestic scrutiny and impeccable moral example is she truly adopted. Lady Davers, for instance, hedges a great deal over calling Pamela sister, even after Pamela has proven her household worth. She slowly learns to call Pamela sister only because she repeatedly observes how unrepresentative Pamela is of her original condition. Ultimately, sisterhood itself becomes a metaphor for Pamela's unsurpassed moral stature, as Lady Davers admits: "instead of my stooping, as I thought it would be, to call *you* Sister, I shall be forced to think in a little while, that you ought not to own *me* as *yours*, till I am nearer your Standard" (II, 3: 99). As always, Pamela's effect on others disrupts their own conception of family status, moral certitude, and even sense of place.

For several family members, Pamela is connected to larger symbolic obstructions of moral, social, and legal order. As Sir Jacob Swynford puts it, "What a Disgrace to a Family ancienter than the Conquest!—*O Tempora! O Mores!* What will this World come to!" (II, 3: 308). Each succeeding relation, then, must witness firsthand the superior gentility of the low-class "Slut" Pamela is reputed to be. That is, she can never become, for Richardson, a general case; her specific experience, despite her conduct-book discourse, must be constantly paraded in order to prevent a duplication of her revolutionary rise in the "Scale of Beings." Only by acting according to the very laws that would have ordinarily disqualified her from her new position in life, and by rigorously maintaining and naturalizing the discourse and conduct she has assumed, can she convince the rest of her new family of her equal status. At first seeming to demonstrate how fragile the limits and reality of class are, Pamela becomes quite her opposite by the end, a rigid opponent of social, sexual, and political permeability.

Nowhere is this retraction of Pamela's revolutionary meaning made clearer than in the gradual modification of her sense of how she relates to her own family. Richardson directs his heroine through well-articulated stages in which she moves from being an obsolete figure of the family-of-origin to an integral member of a new exalted family. Her entire experience is contained by this frame. As we have seen, this movement from one family to another involves complex sexual and class-related adjustments. Thus, at first, Pamela's ascent from her lower-class family to an upper-class one would seem to document a significant moment in class history. As the story unfolds, however, history rewrites itself. When the issue of Pamela's family background intensifies, at the point where a legal and public transformation occurs (Pamela's marriage to Mr. B.), Richardson modifies it to ease the original class conflict. In the latter stages of Part I, Pamela begins to exalt her family heritage, in the same way that she has, in effect, rewritten the character of Mr. B. to reflect a reformed patriarchal ideology.

Though Pamela's parents mention something of their untold past as early as the second letter, needlessly telling their own daughter that "once, as you know, it was better with us" (I, 27), Pamela herself conceals the details until she requires them for self-justification in the critical moment when Lady Davers confronts her with the unsuitability of her marriage to Mr. B. By the time Pamela's family history fully emerges, her heritage has become a matter of public debate between Lady Davers, who wants to prevent "the Disgrace of a Family," and Pamela, who recognizes her temerity in seeking a "high" alliance but wants to defend the moral and behavioral superiority of her parents. Responding to Lady Davers's condescension, Pamela argues most forcefully when her family is mocked: "Good your Ladyship, said I, spare my dear Parents. They are honest and industrious: They were once in a very creditable Way, and never were Beggars. Misfortunes may attend any body: And I can bear the cruellest Imputations on myself, because I know my Innocence; but upon such honest, industrious Parents, who lived thro' the greatest Trials, without being beholden to any thing but God's Blessing, and their own hard Labour; I cannot bear Reflection" (I, 328). Lady

Davers's response emphasizes the importance of this hereditary matter to how the entire plot functions in Richardson's narrative: "What! art thou setting up for a Family, Creature as thou art! God! give me Patience with thee! I suppose my Brother's Folly for thee, and his Wickedness together, will, in a little while, occasion a Search at the Herald's-office, to set out thy wretched Obscurity" (I, 328). Indeed, the entire force of the narrative depends upon the double entendre underlying that "Obscurity"; not only must the class drama be repeatedly reenacted throughout Pamela's history, she must also, for Richardson's ideological purposes, obscure (leave unexplained) her obscure (or lowly) origins.[32] Urged to assume that Pamela's family has always been of a considerably low order (her father digs ditches for a living), the reader does not discover until near the end of Part I that the parents once embraced genteel aspirations, that, in Pamela's words, "they once lived in Credit" (I, 339). As her social trajectory rises, her family background improves; it becomes increasingly difficult for Richardson to reconcile her "wretched" origins with her new station in life.[33]

All the tampering with Pamela's status has a transformative effect on her relation to domesticity and her sense of who legitimately manages the family economy. As in the mock trial, Pamela's household decisions are actually dictated by Mr. B. In a series of what Pamela calls "Curtain-lectures" (II, 3: 73, 102), he directs even the most minute details of the home. In the opening pages of Part II, for instance, he rearranges the Kentish estate for his in-laws, "fitting up" a parlor and three apartments in "plain simple elegance," deciding on new furniture, renovating "old Bow-windows," installing new hinges and locks, selecting appropriate bedding, window curtains, and carpets (II, 3: 2-4); at the Bedfordshire estate he discreetly directs or signals what remuneration Pamela should bestow on the servants (I, 376, 383-85; II, 3: 88, 97); in London, he orders drapery and has "furnish'd out" for her "a little pretty Library" (II, 4: 27). By the end, Mr. B. has given Pamela so many "Cautions and Instructions for [her] Behavior" (II, 3: 229) that she has internalized them as her necessary object in life. As she declares: "you, Sir, act more nobly by your *Pamela*; for you throw in her Way all the Op-

portunities of Improvement that can offer; and she has only to regret, that she cannot make a better Use of them, and, of consequence, render herself more worthy of your generous Indulgence"
(II, 4: 337). The accomplishments of the modern domestic woman
derive, it seems, from what the modern reformed husband throws in
her way.

Pamela herself uses a particularly illuminating metaphor to explain Mr. B.'s delegation of domestic authority. Describing herself as
a "Figure among such lesser Planets, as can only poorly twinkle and
glimmer, for want of the Aids she boasts of," she compares Mr. B.
to the sun whose "mild Benignity" makes "her look up to his own
sunny Sphere" while she "by the Advantages only of his reflected
Glory, in his Absence, which makes a dark Night to her, glides
along with her paler and fainter Beaminess" (II, 4: 384). If the domestic woman in Richardson's philosophy comes to represent a new
and relatively empowered social force, hers is only borrowed power,
the capacity simply to mirror enlightened masculine will back to itself while featuring no personal will herself. At a time when crude
forms of patriarchy seemed to contradict modern Lockean notions
of subjectivity, Richardson defends male domestic authority by
turning it into the source of "reflected glory." Using a symbol of
reason and energy—sunlight—that also retains monarchist connota-
tions, he dovetails ancien regime political vocabulary and contemporary liberal discourse.

Domestic women, according to Richardson's lesser planet analogy, do the ideological work, but men are still the ones who embody it, as figures who properly delegate power. A nurturing force
that enables the woman to run the household, the domestic man is
also the one who finally benefits, who sees that ideological work put
into practice and returned to him with interest. As Pamela observes
to her parents of their relation to Mr. B., "our Gratitude [will] be
the Inspirer of Joy to our common Benefactor; and his Joy will
heighten our Gratitude; and so we shall proceed, as Cause and Effect
to each other's Happiness" (II, 3: 15). The exchange of "Cause and
Effect" here appears equal but actually measures happiness differently. Pamela's and her parents' "Joy" takes the form, as usual, of

"Gratitude"; Mr. B.'s joy, according to the circular economy of his household, arises both from what he gives and from what he receives, joy multiplied on itself. Longman, the manager of Mr. B.'s estate, similarly notes that "all the Good" Mr. B. does "returns upon you in a Trice. It may well be said, *You cast your Bread upon the Waters*; for it presently comes to you again, richer and heavier than when you threw it in" (II, 3: 146). Christ's humble bread is converted here into specific economic gains to the patriarchal estate. This spiritual and material doubling, typical of Richardson's Protestant work ethic, parallels the mixture of liberalism, royal prerogative, Christian typology, and capital investments that the image of Mr. B. as sun king in his own family implies.

Each of Pamela's identifying metaphors, from mirror and cipher to defendant and satellite, emphasizes an unequal notion of exchange. They are the means by which she embellishes and glorifies her inevitable reduction to a figure of speech that serves a larger discourse of economic, political, and moral mastery. There is, similarly, a countermovement in the second half of Part I and all of Part II that defuses the revolutionary implications of Pamela's discourse because it attributes to the "Master" a command of language over and above that of the "Servant." As Lady Davers says to Pamela, "Thou has done Wonders in a little time: Thou hast not only made a Rake a Husband; but thou hast made a Rake a Preacher" (I, 350). Indeed, Mr. B.'s abrupt turnaround swiftly reverses the familial and linguistic dynamics of the first half. The change to a new language and behavior seems effortless for both Pamela and Mr. B. and entails merely inverting the previous antagonistic discourse. Pamela's "Prison" becomes a "Palace"; Mr. B. is transfigured into an "Angel." He in turn regards Pamela as a "dear Charmer" instead of a "Witch" and comes to understand her meaning of words like virtue, honesty, and truth. A word like "Creature," which had been abusive, is converted into the kindly "dearest Creature." Sarcastic exchanges modulate into sentimental expressions of domestic harmony. While the action of the first half reflects Pamela's rhetorical command in the face of Mr. B.'s physical aggressiveness, her function in the latter half is to learn how to speak and act according to her exalted status. At this juncture Mr. B. becomes the authority on language and reveals suddenly a competence in articulate, dignified speech and nearly unimpeachable knowledge about how an aristocratic family ought to be governed. Where before she was sure of her conduct, Pamela now worries that her language and behavior are inferior. The irony of her final acquisition of a place in the social hierarchy consists in knowing that what allowed her ascent—the fluidity of her social identity—can just as easily revoke her newly attained status. As her new family obligations widen, she feels that she must guard against a sudden return of the pert, lower-class servant.

This alteration in Pamela's attitude to language also changes her relation to the "familiar letter." In the second half, letter-writing for Pamela turns into a consciously public event in which she constructs a new role for herself (dutiful wife) instead of expressing the disruptive energies of her old self. The letter, once the document of her individual struggle to implement a moral vision in social circumstances that challenged her convictions, becomes a vehicle for deliberate observations whose purpose is to shape the future in terms of a now stable present. To a large extent she stops "writing to the moment" and adopts a style of writing and speech that is studied, homiletic, and resistant to Richardson's prior claims that epistolarity must address "the Immediate Impression of every Circumstance which occasioned them" (I, 4). Part I concludes with Pamela facing the "awful" task of living up to her husband's forty-eight "Rules"; and as she writes to her parents she suspects that such duties will coincide with her having to stop writing letters altogether: "I will continue writing till I am settled, and you are determin'd; and then I shall apply myself to the Duties of the Family" (I, 387). By the end of Part II, instead of writing in response to the behavior of others, she writes, on her husband's suggestion, about the works of others (Locke's treatise on education, for example). What empowers her and makes her attractive to the reader as well as to Mr. B. and Lady Davers—her facility with words—must be quietly transmuted. Where her letters had been a means to sustain her identity by linking her to her family, they become after marriage a burden to the new family in which she now has a vested interest. Richardson thus closes his narrative by returning to the model of the didactic tract that inspired the fiction initially and by employing the same tutelary language to which he returned at the end of his literary career by extracting moral sentiments from his own collected fiction (including *Pamela* I and II).

In many respects, then, Pamela's reward is a kind of self-annihilation, a willed subjection to the system that victimized her in the first place. But this renunciation takes the form not of necessarily speaking less but of speaking differently. As she says to Miss Darnford: "See . . . from the humble Cottager, what a publick Person your favour'd Friend is grown" (II, 3: 107). The new language of subjection must have public iteration (and reiteration). Clarissa goes through much the same process as her final letters turn into sermons, moral fables, coffin insignia, and testaments. One of the paradoxes of Richardson's texts is that the heroine, who incorporates many of the principles of individualism, particularly in the belief that personal rights should not be arbitrated by property, also voices the opposing principles of hierarchy. The narrative seems to move ideologically in at least two incompatible directions, one toward a revolutionary perception of autonomy and matrimony based on equality, the other toward patriarchal empowerment. Pamela's story is one in which a system of status seems emphatically subverted but that, nonetheless, strengthens the very system it challenges. If the conflict dramatized in Richardson's text represents a political battle over language, the success of Pamela's assimilation depends on a failure to retain the voice she begins with and that for a large portion of the text articulates her distinctive self. Like Richardson's clamorous defense of his fiction as a "new species of writing," Pamela's work eventually resorts to an older symbolic order.

The political, economic, sexual, and household systems of exchange figured in *Pamela* are ultimately intended to increase the value of the masculine state without causing a consequent drain of male resources. In Richardson, the modern domestic woman embodies an enlightenment view of economy as an invisible network of highly rational, even mathematically precise relations that maximize gain. She is, however, also made to appear a radical force of self-determination, defending freedoms of action and speech. This appearance preserves the illusion that she extols a new libertarian doctrine in social relations while still serving (literally as well as metaphorically) the economic needs of domestic patriarchy. By drawing out the conversion of his heroine from maid to mistress, Richardson emphasizes the homology of wife, mother, and servant. Similar to the domestic woman in the conduct material of the second half of the century, Pamela, one of the most revered and defamed characters in eighteenth-century literature, mystifies the unpaid domestic labor necessary to a patriarchal system of capital growth. Merging these roles, she becomes the ideal emblem of a household order that centralizes domestic functions, reinforces the nuclear family that was supposedly replacing extended kinship as the dominant form of social classification, and consolidates economic practice. If writing is an ontological condition for Pamela, it is one of giving as much as being; or, to be more precise, giving *is* being for her. In the latter stages of her correspondence this gift requires a suppression of her original writing voice. She is a fully modern subject who is made a willing participant in the mystification of personal domestic identity, a selfless figure (like a cipher, mirror, or lesser planet) who is linked to ideology, though not, at least in appearance, simply acted upon by it.

5

The Erotic and the Domestic in
The History of Miss Betsy Thoughtless

"Into what vexations," cried he, "may not a whole family be
plunged, through the indiscretions of one woman?"
— Eliza Haywood, *The History of Miss Betsy Thoughtless*

Opposing Thoughtlessness

Like Richardson, Eliza Haywood dwells on both the constraints
and the benefits of domestic norms. But where Richardson demonstrates how they reside in the exemplary individual, Haywood
shows them intruding vexatiously upon the barricaded self. To read
Eliza Haywood's 1751 prose fiction *The History of Miss Betsy
Thoughtless* is, according to the book's title, to read the progress of a
female consciousness rendered interesting by its very lack of content. As the story proceeds, it becomes evident that the task of the
narrative is to supply the vacant mind with suitable material. The
protagonist, in other words, resembles Locke's tabula rasa, and her
development, like the work that contains her, is closely related to
the quality of ideas imprinted upon her. Matching the "legitimizing"
strategies of the domestic literature that dominates the second half
of the eighteenth century, Haywood's heroine acquires status as a
proper fictional subject by showing the dynamic internal process required to transform behavioral instruction into willed behavior. As
this chapter argues, both the protagonist and the social environment
she inhabits are crisscrossed by channels of desire that move toward
and away from proper household conduct. Character and setting
duplicate the fiction's representational tactics: each comprises ten-

dencies that reveal norms by constantly deviating from them; and, in doing so, they convert ordinary, at times even mundane, domestic actions into events that are always threatening an eruption into novelty.

What might appropriately occupy the mind of Betsy Thoughtless is suggested by the didactic works that Haywood produced during her years as a writer of fiction. Like those of Defoe and Richardson, Haywood's narratives both nourished and depended on educational literature. By 1749, two years before the appearance of *The History of Miss Betsy Thoughtless*, she had completed eight works that might reasonably be termed conduct books. These include *Mary Stuart* (1725), *The Tea Table* (1725), *Reflections on the Various Effects of Love* (1726), *Love-Letters on All Occasions Lately Passed Between Persons of Distinction* (1730), *A Present for a Servant Maid; or, the Sure Means of Gaining Love and Esteem* (1743), *The Female Spectator* (1744–1746), *The Parrot* (1746), and *Epistles for the Ladies* (1749). At the end of her career in 1756, only three years after completing her last significant prose fiction, *The History of Jemmy and Jenny Jessamy*, Haywood wrote her two authoritative works on domestic relations, *The Wife* and *The Husband. In Answer to the Wife.*[1] Since the period of this conduct writing coincides roughly with the period of Haywood's fictional writing (in which she produced more than sixty romances, secret histories, novels, and translations of continental romances), it is fair to say that for her, as for so many other writers, the relation between narrative discourse and conduct literature was both necessary and vexing.[2] Like Defoe, she experimented with fabricated stories that served to illustrate moral and immoral conduct. Like Richardson (and on several occasions before him), she used model forms of writing (letters, for instance) to personalize didactic guidance. Like Fielding, she sought to instruct as well as delight her readers, but found that such objectives were frequently incompatible. Her conduct literature, no less than her imaginary prose, shows that the pleasures of fiction have a tendency to swamp the obligations of instruction. The requirements of morality may even have been an unwelcome necessity; critics frequently suggest that the increased moralizing in Haywood's later fiction is a measure of the pressures she may have encountered in her career to make her work conform to "more conservative" standards of conduct.[3] According to Clara Reeve, writing in 1785, Haywood "repented of her faults, and employed the latter part of her life in expiating the offenses of the former."[4]

The subtler domestic subterfuge of her mature fiction may in fact symbolically represent Haywood's complicated and conflicted feelings about having to purge her own writing of its "immoral" content in order to survive in the literary marketplace. Unlike her male counterparts, Haywood's direct infusion of didactic household commentary seems more self-conscious and is linked more directly to the paradoxes of female literary subjectivity. Unlike Behn, she strives to position the scandalous woman within family ideology through a complex (and sometimes problematic) subjection of the desiring woman to an explicit system of domestic obligations. In *The History of Miss Betsy Thoughtless*, for example, Haywood makes the moral purpose of the heroine's story clear in an authorial address that opens the text: "It was always my opinion, that fewer women were undone by love, than vanity; and that those mistakes the sex are sometimes guilty of, proceed, for the most part, rather from inadvertancy, than a vicious inclination" (1: 1). Throughout the four volumes, Haywood continually refers to the instructional merit of her story in language that derives specifically from conduct books. She interrupts the story at one point, for instance, to emphasize the didactic purpose of a passage on Betsy's vanity: "Though it is certain, that few young handsome ladies are without some share of the vanity here described, yet it is to be hoped, there are not many who are possessed of it in that immoderate degree miss Betsy was. It is, however, for the sake of those who are so, that these pages are wrote, to the end they may use their utmost endeavours to correct that error, as they will find it so fatal to the happiness of one, who had scarce any other blameable propensity in her whole composition" (1: 129). A large number of Haywood's chapter titles, similarly, reflect the narrative's instructive aims, such as the one that asserts: "[It] May be of some service to the ladies, especially the younger sort, if well attended to" (1: 56). Repeatedly, the titles not only alert the reader to ideal demeanor, but use key words that signal this concern: behavior, conduct, principles, disposition, manner, character, management, sentiments. These words, in fact, are meant to guide the reader's own capacity to make moral judgments or draw lessons and are part of the "objective" narrative frame that reinforces the domestic tutelage of the story as a whole. They furthermore mirror the control over narrative structure, sequence, and intention that Haywood regards as necessary to the pedagogical impact of the story. Chapter 11 in the first volume, for example, "Lays a foundation for many events to be produced by time, and waited for with patience" (1: 116). Behavioral and storytelling principles are thus made complementary. Many of the chapter titles are, in fact, intensely aware of reader responses and seek to shape the reader's awareness of the effects and consequences of specific textual details. One typical chapter heading even admits that it "Seems to be calculated rather for the instruction than entertainment of the reader" (3: 51). In these narrative markers, we see a particularly clear example of how self-conscious mid-century prose fiction was about the correspondence between domestic relations and narrative form.

"What a Wilderness Is This House"

For all its paratextual insistence on the monitory value of the work, however, *The History of Miss Betsy Thoughtless* reverts to the image of domestic anarchy. Toward the beginning, the heroine draws a comparison between her guardian's house and an arid wilderness. This interpenetration of untamed and domesticated spaces establishes an opposition that structures the entire narrative while, paradoxically, seeming to confound the distinctions between worldly chaos and household uniformity. The dichotomy not only characterizes the environment in which the heroine is placed but defines her mental state as well. Capable of reasoned thought, she continually mismanages her ideas; destined, like Pamela, to acquire a well-ordered household through marriage, she persists in wreaking havoc upon the system of courtship by which marriages are arranged. Throughout, she seems willfully opposed, like Miranda, to the structures of conduct that would determine her role in life and that are most effectively symbolized by the house itself. Yet she rebels without ever fully succumbing to the self-destructive habits of female misconduct that, in eighteenth-century literary depictions of society, would remove her irretrievably from the happy home. As Mary Anne Schofield observes in *Masking and Unmasking*, she is "a fallible but unfallen heroine" (101). Her thoughtlessness is, moreover, as much produced by the inadequate measures of her family upbringing as it is constitutional; unlike Miranda and Crusoe, whose anti-familial behavior derives from predisposed inclination or the failure of institutional substitutes for the family, Betsy's need for correction is linked in explicit ways to the family's corresponding lack of direction. And clearly, Betsy is not a Pamela-like figure of virtually unassailable domestic logic; instead, her history represents the beginnings of an ideological shift in which household instruction seeks to accommodate rather than alienate, transform, or ignore female desire.

From the beginning, Haywood indicates that Betsy's lack of early domestic security and reliable authority figures causes her erratic behavior in courtship. When her mother dies, she effectively loses paternal guidance as well because her father then places her in boarding school. When he subsequently dies, as a result of financial anxieties, which he has thoughtlessly allowed to accumulate (the result of constitutional "indolence" according to the narrator), she moves to London to live in Mr. Goodman's house. Instead of moving to the country estate of Sir Ralph and Lady Trusty, she chooses a household that lacks a suitable maternal figure. Goodman's wife, Lady Mellasin, is, as her name amply suggests, a figure of multiple indiscretions. Lady Trusty, Betsy's "second mother," provides the moral antidote to Mellasin's corrupting influence, but she is, unfortunately, a character noted more for her absences than for her continuing presence (and thus both a reminder and a duplication of the absent biological mother). During this same period, Betsy's brothers are also absent—Francis is in Oxford, studying theology, despite the fact that his impetuous temper makes such a vocational choice inadvisable; Thomas, traveling on his Grand Tour, becomes mindlessly obsessed with a mistress who later proves unfaithful. As these circumstances imply, appropriate female guidance is lacking in Betsy's life and male authority is either incompetent or absent. According to Deborah Ross in *The Excellence of Falsehood*, the men "mistake the heroines' sexuality . . . because they do not clearly understand their own" (86). Indeed the "thoughtlessness" of Betsy's father and two brothers suggests that Betsy's thoughtlessness is an inherited by-product that the men in the family only reinforce, despite their hypocritical complaints about Betsy's "inadvertancy." While warning Betsy about the dangers inherent in the masculine world, they fall victim themselves to the very behavior they condemn.

Since the nature of the heroine's conduct toward her lovers and their treatment of her is the fundamental structuring device of Haywood's narrative, these omissions in her upbringing provide the explanatory origins of Betsy's vacuity. As the heroine herself notes: "I have, indeed, no parent to direct, and but few faithful friends to guide me through the perplexing labyrinth of life" (2: 64). Her first contact with sexuality occurs at boarding school when she agrees to be the spy and confidant for Miss Forward in her "amour" with a young man named Master Sparkish who develops an "intercourse" with Forward that leads inevitably to the latter's corruption and ruin. The first fully detailed action in the narrative, it provides the key object lesson that the rest of the work extrapolates. As in later instances of indiscretion, Betsy attracts and finds attractive the company of a female figure with a questionable moral disposition. This gravitation reinforces the link throughout the story between the tempted heroine and the fallen women who serve as her "reflections" (both because they mirror tendencies that Betsy discovers in herself and because they allow her to reflect upon their conduct and hence upon her own). On this particular occasion, Betsy merely observes; she has yet to put into practice what she learns about the nature of courtship and coquetry. But such voyeuristic moments provide the basis for her "real" training at boarding school. While she never "errs" in the way Forward does, Betsy's developing theory of passion takes shape through her intermediary role in the "conversation" between Forward and Sparkish: "Miss Betsy was a witness of all the airs the other gave herself on this occasion, and the artifices she made use of, in order to secure the continuance of his addresses; so that thus early initiated into the mystery of courtship, it is not to be wondered at, that when she came to the practice, she was so little at a loss" (1: 7).

This education in love contrasts sharply with the desultory instruction in the boarding school by a governess on whom "time had set his iron fingers" (1: 9). The narrator, making specific reference to this elderly governess, notes that when the instruction of "young girls" comes from a serious or inappropriate source it loses impact: "I have often remarked, that reproofs from the old and ugly have much less efficacy than when given by persons less advanced in years, and who may be supposed not altogether past sensibility themselves of the gaieties they advise others to avoid" (1: 10). Intervening in typical fashion, the narrator here adopts the tone of the conduct book, in effect providing instruction on effective instruction. The narrator recognizes that the conduct of "young girls" essentially implies sexual matters and concludes that, like the subject being trained, the educator must be susceptible to the very things being tabooed. This curious strategy, in turn, influences how the writer constructs a meaningful story. Whereas a conduct book consciously outlines ideology, prose fiction tends to complicate it, and Haywood appears to be aware of the antithetical purposes of her narratives, insofar as they exploit libidinous and prohibited matters at the same time that they frequently denounce them. Taking the principle of "dulce et decorum" to extremes, the amatory fiction of the kind Haywood produced after she resumed writing in the 1740's assumes that the task of prose narratives is to do exactly what the "old and ugly" governess cannot. Resisting the limitations of didactic discourse, prose fiction seeks to inculcate the same values without appearing to dictate them. In fact, it must often disguise its ideological function by seeming to indulge the vices it ultimately intends to censure.

In Haywood's narrative, this double strategy finds its textual parallel in the "fluctuating" nature of the heroine. Betsy's response to the governess's advice not only makes amply clear both the failures of student and instructor, but also manifests the dialectical nature of her moral and intellectual disposition:

> She was, indeed, as yet too young to consider of the justice of the other's reasoning, and her future conduct shewed, also, she was not of a humour to give her self much pains in examining, or weighing in the balance of judgment, the merit of the arguments she heard urged, whether for or against any point whatsoever. She had a great deal of wit, but was too vola-tile for reflection, and as a ship, without sufficient ballast, is tost about at the pleasure of every wind that blows, so was she hurried thro' the ocean of life, just as each predominant passion directed. (1: 10–11)

Using conventional moral imagery, the narrator here suggests that the dilemmas of young women follow patterns that have long sub-sisted in spiritual autobiography. Always a figure of potential vice and potential virtue, Betsy hovers around the destructive knowledge she must understand and safely exploit in order to rid herself ade-quately of its dangerous influence. Thus, in the opening sequence, Betsy has access to the "mystery of courtship" without becoming ru-ined herself. She gains sexual knowledge in theory without having to acquire that knowledge in practice. The rest of her amatory his-tory until the moment she marries follows this pattern; she repeat-edly toys on a verbal or psychological level with men's desires, often to the point of triggering near violation, but invariably eludes actual physical consequences. Whether Betsy's coquetry derives from cov-ert rebelliousness against male tyranny or is the product of contra-dictory male impulses toward desiring virtue and carnality in the same female body, her behavior expresses a double standard of fe-male conduct in which propriety and libidinousness are strangely compounded.

The corresponding disparities between Betsy's individual under-standing and more public views of the intricate relation between domesticity and sexuality are nowhere more apparent than in the scenes leading up to and including the dissolution of Mr. Good-man's home, when, according to Betsy, it becomes a "wilderness." Having discovered his wife's adultery and embezzlement, Mr. Goodman evicts Lady Mellasin and her daughter, Flora (by a previous marriage); in leaving, they take with them the fops, courtiers, coquettes, and rakes—"the Babel of mixed company" (1: 63)—that have transformed Goodman's house from social order into sexual chaos. Rather than a place of systematic relations, the house has become the repository of false ideology in which "[t]he court, the play, the ball, and opera, with giving and receiving visits, engrossed all the time that could be spared from the toilet" (1: 20). Domestic privacy and "publick diversion" have blurred (1: 20). A world without distinctions, Goodman's home under Mellasin's direction provides neither the right proportion of guidance (there are too many conflicting voices) nor its appropriate type (the language spoken here parallels the divisive and heretical babble of Nimrod and his followers). A domestic carnival, it expresses the same "saturnalian" energies that Stallybrass and White ascribe to the fair, and it sets up a similar contrast between didactic propriety and excessive pleasure (27–79, 171–202). The chattering home duplicates the moral confusion—the symbolic wilderness—to which Puritan sinners were conventionally assigned. This false domesticity highlights the destabilizing effects of mixed company and mixed actions even more pointedly than the fair or masquerade because it occurs within the structure of the house; in other words, it specifically challenges domestic ideology.[5]

Verbal and sexual exchange within the household, the importation of erotic public display, is what has appealed to Betsy. Her disappointment over the vacancy of the house is less the result of Flora and Mellasin's departure (she has all along been dutifully suspicious of their behavior) than of the consequent absence of attentive men. The empty house becomes, in effect, the sign not only of her folly but also of the sterile vacuity of the conventional household, the erasure of what the narrator frequently calls Betsy's "plurality of lovers" (1: 193, 287; 2: 209). On the surface, the eviscerated Goodman home represents the damage done to domestic harmony (and economy) by a woman of Mellasin's character. Yet it also seems to provide a correlative to Betsy's emotional and moral state and permits a strange affinity between the heroine and the female villains in whose company she matures. What Betsy ultimately condemns in their behavior is not so far removed from the coquettish tendency underlying her own encouragement of a "multiplicity" of "admirers" and "lovers" (2: 63, 80). Though redeemable, her polyandrous actions subvert the harmony (and economy) of eighteenth-century courtship as much as Mellasin's destroy marital principles. But because her relations with men are not yet contracted or consummated (unlike Mellasin, who is married, and Flora, who gives up her virginity to Gayland, one of Betsy's rejected suitors), Betsy evades the social condemnation that eventually attends the "fallen" woman.

Despite Goodman's banishment of the offending presence, then, the effect of the company on Betsy has been to transform her sense of a moral environment into a fear of domestic propriety without confirming her in the dissolute behavior of carnal women like Mellasin and Flora. She regards the now empty house, governed only by Goodman and a respectable "old gentlewoman" acting as housekeeper, as a form of punishment. The sexual conduct of the company at Goodman's house thus encourages behavior that is virtually the opposite of that promoted by conduct literature. Betsy's actions throughout the first half of the narrative upset the economic precepts of courtship, especially as they encourage "plurality," as opposed to monogamy, in romantic affairs. As Goodman says to his ward: "I do not understand this way of making gentlemen lose their time" (1: 192). He seems to recognize the threat in Betsy's premarital behavior to the economic function of matrimony. A good merchant, who regards marriage more in fiduciary than in romantic terms (despite his own impulsive marriage to the impoverished Lady Mellasin), Goodman cannot condone the loss of valuable time that romantic play incurs. Betsy confuses Goodman precisely because she reverses the conventional association between pragmatism and masculinity. Betsy's disruption of courtship form is not the result of the usual literary opposition between men's business and women's love. Refusing to choose a single lover, Betsy reveals that love *is* a form of business: "it seemed strange to her, that a young woman who had her fortune to make might not be allowed to hear all the different proposals should be offered to her on that score" (1: 192). In the process of coquetting, she acquires impressive managerial skills. As Goodman himself notes about her manipulation of lovers: "it was a pity she was not a man, she would have made a rare minister of state" (1: 210). Similarly, Flora, of all people, calls Betsy "a perfect Machiavel in love affairs" (1: 200). The quest for power in a world that denies women access to the means of power underlies the coquette's business, as Betsy acknowledges: "when [her lovers] came to address her, she should play the one against the other, and give herself a constant round of diversion, by their alternate contentment or disquiet. As the barometer, said she to herself, is governed by the weather, so is the man in love governed by the woman he admires: he is a meer machine,—acts nothing of himself,—has no will or power of his own, but is lifted up, or depressed, just as the charmer of his heart is in the humour" (1: 143). Depriving men of their autonomy, and turning them into unreflective machines, Betsy measures her sexual power against their mechanical desires. Customarily the object of men's dominion (particularly in her encounters with near rape), she reverses roles in courtship, seeing in male victimage both a measure of her own suppressed capacities and the realities of her own gendered condition.

What makes Betsy so fascinating, in part, therefore, is her resemblance to the scandalous creatures whose utter mortification seems to be one of the narrative's chief purposes. In fact, Haywood emphasizes the symbolic connection between Betsy and the women in Goodman's house early in volume 1 when Betsy, having just recovered from the "rude impertinencies" of Gayland, takes momentary stock of her own behavior in relation to that of Flora's: "Her good sense had now scope to operate;—she saw, as in a mirror, her own late follies in those of miss Flora, who swelled with all the pride of flattered vanity, on this new imaginary conquest over the heart of the accomplished Gayland, as he was generally esteemed, and perceived the errors of such a way of thinking and acting, in so clear a light, as had it continued, would, doubtless, have spared her those anxieties her relapse from it afterwards occasioned" (1: 36). The misconduct of Mellasin's daughter appears here to suggest a misguided sisterhood (and daughterhood) that Betsy must consciously exorcise in order to save herself. The confused grammatical subordination and technically unclear use of pronouns in the second half of the sentence seems to emphasize the nearly interchangeable nature of Betsy and Flora. Metaphorically gazing into the glass, Betsy perceives Mellasin's offspring where her own features ought to be, in a manner reminiscent of the fair jilt's conversion of a priest's imagined lust into a mirror image of herself. As Ross suggests, the sexuality of women in Haywood's narrative is essentially "autoerotic" (or, perhaps, I would argue, projected onto other women) because heterosexual desire is so confused (86). Betsy seems able, upon reflection, to correct—or at least to examine—the distorted image presented to her in the guise of her alter ego, but typically she allows those moral reckonings to lapse. The coquette and the proper lady confront each other over a domestic wasteland, a space waiting to be appropriately populated. Unlike Miranda, who parodies household duty, and Pamela, who enshrines it, Betsy struggles for a middle ground between stimulating and erasing social exchange within the household.

The issue on which the narrative's suspense depends is whether the vain coquette will succumb to the rational self-mortifying adult. In the gap between coming of age and entering marriage Betsy finds a momentary space (which the narrator prolongs) that allows her to cross genres and act the part of a scandal heroine while all the time acquiring a better sense of how to become a proper wife. To some degree, Betsy's encouragement of plural lovers before marriage, though not exactly sanctioned by society, constitutes the only viable means by which she can test her passion, and the entire shape of the work, extending the moments of potential infamy, suggests a covert means by which women could plot their amatory history in advance of marriage. In a society that narrowly defines female subjectivity in relation to its domestic potential, such "freedom" acts as a kind of safety valve. It exercises rebel passions and provides the illusion of self-determination in a marital market that considerably restricts women's power of choice. The indulgence of coquetry provides a certain limited amount of social agency upon which the heroine capitalizes.

In assuming this power, however, Betsy aligns herself with those who destroy house and home (the end points of her fictional destiny); and when they leave she finds that the house, governed by thoughtful and prudent means once the chastened Mr. Goodman dismisses his wife, becomes intolerable. Despite her guardian's revealing name, she is unable to distinguish the value of a "good man's" home; rather than attempting to claim a role in its reestablishment, she merely dismisses it. That is, Betsy experiences (almost as if she were its avatar) the liberating effects of sexual extroversion and, at the same time, witnesses the effects of desire if exercised against the interests of the family, but she is unable to envision any coupling of legitimate female desire and the management of domestic space. That the government of the household falls to Mr. Goodman, a man more suited to the public activity of mercantile business, only signals the more complicated breach in sexual order that Mellasin's vices prompt. Indeed, it is not long before Goodman simply falls ill and dies. The lack of a woman who can actively shape her passion to the requirements of domestic government is as baleful to the family's effective administration as a woman whose appetite destroys it.

In terms of fictional typology, then, Betsy's moments of self-determination poise her between seemingly incompatible generic alternatives (Ross calls her a "mixed" heroine whose "unmixing" occurs only when she is safely married at the end and romance and realism are effectively separated [73, 87]). As a heroine, Betsy mediates the sexual extravagance of the romance (and its permutations in the scandal chronicle) and the repressive aims of domestic fiction. Where one dismantles home, the other constitutes it. She is, in a sense, an attempt to fuse the characters of Miranda and Pamela. To a large extent, her history marks prose fiction's shift in balance from scandal chronicle (the subversion of family ideology) to courtship narrative (the conversion to family ideology). Indeed, Haywood, more than any other eighteenth-century writer, I would argue, bridges the fictional narratives of Behn or Defoe and the works of Burney and Austen. A narrative like *The History of Miss Betsy Thoughtless* effectively inscribes the dynamic transference between sexuality and propriety that obsesses eighteenth-century prose fiction in general; its heroine dramatizes the developmental capacities of the literary form that contains her. Rationalizing her misconduct, the narrative rationalizes its own generic aims, and incorporates (or tries to) the radical energy of earlier types of the scandalous woman.

Haywood thus uses the critical absence of an authentic home to explain the formation of her heroine's character in terms of an uncertain historical progression. The houses Betsy occupies are all substitute homes: from the boarding school, to Goodman's house, to the private quarters she takes after Goodman's death, and ultimately to her older brother's residence where she flees after the failure of her first marriage. Each place accentuates either her orphan status or her continuing debarment from a stable home. Indeed, her shifting among these residences is reminiscent of the epic homelessness that Lukács and Bahktin regard as the principal constituent of narrative relations and that is particularly featured in prose fiction itself (although here in domestic rather than epic form).[6] Betsy's homelessness promotes her thoughtlessness; she lacks the adequate parental, and particularly maternal, guidance that would expunge what makes her interesting as a character but dangerous as a daughter. As the narrator observes, fourteen is "a nice and delicate time, in persons of her sex; since it is then they are most apt to take the bent of impression, which, according as it is well or ill directed, makes, or marrs, the future prospect of their lives" (1: 19). Echoing Locke's strictures on education, Haywood nonetheless foresees that the function of didacticism and the requirements of popular literature do not happily correspond. Her fiction typically depends on a form of moral absenteeism. We are reminded continually of the failures attending conventional forms of "tuition." Haywood would seem to be implying that prose fiction itself could assume, or at least assist in, the education of wayward daughters; but the story nonetheless works because it indulges that very waywardness in Betsy, thus capitalizing on the heroine's homelessness.

The Company She Keeps

Betsy's native attraction to "promiscuous enjoyment" and "pub-lick diversion" (1: 20), in addition to deranging conventional expec-tations about courtship, confounds linear plotting. Repeatedly, the progressive story of her relationship with her preferred suitor, True-worth, is subverted by her experiences with other potential lovers or by her exposure to dangerous sexual threats. *The History of Miss Betsy Thoughtless* is, in fact, uncharacteristic of the classical courtship plot insofar as it marries off the lovers to other partners (and the woman to a brutal husband) before uniting them at the conclusion. Instead of sharply dividing characters into licit and illicit types, Hay-wood creates figures on the boundary of proper conduct who strug-gle to reconcile desire and domestic stricture.

The tendency in Betsy to dramatize this conflict in public is dem-onstrated by the long sequence in which Trueworth observes her at-tendance at a play. Having warned Betsy of the impropriety of a con-tinued friendship with Miss Forward, Trueworth witnesses Betsy at the theater with her "indecent" friend and a consort of "gay young gentlemen" (2: 112). Betsy fulfills this assignation with Forward in part to chasten Trueworth for his presumption in assuming the guise of, as she puts it, "a spy to inspect, or a governor to direct my actions" (2: 108); she also wants to scrutinize Forward's actions in order to make her own judgment. But the shift in venue here, from the inte-rior of a house to a place of public contact, symbolizes the dangers Betsy encounters when she alienates Trueworth, the one figure who can assure her of a "proper" house of her own (the teleological value that most eighteenth-century narratives recommend).

The theatrical setting of Betsy's indiscretion heightens the public nature of her folly and sets up a complex sequence of observational gazes that intensify the specular nature of the event. Reproducing the "Babel of mixed company" that contaminates Goodman's house, the theater magnifies the corrupting influence of public assembly. Indeed, Betsy immediately recognizes her error when she enters the playhouse: "In fine, they went, but the house being very full, and the fellow, who had been sent to keep places for them, going somewhat too late, they were obliged to content themselves with sitting in the third row.—This, at another time, would have been a matter of some mortification to miss Betsy; but in the humour she now was, to shew herself was the least of her care.—Never had she entered any place of publick entertainment with so little satisfaction;— mr. Trueworth's words ran very much in her mind" (2: 111). The failure to find their right places reaffirms her dissatisfaction with this entrance into "publick entertainment." She has literally and figuratively lost her place. Her proximity to the stage accentuates her troubling association with the theatrical art of having to "shew herself" and sanctions the "low" company that her association with Forward attracts. She has become, in part, the "publick entertainment" (just as Goodman's house earlier became confused with "publick diversions"). That her mind turns to Trueworth's warnings at this time further denotes her need of (and instinctive regard for) male guidance and validates the qualities of governorship that repose in him. As in an advice manual, Trueworth links his concern for a woman's reputation to her family's honor: "I shall never, madam, presume to prescribe . . . but shall always think it my duty to advise you, in a matter, which so nearly concerns, not only yourself, but all who have any relation to you, either by blood or affection" (2: 105–6). In thinking about his "advice" at the theater, Betsy has already begun to internalize the voice of behavioral instruction, much as the domestic woman in the eighteenth century was intended to naturalize conduct-book rhetoric.

Initially, Betsy attends the theater in order to study Flora's behavior, but as the drama on stage proceeds and the liveliness of the company intensifies she is absorbed by, and ultimately becomes, the entertainment: "But, alas! those serious considerations were but of short duration:—the brilliant audience—the musick,—the moving scenes exhibited on the stage, and above all the gallantries, with which herself and miss Forward were treated, by several gay young gentlemen, who, between the acts, presented them with fruits and sweetmeats, soon dissipated all those reflections, which it was so much her interest to have cherished, and she once more relapsed into her former self" (2: 112). Her gaze is thus divided between

Forward as object of scrutiny and the actions on stage and among the gallants as sources of entertainment. Seduced by the fruit of strangers, she allows moral thought to evaporate, and we discover that she has "relapsed" into her former self. The word "relapsed" here suggests not only moral "lapsing" and cessation of thought but also recurring states of a formidable disease. "Dissipation," in addition to describing the ephemerality of her thought, further emphasizes her moral delinquency. In the process of "shewing herself" Betsy's inappropriate conduct becomes the object of social scrutiny by members of the audience around her whose gazes are equally divided between Betsy and the actions upon the stage. She turns into a public figure, in a sense, precisely because her behavior contravenes domestic principles.

As Betsy succumbs to the theater, she becomes the specific object of scrutiny to two men in the audience whose motives for observing her narrowly are diametrically opposed and whose opinions of her behavior have much greater consequences than the audience's reproving stares. These two opposed viewings mark out two prevalent ways in which eighteenth-century male characters tend to regard women: either as quarry for sexual gratification or as potential victims needing to be supervised and tutored in the ways of designing gentlemen. From these viewpoints, women are either innately sinful or, if virtuous, inevitably at risk unless enlightened by better-informed men. Toward the conclusion of the play some "rakes of distinction" attend the two women; one of these has, in fact, both watched the play and observed Betsy's conduct, assuming from her company with Forward that she, like her companion, is advertising herself. The added viewpoint of the rake adds ironic distance to the heroine's professed aim of watching her suspected female companion. What Betsy fails to observe is that her conduct needs as much "careful" surveillance as Forward's—she cannot recognize the affinities between herself and the woman she is ostensibly watching. Nor does she understand her own "visibility." As she unwittingly says to the gentleman-rake: "I went to see the play, not to be seen myself" (2: 114). Co-opting the language of romance, he responds by accentuating the public aspects of Betsy's (un)conscious flaunting: "'Not to be seen!' cried he, 'why then have you taken all this pains to . . . [make yourself charming] . . . but to attract, and allure us poor, admiring men, into a pleasing ruin?'" (2: 114). Explicitly drawing parallels between her performance and the theater, he measures her histrionics against the moral actions of proper ladies: "What a pity it is you did not shine in the front to-night? By my soul you would have out-dazzled all the titled prudes about you" (2: 114). Like the commodity she becomes in his eyes, Betsy out-dazzles drama and audience alike; her value in this instance increases according to her departures from feminine decorum. Part of her error, then, is that she does not consciously adopt the exemplary public stance of the proper lady.

The gentleman-rake's comments are more perceptive than he realizes, since Betsy has indeed been a general source of entertainment. In effect, she is implicated in the voyeuristic economy of theater and art by presenting herself as a noteworthy subject. She seems too much like a woman in want of a lover. Like the literary form in which she is figured, both Betsy's attraction and her moral susceptibility heighten as she enters a public field of vision. And with each added gaze, the dangers to Betsy's honor increase: first, she loses sight herself of Forward's dangerous influence; second, she forfeits her social reputation in the eyes of the audience; and, third, she arouses illicit male desire.

One might expect the narrative to maintain a clearly focused view of Betsy's moral failings here. Yet Haywood also uses the occasion at the theater to highlight Betsy's seductiveness, making her seem increasingly desirable while condemning the lapse by which she reveals herself to the world. As Trueworth, the other significant symbol of male gazing, notices, her behavior mortifies him at the same time that it arouses his jealousy: "he thought he had more right to the honour of conducting her, than those to whom she gave permission . . . he thought miss Betsy unworthy of his love, yet still he loved her" (2: 131). His claim to the right of "conducting" her parallels his urge to teach her proper conduct. In part, that is the reason for Trueworth's presence at this scene. Having refused to attend the theater with Betsy in the company of Forward, he decides to go dressed in "a black perriwig, and muffled up in a cloak, so as to render it almost an impossibility for him to be known by any one" (2: 130). Literally assuming the role of spy that Betsy has metaphorically accused him of, he gazes down upon Betsy's indiscretion from the gallery, where he is stationed in his appropriate social circle. His view is comprehensive: unlike the gazes of the others, his commands at least three points of interest. He observes the theater and Betsy's actions; he also observes the audience (and among them the "rakes of distinction") as they observe Betsy. But if his gaze represents a sobering moral perspective, it also heightens Betsy's desirability by making her the subject of a complex and sexualized drama. It appears, therefore, to parallel the nature of narrative art in general; choosing subjects that persistently challenge moral limits—scandal, pornography, civic and familial disobedience, crime— eighteenth-century prose fiction seems to condemn and desire female misconduct at the same time. If we consider ourselves, in the role of readers, as adding yet another perspective to the narrative process, then, like Trueworth, we too become paradoxical moral censors of the literary subject, both desiring and judging her "world." In measuring her promise as a domestic subject as she simultaneously measures another woman for hers, we may, as an audience, be ignoring our own complicity with, or susceptibility to, a system of moral management that fuses the rectifying and desiring eye.

Representing the antithesis of the "rake of distinction," since his concern lies with Betsy's moral rather than immoral conduct, Trueworth's empyrean position denotes the extent to which Betsy has become a fallen subject. Her current behavior attracts companions who are on the same moral level that her own actions seem to confirm—she is in the pit with them. Yet despite this, she remains an alluring object to the male viewer who condemns her behavior. In this highly symbolic sequence of events, Betsy finds herself, then, unwittingly caught between censorious male opinion and dangerous male lust. Gazing performs such a prominent role in the text because, representing women in general, Betsy is chiefly an object to be viewed; moreover, as a potentially exemplary figure, she suffers the fate of all literary heroines of the eighteenth century. The looks she receives either "discover" her concupiscent nature or measure her as an object lesson. Even as a model of decorum, she must merge her roles as a domestic woman made sufficiently alluring and an alluring woman made sufficiently domestic. Conversely, male judgment, combining aspects of both the voyeur and panopticon, is allowed to maintain its contradictory status. As long as she presents herself outside of the home, then, Betsy offers herself up to public scrutiny and will be judged only according to her promotion of or deviation from positive female manners. Either she supervises the myth of the regulated house or she succumbs to the treacheries of the wilderness.

Of the rising consequences that Betsy's "visibility" has caused, the last one, the one she is initially least aware of, has the greatest impact on her future. First of all, by convincing Trueworth of her unworthiness she deprives herself of his protection from indecent male attentions. As it turns out, Trueworth has rightly questioned her safety with Forward; the rake that attends her home in his carriage attempts to rape her, having assumed, as he later states, that Betsy was "a woman of the town, by seeing her with one who was so; and her too great freedom in conversation" (2: 119). Though he does not follow through with his intent because of ethical compunctions, and because she manages to disabuse him of a belief in her wantonness by her willingness to forfeit her life in protection of her virtue, Betsy is mortified by the encounter. The occasion dramatizes the dangers she has succumbed to and the contradictory way in which she represents herself to the world while in the company of Forward (or Flora, for that matter). She seems to testify to the conduct book's concern not only with correcting the woman but also with separating her from other suspicious women who might influence her as part of the increased seclusion from a public world symbolized by the theater. The rake emphasizes this point when, astonished to find a chaste woman on his hands, he exclaims "Is it possible . . . that you are virtuous?" (2: 119) and goes on to warn her, reiterating the advice of Trueworth, to regulate her company more carefully. "He . . . took the liberty of reminding her, that a young lady more endangered her reputation, by an acquaintance with one woman of ill fame, than by receiving the visits of twenty men, though professed libertines.—To which she replied, that for the future she should be very careful what company she kept, of both sexes" (2: 122). And, indeed, upon her return home she seriously muses on the consequences of her actions and their relation to Trueworth's exhortations, finally deciding to end her friendship with Forward:

[S]he looked back with horror on the precipice she had fallen into, and considered it as a kind of miracle, that she had recovered from it unhurt;— she could not reflect on what had passed, that by the levity of her conduct she had been thought a common prostitute, had been treated as such, and preserved from irrecoverable ruin, by the meer mercy of a man, who was a perfect stranger to her, without feeling anew that confusion, which the most shocking moments of her distress inflicted.—The most bitter of her enemies could not have passed censures more severe than she did on herself, and in this fit of humiliation, and repentance, would even have asked mr. Trueworth pardon for the little regard she had paid to his advice. (2: 123–24)

Not as dramatic as Miranda's public exposure in *The Fair Jilt*, Betsy's "shewing" at the theater constitutes an equally hazardous confrontation with opinion, though already made much more private as an encounter within a curtained carriage. Having been thought a prostitute approximates being one. This forces her to "reflect" on the strange providence—"a kind of miracle"—that rescues her from "irrecoverable ruin." Though not publicly disgraced, Betsy suffers private shame—a personal fall that is compressed into her "fit of humiliation." Like Crusoe ruminating on his physical and moral shipwrecks, Betsy compares her encounter with the rake to a physical fall that signifies a spiritual misstep.

A Good Man Is Hard to Find

Comprising a feminocentric version of Defoe's male journeys, Betsy's continual approach to and retreat from the precipice defines the spiritual conditions of a woman's experience in eighteenth-century fictional worlds. Though entirely secularized and sexualized, the multiple contacts with male rapacity, beyond the reassuring confines of home, represent a kind of religious event in which providence intervenes. What shocks Betsy the most is that her salvation comes about through the "meer mercy of a man, who was a perfect stranger to her." For in this, as in all other instances, she must either be prepared to kill herself (as Pamela and Clarissa are) or rely on the generosity of a man in order to avoid ruin. The mercies of men thus reflect the powerlessness of women, and more important, suggest that the moral conscience of men, not the actions of women, regulate female providence. However, though action and instigation always lie with the male, women are assigned negative agency for "encouraging" the immoral actions of men. In this way, the rapist (and frequently the law) justifies his assault; this reasoning re-encodes masculine myths of potency and "activity" yet finds that active blame resides in the passive (and usually desiring) victim.[7] Unlike Crusoe, Haywood's representative woman must base her adventures on a sequence of human interventions that decrease, rather than increase, her sense of personal resourcefulness, and align salvation and moral development with passive resistance.

The confrontation with the rake, however, is not the only dire result of Betsy's attendance at the play. It also ends Trueworth's marital suit, despite his abiding love for Betsy: "His good sense, however, at last convinced him, that as no solid happiness could be expected with a woman of miss Betsy's temper, he ought to conquer his passion for her" (2: 132). Employing his own reason to control his passion he discovers that his rationality—and his true worth—cannot be matched by hers. When Betsy fails to demonstrate her good sense at the theater she forfeits her right to an auspicious marriage and model family life with Trueworth, revealing a constitutional weakness that is reflected in the transitoriness of her lovers: "It was the fate of miss Betsy to attract a great number of admirers, but never to keep alive, for any length of time, the flame she had inspired them with.—Whether this was owing to the inconstancy of the addressers, or the ill conduct of the person addressed, cannot absolutely be determined; but it is highly probable, that both these

motives might sometimes concur to the losing her so many con-
quests" (2: 195). Originally, Trueworth is merely one among Betsy's
"plurality of lovers," but the more he establishes himself as a prospect of true worth (both in a moral and an economic sense), the
more Betsy appreciates his superior merit. The ascension of his
value in her eyes, however, coincides with the depreciation of her
eligibility in his. As he declares, after being falsely convinced that
Betsy is secretly maintaining an illegitimate child, a marriage with
such a woman is "quite out of the question" (2: 206). Ending his
courtship with Betsy in a letter, he decides to retire to his country
seat and "lose the remembrance of all that had been displeasing to
him since he left it" (2: 208). Ironically, at the very moment in
which Trueworth seeks oblivion and finality, Betsy consoles herself
with speculating about romantic and domestic possibilities with
him:

While mr. Trueworth was employing himself in exploring the truth of
miss Betsy's imaginary crime, and hunting after secrets to render her more
unworthy of his love, that young lady's head was no less taken up with
him, though in a widely different manner;—she wanted not a just sense of
the merits, both of his person and passion; and though a plurality of lovers,
the power of flattering the timid with vain hopes, and awing the proudest
into submission, seemed to her a greater triumph, than to be the wife of
the most deserving man on earth, yet when she consulted her heart, she
found, and avowed within herself, she could part with that triumph, with
less reluctance in favour of mr. Trueworth, than of any other she yet had
seen. (2: 209)

The variance between Betsy's and Trueworth's perceptions of each
other is, of course, a stock component of romantic narrative, one of
the necessary obstructions that temporarily blocks the denouement
of the lovers' "engagement" and provides the requisite misunder-
standings, confusions, and hindrances that constitute plot and that
delay the representation of family life while always seeming to move
inexorably toward it. Moreover, the symmetry produced by the
protagonists' diametric progression in each other's estimation both
creates and threatens narrative balance and makes their unity at the
end seem that much more imperative.[8]

The seemingly irrevocable nature of Trueworth's decision to abandon Betsy is, of course, substantiated by his marriage to Harriot (which concludes the third volume and marks the crucial climax—or crisis—of the narrative). Almost a precise reversal of the theater scene, Betsy accidentally witnesses the post-wedding procession from a hidden "hallway" on a visit to her brothers in Golden Square, having heard of the match only moments before (which news almost makes her lose consciousness). Unlike her own condition at the theater, the "spectacle she was to be presented with" (3: 285) in Golden Square denotes the acceptable public nature of Trueworth's relationship with Harriot (as opposed to the disreputable one of Betsy's suitors). Rather than creating theater, he creates family—in a golden square, no less. Indeed, in almost all respects, hero and heroine are contrasted. Whereas Trueworth spies on Betsy intentionally, she happens suddenly upon his public "spectacle." Whereas his invisibility is the result of a conscious decision to disguise himself, her hidden presence at the procession denotes an unconscious self-abnegation. When she ascends to visit her brothers moments later, a noticeable "paleness, mixed with a certain confusion" appears in her countenance, despite her prior assertions that "all is over" and that "he has long since been lost to me, nor did I love him" (3: 287, 286–87). Rather than use rational thought to overcome passion, as he has, she represses knowledge. Where he employs thought, she indulges thoughtlessness. Moreover, in contrast to her debased social status at the theater, Trueworth's "spectacle" manifests his superior social standing. Like Betsy, we are made painfully aware of how worthy a match he is when the narrator describes the wedding party in rich detail.[9] This material substantiation of his "true worth" adds to her mortification: she has "an opportunity of seeing much more than she desired" (3: 286). It is a moment very like Elizabeth Bennet's examination of Pemberley in Jane Austen's *Pride and Prejudice*: both scenes manifest the extent of the heroine's lost opportunity to create a morally and materially enriching home.

By observing Trueworth's marriage from the wings, as it were, Betsy experiences at a remove what is, after all, an event of central importance to her happiness (whether she admits it or not). That distance is, in part, what makes it so effective as a form of mortification. Indeed, the entire encounter is set up as a fatal act, because of both its coincidental nature and its lethal consequences: "It seemed as if fate interested itself in a peculiar manner, for the mortification of this young lady;—every thing contributed to give her the most poignant shock her soul could possibly sustain:—it was not enough that she had heard the cruel tidings of what she looked upon as the greatest of misfortunes, her eyes must also be witness of the stabbing confirmation" (3: 285). Read in a religious context, this passage verifies the heroine's sanctity. To be a witness on this particular occasion is to suffer a "shock" to the "soul." Saintly martyrdom, along with its physical punishment (metaphorically reproduced here by a "stabbing confirmation") is transcribed to the secular condition of a woman's search for marital transcendence. Both the sordid encounter with the gentleman-rake and the ensuing loss of Trueworth's attentions emphasize the domestic ideology underlying Betsy's history. The more she betrays conventions of courtship and sexual propriety, the more she endangers her marital opportunities; the more she endangers her marital opportunities, the more she acquires a substantial respect for them. If Betsy seems to experience her affliction as if it were part of someone else's prescripted drama, it is because, having no settled character, she is split between competing models of female behavior.

The relationship between Betsy's failure to maintain Trueworth's interest and her best offer of marriage is reinforced by the events following his departure and the death of Mr. Goodman. Alone, and vowing that love is "a ridiculous thing" (3: 7), Betsy encourages the attentions of Sir Frederick Fineer and Mr. Munden solely for her own amusement, thinking she can manage her affairs without help from family and friends. But when Fineer proves to be a "valet de chambre" merely posturing as a gentleman of fortune and tries first to trap Betsy into marriage and then to rape her, Betsy's brothers successfully pressure her into marrying Munden, who eventually proves to be a tyrannical husband. By rejecting the appropriate conventions of courtship she thus projects herself into a marriage of convenience. Having failed to affirm the ideology of marriage in the first place, Betsy's punishment is symbolized by a marriage that reminds her constantly of her ideological shortcomings.

The brothers justify their pressure to marry off Betsy on the grounds of their sister's prior history of endangerment, evidently assuming that only marriage will protect her from future assaults. Pointing out the "perpetual dangers to which, through the baseness of the world, and her own inadvertency, she was liable every day to be exposed" (3: 230), they follow the advice of Goodman and urge Betsy to accept Mr. Munden. All the men in or concerned with the Thoughtless family thus agree that only marriage will save Betsy both from the world and from herself. Even the narrator observes that dangers arise when Betsy is "left entirely to her own management" (2: 233), and Lady Trusty is forced to concur: she tells Betsy, "[you] are but too much mistress of yourself" (2: 54). Francis Thoughtless regards marriage, moreover, as the only means to contain and correct Betsy's dangerous inclinations. Referring to her near disastrous encounter with Fineer, he describes Betsy's character in the conventional terms of female intransigence: "'If she were either a fool,' said he, stamping with extremity of vexation, 'or of a vicious inclination, her conduct would leave no room for wonder;— but for a girl, who wants neither wit nor virtue, to expose herself in this manner, has something in it inconsistent!—unnatural!—monstrous!'" (3: 203). Francis assumes that marriage, any marriage, will adequately structure and channel female deviance. His list of adjectives reflects how far removed a woman is from rational male ideals when she fails to employ "wit" (reason) and "virtue" (chastity): she becomes inconstant, unnatural, and monstrous.

Marriage and family are thus conceived as natural means for persuading women to act in opposition to their desire; in the process, marriage becomes both a regulative institution and a corrective one and, according to narrative logic—whereby Betsy's misconduct leads not only to the missed opportunity with Trueworth but to the mortifying union with Munden encouraged by her own family—a punitive one. The brothers, and Francis in particular, represent a conventional, and somewhat outmoded, eighteenth-century view that

family considerations and the sanctity of marriage outweigh wom-
en's individual choice and concern.[10] The brothers understand that,
as Thomas Thoughtless notes, "the honour of a family depended
greatly on the female part of it" (3: 18), and they are deeply concerned with protecting that honor. Again, Lady Trusty grudgingly
agrees, adding to the disapproving chorus of male voices her confirming female voice: "though she laid the blame of her ill-conduct
chiefly on her having lived so long under the tuition and example of
a woman, such as lady Mellasin; yet she could not but allow there
was a certain vanity in her composition, as dangerous to virtue, as to
reputation, and that marriage was the only defence for both" (4: 11).
Betsy's wildness, it would seem, can only be contained and thus
eradicated in a house ruled by a husband.

Betsy herself is not without the powers or acumen to decode the
false behavior of her "mixed company" and the corrupting influences that threaten her well-being, but she continually misdirects
her abilities and, as a result, finds herself repeatedly in compromising situations. On four occasions she barely escapes being raped, and
on each occasion her distress derives from some observable indiscretion on her part. Not only has she failed to be discreet in a world
where, as her brother crudely puts it, "a woman brings less dishon-
our upon a family, by twenty private sins, than by one public indiscretion" (3: 109), she also fails to make proper distinctions. The fascination for the reader lies in watching her teeter on the verge of
moral collapse. Unlike either the unregenerate Miranda of Behn's
The Fair Jilt or the female idols of compunction populating the
works of Richardson and Fielding, Betsy assumes a transitory character—she suffers, as the narrator observes, from "a fluctuating
mind." The aim of the book, in part, is to rationalize the heroine's
amatory latitude and resituate her in a proper romantic economy.
Consequently, when she finally recognizes her faults toward the end
of the narrative she observes how they controvert principles of reason and enlightenment. It is her awakening, an Austenian moment
of climactic insight, conversion, alarming self-disgust, and mortification of pride:

In fine, she now saw herself, and the errors of her past conduct in their true light:—"How strange a creature have I been!" cried she, "how inconsistent with myself! I knew the character of a coquet both silly and insignificant, yet did every thing in my power to acquire it:—I aimed to inspire awe and reverence in the men, yet by my imprudence emboldened them to the utmost unbecoming freedoms with me:—I had sense enough to discern real merit in those who profest themselves my lovers, yet affected to treat most ill those, in whom I found the greatest share of it.—Nature has made me no fool, yet not one action of my life has given any proof of common reason. (4: 159–60)

This important passage is flooded with Enlightenment sentiment. Seeing her coquetry as Trueworth saw it at the theater, in its "true light," Betsy presumably encounters her "authentic" self, the one that has for so long given no "proof" of existence. Recognizing how her actions have obstructed natural patterns of courtship—in which those who genuinely "merit" passion receive it—she finally observes that "common reason" best manages the promptings of desire. This pivotal insight, consequently, not only mortifies her but also gives birth to a new enlightened self. It is the revelatory moment (common to spiritual autobiography and bildungsroman alike) in which the protagonist discovers her natural reason and in which consciousness triumphantly replaces thoughtlessness. It is the moral revelation that regenerates Betsy for the task that her society assumed was the proper one for women to undertake, creating and maintaining a home.

The Injurious Husband

Having thus mortified the heroine into a proper estimation of matrimony, the narrative then proceeds to deconstruct the institutional validity of the domestic sphere. When Betsy at last agrees to marry Mr. Munden for what we are encouraged to regard as altogether misguided reasoning ("since my marriage is a thing so much desired by those, to whose will I shall always be ready to submit" [4: 15]), she succumbs to family pressure in a manner that the context (and Munden's vapidity) clearly argues against. Though voiced by

an "inconsistent" woman, Betsy's ruminations about her family's
tactics imply a resilient opposition to the conventional principles
she accepts for the sake of maintaining family consensus: "One has
no sooner left off one's bib and apron, than people cry,—'Miss will
soon be married.'—And this man, and that man, is presently picked
out for a husband.—Mighty ridiculous!—they want to deprive us of
all the pleasures of life, just when one begins to have a relish for
them" (4: 24). From depending too little on the advice of family and
friends, Betsy shifts to depending on them entirely too much. "Even
in the greatest, and most serious affair of life—that of marriage," she
later laments, "have I not been governed wholly by caprice!" (4:
160). Though she assumes the blame here, the caprice stems as much
from her family's thoughtlessness as from hers. As if to affirm the
dangers of this mistake, Betsy prognosticates the future with Munden in her "splenetic" dreams: "sometimes she imagined herself
standing on the brink of muddy, troubled waters;—at others, that
she was wandering through deserts, overgrown with thorns and bri-
ars; or seeking to find a passage through some ruin'd building,
whose tottering roof seemed ready to fall upon her head, and crush
her to pieces" (4: 24). Reminding us of Betsy's forlorn cry about
Goodman's deserted home, the combined imagery of wilderness and
house here foreshadows the domestic ruin to which Munden inevitably conducts her. The muddied river, the vast deserts, and the
crumbling mansion (however much they anticipate the thrills of
gothic and romantic literature) denote the dysphoric implications of
her marriage to a man she neither loves nor esteems. When she
should be dreaming of constructing the proverbial happy home,
Betsy has nightmares about obscure or unruly landscapes and buildings that crumble away in the dark. Her marital future portends not
the self-affirming joys of conduct-book domesticity but the violent
annihilation of self. In part also, these "gloomy representations" record the passivity of her decision to marry Munden; as in life, where
her family decides the course of her romantic experience, so in her
dreams external forces beyond her control seem to determine her
fate. Mostly, however, the dream sequence predicts the disastrous
consequences of what the family dictates. Even her abstract criti-

cisms of marriage foretell Betsy's specific future with Munden: "'I wonder,' continued she, 'what can make the generality of Women so fond of marrying?—It looks to me like an infatuation.—Just as if it were not a greater pleasure to be courted, complimented, admired, and addressed by a number, than be confined to one, who from a slave becomes a master, and, perhaps, uses his authority in a manner disagreeable enough'" (4: 23–24). This is, of course, precisely what happens to Betsy. Representing the "generality of Women," she regards women's anticipated subjection through marriage and family pressure as a social delusion specifically aimed at confirming patriarchal pretensions. The reader, already privy to Munden's authoritarian notions of marriage—which allow him to submit before the wedding "to every thing his tyrant should inflict, in the hope, that it would one day be his turn to impose laws" (2: 228)—is urged to regard Betsy's pleasure-seeking as an extension of a real political desire to challenge oppressive legal codes.

Munden's domestic tyrannies increase exponentially as time passes. The first indications of his autocratic behavior occur when he argues with Betsy about the keeping of servants and equipage. As with all later domestic costs, Munden seeks to retrench the domestic economy in those areas that affect Betsy's comforts and expectations while preserving expenses that support his customary habits. What the narrator calls Munden's "parsimonious" attitude toward housekeeping reveals retentive habits for which one of Defoe's protagonists would be commended, but which for Haywood indicate an impoverished spirit. The conflict between husband and wife on this issue explodes finally into an angry confrontation over the suitable use of Betsy's pin money (Munden wants her to pay for pantry necessities and personal servants out of her pocket, even though he controls the substantial financial resources that legally pass from her to him through their marriage).[11] This, in turn, leads to perhaps the narrative's most shocking domestic event, when Munden dashes out the brains of Betsy's pet squirrel during an argument over unnecessary domestic costs: "'Here is one domestic, at least, that may be spared'" (4: 61). His act of displacement, where the squirrel denotes the servants that, in turn, represent his wife, indicates how brutally he yokes wifehood with servitude. Betsy recognizes that Munden's violence here masks a desire to assault her, which is barely checked by his fear of social reprisals: "the bloody and inhuman deed being perpetrated by this injurious husband, merely in opposition to his wife, and because he knew it would give her some sort of affliction, was sufficient to convince her, that he took pleasure in giving pain to her, and also made her not doubt, but he would stop at nothing for that purpose, provided it were safe, and came within the letter of the law" (4: 63–64). Betsy's recognition of Munden's domestic sadism leads her eventually to vow "that she would never eat, or sleep with him again" (4: 62). Without exonerating Betsy's coquetry, Haywood suggests that automatic assumptions about marriage's utopian capacity to protect and correct women are equally delusive. Indeed, the concluding volume of the work criticizes arranged wedlock by focusing on the heroine's disastrous marriage, rather than on the domestic failure of the various minor characters who have served as foils. That is, the narrative pointedly shifts from the relapses of the female subject to the shortcomings of cultural forces that are meant to instruct her.

The pomposity of Munden (whose mundane name accentuates the links in the narrative between a character's actions, personality, and nomenclature) corresponds to the kind of house he creates. It is a place Betsy likens to "an Egyptian bondage" (4: 47). Punning ruefully on the word "wedlock," she draws on the imprisoning implications of marriage to describe her relationship with her "domestic tyrant" (4: 182). Later she compares this marriage to a "fall": "And into what an abyss of wretchedness am I now plunged!—Irretrievably undone, married without loving or being loved, lost in my bloom of years to every joy that can make life a blessing" (4: 252). Like Goodman's house, Betsy's connubial home becomes a wilderness, both existentially bleak and morally chaotic, as Munden commits acts of violence, seems to encourage the prostitution of his wife to an influential lord for pecuniary reasons, and commits adultery with a manipulative French woman whom Betsy has naively sheltered in their home.

While domestic life with Munden constitutes Betsy's final and worst mortification, and although it occurs partly as a result of her own behavioral lapses, it chiefly represents the dismal failure of male forms of familial pressure. Thus, when Munden kills Betsy's pet squirrel (which, to add further insult to injury, is an old gift from Trueworth), he reveals the latent violence that the family unwittingly sanctions and that Haywood seems to ascribe to patriarchy. The killing of the courtship gift becomes a symbolic murder of Betsy's days as a playful maid. Even though Munden's violence is exposed, Betsy's family initially attempts to reconcile the estranged pair for the sake of reputation, at the expense of Betsy's happiness. When Betsy complains of Munden's "low" and "groveling" mind and threatens to "separate" from him, Lady Trusty (Betsy's "second mother") warns her "not to think, nor talk in this fashion" and asks her to "consider how odd a figure a woman makes, who lives apart from her husband" (4: 68). Apart from paralleling in tantalizing ways the popularized "life" of Haywood herself, who supposedly "eloped" from her husband at the age of twenty-eight and lived separately from him for the rest of her life, the family's response to Betsy's misery reflects the limited resources available to a disaffected wife in the eighteenth century. However justifiable the complaint, or however willing the woman was to forfeit her estate to the husband, both legal prescriptions and public opinion essentially "outlawed" those who sought separation from their husbands.[12]

The marriage to and separation from Munden—in some senses, the most provocative and radical element of Haywood's text—sharpens Betsy's sense of how different her marriage is from what marriage ought to have been. The scenes following the squirrel incident compose a harrowing portrait of unhappy marriage. No longer a reflection of the heroine's vacuousness, the household serves, like the negative examples of behavior frequently introduced in the conduct literature, to emphasize the cruelties of misapplied patriarchal authority and Filmerian logic. As Munden bluntly observes, dismissing all rational evidence that the meanness of their home is owing to his parsimony and not to Betsy's "want of management" (4: 44), a wife is "no more than an upper servant, bound to study and obey, in all things, the will of him to whom she had given her hand" (4:

60). Calling her "a bad oeconomist" (4: 43), Munden reveals the very pragmatic basis of marriage and the tendency for it to shed its romantic luster in the light of conflicting views over "economy" and "management." When Munden suggests that Betsy use her "pin money" to purchase domestic necessities so as to allow him to "retrench somewhere" (4: 42), he not only betrays a legal contract but also challenges her matrimonial self-definition. As the narrator points out, "Nothing can be more galling to a woman of any spirit, than to see herself at the head of a family without sufficient means to support her character" (4: 43). Munden's retrenchment is Betsy's effacement; as long as he asserts his economic privilege, she can no longer maintain her "character."

This struggle for limited power finally becomes the focus of Betsy's marital experience. It reaches an irreversible point of conflict when Munden prefers the household authority of the "base" French woman, Mademoiselle de Roquelair, to the marital authority invested in Betsy. Initially, the confrontation between the women occurs when Betsy, attempting to make Roquelair leave the house, provokes an argument about household power and the women's triangular relation to the man who owns the home: "'You will not turn me out of doors?' cried mademoiselle de Roquelair.—'I hope you will not oblige me to an act, so contrary to my nature,' replied mrs. Munden.—'Say rather contrary to your power,' returned that audacious woman, and coming up to her with the most unparalleled assurance, 'This house, which you forbid me,' pursued she, 'I think mr. Munden is the master of, and I shall therefore continue in it till my convenience call me from it, or he shall tell me I am no longer welcome'" (4: 222–23). Once more, Betsy's relation to a house expresses how she conceives herself socially. Possession over domestic space, in this particular instance, implies self-possession. When that dissolves in the face of Roquelair's audacity, Betsy's only recourse is to seek retribution from the "genuine" master of the house. Turning to her husband she says, "I hope . . . you will do me that justice which every wife has a right to expect, and convince that French hypocrite, that I am too much the mistress of this house for any one to remain in it without my permission" (4: 224). When he fails to substantiate her "rights" and her authority, she can no longer regard herself as the appropriate mistress of the house. And as she has no recognizable status or identity within it, she becomes a "feme covert" in the most literal of ways—she vanishes. Assuming that Munden's behavior can only signify a "criminal correspondence" with Mademoiselle Roquelair, she quits the house and begins legal action for separating from him. If in Behn's fiction carnal and marital women are not insistently separated, in Haywood (as in Richardson), there is a problematic demarcation, a specialization of sexual labor in which the married woman exiles either herself or the concupiscent other, while fully recognizing the latent capacity for carnal behavior in herself. She consciously chooses to limit her access to a public world teeming with irresponsible women. Implicit in Haywood's depiction of Betsy, however, is the conviction that the domestic woman should supplant those carnal women who, like Roquelair, prey on marriages by channeling, rather than disowning, their own sexual identity.

The language of "rights," "power," and "mastery" in this triangular exchange suggests that the political dimension of domestic power evolves out of the preceding economic concerns that have shaped Betsy's marriage to Munden. Betsy discovers Munden's infidelity after, and as a result of, his dismissive attitude toward her household authority. Not surprisingly, then, Betsy's justification for leaving Munden involves contractual language: "'Neither divine, nor human laws,' said she, 'nor any of those obligations by which I have hitherto looked upon myself as bound, can now compel me any longer to endure the cold neglects, the insults, the tyranny of this most ungrateful—most perfidious man.—I have discharged the duties of my station; I have fully proved I know how to be a good wife, if he had known how to be even a tolerable husband'" (4: 226). How to be a dutiful wife or a tolerable husband (apparently, the minimum requirements for a functioning society) is here presented in the context of political belief. Betsy is able to justify her revolt because her knowledge of domestic conduct is superior to her husband's; her actions have been exemplary. By evincing her domestic capabilities (and thereby reminding us how deeply entrenched in conduct-book practice the narrative that describes her really is), she demonstrates that women must actively encode the moral and behavioral values that ostensibly justify bourgeois culture. Whereas the man must be merely "tolerable," the woman has to manifest a complete mastery of domestic ideology, synthesizing the roles of manager, teacher, and lover. And when husbands fail to adhere to their basic familial obligations—when they break contract and exclude their wives from domestic governance—they relinquish (or ought to) their rights to those women who are their potential saviors. That is, when patriarchy fails to observe the principles of enlightenment it should render itself obsolete, at least in the fantasy world of eighteenth-century fiction. In Haywood's narrative just such expectations are fulfilled: not only does Munden conveniently die before the Thoughtless family can bring legal action against him, he also begs forgiveness from his estranged wife. Betsy's demand to control private space (and lewd public intrusions upon it) or be contractually released from it suggests that the process of internalization in Haywood's story is, in some ways, much more dynamic and compelling than in *Pamela*, where the heroine's domestic virtue is already given and can be defended only in a private mock trial within the home.

A Good Husband Is Never Unseasonable

There are few, if any, examples before Wollstonecraft's heroines of a female character who actively separates from her husband and is both exonerated and wedded successfully to another man. Certainly no fiction by a male writer before the inception of the "Jacobin novel" considers the possibility.[13] Of course, Haywood cautiously emphasizes the magnitude of Betsy's decision; nonetheless, the story affirms the heroine's recourse to a legal action that was customarily derogated and that, in fact, required the husband's legal consent.[14]

To shield Betsy from moral judgment, Haywood reiterates the special circumstances that impel her separation from Munden. Despite Munden's derelict behavior, Betsy determines to observe her wifely duties as long as possible and anxiously wonders about the legitimacy of her decision to separate: "the violence of that passion, which had made her resolve to leave mr. Munden being a little evaporated, the vows she had made to him at the altar were continually in her thoughts;—she could not quite assure herself, that a breach of that solemn covenant was to be justified by any provocations; nor whether the worst usage on the part of the husband could authorize resentment in that of a wife" (4: 248). These reflections occur to her after Munden has already killed her pet squirrel, accused her unjustly of mismanaging the household finances, attempted to extort her pin money, tacitly supported Lord ****'s attempted rape, and committed adultery with a woman living in their own home. Such accumulated provocations are a sign, perhaps, of the extraordinary circumstances needed to justify a woman's bid for separation in eighteenth-century jurisprudence, even though the legal rights for it existed. To further indicate her devotion to domestic ideals, Betsy returns to her husband on his sickbed and comforts him in his last hours. She even dutifully observes a year of mourning after his sudden repentance and death. This suggests that the steps she takes to free herself from Munden, even when justified by his gross misconduct and by the eventual support of her family (she first finds "asylum" at her older brother's house), are barely acceptable to her. It suggests, further, that the double standard of female perfection and male tolerability in marriage severely restricted women's recourse to the legal actions that were ostensibly available to them.

Ultimately, fortuitous events like Munden's death, rather than judicial action, must save Betsy from her domestic wasteland. Haywood retreats, in other words, from the fully radical implications of making her heroine exploit legal resources to shift the balance of domestic power, relying instead on happenstance to resolve marital conflict. Similarly, Trueworth's sudden availability for remarriage (his wife having died four months after their wedding) substantiates the story's early avowal that "a good husband" can "never come unseasonably" (1: 142). Nevertheless, such happy coincidences occur only after a long period of mortification, both for the heroine and for the male advisers in her family. In the resolution, Trueworth conveniently returns to Betsy after all members of the Thoughtless

clan—not just the errant sister alone—have proven themselves fallible (though not fallen). The closing scenes have a resonant if improbable impact, because Trueworth now appears to be both the
family's choice and the heroine's preference. Everyone has been
duly corrected. The implication of the family's double incompe-
tence (neither family nor daughter seems to be able to make rational
choices) is that, conversely, both family and daughter must participate equally in the choice of husband. Seeking a rapprochement between authoritarian domestic politics and progressive doctrines
about marital choice, Haywood provides a compromise that critiques and exonerates institutional authority (in the form of the family) while it simultaneously critiques and exonerates democratic autonomy (in the figure of the heroine).

The History of Miss Betsy Thoughtless achieves this momentary balance by erasing noisy social exchange, and therefore female con-
tamination, within the home, not only reducing the heroine's plural
sexuality to monogamous relations but also making her increasingly
self-contained. A chastened Betsy directs her second courtship to
Trueworth through a series of formal letters during her year-long retreat at her aunt and uncle's estate in the country (what Trueworth
calls a "painful penance" [4: 586]). By merging in Betsy the carnal
woman and domestic ideologue, Haywood attempts to harness active female will to the supervision of family, avoiding Pamela's passive facilitation, Miranda's adulteration, and Crusoe's evasion of female domestic government. By internalizing household law in the
female subject, as a means both to solidify domestic ideology and to
incorporate narrative form and family structure, *The History of Miss
Betsy Thoughtless* also preserves patriarchy from its tendency to disgrace itself through brutal authoritarianism. Trying to solve the dilemma of Pamela's inert moral management, Haywood maneuvers a
woman's access to legal, social, and political action within an admittedly limited structure of self-determination. A woman's fall from
perfection, consequently, is that much more critically significant
than a man's. As Trueworth exclaims: "[the female sex] are endued
by nature with many perfections, which our's cannot boast of,—it is
their own faults when they sink beneath us in value;—but the best

things, when once corrupted, become the worst.—How dear, therefore, ought a woman prize her innocence!" (3: 269). On one hand,
Haywood's narrative seems to support this moral perspective, putting it in the mouth of the nearly infallible hero; on the other hand,
it appears to challenge the supposition of female culpability by repeatedly revealing the brute insensibilities of male ideology.

The four volumes constituting *The History of Miss Betsy Thoughtless* chart the heroine's labyrinthine progress from thoughtless youth
to mature womanhood; thus, each volume also becomes a significant
structural marker in the heroine's symbolic enactment of female experience. Beginning from the point of her homelessness, the work
describes a series of incidents (either involving or associated with
rape, each more dangerous than the one before) that build climacti-
cally toward the heroine's transcendent understanding of herself and
her place in a world that demands that she either obey the dictates
of marital conformity or suffer for her transgressions against them.
Each volume contains one attempted rape of the heroine. In the first
volume Betsy is accosted by a "gentleman-commoner" in one of the
public gardens of Oxford but is saved by the fortuitous arrival of
her brother Francis (who later engages the man in a near-fatal duel).
Volume 2 contains the near disastrous encounter with the gentleman-rake who joins Betsy at the theater. In the third volume, Betsy
nearly falls victim to the sham Sir Frederick Fineer until Trueworth
miraculously arrives to rescue her. In the final volume, Betsy narrowly escapes the violence of Lord ****, an influential man that her
husband, Mr. Munden, has been trying desperately to court, and to
whom her husband seems willing to make her virtue a sacrifice. In
each case Betsy confronts men of increasing social power; the dangers to her reputation consequently mount with each encounter. On
the first three occasions, instead of freeing herself, she must rely on
fortune, other men, or the compassion of her attacker to escape
"ruin"; it is only in the last episode with Lord **** that she finally
learns how to liberate herself, and it is only then that she seriously
takes responsibility for her actions, vowing never to be caught again
in compromising situations.[15] External male threats to her domestic

virtue thus evolve to the point where she must rely on her own internal resources of defense: her maturing thoughtfulness.

That so many eighteenth-century writers like Haywood organize their courtship narratives on patterns of threatened rape suggests that the domestic world these works ultimately affirmed was beset by complex forces working actively against it. It may be that repeated resistance to rape generates a form of intellectual recuperation, insofar as a narrative structured on patterns of obstructed violence safely delivers the reader from anxieties and fears and even, perhaps, illicit desires. It fulfills what Janice Radway refers to as the "need to read one's way out of a bad situation and to resolve or contain all of the unpleasant feelings aroused by it" (71).[16] Moreover, the recurrence of attempted rape sharpens the sense that marriage itself, by providing the correct mate, who will protect the distressed heroine from a world of male brutality, offers the only possible means of creating a safe world. Dramatizing the lurid consequences of illicit sexuality and indiscretions, prose narratives reinforce the ideological preeminence of marriage in bourgeois culture. Of course, this solution nullifies the woman's powers of self-determination and makes the rapist and the husband seem complicit figures in a sexual system that disposes female sexuality. As Radway notes: "Romantic violence may also be the product of a continuing inability to imagine any situation in which a woman might acquire and use resources that would enable her to withstand male opposition and coercion" (72). On the other hand, it is even possible that the frequent thwarting of rape, particularly when it occurs because of the heroine's courage or ingenuity, satisfies the reader's desire to witness female power in a situation that ordinarily denies it. "The romance may express misogynistic attitudes not because women share them but because they increasingly need to know how to deal with them" (72). In discussing the scandal material of which Haywood's early fiction is a preeminent example, John Richetti argues that "the seduction we are witnessing is the tragic conflict which female virtue is forever doomed to engage in with irresistible masculine evil. The mythology [of persecuted innocence] thus persistently evoked acts as a compensation for the erotic fantasy, a displacement, as it were, of the central task of the narrative to provide vicarious sexual pleasure" (21). Richetti links this opposition (and convergence) of female innocence and male rapacity to an ideological antithesis in the eighteenth century between the religious and the secular: "[the popular books of the period] resolve themselves into pictures of the embattled individual in a hostile and vicious world, and . . . dramatize the natural and spontaneous urgings of an inner spirit versus the mechanized and corruptly efficient institutions of the world" (21). In this light the anti-familial bias and semi-pornographic appearance of works like Haywood's serve as much to exonerate heroic female virtue and demean male conduct as to arouse (or safely vent) sexual desire in the reader.[17] In Haywood's narrative, Betsy's sexual encounters are associated with the development of thought itself. Each stage in her dawning awareness of propriety is signaled by a dangerous or manipulative act of male aggression. Since Betsy's increased "thoughtfulness" is coupled with her increased awareness of male rapacity, her history stems as much from male misconduct as from female "inadvertency" (1: 1). Significantly, all of her near rapes occur when she is away from home and unattended by a family member; and only in the last attempt, when she secures her own deliverance, is she a married woman, one who has finally internalized marital propriety (even despite her husband's cynical view of matrimony).

Similarly, on the narrative level, the book manages to titillate the reader with the possibility of the heroine's scandalous fall, all the while shaping her as a moral receptacle. In this respect, the work consciously shapes its own theory of narrative on the exemplary experiences of the female it is portraying. The narrator confirms this parallel when she describes the nature of her storytelling: "But I will not anticipate that gratification, which ought to be the reward of a long curiosity. The reader, if he has patience to go thro' the following pages, will see into the secret springs which set this fair machine in motion, and produced many actions, which were ascribed, by the ill-judging and malicious world, to causes very different from the real ones" (1: 11). This paragraph mirrors the heroine's life and narrative process in several ways. For one, given the context, it is not entirely clear whether "this fair machine" refers to Betsy or to the book itself. What makes the narrative a "fair machine" is intricately linked with what makes the heroine one. Furthermore, the narrator will not, like Betsy, "anticipate that gratification" of those who are most curious about what she has to say. Like the coquette, the story arouses desires (principally about what will happen) that are never gratified quite in the ways one is led to expect. It is also arguable that the narrator's suppression of knowledge here matches the moments of "thoughtlessness" by which the heroine allows her actions to be "ascribed, by the ill-judging and malicious world, to causes very different from the real ones." As the narrator notes, all "will be revealed in time; but it would be as absurd in a writer to rush all at once into the catastrophe of the adventures he would relate, as it would be impracticable in a traveller to reach the end of a long journey, without sometimes stopping at the inns in his way to it" (1: 11). Echoing Fielding's comparison of *Tom Jones* to a stagecoach journey and mimicking his self-conscious narrator, Haywood not only situates her writing in the "new" species of prose fiction but also relates such writing to the dynamics of seduction and deferral, storytelling, and didacticism.

Eighteenth-century prose fiction in general, like the specific "history" of Betsy's amorous experiences, adhered increasingly to just the same ideological accommodation, seeking to express its radical potential within traditional structures of belief that simultaneously authorize discreet amounts of resistance and check their tendency to become chaotic. Many of the sentimental and domestic (and even gothic) narratives that dominate the latter part of the century sponsor comforting myths of domesticity even while they explore marital tyranny and domestic anarchy. In many ways, then, *The History of Miss Betsy Thoughtless* is one of the best examples of the intimate relationship between prose fiction and the conduct book, and a significant instance of the shift from illicit to domestic narrative subjects. An amalgam of scandal chronicle, bildungsroman, roman à clef, and domestic fiction, it combines Behn's erotic ideology, Defoe's rapid plotting, Fielding's self-conscious narrator, and Richardson's dialogic intensity (and occasionally his epistolarity), while preserving Haywood's own contributions to the development of prose fiction (particularly in terms of structural efficiency).[18] By confirming and exploiting the inevitable tensions between fictional and didactic aims, it provides a technical synthesis that mediates the conduct book and prose fiction. Haywood's mature work, while capitalizing extensively upon prior narrative methodology, looks forward, perhaps even more effectively than the fiction of either Fielding or Richardson, to the accomplishments of Burney and Austen and the so-called "domestication of the novel." It records the increasing pressure on prose fiction to inculcate moral habits yet preserve the radical potential of female desire, as it exchanges the sexual wilderness of the scandal chronicle or amatory history for the regularities of domestic fictions and the proprieties of courtship narratives.

6

Disavowing Kinship, 1760-1798

All we can do, is to appeal to that undutiful urchin, posterity.
　　　　　　　　　　　　—Horace Walpole, *Correspondence*

It must have been observed by many a peripatetic philosopher,
That nature has set up by her own unquestionable authority
certain boundaries and fences to circumscribe the discontent of
man: she has effected her purpose in the quietest and easiest
manner by laying him under almost insuperable obligations to
work out his ease, and to sustain his sufferings at home.
　　　　　　　　　—Laurence Sterne, *A Sentimental Journey*

A man has been termed a microcosm; and every family might also
be called a state. States, it is true, have mostly been governed by
arts that disgrace the character of man and the want of a just
constitution, and equal laws, have so perplexed the notions of the
worldly wise, that they more than question the reasonableness of
contending for the rights of humanity. Thus morality, polluted in
the national reservoir, sends off streams of vice to corrupt the
constituent parts of the body politic; but should more noble, or
rather, more just principles regulate the laws, which ought to be
the government of society, and not those who execute them, duty
might become the rule of private conduct.
　　　—Mary Wollstonecraft, *A Vindication of the Rights of Woman*

Antecedents

In the four preceding chapters, I have argued that eighteenth-
century British prose fiction often charted the effect of the family
on the protagonist by either diminishing its direct moral influence
on individual consciousness or emphasizing its intimate and continuous contact with a burgeoning self. Examples of the first type,

Defoe's *Robinson Crusoe* and Behn's *Fair Jilt* use certain narrative patterns to document the marginalization of family in constructing a provisional identity that either resists social and institutional determinations of character or works to transmute family relations exclusively into political and economic ones. Both works resist utopian readings; closure is indefinite, and the fulfillment of individual desire remains merely potential or unutterable. While such narratives push family to the side, they do not, in the end, imagine a satisfying alternative domain. The forms of these narratives, the imaginary voyage and the scandal chronicle, dramatize the distance from which the family is regarded; but these forms are also invariably marked by metaphorical or institutional re-creations of the family. They return wearily to the sites of their initial withdrawal.

By contrast, the "legitimation" of the family as a model of narrative and personal relations explicitly shapes the discursive structures of Richardson's *Pamela* or Haywood's *Miss Betsy Thoughtless*. The very organizing units of these works—the "familiar letters" that Pamela specifically addresses to her parents and the chapters in Betsy's "history," whose titles underline the narrative and didactic purposes of the story—repeatedly remind the reader of the correlation between domesticity, narrative structure, and subjectivity. The ends of these stories are utopian only insofar as they align individual and institutional intent. It is not just that they contain, manage, or subsume desire within a conclusive family harmony such as Pamela's well-ordered domestic machine or Betsy's final connubial reward; it is that they make general categories of ideal social behavior emerge explicitly from the particular experience of solitary figures. The personal development of these characters over the course of a narrative, in turn, exposes an affinity to the family unity they seem to be themselves shaping. The domestic realm therefore constitutes an already established "happiness," to borrow Haywood's language, for which the protagonist must have "rendered herself wholly worthy of receiving" (594). While this process may appear circular in structure, individual characters are, in fact, working out a logic in their private lives that is coeval with, though not simply reducible to, developments in public norms of domestic conduct.

These narrative paradigms are, in other words, occasions for a more general appraisal of the shifting and problematic relationship between subjective agency and social determinacy. Collectively, they reveal some of the multiple and mobile tactics used in the eighteenth century to represent the effect of changes in how the family might be configured. They are speculative responses to a widespread cultural reassessment of kinship and affective behavior. John Zomchick has argued in *Family and the Law in Eighteenth-Century Fiction* that "[t]ogether the law and the eighteenth-century novel displace the subject from a contentious civil society to the newly emergent nuclear family, which is in turn represented as the natural home of the rational, pleasure-seeking individual" (10). According to Zomchick, this "double predication" (xii) serves to produce an internally coherent model of subjectivity necessary to reconcile individuals (who must internalize juridical norms and then externalize them in their management of self and home) to what Foucault would consider the discursive strategies of power that work upon and through the individual subject.[1] I want to extend Zomchick's remarks to argue that between positioning the subject in the "newly emergent nuclear family" and characterizing that set of symbolic relations as "natural" lies an extended and mystifying process where the concerted historical marketing of an intimate family sphere makes that domain seem self-evident, antecedent, and innate. On the one hand, because this process occurs very gradually in a wide variety of representational events—such as conduct books, domestic prose fiction, sermons on household matters, family portraits, new marriage legislation and divorce settlements, architectural advances in household privacy, sentimental family drama, and the popularization of maternal breast-feeding—the blurring of what is natural and coherent with what is socially determined and diffuse can seem invisible since it is, in a sense, present everywhere. On the other hand, the act of internalization that Zomchick describes signals the subject's indispensable need to participate in a "coherent" process that might otherwise reveal too blatantly how much the individual is merely the heterogeneous bearer of various structures of social signification. What these complementary processes obscure is that social life is so complex and changeable, so connected to shifting historical conditions, that individuals require imaginary models of its presumed coherence, usually in the form of comprehensible fragments of a whole culture. Individual subjects may need those models, as well, to fashion their own sense of internal uniformity; given such models, one need not acknowledge the provisional, multiple, and sometimes contradictory nature of one's own personal identity. What I am claiming, therefore, is that the "coherent" stories that shape social and personal relations are frequently at odds both with each other *and* with the individual and institutional events that ostensibly produce them.

The narratives I examine in this final chapter confront this double bind directly. They speculate on what occurs when a fictional subject explicitly recognizes his or her divided state in the face of a family that is also impossibly unruly. Does the world consequently become unassimilable? Narratives of this kind employ a third mode for narrating the relation between a singular self and its original family: the disavowal of kinship. Here, the omnipresence of the family in both social and narrative formation is acknowledged, even by resistant characters, but is simultaneously made to seem restrictive and incurable. Texts such as *The Castle of Otranto*; *The Life and Opinions of Tristram Shandy, Gentleman*; and *The Wrongs of Woman: or, Maria* repeatedly create situations in which self and family are utterly irreconcilable and yet inevitably joined. These works, unlike those in which the diegetic force of the family is pushed to the margins or those where it plays a central role through the legitimation of domestic discourse, are characterized by metaphoric or discursive fragmentation. That is, the formal and thematic character of the narrative parallels the inevitable ruptures in personal and household relations that the author aligns with social practice. In such narratives, the writer avows the seemingly inescapable coupling of family and narrative paradigms but emphasizes their mutual disruption. Instead of internalized coherence between individual consciousness and social commonality, we see a simultaneous ransacking of self and family.

"Some Strange Revolution": Household Disorder in 'The Castle of Otranto'

Gothic literature is perhaps most famous for its historical trans-figuration of eighteenth-century family relations into objects of terror and melancholy.[2] As in much sentimental fiction, the purpose is to saturate the domestic sphere with special emotional significance and prevent it from being reduced to the wholly rational form usually advocated in the conduct books.[3] In *The Castle of Otranto* (1764), for example, a mysterious principle of household possession produces an equally baffling change in object relations. An obscure ancient prophecy, *"That the castle and lordship of Otranto should pass from the present family, whenever the real owner should be grown too large to inhabit it"* (15–16), is manifested in the current "house of Manfred" through the strange mutation of domestic artifacts. An ancestral portrait descends from its canvas; a statue is brought to life and roams the household; the castle itself groans and sighs. This incarnation of common objects is particularly disturbing because it converts familiar surroundings into alien territory; domestic space becomes the site of ruptures in the individual's sense of belonging.[4]

Such instances of objectification and defamiliarization in *The Castle of Otranto* were, as it turns out, the moments that did indeed electrify eighteenth-century readers. As an enthralled Thomas Gray wrote to Walpole when the book first appeared, "It engages our attention here, makes some of us cry a little, and all in general afraid to go to bed o' nights" (*Walpole's Correspondence*, 14, pt. 2: 137). In 1789 the first Lord Stanley, as reported by his sister, claimed that a party reading the narrative on a foggy atmospheric boat trip through the Faroe Islands were "sorry to leave off the story before we knew to whom the great enchanted helmet belonged" (65). The dramatic versions of Walpole's story, Robert Jephson's *The Count of Narbonne* (1781), Miles Peter Andrews's *The Enchanted Castle* (1786), which appeared later as *The Mysteries of the Castle* (1795), and Matthew Lewis's *The Castle Spectre* (1797), repeatedly dwell on the ancestral portrait that descends from its frame to pester the members of the household and generally disrupt domestic order. As late as

1811, Walter Scott was still marveling at the "manner in which the various prodigious appearances, bearing each upon the other, and all upon the accomplishment of the ancient prophecy, denouncing the ruin of the house of Manfred, gradually prepare us for the grand catastrophe. The moon-light vision of Alfonso dilated to immense magnitude, the astonished group of astonished spectators in the front, and the shattered ruins of the castle in the back-ground, is briefly and sublimely described" (96). In these remarks we glimpse what may have made the gothic so compelling to enlightenment culture, its deracination of family structure. As Scott suggests, the disclosure of the home transforms those who watch into estranged spectators. By representing the relation of past to present through the cumulative effect of family relics that assume the appearance of vast animated objects, Walpole envisions historical shifts in domestic behavior not as a triumph of progressive clarification but as a shattering reversal of temporal and aesthetic order. Although the gothic reconstructs a time of powerful affective energy among family members, it always regards that emotional intensity as a receding historical fact. At the same time, preserved in objects that literally become larger than life, family history transcends the future it is supposed to validate; the more it grows in symbolic stature the more it diminishes the contemporary subjects who watch its astonishing mythic expansion.

The violent dislocation of ancestral portraits, statuary, and architecture in the gothic to represent the impact of dead relations on living ones marks the extent to which the image of kinship, in both its historical and contemporary forms, has, like Oliver Goldsmith's unruly "family piece" in *The Vicar of Wakefield*, become an uncontrollable element of private as well as public history. Critics have long observed the scrupulous treatment of historical reconstruction in *The Castle of Otranto*, often focusing on the same fragmentary images that fascinated Walpole's contemporary readers. Scott's impression of the book, for instance, was based in part on his admiration for "the singular attention to the costume of the period in which the scene was laid" (92). Walpole's remaking of medieval culture, however, is also a reverie about the unmaking of historical meaning. In

Otranto, one's forebears are colossal, broken, and ghostly; they have ruptured the boundaries of the body, of totalization, and of life expectancy; they become the immaterial referents of a harrowing but obsolete set of material signs. As representatives of a dead past, preserved in art, they have a palpable solidity; but as contemporaries they escape the limits of art and enter into the lived relations of their distant progeny. In the present, they assume the form of radically unstable figures whose images become dilated, spectralized, and fragmentary.

The moments of contact between uncanny ancestors and living family members are thus impelled by an impossible yearning to communicate with the past, or, in Walpole's words, to "live back into centuries that cannot disappoint one" (*Walpole's Correspondence*, 10, pt. 2: 192). Such encounters are therefore almost invariably marked by silence and obstruction. They are scenes of aborted affiliation. When the large portrait of Otranto's original usurper, Don Ricardo, detaches itself from the castle wall and walks mournfully into an inner chamber while beckoning to his grandson Manfred, the latter follows in "anxiety and horror" until an invisible hand claps shut the door that separates the two figures (24). As with all the other phantasms that stalk Otranto, Don Ricardo seems to invite a dialogue between the dead and the living. But his purpose is instead to signal the impediments, mysteries, silences, and gaps that lie between "history" and its offspring. Dislocated from his semiotic context, Don Ricardo is converted into a mute and partial sign of hereditary sorrow and guilt, a parody of accurate historical detail. In a narrative that seeks to reconstruct the past in the rational light of the present, Ricardo stands as a mournful reminder that cherished fragments of history often become evidence of one's misperceptions about lived experience. Signs are given, but are understood only after the events they herald are irrevocably past. Symbolic language is suffused with mystery, and even a kind of sad majesty, but it is also superfluous, expending itself without either the hope or the intention of making sense.

We are thus confronted by a rift between two kinds of history, the experiential and the archeological, a distinction that is clearly important to Walpole (otherwise the spectral figures would simply appear, like the ghost of Hamlet's father, separate from a complicating secondary realm of symbolic reproduction). It is never clear, in fact, whether the ghosts in Otranto are the spirits of the real ancestors or merely specters emanating from the artistic re-creation of Otranto's precursors, forms twice removed from their original embodiment. They objectify strong emotions—violent anger and profound melancholy—that seem to be rooted in specific historical events, such as Alfonso's betrayal by Manfred's father, Don Ricardo. But these emotions are also strangely detached from their determining occasions, passing from the original actors through the objects representing them and into physically indeterminate projections of those images. As such, the emotions generated by the family scene become generalized responses to an ongoing domestic and political crisis that cannot be felt fully enough by the current generation without some spectral prodding. They provide a kind of permanent affective register for the family that transcends particular events, particular generations, even perhaps particular kin. Families must always be in a state of sublimated emotional contact with a domestic sphere that is both uniquely expressive and yet historically produced. Walpole may, in fact, be critiquing the tendency in late-eighteenth-century British culture to organize the family around precisely disposed signs by fetishizing the household object in such a way as to uncouple it from the system of meanings that customarily stabilizes it. Hence the silence, the breaking of symbols into component parts whose affective significance outweighs their semantic purpose, the mysterious closing of doors.

The unsettling effect of antiquarian objects in the household—what one of the servants calls "some strange revolution" (100)—is dramatized almost immediately by the notorious sequence that initiates the main action of Walpole's narrative. Here, history not only exerts its impact on the present through the violent displacement of a relic from the past; it also lays bare the unsuspected fragility of the present and then begins to wreak havoc on the spatial relations it is evidently supposed to restore. A helmet, reportedly from the large memorial statue in black marble of the usurped prince Alfonso the

Good, expands tenfold, turns to steel, and plummets mysteriously from above the castle's courtyard to kill Manfred's heir, Conrad, on the morning of his wedding and fifteenth birthday. The sudden changes in size, material, and location of the object imply a connected sequence of transformations in perceptual categories that customarily shape human understanding: material solidity, temporal succession, and spatial order are all defied. The helmet's immediate effect on the family is similarly disassociating. In the narrative's pervasive language of fragmentation, the son is "dashed to pieces, and almost buried" (17), as, of course, are the dynastic hopes of his father. By reviving history, it appears, one can radically change existing circumstances, alter domestic and political structures of control, even transform modes of empirical understanding.

Mediated through a domestic icon, family history is thus made a force at once mechanical in its inexorable administering of ancestral politics and arbitrary in its volatile and emotionally charged appearances. The death of Conrad is a powerful fissuring moment, interrupting perhaps the most evocative symbol of family unity and progress: a marriage. The martial imagery of the helmet, like almost all "strange phaenomena" that interrupt the lives of the central characters, suggests the dangerous capacity of the family's symbolized forms. At the beginning of the story, then, Walpole attributes to his apparitional objects the power to reinscribe history and use it to correct abuses from the past that continue to shape the present. The familiar past is made alien, divorced from the present; it thus forces the present into an estranged view of its own systems of order and compunction.

But just as the ghosts may be doubly removed from a historical referent, their promise of explosive action is, over the course of the story, similarly diminished, despite their frequent if erratic physical expansion. After its dramatic descent from the sky, for example, the helmet subsequently serves only to mark critical moments of human agency or intention, agitating its plumes whenever someone says or does something particularly significant. When a massive steel saber is later joined to the helmet, it demonstrates its signifying power through a similar shift from aggressive action to inertia: "the gigan-

tic sword burst from the supporters, and, falling to the ground opposite to the helmet, remained immovable" (63). (Manfred, becoming gradually "hardened to preternatural appearances," even begins
to ignore each "new prodigy," as if it was no different from other
tiresome idiosyncrasies of the household, like a noisy door or talka-
tive servant.) Ultimately, Alfonso's ghost (or the ghost of his monument) cannot find comfort in the house from which he is estranged
because his increasing conceptual bulk conflicts with his ultimate
purpose of reclaiming the "house" and restoring order. At one point,
the spirit, reverting to his original size, substance, and location, simply watches from his tomb in the church adjoining the castle and
quietly bleeds exactly three drops of blood from the nose (93).
There seems to be a rueful admission throughout Walpole's narrative that reasserting historical truth may alter the present but that it
can never reinstate the past.

Much of the narrative's despairing attitude toward history is
implicit in the dispirited behavior of the spirits haunting Otranto.
When Manfred's servants report their discovery of Alfonso's apparition in the "great chamber," they note that it is prostrate, visible
only in parts: "it is a giant, I believe; he is all clad in armour, for I
saw his foot and part of his leg, and they are as large as the helmet
below . . . we heard a violent motion and the rattling of armour, as
if the giant was rising; for Diego has told me since, that he believes
the giant was lying down, for the foot and leg were stretched at
length on the floor. Before we could get to the end of the gallery, we
heard the door of the great chamber clap behind us, but we did not
dare turn back to see if the giant was following us" (33). Though
dressed for battle, and evidently willing to kill (as Conrad's "man-
gled remains" attest), the apparition is most noteworthy for its melancholy disposition. It lies about the castle in untidy fragments,
slamming doors when impertinent servants intrude on its privacy,
rattling armor in peevish disgust and acting more like a shiftless dependent son than the stern retributive grandsire whose interests it is
supposed to represent. Though modeled after the ghost of Hamlet's
father, it behaves like the inactive hero of Elsinore, unwilling, as it
were, to pick up the pieces. Rather than a symbol of proper history

reasserting itself, it comes to represent a form of cultural inertia.

History as Walpole's characters experience it is thus a peculiar compound of social continuity, animistic rupture, and stagnation, creating moments of recognized kinship only to mourn them. On the one hand it strives to complete the telic structure of prophecy; on the other hand, it promotes a domestic turmoil that extends far into the future. Theodore, it turns out, exactly resembles his grandfather, and is himself mistaken for a supernatural embodiment of the paintings and statues of Alfonso, particularly when he is suited in armor. At one point, Manfred's daughter Matilda is amazed at the resemblance: "[D]o I dream? or is not that youth the exact resemblance of Alfonso's picture in the gallery?" (52). And Manfred is later staggered by Theodore's spectral appearance: "What, is not that Alfonso? cried Manfred: dost thou not see him? Can it be my brain's delirium?—This! my lord, said Hippolita: this is Theodore, the youth who has been so unfortunate—Theodore! said Manfred mournfully, and striking his forehead—Theodore, or a phantom, he has unhinged the soul of Manfred" (80). Characteristically, neither past nor present is stable. Personality appears mutable; nor can flesh and blood be entirely distinguishable from the artifactual forms to which history reduces them. A radical temporal inversion, in which the past solidifies as the present vanishes into it, reshapes not only the living family but also the history on which it is based. Domestic history is not simply a set of hidden facts that eventually reorder the narrative world but a body of images, stories, and pieces of evidence that are also transformed in time, obliterating an imagined future. Theodore enters the story as a peasant knowing nothing of his own royal patrilineage, but he is the first to recognize that the helmet belongs to the statue of Alfonso. By the end, he is the restored but crushed owner of Otranto, a castle whose walls have already begun to collapse from the strain of accommodating the spiritual revival of its scion.

The concluding vision of Alfonso, repossessed at last of his helmet, sword, leg, and foot, and rising up in full regalia to acknowledge Theodore as legitimate heir, is the culminating moment in a series of extravagant family reunions. Throughout *The Castle of Otran-*

to, Walpole builds a sequence of emotionally charged scenes in which parents and children suddenly recognize one another after periods of separation or misidentification. In every case, however, the reunion is immediately menaced by further separation, usually the threat of death. Friar Jerome (once the Count of Falconara) discovers that Theodore is his son by the mark of a bloody arrow exposed when the young man's shirt is loosened for execution. "Canst thou be unmoved," the father asks Manfred, "at such a scene as this?" (55). Similarly, the mysterious knight who challenges Manfred in the name of Duke Frederic (and is in fact Frederic) reveals himself as Isabella's father after being violently wounded in battle. "Oh! amazement! horror! what do I hear? what do I see? cried Isabella. My father! You my father!" (75). Perhaps the most dramatic instance of such recognition occurs when Manfred stabs his own daughter, thinking she is Isabella. This "accident" instantly converts Manfred's feelings for Matilda, toward whom he "never showed any symptoms of affection" (15), into paternal emotions so acute he tries to lay "violent hands on himself" (104). Matilda subsequently uses the event of her death to briefly establish the sentimental unity of the family that Manfred's actions have disrupted: "seizing his hand and her mother's, [she] locked them in her own, and then clasped them to her heart" (106). These are heightened moments of discovery, as if domestic relations were always disposed to such mysteries of attachment. Individuals not only relocate cherished relations, they rediscover themselves.

Almost every instance of domestic affiliation is thus constructed to amplify the affective thrill of parental bonds, as if intense family feeling could only be experienced in moments of extreme crisis. Family members are made strangers to one another, rejoined in moments of exquisite reunion, and then confronted immediately by loss in a dizzying spiral of emotional extremes. In each instance, the individual is reunited with his or her origins, but those origins have undergone an irrevocable change that makes the reconnection of domestic ties the prelude merely to a painful realization that all family relations are marked by irreversible historical disjunctions. What is remarkable about the popularity of the gothic is its implicit (though circumspect) objection that the new rhetoric of nuclear affect was in fact aimed at delimiting feeling and that the past rather than the future could best serve as a projection of the present urge to extol domestic affect. Using a past so distant that it could enliven household feeling without seeming to threaten contemporary domestic ideology, the gothic nonetheless opened to view the strangeness of advocating family affect while at the same time organizing it into economical public display. One contemporary observer considered parts of Walpole's narrative suitable guidance for the education of "young ladies": "a mother would surely be glad to select for her daughter such sentiments as may be met with in the mouths of that constellation of exalted characters, *Theodore, Hippolita, Matilda*, and *Jerome*." But such didactic purposes could only be adduced by selecting "interspersed" passages from the text, stripped of their alarming narrative context.[5]

Walpole understood, at the very least, that reverting to the past entailed both enchantments and hazards. The culminating recognition between a parent and child in *The Castle of Otranto*, Alfonso's public acknowledgment of Theodore, is also the most fully emblematic. Its symbolic preeminence is underlined by the fact that the apparition speaks for the first time at this instant and that he only now appears as a visible gargantuan totality: "The moment Theodore appeared, the walls of the castle behind Manfred were thrown down with a mighty force, and the form of Alfonso, dilated to an immense magnitude, appeared in the centre of the ruins. Behold in Theodore, the true heir of Alfonso! said the vision: and having pronounced those words, accompanied by a clap of thunder, it ascended solemnly towards heaven" (108). Susan Stewart has pointed out how often the invention or presence of the gigantic reduces the observer, the self whose body is belittled and whose perceptions become fragmented, to a figure confronting an infinite, exterior, public, and overly natural history. That such history is embodied in a hyperbolic form whose undisclosable nature is beyond imagining implies that systems of cultural constraint have a signifying power and cohesion that could be seen in totality were individual human comprehension sufficiently adequate (70–103). Similarly, Terry Castle has shown that the spectralization of the human figure is also frequently a sign of its transformation into a radical otherness (*Apparitional Lesbian*, 28–65). But in Walpole's narrative the gigantic is itself fragmented, a vestige of the past that has grown too large for the present but that must be appeased by the efforts of a current generation to restore it, or failing that, acknowledge its precedence. The moment it finally gathers itself together and achieves comprehensive form it vanishes with a clap of thunder, revealing yet another form of insubstantiality, separation, and inconclusiveness: the divide between heaven and earth. It is, moreover, in its ghostliness, a sign not only of the alien other but also of legitimate birth, the biological origins of the self. Here, the gigantic, the spectral, and the incomplete do not signal the distinctions between private and public, present and past, body and spirit, self and other so much as their uneasy cohabitation.

Lineal succession is thus validated simultaneously through the bodies, icons, and architectural structures of the family, but the process is also profoundly violent, in pointed contrast to the teleological progress of a conventional courtship narrative. Recognizing legitimate paternity, the authority of the past, is not consonant with wholly restoring it; the passage of household property from the "rightful owner" (109) to the "true heir" (108) is marked by loss, absence, and misery. Theodore's marriage to Isabella at the very end of *The Castle of Otranto*, rather than a triumphant confirmation of family heritage, is a sign of the narrative's unconsoling tendency to link the creation of family to the reproduction of sorrow: "it was not till after frequent discourses with Isabella, of his dear Matilda, that he was persuaded he could know no happiness but in the society of one with whom he could forever indulge the melancholy that had taken possession of his soul" (110). The rupturing of families, bodies, and memories in Walpole's story is a repudiation of progressive historiography, as if the rewriting of history, however necessary, is so traumatic a process that it can only produce disarticulated social and representational relations. The preponderance of highly dramatic moments of recognition is simply a facet of this mutable nature in Walpole's characters. What Marshall Brown calls the "broken personalities of *The Castle of Otranto*" (100) are thus the signs of the dis-association of character from a cohesive social environment.

As the central force of domestic government, Manfred is the most representative figure of such personal fragmentation. The more he attempts to deflect spectral challenges to the historical character of the family, the more he becomes like them in their volatile de-rangement of household order. At first, this plasticity seems entirely antithetical to the patriarchal rigidity he represents. Throughout the story, in fact, Manfred is repeatedly described in terms that empha-size his obduracy. Where the spectral grandfather exposes a rift in the past, the current father attempts to hide that rift through the ceaseless reproduction of mastery. Manfred is recognized for "the severity" of his "disposition" (15), treats his family with "causeless rigour" (18) and is marveled alternately for his "austerity" (20), "for-titude" (34), "inflexibility" (55), and "intrepidity" (62). This immov-ability derives from his overruling concern with maintaining a strict line of inheritance. It also signals his commitment to a plan that will not be altered by the disruptions manifested in the domestic objects that come alive around him. "Heaven nor hell shall impede my de-signs," he announces when the gallery door shuts him off from Don Ricardo's ghostly painting (23). "Since hell will not satisfy my curi-osity," he adds, "I will use the human means in my power for pre-serving my race" (24). His commitment to design is, of course, manifested in his obsession with controlling the future through the system of genealogy that sustains his own power. Calling his inten-tion of divorcing Hippolita and marrying Isabella "policy" (59) and citing "reasons of state" (47), he exploits the purely secular logic of marriage and property laws. That is, he strives to embody linear or-der, temporal succession, and predictive family structure.

Manfred appears then to represent an extreme of rational cogni-tion. He attempts to shape his character on principles that derive from the household (and that, ironically, his main spectral nemesis also strives to uphold); he is concerned, in other words, with mak-ing his subjective state coincide with the objective conditions of the family. Of all the characters in the story, he is the one who most ac-tively seeks to impose a linear and unified order on domestic experi-

ence, seeking to model private space on the institutional clarity of
the public sphere. For many critics he is emblematic of the excessive, and ultimately futile, exercise of rationality, one that is finally
blind to actual circumstances.[6] There is indeed something both perverse and impressive in Manfred's determination to convert every
sign of a power greater than his into verification of his own dominion. Only moments after Conrad's death, he begins to regard this
"portent" (17) as divine confirmation of his own domestic policy:
"he was a sickly puny child, and heaven has perhaps taken him
away that I might not trust the honours of my house on so frail a
foundation. The line of Manfred calls for numerous supports. My
foolish fondness for that boy blinded the eyes of my prudence" (22).
His subsequent attempts to preserve "his dominions" to "his posterity" (95) are thus part of a willed effort to make his fond eyes become wholly rational organs, to see the family as a set of logical
rather than affective relations.

However, what is equally characteristic of Manfred is his inability
to cohere, invariably because of passions that make him "disordered" (21, 22, 34, 64, 101). One of the book's central ironies is that
despite his obsessive devotion to the family in abstract terms as an
assurance of future continuity, all his acts in fact destroy family
harmony and therefore social order. His fixation on divorce is a
measure of this tendency to divide the present world at the expense
of a future confirmation of the self. Jerome is quick to point out
that Manfred's plan to divorce his wife and marry his intended
daughter-in-law signals an irrational passion as much as it demonstrates Manfred's systematic concern with preserving the family: "a
marriage, which, founded on lust or policy, could never prosper"
(48). The one is the obverse of the other; and they denote a subject
constituted by extremes. As the narrator indicates early in the story,
this is a condition forced upon Otranto's patriarch by context:
"Manfred was not one of those savage tyrants who wanton in cru-
elty unprovoked. The circumstances of his fortune had given an as-
perity to his temper, which was naturally humane; and his virtues
were always ready to operate, when his passion did not obscure his
reason" (30). The surprising insight of *The Castle of Otranto* is that

the "cruel father" is as much a victim as an abuser of the "rational" order by which the family's future is secured; he is dehumanized by a system that would organize domestic affect on a logic of behavior.

This volatility in and between the patriarch's affective and rational conduct is conveyed throughout the narrative in the adjectives denoting Manfred's emotional extremes. He is repeatedly "frantic" (19, 34), "disturbed" (34), in a state of "confusion" (22, 45, 108), "distracted" (24, 31, 67, 104, 108), "staggered" (30), "overwhelmed" (68), "agitated" (95), and at one point capable of uttering "nothing but incoherent sentences" (67). All these characterizations emphasize the strain put upon the figure of the gothic father in his effort to reconcile a system of family management, one based on futurity, with the sudden eruptions of emotion incited by domestic relations; he is haunted as much by family affect as by the spectral artifacts closing off the household into deracinated zones. Spectral dissolution seems to pass from the apparitional to the human world and back as if both were operating under the same uncanny mode of behavior. Manfred's climactic stabbing of his daughter is thus the corollary to Alfonso's mutilation of Conrad. Like the ghost, Manfred has become the unstable agent of his own family's destruction; the power to intrude a revisionary past onto the present has shifted from the supernatural figure to the father and is now enacted in explicable human form.

If the genealogical rationale works on Manfred to bring him into crisis with his natural affinity toward sentimental concern for the family, the confusion that results also works outward into the domestic world (widely construed in the book as the social interactions among the nuclear family, the servants, guests of the house, and an indeterminate public economically and politically dependent on the castle). That is, Manfred's internal incoherence (the product of external principles of genealogy) is communicated to the public sphere (itself a blurring of domestic and community relations) in the form of unruly tendencies that are passed to others. He "sought a subject on which to vent the tempest within him. ... The mob, who wanted some object within the scope of their capacities on whom they might discharge their bewildered reasonings, caught the words from the mouth of their lord" (19). The father's own emotional transference, like the affective displacement of the occult artifact, reveals how the uncontrollable feelings, as well as the systematic structuring, of patriarchal ideology are conveyed through individuals who are both internally disordered and subject to entropic external pressures.

Gothic literature typically dwells on symbolic figures of paternity. It is, in fact, one of the few fictional genres that positions older fathers (or their surrogates) as characters of central dramatic importance. Of course, the gothic patriarch is also invariably a domestic and political tyrant who serves to emphasize the problematic blurring of private and public domains that domestic literature and advice books persistently segregate (and of which the Otranto castle and principality are preeminent emblems). As a fairly explicit representative of ideology, he is often used to reveal the massive paradoxes that are frequently associated with ideological practice. In the same way that ideology can be described as both an excessively unfeeling system of mechanical forces (thereby distorting reality) and a passionate rhetoric that incites dogmatic zealots (in turn distorting reality), Manfred is both the shaper of public consciousness and the sign of its porousness.[7] He oscillates between dogmatic conviction and bewildered passion, unable to center his own identity.

It is interesting, therefore, that Manfred is the only significant male figure in Walpole's story not to appear at some point unnamed, in disguise, or ignorant of his patrimony. He stands apart, fully exposed to view, even contemptuous of the subterfuges that occupy other characters. There is no mistaking him: "Oh, heavens! cried Isabella, it is the voice of Manfred!" (28); "Stop, stop thy impious hand, cried Matilda; it is my father!" (104). With such characterizations, the gothic, which reached popularity at a time when images of the family were governed by a complex reconsideration of paternity, seemed to offer a counterpart to that reevaluation. As it implicitly critiques the conventional patriarch, it also evinces a desire to retain him, to have and overcome the father at the same time, reaching back in history for an image of his power. The ghosts, representing historically legitimate paternalism, and Manfred, connoting a "started-up" form of patriarchy (94), are thus enmeshed as complementary versions of a model of a fatherhood simultaneously deplored and yet coveted. Gothic literature of this nature is, arguably, the obverse of the conduct book's reformist treatment of fathers, reminding us of the persistence (and sometimes attractive energy) of tyrannical patriarchs, even as it distances them in time.

The gothic, we might say, is itself haunted by an image of fatherhood it can neither emend nor eradicate, and it suggests that the same readership that was consuming conduct books at an alarmingly rapid pace was also drawn to images of domestic discord. In *The Castle of Otranto*, the strains of Manfred's ideological pressure are found in the family members that surround him. Theodore, we have already seen, is aligned with melancholy apparitions who can only submit to their sorrow and paralysis until they are saved by otherworldly ascendance. Moreover, though the Otranto prophecy resolves in his favor, it coincides with Manfred's instrumental role in destroying Theodore's peace of mind, reducing the "true heir" to a broken figure who can only re-create his sorrow endlessly in conversation with Isabella, a symbol of compensation herself for the inconsolable loss of Matilda. The Otranto women are no less plagued by contrary impulses and feelings that always exceed the possibility of fulfillment. The female characters have often been regarded as Manfred's counterweights, establishing an opposing model of sentiment, decorum, and common sense. Where he engenders fragmentary, violent consciousness, they ensure compassion, restraint, and harmony.[8] Yet the ending of the story, with Matilda accidentally killed, Hippolita sadly resigned to living out the rest of her sterile life in a convent, and Isabella united in a somber marriage to Theodore devoted only to recalling the past, substantially diminishes the sense of feminine power and authority implied in the restoration of Alfonso's family line.

In their effort to uphold family duty, moreover, the women are torn between their emotional resistance to patriarchal coercion and their profound allegiance to such authority. As the excruciatingly patient Hippolita informs Matilda and Isabella, "It is not ours to make election for ourselves; heaven, our fathers, and our husbands, must decide for us" (88). She herself is willing to facilitate what Jerome calls the "adulterous intention" and "incestuous design" of Manfred's plans solely because her husband commands her: "I have no will but that of my lord and the church" (94). Matilda is similarly divided. She can affirm repeatedly her "affectionate duty" to Manfred (20) and her belief that "a child ought to have no ears or eyes but as a parent directs" (39), and then liberate Theodore against the express commands of her father. That she is acutely conscious of the contradiction suggests the adverse obligations that regulate her behavior: "though filial duty and womanly modesty condemn the step I am taking, yet holy charity, surmounting all other ties, justifies this act" (68). When Manfred stabs her, she even begs forgiveness from him for her clandestine rendezvous with Theodore, not wanting to "aggravate the woes of a parent" (105). Isabella herself, though the most rebellious of the three Otranto women, has difficulty reconciling her convictions with the compliant behavior she admires in Matilda and Hippolita. On the one hand, she is able to assert defiantly, "can a father enjoin a cursed act? I was contracted to the son; can I wed the father?—No, madam, no; force should not drag me to Manfred's hated bed. I loathe him, I abhor him: divine and human laws forbid" (87–88). On the other hand, by the end she appears to have lapsed back into her customary role of brokered daughter, even if the final arranged marriage is more to her liking than the first one to Conrad: "Frederic offered his daughter to the new prince, which Hippolita's tenderness for Isabella concurred to promote" (110). Like her substitute mother and sister, Isabella has to channel her desire through the parenting and marital systems imposed on her. To a large extent, the women indicate the ideological inconsistencies in Manfred's particular embodiment of paternal rule. The breakdown in continuity that is manifested in the living father's inability to generate a coherent fiction—"My story," he acknowledges, "has drawn down these judgements" (109)—is similarly imparted by the curtailed signifying force of the women of Otranto. Their eventual destiny is not to announce a new domestic order but to serve as victims or caretakers of the old when it finally breaks. Their unproductive ends foreclose the narrative lines that are customarily augured in the conclusions to conventional domestic fiction.

Walpole's thematic concern with the family's self-consuming impulses intersects with formal considerations only in very complicated ways, but a similar stress between continuity and rupture functions structurally in the text. If he was intent on using the story he had created to signal the breakdown of domestic relations, Walpole was nonetheless concerned with displaying it in a concise and regular fashion. The narrative organization of the story seems to confirm a much greater striving toward unity of form than in any of the narratives by Behn, Defoe, Richardson, or Haywood. It is organized into five chapters of almost equal length corresponding to the five acts of a tragedy and covering only three days. Episodes, character types, and language are frequently and consciously borrowed from Shakespeare.[9] Certain events are symbolically repeated in order to emphasize the uncanny order that underlies the gothic world. Apparitions appear, like clockwork, at even intervals, and the narrative opens and closes with parallel scenes that intermingle marriage and death. Theodore is thrice subjected to and delivered from incarceration. Several other figures, such as Matilda and Isabella, are doubles of each other. Overall, the story appears to move toward synthesis, establishing an architectonic vision of the past in which patterns of correspondence emerge over time. Walpole himself argued that *The Castle of Otranto* was an effort to reconcile "two kinds of romance, the ancient and the modern" so that "the great resources of fancy" could be blended with "the rules of probability" (7–8). That is, he was, at least ostensibly, determined to create a balanced literary form.

At the same time, however, a rift between the desire to duplicate history and awareness of its piecemeal, and hence unreliable, presence in human memory, random texts, and partial objects, characterizes Walpole's evocation of the past. The syntactical and stylistic patterns of the text repeatedly produce formal disjunctions that correspond to the spectral and human disruptions of family structure. David Morris has pointed out how Walpole's characteristic hyperbole and repetition arouse unease as much as they create legible

patterns (302–5). Interruptions and questions are equally pervasive
as modes of discourse, and Walpole's use of short and long dashes, while not as variable and nuanced as Sterne's, plays a significant
role in conveying the rhythms of suspended discourse. Along with
the extraordinarily frequent appearance of the word "interrupted,"
dashes signal the breakdown between signifier and signified; they
are measures of silence that record inarticulate mortal responses to
shocking "preternatural appearances" (63) and human "excesses"
(103) that abort language altogether. Of all the heightened rhetorical
effects, however, Walpole's compulsive interrogatories may be the
most representative. Indeed, the fundamental means of verbal exchange in the story is the question, for which there is rarely a direct
answer. In fewer than 100 pages, more than 340 direct questions are
asked. The first words spoken in the text are Manfred's, and they
form a query that summarizes all the anxious questions subsequently asked in and by the book as a whole: "What was the matter?" (16).
Most of these questions concern the disposition of family members
within the household. Isabella's whereabouts alone are demanded
more than a dozen times, her state of mind another seven. The cumulative effect of the questions is to convert home into a mysterious
space, in which blood relations or contracted alliances are physically
and ontologically severed. We are reminded constantly that the ideal
of the harmonious domestic interior is fracturing into secret or prohibited recesses, divided between those anxiously fleeing and those
actively pursuing each other, those seeking information and those
hiding it.

The temporal, spatial, and bodily fragmentation within the story,
provided by the startling interventions of dead family members and
the destructive behavior of living ones, is thus reenacted by Walpole
in the dispersal of the text's form and language.[10] The disorder of the
household is not restricted to the domain of objects or figures but
invades the structure of discourse itself. It is also manifested in the
problem of knowledge that Walpole's narrative persistently emphasizes and that is triggered by the appearance of ancestral ghosts. The
thematic, syntactical, and contextual confusions are all of a piece,
expressing the contradictory strategy, customary in eighteenth-cen-

tury domestic theory, of locating in family structure the fullest expression of desire and, at the same time, using it to shape normative behavior. To some extent, the gothic's uneasy relationship to authentic history is a measure both of its yearning for a total structure of rational principles and a rejection of those principles. Gothic "performances" (7) such as *The Castle of Otranto* are at once a vindication of domestic order and a condemnation of household systems in which the rationalization of family structure strains against the investment of emotion in domestic relations.

Tristram Shandy and "This Fragment of Life"

If gothic literature like *The Castle of Otranto* employs metaphors of disarticulation to express a variety of rifts in the historical representation of domestic relations, *Tristram Shandy*, as has long been noted, literally fragments the text in order to pair the breakdown of family with the breakdown of communication (entire chapters vanish from one place and appear in another).[11] Sterne's narrative is, of course, punctuated by a vast number of displaced events, characters, and textual conventions. It begins, "*ab Ovo*," with an aborted account of the interrupted, and therefore feeble, insemination that produces the text's digressive author. In the same way that gothic literature often depicts what Patricia Spacks calls "ludicrously phallic" images to emphasize how the supernatural "embodies power," Sterne's fiction obsessively couples male virility with narrative control (*Desire and Truth*, 150). *Tristram Shandy*, however, like the most aggressive gothic works, also reveals a counterplot in which masculine energy is dispersed. It thus ends with an anecdote about the economic consequences of sterility, attributed to the bull the Shandy family must maintain "for the service of the parish." This latter story provides the famous metaphor of the "COCK and BULL," which appears both to characterize and conclude Tristram's biography at a moment four years before he is begotten (614–15).[12] That is, the author's "history of myself" (41) is not only legitimated by family history but also profoundly disordered by it, relegated to a secondary position in time, space, and narrative order. Tristram is a descriptive absence because his family background is a series of discontinuities that cannot produce a foundational subject.

Such dislocation is the order of writing in *Tristram Shandy*. In the opening dedication to Pitt, Sterne (or is it Tristram?) begins his opinions with a complaint about the fragmentary nature of life, the infirmities of the body, and the retirement of the "house" in "a bye corner of the kingdom" from which he writes (33). His text is a "fence" against these. That is, the existential, somatic, and domestic dimensions of life are linked together by virtue of their displacement from a center: psychic wholeness, physical health, public affairs. Writing ostensibly draws an order around these eccentric conditions, adding "something" to this "Fragment of Life" (33). Like Walpole, Tristram writes the history of a family in order to escape the present and return to a time that cannot disappoint. Unlike Walpole, however, Tristram cannot safely distance himself from the historical process he engenders. The "domestic misadventures" (122, 240) he describes in the rest of the book impinge directly on his present character (his life and opinions) though that is something he chooses to repress. He can only become known to us through reflections on his family. As he admits, to "live or write" is in his case "the same thing" (175). His own immediate state of mind is, like his immediate surroundings, a subject on which he is generally evasive—except when describing his trip through France and his efforts to elude death (vol. 7). That is, only when he is dramatically removed from a familiar landscape, as the result of a crisis that threatens the self altogether, can he stand out as a subject. At such a time, his assertions of identity are the result of a future end rather than a labyrinthine family past.

At almost all other times, however, Tristram collapses the immediate experience of writing onto the history about which he is writing. Unlike Defoe's autobiographical narrators or Richardson's epistolary subjects, Sterne, for all his apparent writing to the moment, never really tries to flesh out the temporal intimacy between one's self and one's pen. Where exactly is Tristram when he writes and what are the conditions of his household? He mentions a companion, "Jenny," but cautions the reader not to assume what role she plays in his life. She may be a wife, a mistress, a daughter, or a friend. All Tristram concedes is the "impossibility" that the reader "should know how this matter really stands" (76).[13] About other "family concernments" (39) he is silent. Yet he is determined, at the same time, to remind us of the narrator's precise time and place. Where the past household is made a domain of particularly meaningful objects—the large house-clock (39), the parlour fireplace (87, 113, 120, 128, 202, 244, 381), a creaking door (211–13, 285), Walter's bed (223, 275, 278, 422), various stairs (281–85, 327), and a window sash (369, 371, 376)—the present one, the scene of authorship itself, is limited to details that relate only to Tristram's writing habits: his cane chair (209); his spurting pen (222); a table, an inkhorn, and a writing cap (222, 240, 332, 515), the fire that alternately warms him and burns pages of his manuscript (291, 332), his state of dress (572, 587–88, 602).

These instances in which Tristram makes us aware of his body, authorship, and subjectivity are also, frequently, moments of intense temporal specificity: "it is no more than a week from this very day, in which I am now writing this book for the edification of the world—which is March 9, 1759" (72). The exactness, however, is a distraction from the fact that the narrator's world is essentially empty of content, a series of discontinuous though chronological moments of time, rarely filled in with detail or describing anything more than an isolated reaction to the act of writing family history itself: "Instantly I snatched off my wig, and threw it perpendicularly, with all imaginable violence, up to the top of the room—indeed I caught it as it fell—but there was an end of the matter" (291); "I stop it [the reader's anticipation], by pulling off one of my yellow slippers and throwing it with all my violence to the opposite side of my room, with a declaration at the heel of it—" (602). The emphatic and interruptive nature of these allusions, moreover, signals the extent to which they are exceptions to, rather than affirmations of, present awareness. Consciousness is, in a sense, always lived elsewhere.

The autobiographical act in *Tristram Shandy* is thus always saturated in early family scenes, which no amount of ink can exorcise.

Speaking of an aborted discourse by his father, for example, Tristram complains: "And, at this hour, it is a thing full as problematical as the subject of the dissertation itself,—(considering the confusion and distresses of our domestic misadventures, which are now coming thick one upon the back of another) whether I shall be able to find a place for it in the third volume or not" (122). Here, the written past emerges as a present urgency that supplants the creative will. Events already ended "are now coming" once again. They achieve a grammatical rebirth and shape the writer's forthcoming work as if they were active determining events that force the author along certain lines. Tristram may claim that the nature of writing is such that he is allowed to "tell my story my own way" (41), but repeatedly we observe him anxiously trying to arrange family narratives that intrude forcibly upon his mind, situating them in their "proper place." His memories of family life become a force that shapes his writerly consciousness rather than a resource he shapes to enable his unique creative efforts, and they push aside the possibility for other forms of productive life: "Time wastes too fast: every letter I trace tells me with what rapidity Life follows my pen" (582).

Typically, it is the father's life and opinions that intrude most forcibly on the author's creative process; the son is forever writing out/of the father. It is true that Tristram wishes that both his father and mother had "minded what they were about when they begot me," but only because he thinks them "equally bound" to ensure the vigor of the homunculus—that is, the "muscular strength and virility" of the father's seed. What weaknesses "both of body and mind" might befall, he asks, should paternal heritability be "worn down to a thread" (35–37). In effect, Locke's liberating doctrines of "tabula rasa" and associative cognitive development are rewritten as a revision of a patriarchal logic whose power seems to be waning but still provides the only measure of identity. As we will see, the flawed "thread" Walter provides is a sign of the perpetually unstable domestic governance he offers. That a father who did not properly mind what he was about could have the debilitating effect Walter has on Tristram's "body and mind" confirms as much as ridicules the continuing masculinist assumptions of patriarchy's naturalizing rhetoric. Effective or not, the father's will determines his offspring's social as well as biological destiny, converting the younger generation's cognitive behavior into an anxious imitation of the older, trapping it in the time and thoughts of his predecessor: "From the first moment I sat down to write my life for the amusement of the world, and my opinions for its instruction, has a cloud insensibly been gathering over my father . . . now is the storm thickened, and going to break, and pour down full upon his head" (222). We have seen that the archaeological urge in Walpole's fiction is partly the sign of a cultural dilemma: the more you know of your past the less you know yourself. In Sterne that archaeological impulse is not removed to a distant past, mediated by a series of authorial or editorial personae; it is, instead, made an explosive and comic aspect of lived consciousness, one that produces "so much unfixed and equivocal matter starting up, with so many breaks and gaps in it" (444).

Almost all the ruptures in Sterne's work, then, are located in and around the complex integration of family life and social behavior, but they tend to be most concentrated on the father's vexed attempts to regulate his son's character. Walter Shandy's hopelessly comprehensive primer, the incomplete and unused *Tristrapædia* suggests that part (and only part) of the characteristic fragmentation in Tristram's "life" derives from the equally encyclopedic, piecemeal, and often contradictory nature of the conduct books that were widely read in the latter half of the century.[14] Walter initially constructs his "system of education" from "his own scattered thoughts, counsels, and notions . . . binding them together, so as to form an INSTITUTE for the government of my [Tristram's] childhood and adolescence" (366). That is, the conduct materials simply confirm the two contrary impulses that induce the father to collect advice. On the one hand, they denote a totalizing urge; on the other hand, they signal a historical decline into a fetishizing accumulation of disconnected informational fragments. They imply, moreover, a foundational instability in the institution of government through the domestic training of individual subjects. Walter's metaphoric alignment of civil society with Tristram's childhood and adolescence belies the reciprocal exchange implied in the comparison. Both the authoritative sources of government (national or domestic) and the constitution of the private individual self (paternal or filial) are equally "scattered."

Walter's conduct book suggests that his beliefs about family are not commensurate with his philosophical assumptions. Sterne does refer implicitly to *Some Thoughts on Education*, but the *Tristrapædia* owes much more to Filmer's *Patriarcha*. Reading his work aloud, Walter acknowledges in an aside that its acceptance of "the natural relation between a father and his child" confirms "the right and jurisdiction" of the patriarch "over" his offspring (383). This power derives from the "original of society," which is "merely conjugal" and the "foundation" of "political or civil government" (382). Earlier Tristram affirms more directly that his father "was entirely of Sir Robert Filmer's opinion" that the "greatest monarchies" were "originally, all stolen" from the "system of domestic government established in the first creation," a "prototype" of "household and paternal power" that had "been gradually degenerating away into a mixed government" (75). Elsewhere, however, Walter relies nearly verbatim on *An Essay on Human Understanding* to explain "duration and its modes," the sensation that subjective time is different from clock time, "owing . . . to the succession of our ideas" (199–201). His source of political and domestic theory, in other words, is at odds with his philosophical references to individual identity. One of the many ironies of the *Tristrapædia* is that it constitutes the very "mixed government" the father deplores and produces a subject who is similarly "degenerating away." That Walter can move effortlessly from Lockean doctrines about temporality and consciousness to patriarchal theories of family instruction emphasizes not only his shifting ideological positions but also the strategic deviations that govern Locke's treatment of parental power in different discursive contexts. As in Locke, competing structures of domestic government are distributed over a body of claims (from philosophical to political and instructional arguments) in which patriarchal authority is variously rejected or invoked.

Walter Shandy's modern conduct book, it seems, is as reliable an image of his family as the instructional literature of the period could

provide. Based on fragments of advice marshalled from traditional sources, Walter's book is both novel and obsolete; the more it
attempts to establish a uniform character, the more it produces a
divided subject. Like the contemporary behavioral literature, it
grounds its innovation on a refashioning of domestic principles that
become increasingly attenuated as they are reworked or combined
with other antithetical precepts. Though patriarchy is, in a sense,
driven underground, it continues to exert pressure through the
methods apparently displacing it (a sign of this influence is Tristram's determination to have the *Tristrapædia* published [388]). Walter believes he is preempting disorderly instruction that might mud-
dle his son's character, and he emphasizes the rigorous clarity of his
own system by juxtaposing it to the chaotic practice of modern female rearing. In other words, he tries to modify a traditional mode
of tutelage by proposing it as a novel alternative to effeminate custom:

Prejudice of education, he would say, *is the devil*,—and the multitudes of
them which we suck in with our mother's milk—*are the devil and all.*—We
are haunted with them brother Toby, in all our lucubrations and researches; and was a man fool enough to submit tamely to what they ob-
truded upon him,—what would his book be? Nothing,—he would add,
throwing his pen away with vengeance,—nothing but a farrago of the clack
of nurses, and of the old women (of both sexes) throughout the kingdom.
(368)

Wanting to obviate an instinctual maternal orality, in which physical fluids replace the succor of words and turn language into babble,
Walter offers a wholly rational exchange of language. The multitu-
dinous prejudices imbibed from the mother are countered by the father's singular train of reasoning: "['T]is high time . . . to take this
young creature out of these women's hands, and put him into those
of a private governor" (401). Walter simply ignores the fact that he
himself has naturalized phallic prejudices imbibed from his own
mother; referring to the "*tenet* in favour of long noses," Tristram
observes that his father "might be said to have sucked this in with
his mother's milk" (227). Moreover, Walter has already confused his

concern for his offspring with concern for his own work: he asks, "what would his book be?" rather than wondering what would happen to his child.

The father's absorption for more than three years in the first part of the *Tristrapædia*, so that Tristram outgrows its utility, reflects, therefore, the extent to which a philosophical system of rearing and an idealized image of domesticity have come to displace the living family, forcing it into a subsidiary existence. That Tristram becomes a fissured personality without having been raised by the book implies that the education he receives at Shandy Hall, "neglected and abandoned" to his mother (368), is no less random than the systematic attempts to regulate domestic government through calculated authorial synthesis. Moreover, the book itself, like the clack of nurses and old women, is a farrago. Here is how Tristram describes the various educational stages proposed by his father:

> —Five years with a bib under his chin;
> Four years in travelling from Christ-cross-row to Malachi;
> A year and a half in learning to write his own name;
> Seven long years and more τυπτω-ing it, at Greek and Latin;
> Four years at his *probations* and his *negations*. (393)

Patriarchal discourse has succumbed to the arbitrary and automatic forms of household instruction it seeks to correct.

If eighteenth-century prose narrative is generally evasive about paternal relations (usually projecting them onto avuncular substitutes), Sterne's sentimental fiction, like Walpole's gothic phantasmagoria, marks the return of the repressed patriarch with a vengeance. Just as Locke's domestic philosophy complicates the rebellion against strict patriarchy in his philosophical and political work by naturalizing filial obedience, Sterne's fiction exposes the stubborn paternalism that is sublimated in both eighteenth-century family instruction and realistic narrative. Sterne's supra-realism, like the gothic's supernaturalism, highlights the strange absence of a fully imagined role for fathers in both the conduct literature and domestic fiction by exaggerating filial subjection to the father's prior being. The family in these counterplots repeatedly becomes the site of the practical dilemmas that emerge from the complex mystification of male household power in the didactic characterizations of domestic relations appearing in the second half of the eighteenth century. Tristram, then, is as haunted as Manfred or Theodore by a destructive paternity, the oxymoronic nature of Sternean fatherhood. The patriarch has become a politically embarrassing figure who disrupts household order but whose presence is, nonetheless, required by the policies of the nuclear family.

One of the signs of this domestic chaos in Sterne's work is the pervasive division of space in the Shandy household. Frequently, in moments of crisis, the narrative draws striking distinctions between upstairs and downstairs, or closed and open areas, each temporarily corresponding to feminine or masculine understanding. Walter and Slop are perpetually wondering about the noise "above stairs" as Tristram is being born or accidentally circumcised (87, 119, 179, 291, 376); Tristram himself focuses on the male discourse in the parlour while the women attend to Mrs. Shandy's childbirth in an upper room; Dr. Slop worries about having a midwife "put over" his head and insists she come down to explain complications in the delivery (195). As Walter notes, when "the mistress of the house is brought to bed, every female in it, from my lady's gentle-woman down to the cinder-wench, becomes an inch taller for it" (285). Similarly, throughout the story, the doors in Shandy Hall act as barriers to shared sentiments about the family's united concerns. The parlour door alternately seals the men off from or noisily reminds them of household business; Trim habitually leaves the door to the kitchen open, enabling the servants to spy on the family's activities. If the nuclear family was in fact becoming the dominant model of domestic relations in the eighteenth century, it also served paradoxically as a symbol of desocialized experience; the more it shrank into its own space, the more it divided that space into individual preserves, forcing knowledge about the family to cross demarcated zones of self-interest.

In *Tristram Shandy* this acute awareness of the complex isolation and exposure of household members is perhaps most effectively exploited in the scene where Tristram's mother stands outside the par-

lour door eavesdropping on a conversation between Walter and Toby. Bobby's death has just been announced and, typically, Walter is
seeking consolation in classical precedents, discussing Cornelius Gal-
lus's wife and Socrates' children:

My mother was going very gingerly in the dark along the passage which
led to the parlour, as my uncle Toby pronounced the word *wife*.—'Tis a
shrill penetrating sound of itself, and Obadiah had helped it by leaving the
door a little ajar, so that my mother heard enough of it, to imagine herself
the subject of the conversation: so laying the edge of her finger across her
two lips—holding in her breath, and bending her head a little downwards,
with a twist of her neck—(not towards the door, but from it, by which
means her ear was brought to the chink)—she listened with all her powers.
(352)

Here, Sterne's precise attention to the relation between Mrs. Shandy's posture and the exact placement of the door heightens the significance of the household's spatial distribution, its tendency to in-
cite secrecy, espial, and murky communication. The door appears to
be a measure of divisive forces inhabiting what otherwise would be
an exclusively rational or human organization of space, emphasizing
both the mysteries and paradoxes of domestic privacy. The closed
(or nearly closed) door is a sign of obstructed communication, of the
separation of bodies and the diminution of affective space. It can, of
course, as happens frequently in the gothic and famously in *Clarissa*,
signify the abuse of family authority, the conversion of home into
prison. But it also intensifies issues of communication because it
heightens the reading of muffled sounds, imperfectly overheard
conversations, and recondite allusions. That is, it intensifies the act
of interpretation, the reading of affective behavior through disrupted signs. Various spaces in the household structure are thus being
marked off into discrete and disconnected territories. When Walter,
quoting Socrates, says "I have three desolate children," Mrs. Shandy
misapprehends and, understandably alarmed by the discovery of
Walter's apparent infidelity, quickly interrupts:

—Then, cried my mother, opening the door,—you have one more, Mr
Shandy, than I know of.

By heaven! I have one less,—said my father, getting up and walking out of the room. (364)

The chapter concludes on this note of discord; and the enjambment, as well as the abrupt walking in and out of rooms, enhances the breakdown in marital communication. At the beginning of the next chapter Uncle Toby tries to clarify matters to Mrs. Shandy; when he fails, he leads her out the door after Walter "that he might finish the ecclaircissement himself" (364). What should be the feeling exchange of sorrow between husband and wife over the death of their son becomes a moment of contentious emotion that must be mediated by the brother-in-law.

In such exchanges, we are reminded that the ideal of the harmonious domestic interior is fracturing into secret or prohibited recesses. While this certainly creates claustrophobia it also magnifies interior domestic space by making it the site not only of shrinkage but of a complicated network of cross purposes. This is precisely the structure of communication that Tristram internalizes in his own writing. His text is also organized around moments of abrupt closure and intensified emotional outburst that continually expand, as well as crowd, the boundaries of the text. At one point, when he begins to pinpoint the exact moment of his begetting (38), Tristram even treats the reader to the textual equivalent of spatial divide, of being on one side or the other yet not knowing where one stands, by drawing straight lines around a command for privacy:

_____Shut the door_____

It is as if the closing off of space between male discourse and female procreation that we have observed in the family is transmuted into authorial consciousness. Textual relations between reader and author are worked out in the same terms of domestic arrangement that condition the author's upbringing. Family has crept into the minutest aspects of literary production.

The division of household space at Shandy Hall further confirms the central metaphor Tristram employs to describe the family, a machine whose parts work against rather than for the progressive functioning of the whole:

> Though in one sense, our family was certainly a simple machine, as it consisted of a few wheels; yet there was thus much to be said for it, that these wheels were set in motion by so many different springs, and acted one upon the other from such a variety of strange principles and impulses,— that though it was a simple machine, it had all the honour and advantages of a complex one,—and a number of as odd movements within it, as ever were beheld in the inside of a Dutch silk-mill. (353)

Domestic structure is given a double significance. Everyday experience is both a simple visible phenomenon, a surface reality, and a complex set of hidden interactions whose motivations are not commensurate with the external appearance of order. Using a metaphor common to the conduct literature, Sterne turns the comparison of family relations to mechanical operations into a skeptical reflection on the compatibility between general household laws and sentimental ideals about individual originality. When the functional order commended by the behavioral literature is directly contrasted with an equally strong insistence that each family is unique, the internal inconsistency is made apparent. The fabric of everyday family life may, like the product of "a Dutch silk-mill," appear to have a uniform and seamless quality; on closer examination its uniqueness stems from the inconsistencies of its internal mechanism. The effect of such a contrary model of domestic structure on Tristram is reflected in his understanding of his own mental process, as if the organizational principles and impulses of the family were directly translatable into a mental economy. The mechanistic structure of Tristram's consciousness is in turn duplicated in the work he creates: "the machinery of my work is of a species by itself; two contrary motions are introduced into it, and reconciled, which were thought to be at variance with each other. In a word, my work is digressive, and it is progressive too,—and at the same time" (95); "speaking of my book as a *machine*, and laying my pen and ruler down cross-wise upon the table, in order to gain the greatest credit to it—I swore it should be kept a-going at that rate [two volumes every year] these forty years" (459). The "odd movements" of the family machine thus produce a similarly mechanical self; that self, in turn, creates a verbal machine whose motions are equally odd.

Tristram's reference to textile machinery is, moreover, particularly resonant. One of the metaphors that epitomizes both the tenuous (if nonetheless remarkable) control Tristram has on his disorderly "*machine*" and the ubiquitous strain of paternal disablement that runs throughout the book is the modest domestic image of thread. The plot lines that figure in the text are of course the imagined, abstracted, or truly representative threads of Tristram Shandy's story. These may follow an infinite linear rectitude or the kind of entanglements that separate Dr. Slop from his bag of medical innovations and prevent Tristram from finishing his story in a fully eschatological manner. Whether straight line or knot, Tristram's narrative threads are consistently "mystic" (450). They may draw together or they may break: "—for never poor jerkin has been tickled off, at such a rate . . . had there been the least gumminess in my lining,—by heaven! it had all of it long ago been frayed and fretted to a thread" (174–75). Above all, these lines represent the disarming mundanity of everyday life, where complexities are hidden in simple domestic acts. Thus when Walter, absorbed in one of his many disquisitions, accidentally tosses his wife's thread-paper into the parlour fire, his action suggests his casual disregard for her particular model of household relations. His puzzled question, "What is become of my wife's thread-paper?" serves to conclude the chapter on a note of comical unawareness of self. But Tristram's rhetorical answer at the beginning of the next chapter hints at the bifurcated relationships that articulate sexual difference in Shandy Hall: "No matter,—as an appendage to seamstressy, the thread-paper might be of some consequence to my mother,—of none to my father, as a mark in Slawkenbergius" (245). Tristram absorbs his father's dismissive attitude toward female arts. Walter uses the thread-paper to mark the page of Slawkenbergius he is translating, but Mrs. Shandy's sewing aid is a metaphoric book in itself, a piece of paper on which various threads are organized, a symbol of reparative domestic practice; it represents the tale she might weave were it not encompassed by male text or idly destroyed by the father. Like the dramatic tale of childbirth,

which barely makes itself felt through the cloud of words and pipe
smoke weaving about the men gathered downstairs in the parlour,
the female line is minimized, disappearing not only into the father's
book but also into the comparable text produced by the son. It is
"No matter." The creativity upstairs, despite the emblematic spatial
hierarchy that makes it appear dominant, seems inferior to the male
discourses dominating the parlour and organizing Tristram's own
blank sheets of paper, his tabula rasa, the story of his "life and opinions."[15]

Walter's paternal influence on the Shandy household, and Tristram specifically, is thus manifested by his selective concern over
which of the many threads of the family history will be preserved
and documented. We may recall that Walter has "spun" the *Tristrapædia*, "every thread of it, out of his own brain,—or reeled and
cross-twisted what all other spinners and spinsters had spun before
him" (366). This description borrows the same metaphor subsequently used to diminish Mrs. Shandy's domestic significance, but
here it denotes Walter's endless masculine search for a perfect and
comprehensive system of childhood governance (though the pun on
spinsters should warn us to look for evidence of unproductive energy). The book is the father's fourth and final attempt to control
his son's life: "he had lost, by his own computation, full three-
fourths of me—that is, he had been unfortunate in his three first
great casts for me—my geniture, nose, and name" (366). Walter
hopes to gain the son he desires through a tutorial process that will
redress the failures in procreation, physical stature, and patronymic
that have already threatened the family's "second staff" (69). His
concern in the *Tristrapædia* is with the biological, phallic, discursive,
and informational systems of perpetuity that gird paternal order
(though he himself claims to detest all "perpetuities" [213]); this is
the overall strategy that informs the father's "casts" (and we should
keep in mind that the word can signify an act of throwing, fishing,
hawking, moulding, accounting, directing, or weaving—that is, various methods of linear or formal control).

The threads of Walter's book, however, are never sufficiently or
practically ordered. As Tristram explains when his father's text spins

out of control, "Matter grows under our hands" (366). Mixing allusions to gestation, erection, masturbation, husbandry, pottery,
sewing, and physical science, Tristram here assigns to his father the
self-indulgent flaws that engender chaos (even though, at the same
time, the son is accurately characterizing his own book). Walter's
conduct book grows beyond the practical domestic use for which it
is intended, becoming instead a monument to masculine excess, a
crazy quilt of reticulated opinions and cross purposes. Where the
mother's papers are tightly organized but of "No matter," the
father's "Matter" tends to unravel as it gathers size. Ironically, Walter initially believes his book will be so economical that "when it
was finished and bound, it might be rolled up in my mother's
hussive" (366). A phonetic reduction of housewife, the hussive, a
pocket-case for needles, pins, thread, scissors, etc., represents both
the compartmentalized body of the domestic woman and the di-
minutive tools of her labor. In other words, instead of containing
and regulating principles of a specifically feminine activity, the male
logos seeks to inhabit them, to supply their meaning from deep
inside, to occupy the secret spaces of female productivity. Fully
ideological, it nonetheless strives to be at the heart of practical domestic activity, no matter how small or modest. The uncontrolled
spinning of masculine desire, however, invariably produces only an
exterior cover for the housewife's eternally mystified condition.
Male domestic discourse solves the problem of female cultural power simply by belittling it. The tall tales the man creates—the cock
and bull stories, the yarns—are merely compensation for his inadequate hold on matters; they become the dominating structures of
belief from which productive domestic activity cannot emerge. Forever outside or below the woman's direct creativity and pragmatic
certitude, the domestic male compensates by making the wife appear
the outsider, listening on the other side of the door as he turns his
real children into abstract figures in an argumentative discourse; he
thus makes reproduction a mystery to be explained only through
his access to a specialized language owned by men.[16]

The semblance between the father's books and the son's text affirms the extent to which the father's selective system of influence

has overdetermined Tristram. As Tristram notes:

> —and now you see, I am lost myself!——
> —But 'tis my father's fault; and whenever my brains come to be dis-
> sected, you will perceive, without spectacles, that he has left a large uneven
> thread, as you sometimes see in an unsalable piece of cambric, running
> along the whole length of the web. (444–45)

Both men are the products, as well as producers, of a patchwork of
domestic experience that mirrors the kind of work they fashion. But
where the father finds himself in the life he stitches together, the son
loses himself. Indeed, Walter's abstract obsession with the fabric of
experience on one hand and the tendency for the world to see the
fragmentary nature of the family on the other is summed up in his
concern for Tristram's "breeches" (422–26). The word itself epitomizes this double condition because it signifies both the protective
devices that clothe life (specifically the male organ of life), and, by
way of the pun, the ruptures that just as certainly characterize it.
What Tristram is both reproducing and combating in his autobiography is his father's time. His "Life" lies somewhere between the paternal coats bequeathed to the three sons in Swift's *A Tale of a Tub*
(who then rip their patrimony to shreds) and the ultimately affirma-
tive outfitting provided by the father in Carlyle's *Sartor Resartus*.
Tristram is both scornful and utterly dependent on the pattern provided by his father. But as he scorns patriarchy, he accepts it even in
defeat, realizing that it is the only measure of a past irrevocably decided for him. His book is compensation for the life he cannot align
with his father's wishes. As he declares: "I will answer for it the
book shall make its way in the world, much better than its master
has done before it" (332).

In relating his life and opinions Tristram wants to sublimate genealogical time by demystifying both plot and genealogy. Victor
Shklovsky has suggested that Sterne's narrative is remarkable precisely because it "defamiliarizes" the conventions of realistic prose
fiction before they had even yet crystallized ("Sterne's *Tristram
Shandy*," 35). Ironically, this defamiliarization coincides with the

complete familiarization of Tristram's experiences. While the family is regarded as an obstruction to the direct expression of the self, it nonetheless proves to be inescapable as well as absolutely and oppressively dominant—the more Tristram tries to tell his story, the more he is forced to recount the history of his family. And ultimately, the fragmented nature of his narrative reflects the fragmented character of the family, and its failure finally to lend coherence to the lives of its offspring: "To sum up all; there are archives at every stage to be looked into, and rolls, records, documents, and endless genealogies, which justice ever and anon calls [the writer] back to stay the reading of:—In short, there is no end of it;—for my own part, I declare I have been at it these six weeks, making all the speed I possibly could,—and am not yet born" (65). The form of the narrative displays the very same disarray that the "author" (Tristram) experiences in association with the bourgeois family itself. The narrowing of the concept of family to its modern figuration as a closed, domestic, nuclear unit brings with it a crisis of "relation" in which the perennial problem of reconciling individual gratification and social or institutional responsiveness paralyzes the writer. The family destroys coherent lines of communication by, paradoxically, giving the writer too much to relate.

Sterne's book pivots on Tristram's futile effort to create order, a product largely of his failure to reconcile his father's designs and his own history. Every effort has been made to control the circumstances of Tristram's entrance into the world: the specific wording of the marriage contract, the coupling of Mr. and Mrs. Shandy according to a strict schedule, the exhaustive *Tristrapædia*, the careful selection of a name, the choice of forceps for Tristram's delivery, etc. As each precaution leads inexorably into further comic disasters, it becomes clear that the Lockean doctrine underlying Mr. Shandy's attempt to formulate Tristram is at best misguided, at worst destructive. Parodying the language of Locke's *Some Thoughts Concerning Education* at the very outset, Sterne effectively demolishes the optimistic rationalism of Lockean pedagogy by turning its own language and assumptions against itself:

[Y]ou have all, I dare say, heard of the animal spirits, as how they are trans-
fused from father to son &tc. &tc.—and a great deal to that purpose:—
Well, you may take my word, that nine parts in ten of a man's sense or
nonsense, his successes and miscarriages in this world depend upon their
motions and activity, and the different tracts and trains you put them into,
so that when they are set a-going, whether right or wrong, 'tis not a
halfpenny matter,—away they go cluttering like hey-go-mad; and by tread-
ing the same steps over and over again, they presently make a road of it.
(35)

If we compare this passage to the opening remarks in *Some Thoughts*
we can see that in Sterne's narrative the concept of "tabula rasa" is
taken to its logical and absurd conclusion.[17] Unlike *Pamela*, Part II,
which earnestly engages Locke's pedagogical theory, *Tristram Shandy* wreaks mischievous havoc on the theory and in so doing dismantles the family ideology, which underlined social and political order
in England and America throughout the eighteenth century. The
difference between Richardson's treatment of *Some Thoughts* and
Sterne's is not only a matter of temperament but a matter of a more
general change in attitude as well.

What is distinctive about *Tristram Shandy*'s representation of
household government is that it depicts the nuclear family not as a
monolithic form but as a complicated network of divergent conflicts
and affiliations. The family is not an ideological whole against
which the individual struggles but a porous model of social interaction. The difficulties Tristram has with aligning his plot are related
to his insecurities about being the author of his own "life" and relying on his family for exemplary behavior. His rhetorical evasions,
especially the metaphoric and metonymic displacements of anxieties
about reproduction and filiation, signal the interplay between the
linguistic and affective relations that make up his text, "all dispersed,
confused, confounded, scattered, and sent to the devil.——" (295).
Family planning, "beds of justice," rational child care, a rigorously
conceived education, and proper naming only breed chaos; and the
family becomes not an ideal of governance but a symbol of social
entanglement.

Fragments Toward a Vindication
of the *Wrongs of Woman*

Both Walpole's and Sterne's narratives dramatize the problems of creating a coherent record of domestic experience, one by burying the act of writing in a distant foreign past, the other by submerging the writing agent in the family's anecdotal history. Mary Wollstonecraft's "fragment," *The Wrongs of Woman: or, Maria* (1798), similarly construes family relations in terms of separation, but Wollstonecraft's work inverts the customary relation between an individual's identity and the social conditions that the individual's experiences represent. As in *The Castle of Otranto* and *Tristram Shandy*, imagining the family is made a critical act in which domestic ideology (and especially patrilineal succession) is dismantled. But whereas the dissolution of kinship in *Tristram Shandy* (or *The Castle of Otranto*, for that matter) occurs because the male members are unable to produce lasting heirs, the threat to family order in *The Wrongs of Woman* arises because women can reproduce, because they have active sexual desires and social concerns that are unaccommodated by the structure of the bourgeois family and by the rhetoric of the conduct book. The instructions in Walter Shandy's *Tristrapædia*, unlike Maria's addresses to her daughter, are sealed off from the family's immediate historical conditions, constrained by the self-indulgent masculine world that the father re-creates; such limited responses to the subject's temporal context are, in turn, passed on to the son and reproduced in his evasive treatment of the present and his obsessive fascination with the closed male group spinning its endless discourse below stairs. In contrast, Wollstonecraft's narrative specifically traces the connections between family dynamics and contemporary political ideology. When Maria composes her autobiography to enlighten her daughter she links private and public coercion; the text's use of fragmentary images and forms is less a mark of reliving the past than of confronting an ongoing disruption in domestic and political relations.[18]

By the time Wollstonecraft began *The Wrongs of Woman* in 1796, the relation between family government and state hegemony had reemerged fully in political debates, especially those concerning the French Revolution. Edmund Burke, for example, effectively aroused partisan support and ardent opposition with *Reflections on the Revolution in France* through a rhetorical and substantive incorporation of family at all levels of experience, using domestic principles to validate the natural constitution of an authoritarian monarchy. Government should be run like a family "estate," in which each generation receives rights and liberties "as an *entailed inheritance* derived to us from our forefathers, and to be transmitted to our posterity" (119). The correlation between political and domestic order is so fundamental that it saturates the everyday world: "In this choice of inheritance we have given to our frame of polity the image of a relation in blood; binding up the constitution of our country with our domestic ties; adopting our fundamental laws into the bosom of our family affections; keeping inseparable . . . our state, our hearths, our sepulchers, and our altars" (120). Extending Filmer's *Patriarcha*, Burke establishes a systematic pattern of social relations that reproduces the principle of continuance at the cognitive as well as social and political levels. The complicated reciprocality of this exchange between family and state is reflected in the connective language and shifting organization of his clauses. On the one hand, "we" bind "our" nation with family "ties"; on the other hand, "our" families adopt the "fundamental laws" of the state. Fascinated by the "image" of blood relations, Burke assumes that there can be no ideological break, no messy slippage, between the various states of human behavior, so that governing, caring, dying, and believing are all reduced to the same inbred principle. Even the emotional life of the family serves to enhance the affective power of the nation.

Thomas Paine's rebuttal of Burke's theory of "hereditary powers" reveals the intensity with which these debates over family and government were conducted, and the popularity of the *Rights of Man* suggests how widespread was the complementary belief that a radical transformation of both familial and governmental relations was necessary: "The vanity and presumption of governing beyond the grave, is the most ridiculous and insolent of all tyrannies. Man has no property in man; neither has any generation a property in the generations which are to follow" (41–42). To Paine, the conceptual impact of family is of marginal importance in formulating political principles; following Locke, he focuses instead on individual liberties, opposing "the unity or equality of man" (66) to the "family tyranny and injustice" of aristocratic government (83).[19] Where Burke intensifies the temporal permanency of family order to stabilize government and solidify property, Paine emphasizes the provisional nature of domestic relations, linking them to the arbitrary, and presumably convertible laws of property and entailment. Government, and hence political history, is reimagined paradoxically as a sequence of discontinuities in which "every age and generation must be free to act for itself" (41).

Following Paine's direction, late-eighteenth-century radical fiction frequently expressed the need for a "progressive" reevaluation of family government with special urgency. *The Wrongs of Woman: or, Maria*, whose title echoes not only Wollstonecraft's earlier work in *Mary, A Fiction* (1788) and her two *Vindications*, of man and of woman (1790; 1792) but Paine's treatise as well, is particularly emblematic for the way in which it combines critiques of political, familial, and sexual hegemony. Although Burke and Paine use the "image of a relation in blood" to contest England's "frame of polity," the one commemorating "inheritance" while the other derides the gothic tyranny of "governing beyond the grave," they are both more interested in the "spirit of philosophic analogy" (Burke, 120) than in the pragmatic effects of political change on domestic government. Wollstonecraft, by contrast, never loses sight of the material consequences of what she calls "the government of society" on domestic and sentimental behavior. Combining the disruptive patterns of both the gothic and sentimentalism, she uses fiction to advance an ongoing reformation in how domestic conduct could be imagined, repeatedly invoking the revolution in France as a counterpart to the domestic scenes that entrap Maria. Wollstonecraft's work represents, then, a radical instance of the double breakdown in individual and communal efforts to shape history.[20]

The Wrongs of Woman relies on the language of radical political critique to characterize domestic relations, repeatedly using words such as "tyranny," "despot," "oppression," "liberty," "justice," "freedom," "state," "system," and "government" to suggest the ideological function of the conventional family.[21] Maria herself, borrowing one of the most vivid images of arbitrary power from the French Revolution, claims that "marriage had bastilled me for life" (155). Evoking Robespierre's directive of May–June 1794, she complains that marital laws should be framed by "impartial lawgivers" in "the style of a great assembly, who recognized the existence of an *être suprême*, to fix [i.e., correct] the national belief, that the husband should always be wiser and more virtuous than his wife" (159). If Burke employs the family as a natural and sentimental justification for monarchy, Wollstonecraft uses it to demonstrate the unnatural and unfeeling conduct that, like Manfred's seemingly rationalist policies, divides household relations. Where Burke tries to establish a systematic order to personal, social, and political relations, Wollstonecraft seeks to demonstrate the artificial and irreconcilable principles that instill domestic virtue and those systems of government rooted in its conventional elaboration.

The political disorder of the successive households that Maria occupies thus manifests the same crisis in domestic economy that haunts *The Castle of Otranto*—that is, the incongruity of using the family both to accommodate desire and to instill normative behavior, but Wollstonecraft makes it the subject of contemporary ruptures in social relations. Nowhere is this more evident than in Maria's response to her abusive husband's physical transformation. The memoirs are essentially a litany of household betrayals, tracing Maria's early sufferings at the hands of a despotic father who runs the family like a "man of war" (125) to the "domestic tyranny" (128) of her married life with George Venables (whose name underscores his venality and reveals the seamier consequences of advice literature that justified the husband's rights through sentimental and rationalist palliation). Her own "domestic regulations," which give a "glow" to her appearance, are sharply contrasted by his failures of personal management, which, like his continuous indebtedness and penchant for "profligate women" (146), indicate a vaster collapse of economic, sexual, and somatic categories: "The very countenance of my husband changed; his complexion became sallow, and all the charms of youth were vanishing with its vivacity" (145); "I think I now see him lolling in an arm-chair, in a dirty powdering gown, soiled linen, ungartered stockings, and tangled hair, yawning and stretching himself" (147); "his tainted breath, pimpled face, and blood-shot eyes, were not more repugnant to my senses, than his gross manners, and loveless familiarity to my taste" (154). Here, the gradual corruption of one man's appearance matches the more generalized breakdown of the body politic; the "newspaper" that Mr. Venables calls for every morning, like the father's prior occupation in the British navy, becomes a sign of this connection between his material condition and the ongoing decline of the national state (147). Maria's political dissatisfactions are thus mirrored (and perhaps sublimated) in her aesthetic and affective reaction to the patriarch's precise historical degradation. Maria, concerned that certain paternal features, tendencies, and even gestures will reemerge in her child, worries that the "*sins*" of the "father's entailed disgrace" will "be added to the ills to which woman is heir" (160). "Entail" is, in fact, a key word that Wollstonecraft employs periodically, to emphasize parallels between individual and social oppression and to denote the heroine's fear that abstract masculine rules of property will be permanently encoded in the biological, economic, and intellectual inheritance of future generations (104, 124, 160).

Wollstonecraft is, then, one of the few writers in the period to make so clear a causal, or at least complementary, sequence of effects between international events and domestic conduct in its most limited sense. The consequent desire to reimagine family structure, and in so doing reorganize state power, emerges most forcefully in Wollstonecraft's decision to structure *The Wrongs of Woman* on the radical but disturbing submergence of the figure of the mother in that of an enlightened daughter. At the center of the nearly completed first part of the manuscript is the first-person narration of Maria, who uses the story of her life as "the instruction, the counsel, which is meant rather to exercise than influence" the infant daughter from whom she has been separated (124). In devoting her "life" to the noncoercive "instruction" of her child, however, Maria envisions no personal future and regards herself simply as a pedagogical device. Her history is thus subsumed in the unwritten life of another, and the promise of deliverance is deferred to a later state: "the events of her past ... might perhaps instruct her daughter, and shield her from the misery, the tyranny, her mother knew not how to avoid" (82). Relying on the persuasive force of autobiography, Maria's text offers only a defensive posture in which women can perhaps be shielded from, but not actively shape, normative social behavior. Instead of ensuring a productive realignment of the domestic sphere with the public sphere, Maria's conduct book encourages a fugitive strategy whereby public pressures are circumvented in the private sphere. "I write not," she insists, to those "advocates for matrimonial obedience, who, making a distinction between the duty of a wife and of a human being, may blame my conduct" (163). Maria's form of instruction is always rehearsing its difference from conventional domestic literature, and measuring its own limited efficacy in a broader social context. Thus, despite its revolutionary rhetoric, *The Wrongs of Woman* persistently denies the capacity of revolution—in political, sexual, or domestic relations—to transform social structure. Because Wollstonecraft sees "tyranny" so completely entrenched in the conventional family, she regards all other relations of power as necessarily entailed.

The limits of such female resistance are made clear when Maria tries to defend herself in court, seeking a "divorce" that will enable her to raise her daughter on the "property" she has brought to the marriage (196). The public world, as the magistrate's summary judgment in the courtroom scene suggests, uses the family as a social model not to support natural human behavior but to naturalize an illogical rhetoric of male dominance. Attempting to harness domestic ideology to national interests, his decision implies a concerted disciplinary alignment among regulative discourses. Legal pronouncements, acting in loco parentis, reproduce household rules that ensure the stratified relations of power defended by Burke. As the magistrate announces:

We did not want French principles in public or private life—and, if women were allowed to plead their feelings, as an excuse or palliation of infidelity, it was opening a flood-gate of immorality. What virtuous woman thought of her feelings?—It was her duty to love and obey the man chosen by her parents and relations, who were qualified by their experience to judge better for her, than she could for herself. . . . Too many restrictions could not be thrown in the way of divorces, if we wished to maintain the sanctity of marriage; and, though they might bear a little hard on a few, very few individuals, it was evidently for the good of the whole. (199)

Merging jurisprudence, political observation, and the language of the conduct book, however, these remarks ironically undermine the very legal and familial principles that stigmatize the heroine. The claim of the patriarchal family, that it provided a stable foundation for the building of individual identity and that it was a symbol of stability, order, and moral purpose—of a whole concept of objective reality, in fact—loses its force when its practice is measured against its beliefs. The judge's admission that marital laws "might bear a little hard on a few" betrays the very partial logic that "justice" is intended to examine objectively. His legal summary brings sharply into focus the false homology between domestic order and political rule that Maria's own disrupted "life"—the memoirs to her daughter—consistently repudiates. Her story overrides domestic, legal, or national strictures—as she says, "definite rules can never apply to indefinite circumstances" (198)—but because it does, it also has no effective currency in public debate.

The Wrongs of Woman: or, Maria is, then, fundamentally a conduct book, akin to Wollstonecraft's first published work, *Thoughts on the Education of Daughters: With Reflections on Female Conduct, in the More Important Duties of Life*, yet one that aggressively resists the public function that customarily motivates the behavioral literature.[22] Like its more conventional predecessor, the fictional narrative points to the central position of the daughter as an ideological fulcrum, but she is made a symbol more of unrealized private aspirations than of progressive civic values. Unlike *Thoughts on the Education of Daughters* or the later *Vindication of the Rights of Woman*, *The Wrongs of Woman* never really addresses active female conduct but rather promotes techniques of avoidance. The autobiographical subject is employed to convey the collective social needs of women.

The unusual title of the book, which puts the general applicability of the narrative before the specific name of the central character, intensifies this indirect exchange between the private and the social. The singular generic noun blurs the distinction between the personal and the universal and simultaneously modifies the "wrongs" that belong both to the individual figure and to women in general. *The Wrongs of Woman*, with its startling shifts between polemical and sentimental discourse, mercurial readings of feminine sensibility or erotic physical presence, and interpolated and usually aborted first-person narratives, is a textbook for the kind of disassembled consciousness prevalent in later-eighteenth-century fiction. Even taking into account its unfinished state, Wollstonecraft's narrative is remarkable for the intensity with which it invokes the fragmented condition of political and personal existence. Perhaps the most radical hybrid of fiction, conduct book, and political disquisition of the eighteenth century, Wollstonecraft's narrative dramatizes the breakdown of publicly affirmable discourse on female manners precisely at a time when it seemed most popular and effective.[23]

Such corresponding disillusionments about public and private experience inevitably shaped the discursive practice of the work. Wollstonecraft recognized that, however opposed men like Burke and Paine were on political issues, neither revolutionary nor counterrevolutionary dogma sufficiently addressed the rights (and wrongs) of women. For Wollstonecraft, the revolution in France largely became the rhetorical mask for a longer revolution in female conduct, providing her with a complicated model of political agitation. Her own divided response to its social ramifications is reproduced to a large extent in the rhetorical and structural fissures in her work. Even excluding its unfinished state, *The Wrongs of Woman*, like *The Castle of Otranto* and *Tristram Shandy*, relies on an aesthetic of fragmentation that aligns national and domestic incongruities. The "partiality" to which Wollstonecraft refers in the preface, for example, signifies not only the way English law favors men but also the way it breaks the world into unequal parts. Wollstonecraft's repeated use of the words "partial" (73, 125, 130, 153, 155, 159, 187), "torn" (77, 80, 81, 107, 108, 156, 183, 197), and "ruin" (83, 102, 136,

179, 184) provides a stylistic register, typical of romantic and gothic prosody, that equates ideological, physical, and biological rupture. As the narrator observes of Maria, "In proportion as other expectations were torn from her, this tender one [of nurturing her daughter] had been fondly clung to, and knit into her heart" (81).

The same diminishing expectations underlie Wollstonecraft's own expressed intentions for the book. Speaking defensively of her own writing, Wollstonecraft acknowledges that "few" will "advance before the improvement of the age, and grant that my sketches are not the abortion of a distempered fancy, or the strong delineations of a wounded heart" (73). Written as fragments for a preface, these remarks already signal the strange, defiant pessimism that punctuates her narrative, anticipating the "few" that the judge will later sacrifice for the sake of ideological consistency between private and public life. The bristling grammar, marked by complicated double negatives and compound clauses, announces the embattled position of the author who avows principles that will inevitably go unrecognized. It mixes the language of mental deterioration, emotional disorder, and physical rupture. The very tyranny of the sentence, the rational clarity of proper syntax, is defied, regarded as a sign of the systematic entrapment that comes to characterize the heroine's experience. Lurking in the chiasmic phrasing is the possible inference that these are indeed the aborted impressions of a "distempered fancy" and the "strong delineations of a wounded heart," but only for those who read in terms of the ruling majority. The sentence, as with so many others in the narrative, seems to demand that the reader work out its meaning by interpreting against conventional discursive practice, using a kind of sympathetic parsing to locate the feeling behind the words and thus elude the confinements of language. At later points in the narrative, such complicated forms of sympathetic exchange and verbal intercalation are reproduced in even larger syntactic units when the subjects of entire paragraphs oscillate from sentence to sentence. When, for example, the narrator describes Maria's efforts to engage Jemima's sympathies for her daughter, the passage duplicates the intended crossover of feeling, beginning with Maria's intentions and then shifting to Jemima's resulting emotional metamorphosis:

> Though she failed immediately to rouse a lively sense of injustice in the mind of her guard, because it had been sophisticated into misanthropy, she touched her heart. Jemima (she had only a claim to a Christian name, which had not procured her any Christian privileges) could patiently hear of Maria's confinement on false pretences; she had felt the crushing hand of power, hardened by the exercise of injustice, and ceased to wonder at the perversions of the understanding, which systematize oppression; but, when told that her child, only four months old, had been torn from her, even while she was discharging the tenderest maternal office, the woman awoke in a bosom long estranged from feminine emotions. (80)

This passage follows a long paragraph focusing exclusively on Maria's inner thoughts; yet by beginning with a universal female pronoun before shifting to Jemima's consciousness, it provides both a transition between the identities of the two and a stylistic rebellion against rigid theories of discrete personality. The interrupting of "the tenderest maternal office" produces a rebirth of "the woman" in a figure who has become so absorbed by masculine "systematization" that she has lost all "feminine emotions." Echoing earlier references to Maria's maternal breast, the awakening of nurturing feeling in the "bosom" of her "keeper" rescues the maternal imperative underlying Wollstonecraft's fiction from a purely biological rationale; it widens the mother/daughter metaphor to include socially constructed forms of collective resistance. While the pronominal identity of the two figures is retained, the constant switching between them suggests a desire to merge identities without sacrificing the unique personal and social features of each individual. At the same time, however, the intensely personal and constrained nature of this empathy indicates that such revolutions in awareness are limited to intermittent and uncharacteristic moments in the history of women.[24]

To a large degree, then, Wollstonecraft's formal strategies complement the latent capacity of her female subject. She complains in the prefatory fragments that "heroines" are required by literary convention "to be born immaculate; and to act like goddesses of wisdom, just come forth highly finished Minervas from the head of

Jove" (73). While national and literary laws protect men who are only partially formed and find completion only through "a train of events and circumstances" (73), women, who are expected to be naturally complete, confront a world organized to limit and even deny female coherence. That is, they are held to a system of expectations but maneuvered to disappoint and then be made accountable for them. In *The Wrongs of Woman* incoherence is both a sign of radical dissent from systems of sexual, social, and political discipline and the conventional mark of a subject's need for correction.

The hallucinatory, gothic opening to the narrative reinforces the condition of fragmentary existence. It presents *in medias res* the random impressions Maria receives as she emerges from the drug-induced stupor administered by her estranged husband, who has separated her from her daughter and confined her to a madhouse in the hopes of gaining control of her fortune. Like the syntactical obfuscations, Wollstonecraft's decision to begin the narrative abruptly, and only later provide a retrospective account of events leading up to the imprisonment, emphasizes dislocation, enclosure, and rupture as paradigmatic experiences. The description, moreover, seeks to defamiliarize accepted cultural institutions as well as narrative realism itself. "Abodes of horror have frequently been described, and castles, filled with specters and chimeras," but they do not rival the "mansion of despair" in which Maria is trapped (75). Otranto's fantasized historical space is made the inadequate complement to a contemporary asylum that signals not only the hidden divisiveness of patriarchal law but also the particular internal effects of that law on female consciousness. There is no need for the gothic because everyday life is already gothic in form and function.[25] Home is replaced by asylum, and because Maria's husband has put her there, he has unwittingly revealed the complicit relation between the two domains. For Maria the surroundings correspond to emotional conditions that have all along been implicit in her family life: the systematic disruption of affective ties. The terrifying fact of disunion—a mother separated from child—emblematizes not only the unnatural social effects of patriarchy, a counter to the naturalizing rhetoric of Burkean paternalism, heritability, and entailment, but also the near impossibility of sustaining an identity based on maternal succession. Here, the physical space matches the incarcerated heroine's mental condition. Her thoughts are "scattered"; her "surprise" and "astonishment" border on "distraction"; her "faculties" are "suspended"; and recollections follow one another "with frightful velocity" (75): "Her infant's image was continually floating on Maria's sight, and the first smile of intelligence remembered, as none but a mother, an unhappy mother, can conceive. She heard her speaking half cooing, and felt the little twinkling fingers on her burning bosom—a bosom bursting with the nutriment for which this cherished child might now be pining in vain" (75). On the one hand, the blurring of mother and child through the mixing of pronouns, whereby the "speaking half cooing" can be attributed to either, underlines the categorical instability of the two figures. Wollstonecraft's insertion of the general category, "an unhappy mother," also strategically recalls the universality that she insists is the main purpose of the story. These confoundings of self and other imply the narrator's endorsement of a theory of consciousness in which female connectedness rather than male solitariness is extolled. The force of this imagined unity, however, is cut short by the body's recollection of its own physical deprivation, the "burning bosom" that cannot convey "nutriment." The tortures of the particular self—"a mother's self-denial"—ultimately merge with the environmental conditions forced upon it.

When Maria's "self-possession" returns, and she begins to shift from internal absorption to external observation, she begins a critical separation of her self and the decaying environment that surrounds her. As Maria turns her gaze outward from her "mental incarceration" in the asylum, she reproduces the same process of discovering structural decay in an image of patriarchy that she had in watching her husband's physical dissolution: "She approached the small grated window of her chamber, and for a considerable time only regarded the blue expanse; though it commanded a view of a desolate garden, and of part of a huge pile of buildings, that, after having been suffered, for half a century, to fall to decay, had undergone some clumsy repairs, merely to render it habitable. The ivy had been torn off the turrets, and the stones not wanted to patch up the breaches of time, and exclude the warring elements, left in heaps in the disordered court" (77). Although powerless, Maria views the world, even from her partial vantage point, as unstable and incomplete, unable to sustain its own fictions of power. The asylum is both the extension and the inversion of the ideal home, and the logical reflection of England. Speculating on the connections between the fetters of conventional domesticity and the political and social restrictions that domestic conduct engenders, Maria recognizes how the "constraints" of her paternal home lead to the prison-house of marriage. This, in turn, leads to the confinement of an asylum and finally to the awareness that a woman's life is universally circumscribed: "And to what purpose did she rally all her energy?— Was not the world a vast prison, and women born slaves?" (79). Moreover, like the asylum or her father's and husband's systems of domestic order, the "institutions" that govern society are "partial" in all senses of the word. Maria discovers that, while her own mind can perceive the "ruins" of the "human soul" that official mechanisms and structures of social enclosure such as the madhouse foster (83), that institutional world is itself blindly locked into an irrevocable process of contradiction and decline; as it adopts the very forms of incoherence it both engenders and criticizes in its victims, it gradually loses its authoritarian power over the subject. "I execrated the institutions of society, which thus enabled men to tyrannize over women" (164). A powerful image of the domestic interior turned outward, the asylum represents both a perverted representation of home and the institutional support of domestic tyranny, since it is repeatedly used as a means to secrete inconvenient children, spouses, siblings, parents, and relatives. Maria is able to penetrate the apparent logic of institutional laws and uncover their fragmentary "constitution" because she herself has experienced the psychological and social disruption they entail. The difference between Maria and her keepers is that she, by fully becoming their victim, sees the limits of systemic cultural policing: "I should rejoice, conscious that my mind is freed, though confined in Hell itself" (139).

Writing one's life as a conduct book becomes the means of a potential escape from patriarchal and institutional mastery; and since

in Maria's circumstances it requires the participation of a female recipient and a female supplier, it also serves to unite a body of wom-
en in a concerted effort to circumvent those who "systematize oppression" (80). The impositions created by male systems of order are
thus partially contested by an illicit discursive community. As in
Pamela, the intended interlocutor is a cherished member of the family, but the text is read first by a set of intervening interpreters
(including the actual reader, who, by analogy, may adopt the position of the daughter to whom it is addressed). The narrator's relationship to the reader thus duplicates Maria's textual mothering of
her absent daughter. Wollstonecraft's peculiar decision to reserve
the daughter's name, even though Maria herself, on at least one occasion, is described as having "pronounced the name of her child
with pleasurable fondness" (121), reinforces the sense that the intended reader of the memoirs is the anonymous consumer of the
text, a potential beneficiary of a radicalized maternal discourse.[26]

Nonetheless, while Maria's memoirs express a certain faith in the
resisting instincts of the maternal word, they also betray a grim
skepticism about the efficacy of revolutionary instruction. The intended recipient, her infant, is a pre-verbal figure who represents latent political understanding of a very limited order. Unlike Walter
Shandy's dilatory instructional manual for his son (which is rendered obsolete by Tristram's maturation), Maria's "instructions" to
her daughter await the future growth of the child into a literate receptacle; the child, in other words, represents the generation who
might "advance before the improvement of the age" to understand
the full implications of the mother's aberrant life. Her namelessness
is also a measure then of her function as an empty signifier, Locke's
tabula rasa transformed into a poignant absence. The positive effects
of a revolution in sexual relations, marital politics, and social order
are thus displaced onto an inarticulate futurity. Significantly, Maria
stops writing the memoirs when she hears that her daughter has
died; broken off abruptly, with "some lines" that "were crossed
out," her unfinished maternal discourse signals not only the rupture
of her identity by the loss of her child but also the degree to which

her culture's insistence on patterns of male continuance actively obstructs positive models of female transmission.

Wollstonecraft's text, in effect, signals the exhaustion of fruitful crossbreeding between fictional and behavioral literature in the political context of the late eighteenth century; while it shows that conventional domestic ideology fragments individual consciousness, it also recognizes that in the absence of such ideology the self has no stable set of images by which to organize experience and must empty itself into the promise of a future generation. Thus, by the time Maria attempts suicide, in the most finished of Wollstonecraft's proposed endings, she reexperiences (in almost exactly the same language) the hallucinatory, discordant impressions that open the narrative. "One remembrance with frightful velocity followed another—All the incidents of her life were in arms, embodied to assail her. . . . Her murdered child again appeared to her, mourning for the babe of which she was the tomb" (202). The daughter, who has been before her as she writes and lives, still assails her consciousness as a figure of broken promise. Maria does recover from the attempt by seeing her child alive, brought in by Jemima at the last moment. But her cry at the end, "The conflict is over!—I will live for my child" (203), registers both a resistance to the psychological atomism imposed on her by "partial laws" that entomb her and a surrender of personal identity to an abortive cause in which the self must relinquish its own life.

As one of the more volatile depictions of a disrupted family, Wollstonecraft's narrative, like *Tristram Shandy* or *The Castle of Otranto,* belongs to a moment in the development of prose fiction when the limits of the bourgeois family were severely tested. All such works provide models of self-invention that shift restlessly between lived and imagined experience, private and public existence, historical authenticity and modern invention. Their heterogeneous representations of the domestic sphere, as in the "subterraneous" vaults that snake beneath Otranto (25), the labyrinthine family plots Tristram constructs, and the "gloomy pile" that Maria is forced to inhabit (184), challenge the insular private life that was increasingly advocated in the literature on household government. The fragmentation of these texts implies the contrary force that lies at the heart of a signifying system whose function is to knit relations together; they envision historical shifts in domestic behavior not as a triumph of progressive clarification but as a fundamental reversal of temporal and aesthetic order. The dissonant behavior of the characters in these works is inseparable from the defamiliarizing effect produced by such historical revision. Ultimately, the figures in the narrative simply mirror the human family in its strange deviations from explicable affective conduct. Lacking a stable history, the characters necessarily manage themselves in ways that are essentially reactive, improvising personality to accommodate the unexpected events that are symptomatic of a patriarchal social structure apparently in the process of decline. If phantasmal agents in Walpole's fiction evoke the imaginary as a symbolic expression of cultural inconsistencies that destroy any attempts by living individuals to create coherent selves, the family members in Sterne and Wollstonecraft are similarly plagued by internal contradiction. The point where Wollstonecraft differs from Sterne and Walpole—in directly linking the failure of the bourgeois family to the defectiveness of existing political institutions controlled by men—marks precisely where eighteenth-century prose fiction becomes most overtly political. The domestic fiction produced by radical women writers toward the end of the eighteenth century (perhaps the most critical phase of "familiarization" in eighteenth-century prose fiction) was aimed at introducing a powerful new conception of political organization, which attempted, in effect, to redress failed systems of justice in and out of the family. In doing so, however, it simultaneously generated a millennial view of domestic politics that implied the defeat of reformist efforts, bequeathing to the next century a profoundly complex set of issues concerning the fictional relations among the self, the family, and the world.

Afterword

> Far better that your house should begin than it should end with
> you. The best families in the world had to start somewhere.
>
> —Jean Cordier, *La famille saincte*

Jean Cordier's observation about starting a "house" is, like most positive claims concerning originality, complicated by the arbitrary limits drawn around beginnings and endings: he privileges modernity over antiquity yet preserves the family's traditional power to confer social and historical distinction. A similar motive may legitimately be applied to the period's domestic maneuvers, as outlined in this book. Early British prose fiction confronted household relations in strategic ways that ranged from distancing to embracing to indicting them, but it consistently proposed to renew traditional domestic principles by reworking them as novel conceptions of the home. This need to refashion the family was prompted by shifts in the political significance of household representation. Behn and Defoe, for example, were drawn to fictional forms that elided normative family relations in part because their work was produced at a time (1660–1725) when a sequence of crises about family succession rendered the political resonance of domesticity particularly troublesome. Richardson and Haywood's work appeared when national tensions over succession and hereditary right (1725–1750) had abated or were more rapidly quelled; while their fiction engages such concerns, it develops them in relation to a comparatively stable conception of the monarchy's family power.[1] Indeed, the less directly expressed connections between family and national policy in these works suggests a more pervasive synthesis of political and domestic ideology. In the latter part of the century writers such as Walpole, Sterne, and Wollstonecraft became insistently aware (and wary) of the political repercussions of family ideology; without reproducing the tactics of Behn or Defoe, they challenged institutionalized representations of household government. The work of all these writers demonstrates that the fiction of the period both resisted the hegemonic deployment of traditional (and often aristocratic) principles of domestic order and sublimated those very codes for fear that important standards of social obligation were being dismantled.

The works by these authors adopt narrative modes that correspond to the tactics they tend to stress. *The Fair Jilt* and *Robinson Crusoe* favor the scandal chronicle and adventure story because these are well suited to the marginalization of customary family relations. *Pamela* and *Miss Betsy Thoughtless* exploit domestic fiction and courtship narratives because these are consonant with Richardson's and Haywood's incorporation of household norms. Walpole, Sterne, and Wollstonecraft, looking to disavow the family's standard usage in political rhetoric, exploit gothic and sentimental discourse because such modes of writing raised patterns of household government into spectacular relief. Thus, while it has long been commonplace to link the ascendancy of prose fiction in the eighteenth century to its formal capacity to wed domestic realism and bourgeois constructions of power, these texts reveal a much less stable alignment of literary genres and social effects. As part of an alternative approach, this book has sought to articulate, through analysis of individual texts, the malleability of the very structures that inform fictional re-creations of family life, such as the imagined divisions between individual, private, domestic, public, social, and national identities; the critical segregation of romance, realism, satire, and adventure; and the literary uses of the laboring, middling, and aristocratic classes. As a crucial structure mediating these social variables, family is best understood in a relational sense—not as a constant against which other social constructs can be measured, but as a shifting tactical term.

Formal and temporal effects on literary discourse are neither

fixed nor separable from other local pressures and individual idiosyncrasies. The writers I have examined were able to manipulate (or
be manipulated by) both the family's apparent resistance as a concept to external pressures and its flexibility, permeability, and volatile emotional force. Even those writers most commonly associated
with middle-class values were ardent about preserving aristocratic
norms; they were as responsive to the dynamic modulation of aesthetic and political values as writers less easily categorized by ideological affiliation. By moving from early displacements of domesticity to intense consolidations of family ideology, and finally to critiques of conventional household government, I have sought to account for both the progressive and the reactionary features embedded in these works. The family in the eighteenth century was, as it
continues to be, an extremely elastic category, used strategically to
make many different kinds of arguments, political as well as literary.
The diverse expressions of narrative and social experience that we
have dubbed fiction and family are a strange mixture of traditional
and revolutionary matter. Indeed, the formal and ideological conditions of eighteenth-century fiction, like Cordier's newborn "house,"
are best conceived in terms of both beginnings and ends.

Reference Matter

Notes

Introduction

1. On "defamiliarization," see Shklovsky, "Art as Technique," 11–22; and Tomashevsky, "Thematics," 84–87. According to Tomashevsky, defamiliarization is "a special instance of artistic motivation. . . . The old and habitual must be spoken of as if it were new and unusual. One must speak of the ordinary as if it were unfamiliar" (85).

2. For a fuller account of the Primrose portrait's relation to household iconography, see Flint, "'The Family Piece,'" 127–52.

3. See Watt, *The Rise of the Novel*; Davis, *Factual Fictions*; McKeon, *The Origins of the English Novel*; Hunter, *Before Novels*; H. Brown, *Institutions of the English Novel*; Miller, *The Heroine's Text*; N. Armstrong, *Desire and Domestic Fiction*; Gallagher, *Nobody's Story*; Todd, *The Sign of Angellica*; Bender, *Imagining the Penitentiary*.

4. Watt, Armstrong, and McKeon, as well as Nelson, *Children, Parents, and the Rise of the Novel*, for example, parallel the influence of the novel in eighteenth-century English letters with some form of change in family ideology. McKeon, for instance, links the ideological motivation of realism to a familial source. Not only does ideology "give birth" to form, it shapes that form on a genealogical imperative: "The figure of the younger son is central both to the progressive and to the conservative imagination. The rule of primogeniture seemed to many to suggest that the genealogical distinctions of aristocratic ideology had force even at the intrafamilial level" (218). In some measure, "founding a new family" becomes the means by which the progressive plot overthrows the aristocratic one, replacing absolutist family order (in which the father dictates the future of the family estate) with meritocracy—"the new gentry supersede not only the old gentry but also the old conception of gentility; the new conception consists of virtue and is evidenced now most clearly (although by no means exclusively) in efficient estate management" (222). The status inconsistency that this

new family encourages corresponds to changes in social categorization that ensure "the replacement of all the outworn fictions of status orientation by the emergent criteria of class" (223). See also Watt, *The Rise of the Novel*, 135–64, and N. Armstrong, *Desire and Domestic Fiction*, 28–160.

5. It is not perhaps surprising that the fiction should be so consumed by the family. A number of critical or analytic assessments of storytelling incline toward explanations that stem at least partly from family dynamics. In Freudian or Lacanian diegesis, for example, the impulse to narrate often derives from the child's compensatory need to replace parents or to appropriate the law and the word of the father. Feminist accounts of narrative empowerment frequently address the exclusionary tactics of patriarchs and husbands, the reconceptualization of domesticity, and the literary resonance of birthing. Even a structural account of narrative, like Propp's *Morphology of the Folk Tale*, generalizes parental, marital, and sibling relations into functional roles ("actants"). A parent may be a "provider," "villain," or "judge"; a child might be a "protagonist," "victim," or "helper." See Lacan, *Écrits*; Propp, *Morphology of the Folktale*. There are a also number of critical texts that specifically, and precisely, align narrative and family issues. See Beizer, *Family Plots*; Bowers, *The Politics of Motherhood*; Cohen, *The Daughter's Dilemma*; Green, *The Courtship Novel*; Kowaleski-Wallace, *Their Fathers' Daughters*; Nussbaum, *Torrid Zones*; Ragussis, *Acts of Naming*; Tanner, *Adultery in the Novel*; and Zomchick, *Family and the Law in Eighteenth-Century Fiction*.

6. Among the many works that argue this point are Ariès, *Centuries of Childhood*; Shorter, *The Making of the Modern Family*; Stone, *The Family, Sex and Marriage*; Trumbach, *The Rise of the Egalitarian Family*; Zaretsky, *Capitalism, the Family, and Personal Life*. Such arguments can, in turn, be traced back to claims in Durkheim, *The Division of Labor*, and Durkheim, *Incest*; Briffault, *The Mothers*; Engels, *The Origin of the Family*; Morgan, *Ancient Society;* Bachofen, *Das Mutterrecht* (Mother Right); Maine, *Ancient Law*; H. Spencer, *Principles of Sociology*; McLennan, *Primitive Marriage*; LePlay, *Ouvriers Européens*, and LePlay, *La réforme sociale en France*. All of these theorists share one essential premise that has long divided anthropological studies: that is, that there existed a universal stage of sexual promiscuity before human beings entered into more complex and restrictive social/sexual groupings. The heated debate, still waged over the reputed existence of an extended kinship model of family before the affective nuclear one of the modern period would consequently be seen as a part of a civilizing tendency in sexual and procreative human behavior, what Fernand Braudel calls the "shattering" of the "biological ancien régime" (70). For an excellent summary of the various positions see Burguière and Lebrun, "One Hundred and One Families of Europe," 11–94. See also Anderson,

Approaches to the History of the Western Family; Hareven, "Modernization and Family History," 740–50; Hareven, "Cycles, Courses, and Cohorts," 97–109; O. Harris, "Households and Their Boundaries," 143–52; Poster, *Critical Theory of the Family*.

7. See, for example, Laslett, *The World We Have Lost*, 18–22; and Lasch, *Haven in a Heartless World*.

8. This differentiation of literary and statistical evidence is reiterated in Laslett's Introduction to *Household and Family in Past Time*, 11–13.

9. Lautman acknowledges that her claims extend points raised by William J. Goode in *World Revolution and Family Patterns*, 76, 371–72.

10. This central assumption reinforces claims such as that of Michael Mascuch, who convincingly demonstrates from a variety of British autobiographies written between 1600 and 1750 that families of the "middle sort" clung intensely to the basic nuclear model in order to fence off the "abyss of poverty." See Mascuch, "Social Mobility and Middling Self-Identity," 61. This implies that the family was essentially a conservative rather than transformative force.

11. For a more extensive discussion of *Desire and Domestic Fiction* see Chapter 1.

12. An especially polemical instance of this kind of argument can be found in Ferdinand Mount's *Subversive Family*, where the nuclear family's historical continuity is determined by its exclusively subversive function. Mount's conviction that "the family is that into which the state does not intrude" should come as no surprise since he was a member of the Conservative Research Department and head of the prime minister's Policy Unit in 1982 and 1983, during Margaret Thatcher's government. See Mount, *The Subversive Family*, 1–11. Mount's argument is essentially a continuation of the claim made by William J. Goode that "[t]he ideology of the conjugal family is a radical one, destructive of the older traditions in almost every society." See Goode, *World Revolution and Family Patterns*, 19.

13. But as Zvi Razi has argued from his work on medieval and early modern English culture, the family rarely produces a structurally finite norm. While he acknowledges that over time the nuclear family has come to dominate as a household form (a fact he traces back to the fourteenth century) and that by 1700 it seems indisputably present, he also insists that a "functional extended family" (as distinct from one occupying a single domicile) continues to reappear as demographic, economic, and social pressures either encourage or discourage its utility. See Razi, "The Myth of the Immutable English Family," 3–44. Even more pointedly, Peter Earle argues that the average experience of Londoners from 1650 to 1750 suggests that the family might still be "fundamental" but it was also "a very fragile institution." See Earle, *A City Full of People*, 165. For an excellent overview of

the diversity of family structures and the difficulty of reconciling the "universality" of family with its multiple permutations see Zonabend, "An Anthropological Perspective," 8–68.

14. Recent theoretical discussions about the field of family studies have, in fact, emphasized tactical and varied understandings of the family. Though distinct, such methods as "symbolic interactionism," "life-course dynamics," "the life-cycle model," "network theory," and "exchange theory" emphasize the evolving strategies in the decision making of individuals and families over a lifetime. As Tamara Hareven notes: "A study of family strategies enables us to examine the interaction between, on the one hand, the social and economic constructions and external cultural values in the society which dictate these choices; and, on the other hand, the family members' values, to the extent that those values diverge from the external ones." Hareven, "Family History at the Crossroads," xiii. Similar points are made by Cheal, *Family and the State of Theory*, 119–52; and by Broderick, "Family Process Theory"; and Sprey, "Theoretical Practice in Family Studies," both in Sprey, ed., *Fashioning Family Theory*, 171–206, 9–33. In a related vein, Pierre Bourdieu, examining marital behavior among peasants in a remote area of the Pyrenees, argues that "the generating and unifying principle of [such] practices is constituted by a whole system of predispositions inculcated by the material circumstances of life and by family upbringing, i.e., by *habitus*" ("Marriage Strategies," 119). By "*habitus*" he means "the practical mastery of a small number of implicit principles that have spawned an infinite number of practices and follow their own pattern, although they are not based on obedience to any formal rules" (141). Anthony Fletcher has argued that between 1500 and 1800 patriarchy and gender had to be constantly renegotiated, creating variable systems both subjected to continuous pressures and constituted by the tensions and contradictions of early modern ideology. See Fletcher, *Gender, Sex and Subordination*, esp. 283–413.

15. In arguing for a semiotic reading of marriage practices in eighteenth-century Britain, I am stating what John Gillis, in his suggestive remarks about the temporal dimensions of the home, similarly proposes: "If our understanding of family past and present is to be enhanced, the existing history of the families people have lived with physically must be supplemented with a history of the families people have lived symbolically" (J. Gillis, "Making Time," 18).

16. The findings of "evolutionist" writers have not, in fact, been uniformly supported by historical research. Perhaps most damaging to the evolutionist position is the fact that Darwin himself thought the nuclear family was from the beginning an essential component of sexual selection. See Darwin, *The Descent of Man*, 2: 361, 363. If many of the "evolutionists"

implement a "Platonic" model of the family (in which sexual-domestic relations are regarded as an obstruction to ideal state government), the model used here springs from Aristotle, who wrote in the *Politics* that the first household derived from the combination of man's possession of property—in the slave or in domesticated animals—with man's relation to woman. See *The Republic of Plato*, 165–66, and *Aristotle's Politics*, 2, 5. In Aristotle the village is a colony or offshoot of the household, and monarchical government ensues from the monarchy of the eldest male member of the family. The modern articulation of this position can be traced to one of Bachofen's contemporaries, Edward Westermarck, also an insistent critic of the Morgan hypothesis. See Westermarck, *The History of Human Marriage*. Bronislaw Malinowski is, however, probably the most outspoken critic of "evolutionary" theory, basing his criticisms on the principles laid down by Aristotle. He supported the view that monogamy as both a pattern and a prototype of human marriage is universal and vehemently discredited the "illusions" of evolutionists. See, for example, Malinowski, *Sex, Culture, and Myth*, 33, 34.

17. On the Marriage Act see Bannet, "The Marriage Act," 233–54; Harth, "The Virtue of Love," 123–34; Vermillion, "*Clarissa* and the Marriage Act," 395–412. Bannet argues that the act's legislators were more interested in regulating fertility than in developing ethical norms. For an account of Gretna Green elopements and folk traditions regarding marriage see Gottlieb, *The Family in the Western World*, 49–88. For clandestine marriages see R. Brown, "The Rise and Fall of Fleet Marriages," 117–36; J. Gillis, "Conjugal Settlements," 261–86; Schellekens, "Courtship," 433–44. These tend to see eighteenth-century marriage legislation as an inadvertent incitement of illegitimacy.

18. Perhaps the most explicit expression of Freud's point is found in "The Dissection of the Psychical Personality," the thirty-first lecture of his *New Introductory Lectures in Psycho-Analysis*: "Even if conscience is something 'within us,' yet it is not so from the first. In this it is a real contrast to sexual life, which is in fact there from the beginning of life and not only a later addition. But, as is well known, young children are amoral and possess no internal inhibitions against their impulses striving for pleasure. The part which is later taken on by the super-ego is played to begin with by an external power, by parental authority. Parental influence governs the child by offering proofs of love and by threatening punishments which are signs to the child of loss of love and are bound to be feared on their own account. This realistic anxiety is the precursor of the later moral anxiety. So long as it is dominant there is no need to talk of a super-ego and of a conscience. It is only subsequently that the secondary situation develops (which we are all too ready to regard as the normal one), where the exter-

nal restraint is internalized and the super-ego takes the place of the parental agency and observes, directs and threatens the ego in exactly the same way as earlier the parents did with the child" (22: 61–62).

19. For a discussion of women writers and "moralizing the novel," see J. Spencer, *The Rise of the Woman Novelist*, 86.

20. Here I use the concept "ideology" to mean "the set of ideas which arise from a given set of material interests or, more broadly, from a definite class or group," rather than the late-eighteenth- and nineteenth-century meaning of "the science of ideas" or the Marxist sense of "false consciousness." I quote from Williams, "Ideology," in *Keywords*, 153–57. Williams takes the last two quotations from elsewhere: the first, according to the O.E.D.'s citations under "Ideology," is by W. Taylor in the *Monthly Magazine* 3 (1797): 285; the second is by Friedrich Engels from his *Letter to Mehring* (1893). For a more complete discussion of the term's definition see Eagleton, *Ideology*, esp. 1–32. In order to focus the term, Eagleton develops six different but related ways of construing it, the first of which approximates my use of the term in this instance, and generally, though not exclusively, in the rest of *Family Fictions*: "the general material process of production of ideas, beliefs and values in social life . . . [as denoted by] the whole complex of signifying practices and symbolic processes in a particular society" (28). I would, however, add his caveat that such a meaning needs also to account for "the relations between these signs and processes of political power" (29).

21. For an insightful account of the familial dimensions of narrative and literary theory see Jonnes, *The Matrix of Narrative*, 84–112, 121–77, 205–68. Jonnes argues that the linguistic, semantic, and social arrangements that prose fiction both represents and imitates are modeled on a particular order of events consisting of such familial acts as love and courtship, engagement, marriage, intercourse, giving birth, rearing children, and founding a home. Conversely, the death of a family member, the abduction or flight of a child from home, incest, adultery, separation, divorce, and the disruption of the family as a result of external circumstances like war, social intolerance, and economic or natural disasters are events that negatively define the prose fiction's ideological and structural framework. The identities of characters are primarily rendered in terms of their functional roles within or in connection with the family—as parents, children, siblings, lovers, suitors, husbands, and wives. Moreover, the actions of the principal figures in extended prose fiction usually have some kind of decisive effect on the internal organization of the family, whether subverting normal relations (a child fleeing home), reconstituting them (reclaiming a child; discovering a parent), or creating new ones (uniting two families through marriage) (84–88).

22. To be precise, the word "family" derives from *familia*, the Latin word for household, which is derived, in turn, from *famulus*, Latin for servant (see O.E.D., s.v. "family"). For further analysis see Raymond Williams, "Family," in *Keywords*, 131–34.

23. Mark Turner argues in his study of how kinship metaphors occupy the rhetoric of literary theory, cognitive science, and linguistics that "analysis of kinship metaphor reveals a mental model we use to produce and understand certain kinds of language about mind . . . [and] provides the basic metaphors we use to understand 'mental creation.'" He believes that quite frequently "we explain 'metaphor' to ourselves in terms of what we know about 'family.'" Family thus becomes a grounding concept for cognitive activity and, therefore, has a pervasive formative effect on literary discourse. See Turner, *Death Is the Mother of Beauty*, 12. See also Jonnes, *The Matrix of Narrative*, 115–77.

24. Spacks, *Desire and Truth*; and Doody, *The True Story of the Novel*, are recent exceptions, examining the works of male and female authors in approximately equal distribution.

25. For an account of shifts in literary attitudes toward the comparison of writing and parturition see Castle, "Lab'ring Bards: Birth Topoi and English Poetics, 1660–1820," 193–208. Castle argues that by the time Fielding was writing the comparison had gained considerable prestige.

26. That was the original title of the prose fiction work by William Godwin, which is now commonly called *Caleb Williams* (1794). For reflections on the title's bearing see Godwin's Preface in *Caleb Williams*, 1. The full original title was *Things as They Are; or, The Adventures of Caleb Williams*.

Chapter 1

1. The main problem, as Jack Goody observes, "is to understand just what is evolving. The English term 'family' is a polysemic word used to describe a conjugal pair and their young ('starting a family'), the members of a household ('one of the family'), a range of bilateral kin ('relatives') or a patronymic group, usually associated with a title ('The Churchill family'). And there are wider semantic usages, extending to the human ('the family of man') and nonhuman ('the family of sweet peas') species." See Goody, "The Evolution of the Family," 103. Discussing printed material concerned with household size, Richard Wall points out that "[the] failure to distinguish between a building such as a workhouse and the domestic group or family is only one aspect of a much more serious problem—the failure on the part of some writers to make appropriate distinction between the houseful and the household." See Wall, "Mean Household Size," 161. On the etymological background and general resonance of "home," see the es-

says by John Hollander, Joseph Rykwert, Eric Hobsbawm, Gwendolyn Wright, Tamara K. Hareven, and Mary Douglas in Mack, ed., *Home: A Place in the World*. All agree that the conceptual solidity of the term evaporates in practice. See also J. Gillis, *For Better, for Worse*, and "Making Time." As he points out in the latter, "Family time presents itself to us as a neutral cultural practice, when in fact, it is an ideologically constituted form of prescription, with a power to convince us of even that which is contradicted by our everyday experience" (17).

2. By "family chronicle" I mean those prose fictional works like Thomas Mann's *Buddenbrooks* or Gabriel García Marquez's *One Hundred Years of Solitude* that describe several generations of a single "family." For a partial account of these kinds of relatively modern texts see Tobin.

3. In this regard, it is interesting to note that a large proportion of eighteenth-century conduct books employ fictional vignettes or personal anecdotes to communicate their advice. That is, to convey general principles of domestic behavior they repeatedly use a specific and familiar domestic scene.

4. I have amassed these titles from Orr, *A Catalogue Checklist of English Prose Fiction*.

5. My claims here have been argued in different form by Bakhtin, who also applies the notion of familiarizing to the development of the novel itself: "The destruction of epic distance and the transferral of the image of an individual from the distanced plane to the zone of contact with the inconclusive events of the present (and consequently of the future) result in a radical re-structuring of the image of the individual in the novel—and consequently in all literature. Folklore and popular-comic sources for the novel played a huge role in this process. Its first and essential step was the comic familiarization of the image of man. Laughter destroyed epic distance; it began to investigate man freely and familiarly, to turn him inside out, expose the disparity between his surface and his center, between his potential and his reality" (35).

6. These intellectual concerns are part of a comprehensive discursive movement in the eighteenth century toward a confident but utilitarian self-sufficiency. As Weber and Tawney long ago argued, the rise of capitalism and the Protestant ethic coincided largely because individuals were seeking the means to reconcile their faith (in religion and state) with their private economic interests. This is not to say that all human thought became secularized, but that individuals appraised the religious or spiritual content of human experience in terms of their contact with a phenomenological world. Thus for Locke, and later the Deists, the senses circumscribed a person's understanding, including understanding of God—that is, comprehension was gained by the experience of the external world as acquired

through the senses and by the inner psychical world as observed through reflection on the workings of the human mind and less on the family's doctrinaire instruction on such matters. See Weber, *The Protestant Ethic*; Tawney, *Religion and the Rise of Capitalism*.

7. See Pocock, *The Machiavellian Moment*, 423–24. Recently, there has been continued speculation that Locke's theories were not of central importance in contemporary political and social debates. See, for example, Tribe, "Property, Patriarchy, and the Constitution of a Polity," in *Land, Labour, and Economic Discourse*, 35–52; and Clark, *English Society*, 42–64. This skepticism is a necessary corrective to what may have previously been an overemphasis on Locke's centrality in eighteenth-century political debates. Indeed, Locke seems in many ways to have been as much a synthetic thinker as an innovator. I use him here precisely for that reason—he offers a convenient combination of attitudes, some outside the mainstream of thought, some within. At the same time, I still believe that it is unsafe to underestimate Locke's influence on the eighteenth century as a political, philosophical, and social theorist. For an account of Locke's role in the debate about patriarchalism see Gauthier, "The Role of Inheritance in Locke's Political Theory," 38–45; and Schochet, *The Authoritarian Family*, 275. See also Shanley, "Marriage Contract and Social Contract."

8. Lawrence Stone, for example, calls *Patriarcha* "Filmer's last-ditch stand"; see *The Family, Sex and Marriage in England*, 411. James Daly claims in *Sir Robert Filmer and English Political Thought* that by 1690 the "political crisis had rendered a large body of political thinking [like Filmer's] embarrassing if not irrelevant, even to its former following" (11). For a subtle, contrary argument that examines the continued tactical uses of divine right ideology, see Clark, *English Society*, 119–98. Clark describes the metamorphosis of this ideology "in three aspects: as a political strategy; as a doctrine of wide incidence, but which (in one of its forms) became unavailable for use in public debate after 1714; and as a cultural survival, caught up with the social function of religion, in the slow-moving, backward-looking world of popular and rural attitudes" (120–21).

9. Though *Two Treatises of Government* appeared in the wake of the Glorious Revolution and therefore seemed an adjudication of the Protestant succession, it was probably written long before William and Mary ascended the British throne, during the Exclusion Crisis. Peter Laslett argues that it was begun as early as the autumn and winter of 1679–1680 and that it was probably composed at the same time as *An Essay Concerning Human Understanding*, which was also published well after it was first composed (see Laslett, ed., Introduction to *Two Treatises of Government*). Eager to assert general truths in the *Essay*, Locke perhaps thought it better to disassociate the philosophical writing entirely from the contingent truths of po-

litical theory. Both works, however, seem to have been born out of a specific crisis about specific family relations in a specific royal family. On Locke's relation to revolution see Ashcraft, *Revolutionary Politics and Locke's 'Two Treatises of Government'*; Franklin, *John Locke and the Theory of Sovereignty*; Rapaczynski, *Nature and Politics*, 177–90; Simmons, *The Lockean Theory of Rights*, esp. 167–221.

10. See Gee, *The Divine Right and Original of the Civil Magistrate From God*, 180–81; Tyrrell, *Patriarcha Non Monarcha*, 73–75. For a discussion of this debate see Daly, *Robert Filmer*, 88–96.

11. On Locke's theory of individualism see Macpherson, *The Political Theory*, 194–262; for an examination of the philosophical contradictions of Locke's theory of identity see Antony Flew's seminal essay, "Locke and the Problem of Personal Identity," 155–78; as Locke's theory of identity relates to freedom see Polin, "John Locke's Conception of Freedom," 1–18.

12. For an interpretation of Locke that regards the works as much more fully complementary see Grant, *John Locke's Liberalism*. See also I. Harris, *The Mind of John Locke*, esp. 280–317.

13. A similar condition obtains with Descartes, who was perhaps even more emphatic about the philosophic negligibility of the family: "All that, at the most, [my parents] contributed to my origin was the giving of certain dispositions (modifications) to the matter in which I have hitherto judged that I or my mind, which is what alone I now consider to be myself, is enclosed; and thus there can here be no difficulty with respect to them." Descartes, *The Meditations*, 60.

14. Spacks contends that sentimental fiction of the 1760s, particularly that written by women, rejects linear trajectories of plot that produce relations of power, and seeks to create affiliation, especially through maternal feeling. "Plots of power," such as *Robinson Crusoe*, *Clarissa*, and *Tom Jones*, duplicate Lockean notions of linear association, providential design, and paternal privilege. Unlike Spacks, I regard both tactics as themselves divided between establishing and relinquishing power. See Spacks, *Desire and Truth*, 114–46. For an outline of the parallels between Lockean educational doctrine and eighteenth-century fiction see Nelson, *Children, Parents, and the Rise of the Novel*, 85–100.

15. Sir William Temple and Charles Leslie, for example, both claimed that conjugality was an innate tendency, though their views on related issues were radically opposed. See Temple, *Miscellanea*, 63–80; Leslie, *The New Association*, pt. 3, supplement, 7. These passages are referred to by Maximillian Novak in *Defoe and the Nature of Man*, 16.

16. On Locke's complicated relation to natural law see Ashcraft, "Locke's State of Nature," 898–915; Riley, "On Finding an Equilibrium Between Consent and Natural Law," 432–52; Strauss, *Natural Right and*

History, 202–51; Yolton, "Locke on the Law of Nature," 477–98. For a recent and comprehensive account of natural law, and its impact on eighteenth-century thought, see Haakonssen, *Natural Law and Moral Philosophy*.

17. Pufendorf, *De Jure Naturae et Gentium*; and Grotius, *De Jure Belli ac Pacis*, quoted in Novak, *Defoe*, 109.

18. Hobbes's view of family government in primitive societies was bleak: "the savage people in many places of America, except the government of small families, the concord whereof dependeth on natural lust, have no government at all; and live at this day in that brutish manner, as I said before" (83). On Hobbes's dependency on natural law see Warrender, *The Political Philosophy of Hobbes*, 48–79; and Taylor, "The Ethical Doctrine of Hobbes."

19. Novak paraphrases Arthur Lovejoy to explain the various meanings of natural law during the seventeenth and eighteenth centuries: "It could be used in an historical or anthropological sense to refer to the 'primeval condition of man'; in a 'cultural sense' to refer to a stage of society in which the arts and sciences had not yet progressed beyond a few primitive tools; or in a political sense to indicate the relationships between men before the creation of government" (Novak, *Defoe*, 22). See also Lovejoy, "The Supposed Primitivism of Rousseau's *Discourses on Inequality*," 14–15. Grotius distinguishes between natural law, divine law, and municipal law (also called civil or positive law), but admits that, just as municipal law derives from natural law, the latter "can nevertheless rightly be attributed to God, because of His having willed that such traits exist in us" (14–15). Such differentiations allowed for distinct but equally authoritative explanations of human conduct. Preserving the necessity of divine law for original human actions and establishing reason as a source for human conduct, the connected separateness of the various laws offered a flexible explanatory model and protected God from too direct a role in those human actions requiring legal restraints. For a fuller discussion of divine, natural, and positive law in relation to Grotius see Edwards, *Hugo Grotius*, 27–69.

20. Like Locke, Grotius was determined, as Charles Edwards points out, to read into the historical past the social features he observed in the present: "Grotius did not consider human beings as ever having lived outside the bounds of society. Originally, all of humanity composed one vast society characterized by families and family groupings. In true Aristotelian fashion, Grotius maintained that human beings were social by nature, that from the dawn of creation they entered responsively into social relations" (Edwards, *Hugo Grotius*, 97).

21. Adding further to the confusion about domestic space, the distinction between "lodger" and "householder" was notoriously slippery and suggestive in the eighteenth century. See Earle, *A City Full of People*, 167.

22. On the history of population in the period see Anderson, *British Population History*; Wrigley and Schofield, *The Population History of England, 1541–1871*. An excellent and concise summary of one of the crucial claims in Wrigley and Schofield for the eighteenth century—that a rise in fertility is the dominant cause of the period's population explosion, particularly in the latter half, and accounts for the multiplication in both legitimate and illegitimate offspring—can be found in Abelove, "Some Speculations in the History of 'Sexual Intercourse,'" 125–30. Abelove points out that such demographic approaches often ignore the compelling deduction that sexual intercourse increased dramatically both in and out of marriage. He links these phenomena, in turn, to the discursive and phenomenologically central role of capitalist production just before the Industrial Revolution. The demographic material thus points to an increased devaluation of sexual and affective relations within the family, implying that the very evidence often used to demonstrate stability in attitudes toward the nuclear family reveals a much more complicated set of assumptions, tactics, and effects.

23. See "Marriage," in the *Encyclopædia Britannica*, 11th ed., 17: 753.

24. For a trenchant account of Smith's reasoning see Winch, *Adam Smith's Politics*.

25. The most forceful claim of the dominance of women novelists in the period is Dale Spender's declaration that "it was women and not men who made the greater contribution to the development of the novel." Spender, one of the most instrumental scholars in the recent recovery of eighteenth-century women writers, claims that there were "more than one hundred women novelists before Jane Austen and no more than thirty men," but she grants an extra "generous allocation" to the men by allowing the proportion to be "two good women novelists to each man." See Spender, *Mothers of the Novel*, 4, 6. Spender reiterates these claims in the Introduction to *Living by the Pen*, ed. Dale Spender, 31. Jane Spencer is more cautious in her observation that if women "wrote, as one literary historian has estimated, between two-thirds and three-quarters of epistolary novels between 1760 and 1790, that was more than enough to give a general impression that they were taking over." See J. Spencer, *The Rise of the Woman Novelist*, 4. (The historian to whom she and Spender refer is F. G. Black; see Black's *The Epistolary Novel in the Late Eighteenth Century*.) But using the same implicit criteria as Spender (writers of at least one work of prose fiction published between 1700 and Austen's death in 1817), I consulted several fiction checklists and, in only a very brief search, was able to amass another 73 names to supplement her list of 100 good women writers (119–37). With the same sources and criteria, I was able to add more than 200 names to her list of male writers who meet the same requirements. Perhaps

Janet Todd's conclusion is the most reasonable: "I do not believe that feminist literary history should simply reverse the faulty procedure. The novel as a genre has both fathers and mothers"; see Todd, *The Sign of Angellica*, 2. A more exacting search could (and should) be made with the Eighteenth-Century Short-Title Catalog, in the manner of Veylit, *A Statistical Survey and Evaluation of the 'Eighteenth-Century Short-Title Catalog.'*

26. On the nature of spectatorship and domestic ideology in *The Spectator Papers* see Ketcham, *Transparent Designs*, 105–23. On the cultural significance of spectating in the period see Straub, *Sexual Suspects*, 3–23.

27. A good overview of the variety of conduct books prevalent in the seventeenth and early eighteenth centuries can be found in Hunter, *Before Novels*. For later in the period see J. Mason, *Gentlefolk in the Making*, 88–112, 175–219. An account of these works that links them specifically to Samuel Richardson's fiction is Marks, *Sir Charles Grandison*, esp. 26–97. For a recent account of the fluidity of masculine norms of conduct in the early modern period see Fletcher, *Gender, Sex and Subordination*, esp. 322–46.

28. The subtitles to T. Rogers's *The Character of a Good Woman* and *Early Religion* make the pairing of his two works even clearer by suggesting their memorial and exemplary nature: "In a funeral discourse . . . occasion'd by the decease of Mrs. Elizabeth Dunton"; "Proposed in a sermon preach'd upon the death of Mr. Robert Linager."

29. On Austen's admiration for *Sir Charles Grandison* see Marks, *Sir Charles Grandison*, 16. For Blake's enthusiasm see J. Harris, "Introduction," in Jocelyn Harris, ed., *Sir Charles Grandison*, xii. The phrase about "living manners" comes from a letter by Frances Grainger to Samuel Richardson, quoted in Marks, *Sir Charles Grandison*, 34.

30. See, in particular, Laslett's interesting conclusion, "Understanding Ourselves in Time" (*The World We Have Lost*), 241–53, where he points out that certain problems "our ancestors" had with affective familial relations "may well have been worse, not better, than our own. . . . In fact, in tending to look backwards in this way, in diagnosing the difficulties as the outcome of something which has indeed been lost to our society, those concerned with social welfare are suffering from a false understanding of ourselves in time" (249).

Chapter 2

1. For a typical example of this argument see Link, *Aphra Behn*, who comments: "Defoe comes immediately to mind in reading *The Fair Jilt*; he did not originate the technique of circumstantial detail for which he is best known, but merely refined and extended it. The difficulty Mrs. Behn has comes from trying to fit an essentially romantic story into a realistic mold;

Moll Flanders is often improbable, but it is not romantic, and therefore it is more successful" (138–39). Catherine Gallagher argues that Behn's stories cannot be linked to the novel because they are not "self-proclaimed fictional works. . . . When the conventions of novelistic form are truly in place, we do not wonder about a book's referentiality." See Gallagher, *Nobody's Story*, 60. An interesting counterpoint is presented by D. Ross, *The Excellence of Falsehood*, 16–38. That there was still considerable confusion about the categories of fact and fiction as late as 1794 is evident from Michael Crump's statistical analysis of the Eighteenth-Century Short-Title Catalog, "Stranger than Fiction," 59–73.

2. Most critics now assume Behn was writing from personal experience, though Ernest Bernbaum, George Guffey, and Ruth T. Sheffey argue variously that the Surinam and Netherlands incidents that Behn claims to have witnessed in works like *Oroonoko* and *The Fair Jilt* were fictional. See Bernbaum, "Mrs. Behn's Biography a Fiction," 432–53; Guffey, "Aphra Behn's *Oroonoko*: Occasion and Accomplishment," 3–41; and Sheffey, "Some Evidence for a New Source of Aphra Behn's *Oroonoko*," 52–63. For Behn's defenders, those who accept as fact the autobiographical details in the novels, see Adams, *Travel Literature and the Evolution of the Novel*, 116–17 (he refers to *Oroonoko* as "colonial realism"); Summers, "Introduction: Memoir of Mrs. Behn," 1: xv–lxi; Platt, "Astrea and Celadon: An Untouched Portrait of Aphra Behn," 544–59; Hargreaves, "New Evidence of the Realism of Mrs. Behn's *Oroonoko*," 437–44; and Ramsaran, "*Oroonoko*: A Study of the Factual Elements," 142–45. Additional supporting evidence for the veracity of Behn's claims may be found in the biographies. The three most recent, Duffy, *The Passionate Shepherdess*; Goreau, *Reconstructing Aphra*; and Woodcock, *Aphra Behn*, are perhaps the most reliable. William J. Cameron's work on the Surinam and Netherlands aspects of Behn's life is particularly valuable for substantiating Behn's claims in *The Fair Jilt*. See Cameron, *New Light on Aphra Behn*, esp. 18–33.

3. See, for example, Watt, *The Rise of the Novel*, 33.

4. I should clarify that romance is not the only genre in opposition to which (or from which) the novel was ostensibly defining itself. I agree with J. Paul Hunter that a detailed history of the novel must acknowledge an enormous variety of discursive objects as the novel's antecedents, without privileging (or, in Hunter's case, even involving) the romance. For Hunter, these antecedents include "the various traditions of prose and poetry, some fictional, some not; some narrative, some not; some long and comprehensive, some not, that ultimately came to fruition in long prose fictional narratives that we have come to call novels" (*Before Novels*, 26). I would maintain, however, that the romance/novel comparison is one of the most often cited distinctions made by novelists and critics in the eighteenth cen-

tury itself. Such awareness indicates a profound conceptual dependence on the romance to provide an empowering sense of difference and an anxious need to distinguish between romance and novel in order to mask continuities between both modes. For a more extensive analysis of this codependence, see Langbauer, *Women and Romance*, esp. 1–61. I differ substantially from Hunter and somewhat from Langbauer in regarding novel and romance, ultimately, as *modes* of prose fictional discourse rather than discrete, or even generally (if problematically) distinct *genres*. For a similar argument and a good overview of the romance/realism conundrum see D. Ross, *The Excellence of Falsehood*, 1–15.

5. In her own time and throughout the eighteenth century Behn was constantly under attack, mostly on the grounds of her supposed moral laxity. Pope noted in his "Epistle to Augustus" ["The First Epistle of the Second Book of Horace, Imitated"]: "The stage how loosely does Astraea tread,/Who fairly puts all characters to bed." *Imitations of Horace*, 219–20, lines 290–91. In 1738, "The Apotheosis of Milton" appeared in the influential publication, *The Gentleman's Magazine*. The anonymous writer, having fallen asleep in Westminister Abbey, dreams of an assembly for the admission of Milton into the company buried in Poet's Corner. When Behn attempts to join them she is rejected: "Observe that Lady dressed in the loose Robe de Chambre with her Neck and Breasts bare; how much Fire in her Eye! what a passionate Expression in her Motions; And how much Assurance in her Features! Observe what an Indignant Look she bestows on the President [Chaucer], who is telling her, that none of her Sex has any Right to a Seat there. How she throws her Eyes about, to see if she can find out any one to take her Part. No! not one stirs; they who are enclined in her favour are overawed, and the rest shake their Heads; and now she flings out of the Assembly. That extraordinary Woman is Afra Behn" (469). Other detractors included Thomas Shadwell, Matthew Prior, Thomas Brown, the Duke of Buckingham, William Wycherley, Jonathan Swift, Henry Fielding, and John Duncombe. She had, of course, her noteworthy admirers as well: John Dryden, Thomas Otway, Abraham Cowley, Nathaniel Lee, Charles Gildon, Gerard Langbaine, George Granville (Baron Lansdowne), Thomas Southerne, John Evelyn, Daniel Defoe, Colley Cibber, Clara Reeve. But even some of her supporters apologized for her "looseness"; in a letter to Elizabeth Thomas, written in 1699, Dryden referred to the "licence which Mrs. Behn allowed herself, of writing loosely, and giving. . . . some scandal to the modesty of her sex." See Dryden, *The Letters of John Dryden*, 127.

6. Moral outrage against Behn was prolonged. In John Doran's history of the stage (1860), Behn is "a mere harlot, who danced through uncleanness" (see Doran, "Their Majesties' Servants," in *Annals of the English Stage*,

1: 85). Link points out that in response to Pearson's 1871 reprint of the works of Behn and his commendatory pamphlet on her reputation, the *Saturday Review* and the *Athenaeum* made such remarks as "time has not staled the foulness of the ordure" (*Saturday Review* 33 [January 27, 1872]: 109) and "she was . . . one of the original corrupters and polluters of the stage" (*Athenaeum*, March 16, 1872, 303); see Link, *Aphra Behn*, 153. As should be clear by now, Behn's literary reputation was inexorably connected to sexual indulgence as if, in her case, these two conditions were mutually operative. As recently as 1905, Ernest Baker in the Introduction to *The Novels of Mrs. Behn* maintained: "There have been novelists since Mrs. Behn who have written stuff that is quite as false, lurid and depraved, and readers who have gushed over it. Only the sinners begotten of later romancers do not sin with such abandon" (xxvi). Most of the obdurate moral criticism occurred during the nineteenth century; almost all of it was made by male critics who were, it seems, concerned not only with the moral laxity of which they thought Behn guilty but also with the threatening presence of a female intellect in the male domain of letters. In the twentieth century the moral dimension has generally died away, though literary historians continue to believe that Behn was somehow "freakish," to use Sandra M. Gilbert and Susan Gubar's adjective. According to Gilbert and Gubar, "Aphra Behn—the first really 'professional' literary woman in England—was and is always considered a somewhat 'shady lady,' no doubt promiscuous, probably self-indulgent, and certainly 'indecent'"; see Gilbert and Gubar, *The Madwoman in the Attic*, 65, 63. See also Jacobs, "The Seduction of Aphra Behn," 395–403.

7. For a good overview of sixteenth- and early-seventeenth-century "Instruction in Domestic Relations" see Wright, *Middle-Class Culture in Elizabethan England*, 201–27; and A. Jones, "Nets and Bridles," 39–72. For a specific account of Gouge's, Swetnam's, and Whately's books (and others like them) see Stenton, *The English Woman in History*, 107–45.

8. See MacCarthy, *Women Writers*, 161.

9. According to Paul Salzman, "the full range of [Behn's] work is an excellent illustration of the various approaches to the novel form taken by Restoration writers." See Salzman, *English Prose Fiction*, 314. Recently, Behn has been well served by edited collections that showcase the range and relevance of her work. See Hutner, ed., *Rereading Aphra Behn*; Todd, ed., *Aphra Behn Studies*. See also Chernaik, *Sexual Freedom in Restoration Literature*.

10. *Oroonoko*, the exception to this rule in that it consistently focuses on the dilemmas of the black male titular hero, is in fact the least characteristic of Behn's fiction. In the body of prose texts attributed to Behn, female characters dominate the action; at the very least, male characters serve to

highlight the activities or disposition of a female character. In any event, it is possible to argue, as Laura Brown does, that as an exilic tale narrated by a woman, *Oroonoko* simply encodes its concern with female experience. The royal slave embodies the marginalized position of even the most privileged women in Restoration England. Indeed, much of the anomalous tone of that work derives from its merging of emancipatory yearning and reactionary political arguments. See L. Brown, "The Romance of Empire," 41–61. See also Ferguson, "*Oroonoko*: Birth of a Paradigm," 339–59; and Gallagher, *Nobody's Story*, 66–87.

11. Gallagher also quotes these lines and, interestingly, regards them as an exemplary instance of how Behn's male competitors cooperated in supplying the anti-feminist invective that Behn herself strategically employed, particularly in aligning authorship with prostitution, in order to establish her visible presence as a professional author. See Gallagher, *Nobody's Story*, 26–27.

12. To a large extent, of course, the attacks on Behn were the result of partisan politics, to which she also contributed. Nonetheless, Behn received an extraordinary amount of critical opprobrium from critics that was not at all commensurate with the amount of political and sexual invective she engaged in herself.

13. Gallagher assesses Behn's rhetorical uses of the prostituted and the sovereign self to articulate her position as a professional woman writer within the seventeenth-century literary marketplace (1–87). Miranda similarly embodies these twin metaphors of illicit appeal and righteous authority, and figures as a type for the author. But while I agree that Behn often used both of these tropes, I would also contend that she frequently extended her metaphoric allusions about authorship to include androgyny and cross-dressing, in an attempt to finesse the sexual limitations implied by both whoredom and kingship.

14. A notorious critical debate about the truthfulness of *Oroonoko*, and to a lesser extent *The Fair Jilt*, was inaugurated by Bernbaum. He and others claimed that Behn falsified, plagiarized, and invented evidence and therefore failed to write successful works of art. This is a point more subtly developed by Davis, *Factual Fictions*, 109–10. Others see a merging of romance and realism in Behn's fiction. See McKeon, *The Origins of the English Novel*, 111–13; and K. Rogers, "Fact and Fiction in Aphra Behn's *Oroonoko*," 1–15. Maureen Duffy has shown that the failed execution of a Prince Tarquino "for endeavoring the death of his sister-in-law" was reported in the *London Gazette* for the week of May 28–31, 1666. See Duffy, *The Passionate Shepherdess*, 54.

15. Payne (spelled Pain in the dedication), a fairly influential friend of Behn's, was a Catholic playwright and alleged conspirator in the "Popish

Plot" (1678) and spent several years in prison as a result. He was renowned for his support of William Howard, Lord Stafford, one of five convicted Catholic peers, who was executed for his apparent involvement in the plot. Payne was only convicted and imprisoned, mostly for carrying seditious material: an elegy to Edward Coleman, secretary to the Duchess of York and one of the principal "supposed" conspirators who was executed. According to Duffy, while in prison Payne "seems to have used his theatrical talents to help with the construction of a counterplot whose purpose was to discredit Oates and company and shift the hunt on to the protestant non-conformists" (183). For further details see Duffy, *The Passionate Shepherdess*, 174–76, 189–90; and Thorp, "Henry Nevil Payne, Dramatist and Jacobite Conspirator," 57–79. For an excellent account of the political import of Behn's fiction see Ballaster, "Pretences of State," 187–211.

16. Lincoln Faller divides criminal biographies produced between the early seventeenth and nineteenth centuries into two categories, one that he associates with the "picaresque," the other he terms "familial." The latter is distinguished from the former by its relatively greater narrative cohesion and psychological insight; it follows a pattern of what Faller calls "familiar murder." The familial myth differs from the picaresque one in that the murderers are placed "within the context of the 'real world,'" and speak to a cultural interest in "consciousness" (4). Here we see the particular aspects of the familiarizing process that so strongly mark prose fiction in the period: the insistence on factuality (even if it has to be fabricated); the articulation of a credible personality (based on the peculiar effects of kinship); the valorization of continuity (on the levels of both narrative and characterization). See Faller, *Turned to Account*.

17. McKeon argues that such a shift toward anti-romance elements in romance material can occur because romance "has become a simple abstraction" (56).

Chapter 3

1. Ian Watt claims that the didactic works had little effect on the narratives: "The fundamental tendency of economic individualism . . . prevents Crusoe from paying much heed to the ties of family, whether as a son or a husband. This is in direct contradiction to the great stress which Defoe lays on the social and religious importance of the family in his didactic works such as the *The Family Instructor*; but his novels reflect not theory but practice, and they accord these ties a very minor, and on the whole obstructive, role." Watt, *The Rise of the Novel*, 66. Since Watt, the influence of domestic literature in Defoe's fiction has received more positive treatment. See Blewett, *Defoe's Art of Fiction*, 6–8, 24–25; Curtis, ed., *The Versatile Defoe*, 419–60; Novak, "Love, Marriage, and Natural Standards in Society," in *Defoe*

and the Nature of Man, 89–112; and Richetti, "The Family, Sex, and Marriage in Defoe's *Moll Flanders* and *Roxana*," 19–35. A particularly pertinent treatment is Flynn, "Defoe's Idea of Conduct," 73–95.

2. As Austin Flanders argues: "Plot structures and the situations of characters in the developing novel are defined to a great extent by a social dialectic strengthening the conjugal family as a social and economic unit but rendering it inadequate as a structure within which individual self-development—now becoming a primary moral and social demand—could be encouraged"; Flanders, *Structures of Experience,* 115. This view parallels to some extent what John J. Richetti has said of Defoe's fiction in general: "The mimetic act in modern narrative begins in the imagination of a self which is somehow apart from the very things which define it, that is, from the constellation of causes and circumstances which it must use to present itself"; see Richetti, *Defoe's Narratives,* 18.

3. Much attention has been paid to the secretiveness of Defoe's characters, their desire to withhold information (especially about money and children), disguise their intentions, or act as spectators. Richetti argues in *Defoe's Narratives* that self-reservation is characteristic of the Defoe protagonist and is a response to socially imposed necessities that continually challenge a person's sense of unique, even exalted identity. Secrecy becomes the means by which the individual who is subjected to circumstance comes to reverse the pattern and dominate circumstance (128). The inference here is that fictional characters have in the reader's mind a certain independence from the text. Part of what makes Defoe's texts successful as mimetic acts is this pretense to extra-textual realities. In arguing that pseudo-autobiography enables Defoe's characters to achieve their personal identities, Leo Braudy claims that they use disguise to package and merchandise themselves in a publicly acceptable way while still preserving a "private self." See Braudy, "Daniel Defoe and the Anxieties of Autobiography," 76–97. See also H. Brown, "The Displaced Self in the Novels of Daniel Defoe," 562–90; Karl, "Moll's Many-Colored Coat," 86–97; Uphaus, *The Impossible Observer,* 46–70.

4. This quotation comes from Defoe, *Colonel Jack,* pt. 2, 123. Crusoe's version is slightly different. He asks: "What is this Earth and Sea of which I have seen so much, whence is it produc'd, and what am I, and all the other Creatures, wild and tame, humane and brutal, whence are we?" (Defoe, *Robinson Crusoe,* pt. 1, 105).

5. On the political import of Crusoe's narrative see Bell, "King Crusoe: Locke's Political Theory in *Robinson Crusoe*," 27–36; Braverman, *Plots and Counterplots;* Braverman, "Crusoe's Legacy," 1–26; Kay, *Political Constructions,* 75–92; Schonhorn, *Defoe's Politics;* Sim, "Interrogating an Ideology," 163–73. Schonhorn argues against the assumption that *Robinson Crusoe*

represents Defoe's "modern" political sensibility, claiming instead that it reflects more conservative and anti-Lockean ideas.

6. There has been much discussion about exactly what Crusoe's break from his family means. Watt argues in *The Rise of the Novel* that it is a decisive moment in the awakening of "homo economicus" (60–92). See especially his remark that "Crusoe's 'original sin' is really the dynamic tendency of capitalism itself, whose aim is never merely to maintain the status quo, but to transform it incessantly. Leaving home, improving on the lot one was born to, is a vital feature of the individualist pattern of life" (65). Richetti goes even further in *Defoe's Narratives* by suggesting that Crusoe's leaving home is a way of economically surpassing and therefore destroying his father: "Capitalist ideology may be said to encourage this natural tendency much more strongly than other ideologies, but at the same time it preserves a hesitancy about the destructive implications of such ambitious energies" (26–27). Maximillian Novak argues on the other hand that "any view of Crusoe as the embodiment of the capitalistic spirit or as economic man must take into account his penchant for traveling and his hatred of a steady life. Crusoe does not disobey his parents in the name of free enterprise or economic freedom, but for a strangely adventurous, romantic, and unprofitable desire to see foreign lands"; see Novak, *Economics and the Fiction of Daniel Defoe*, 48. Finally, George A. Starr maintains that Crusoe's "original sin" can only be understood in relation to typological figures like the prodigal son or Jonah (both of which are alluded to in the text) and that, therefore, the symbolic weight of the disobedience is mostly religious. The father represents a divine order of rule that is headed ultimately by God. Crusoe's failure to follow his father's advice is also a failure to follow God's dictates; see Starr, *Defoe and Spiritual Autobiography*, 74–85. That this symbolism resonates throughout Crusoe's account is unquestionable, yet it is also the case that Defoe paradoxically affirms the act of rebellion that haunts Crusoe. Hence the critical disagreement about what his "original sin" constitutes, since he is both rewarded and punished for it.

7. This sense of personalizing, of fathering the world is of importance to an understanding of prose fiction's historical development. *Robinson Crusoe* has so often been taken for the first true example of the English novel, miraculously born out of the inchoate mass of narrative fiction in the early eighteenth-century as the origin or inviolable precursor of later refinements in novelistic form, that we forget how flexible the term "novel" is, how it seems always to have been and continues to be a synthetic term, so that its historical aspect often seems at variance with its theoretical explications. Given the genetic model that repeatedly influences critical conceptions of the origins of the novel, it is especially interesting that Crusoe should act in loco parentis. Once orphaned from the literary canon,

Defoe's works are now established members. And given the insistence with which *Robinson Crusoe* has been declared the source of the English novel, it is perhaps relevant that it is a source that thoroughly absents female and non-Western culture from a definition of universal experience at the same time that it exploits them, since Friday and Crusoe's own domestic activities play such a prominent role in the storytelling.

8. See P. Rogers, "Crusoe's Home," 375–90. Rogers claims that Crusoe's narrative is the epic of bourgeois domesticity. On Crusoe's reconstruction of home see also Seidel, "Crusoe in Exile," 363–74. Seidel argues that in transforming "domestic withdrawal" into a comfortable version of home life Crusoe's domestic actions are "allegorically analogous to patterns in biblical history, various national histories, and spiritual and personal 'lives.'"

9. See, for example, Richetti, *Defoe's Narratives*, 61–62; Watt, *The Rise of the Novel*, 65.

10. The same analogous links between family discourse, piety, and identity are made by Crusoe in *Serious Reflections*. In one of the stories from the first essay, "Of Solitude," the vows of silence by a father in response to his family's "unsuitable" language lead eventually to his estrangement from his kin, thus ruining his family and breaking up his home (7). This short, paradigmatic tale encapsulates much of the basic thrust of *Serious Reflections*. Any perverse insistence on total self-autonomy, figured here in the man who refuses to talk with his family, leads to a disabling loss of force and an emptying of content. According to Crusoe, the man is right to object to his family's impious talk; he is wrong, however, in cutting off family discourse, which would have been the means by which he could have amended the errors of his kin.

In another of the essays, "Of the Immorality of Conversation, and the Vulgar Errors of Behaviour," the use of language even conforms to a psycho-sexual drama of the family. In this essay Crusoe compares abusive language to incest: "This talking bawdy is like a man going to debauch his own mother; for it is raking into the arcana and exposing the nakedness of Nature, the common mother of us all" (100). Later, in equating false language with false reality Crusoe continues the metaphor of verbal and sexual transmission by arguing that a man who lies may give birth to a whole line of mistruths: "These men know not what foundations they are laying for handing on the sport of lying, for such they make of it to posterity, not only leaving the example, but dictating the very materials for the practice; like family lies handed on from father to son, till what begun in forgery ends in history, and we make our lies be told for truth by all our children that come after us" (108–9). Seeking to construct an original story leads the liar to propagate a world of false consciousness, a world that cannot be

verified "according to the text." Of course, Crusoe excepts his own story
from this pattern: "The selling or writing a parable, or an illusive allegoric
history, is quite a different case, and is always distinguished from this other
jesting with truth, that it is designed and effectually turned for instructive
and upright ends, and has its moral justly applied. Such are the historical
parables in the Holy Scripture, such 'The Pilgrim's Progress,' and such, in
a word, the adventures of your fugitive friend, Robinson Crusoe" (107).

   11. Critics have frequently noted Crusoe's paternal deification. Virginia
Ogden Birdsall, in *Defoe's Perpetual Seekers*, argues that "Crusoe often sees
himself, or suggests that others see him, as a powerful and even godlike figure, the center of a perfectly ordered and wholly nourishing life" (30). John
Richetti, writing about the rescue of Friday, says: "Crusoe here begins his
final transformation into a quasi-divine, autonomous hero whose desires
are no longer self-destructive in their determinate independence but fulfilling and self-constructive in their free dependence on reality" (Richetti, *Defoe's Narratives*, 56). See also Braverman, "Locke, Defoe, and the Politics of
Childhood," 36–48; Reiss, *The Discourse of Modernism*, 294–327.

   12. The moment Crusoe puts his foot into the mysterious footprint he
discovers on the beach, hoping to recognize in this dangerous sign of otherness his own outline, is perhaps the most evocative instance of Crusoe's
desire to reproduce the world in his own image. This kind of appropriation is, as Abdul R. JanMohamed argues in "The Economy of Manichean
Allegory," the basis of colonialism: "If every desire is at base a desire to
impose oneself on another and to be recognized by the Other, then the colonial situation provides an ideal context for the fulfillment of that fundamental drive. The colonialist's military superiority ensures a complete projection of his self on the Other: exercising his assumed superiority, he destroys without any significant qualms the effectiveness of indigenous economic, social, political, legal, and moral systems and imposes his own versions of these structures on the Other" (66). For further elaborations of the
colonial theme see D. Armstrong, "The Myth of Cronus," 207–20; Egan,
"Crusoe's Monarchy," 451–60.

   13. For a discussion of gratitude in Defoe's works and in eighteenth-
century philosophy in general see Novak, *Defoe and the Nature of Man*,
113–28.

   14. Part of Defoe's ethical and narrative technique, the incisive catechis-
tic questioning of an authority figure by a naive inquirer appears in Defoe's
fiction to be a means by which, according to George A. Starr, "casuistry"
becomes a "heuristic mode." As Starr points out: "Defoe himself may finally be 'The Family Instructor,' but he is careful to keep from delivering
his instructions *ex cathedra*, or even from above. Rather, he is fond of making it move in the opposite direction; and instead of fathers, husbands, and

masters laying down the law to children, wives, and servants, it is 'from the mouths of babes' that wisdom most commonly—and most convincingly—comes. The native woman who converts Will Atkins in *The Farther Adventures of Robinson Crusoe* is one well-known instance of a pattern characteristic of all the conduct manuals: the slave, the child, the youngest sibling, the apprentice, the unlettered peasant, and the savage are Defoe's favorite spokesmen." See Starr, *Defoe and Casuistry*, 4, 37–38.

15. On sexuality in *Robinson Crusoe* see Hunter, *The Reluctant Pilgrim*, 205–7; Karl, *The Adversary Literature*, 82–83; Novak, *Defoe and the Nature of Man*, 89–112; Sill, "Crusoe in the Cave: Defoe and the Semiotics of Desire," 215–32; Watt, *The Rise of the Novel*, 67–70; Wiegman, "Economies of the Body: Gendered Sites in *Robinson Crusoe* and *Roxana*," 33–51. For a fictional recreation of Defoe's experience on the island in which sexuality is a pervasive issue see Tournier, *Friday*, esp. 97–116.

16. Novak is one of the few critics who has argued that the *Surprizing Adventures* and the *Farther Adventures of Robinson Crusoe* "must be regarded as a single work concerned with the political evolution of society in the state of nature" (Novak, *Defoe and the Nature of Man*, 51).

17. For background on Defoe's views of marriage see Curtis, ed., *The Versatile Defoe*, 419–60; S. Mason, *Daniel Defoe and the Status of Women*; Novak, *Defoe and the Nature of Man*, 89–112. It is interesting to note in relation to Crusoe's juxtaposition of operating a government and running a family that the *O.E.D.*, under the heading "Family," credits Defoe with the first use of the phrase "family government" in *The Family Instructor*: "We must set up a family government entirely new." See Defoe, *The Family Instructor*, 1: 106.

18. Using *Moll Flanders*, Novak points out that the matter of incest was one that both interested Defoe and played a significant part in the theories of writers on behavior and ethics. See Novak, *Defoe and the Nature of Man*, 108–10. As Novak's example shows, Defoe's attitude toward the incest prohibition has been most fruitfully explored in relation to Moll's early Virginia experience. For a discussion of Defoe's use of incest in this work see Pollak, "*Moll Flanders*, Incest, and the Structure of Exchange," 3–21.

19. See Novak, *Defoe and the Nature of Man*, 84, 125.

20. On the problematic nature of *Roxana*'s ending see Boardman, *Defoe and the Uses of Narrative*, 151–55; Furbank and Owens, "The 'Lost' Continuation," 299–308; R. Hume, "The Conclusion of Defoe's *Roxana*," 475–90; Jenkins, "The Structure of *Roxana*," 145–58; Kropf, "Theme and Structure in Defoe's *Roxana*," 467–80; Richetti, *Defoe's Narratives*, 229–32; Stephanson, "Defoe's *Roxana*," 279–88.

Chapter 4

1. On the relation between Richardson's fiction and conduct literature see N. Armstrong, *Desire and Domestic Fiction*, 96–134; Doody, *A Natural Passion*, 43–59; Folkenflik, "*Pamela*: Domestic Servitude, Marriage, and the Novel," 253–68; Hornbeak, "Richardson's *Familiar Letters* and the Domestic Conduct Books," 1–50; Schücking, *The Puritan Family*, 145–58; Wolff, *Samuel Richardson and the Eighteenth-Century Puritan Character*, 14–57. For a very particular account of the relation between Richardson's interest in domestic conduct and writing fiction see Marks, *Sir Charles Grandison: The Compleat Conduct Book*. Recently, in *Torrid Zones*, Felicity Nussbaum has linked the conventions that shaped eighteenth-century British womanhood in such works as *Pamela* (Parts 1 and 2) to the needs of empire building, suggesting that the trope of the maternal "other" allowed women to participate, even if indirectly for the most part, in colonial expansion and domestic patriarchy. See esp. 73–94.

2. Alan Dugald McKillop prints Richardson's account of the genesis of *Pamela* in *Samuel Richardson*. Richardson explained that while writing "a little Volume of Letters, in a common Style, on such Subjects as might be of Use to those Country Readers who were unable to indite for themselves," a true story about a servant girl trying "to avoid the Snares that might be laid against their Virtue . . . recurred to my Thought: And hence sprung Pamela" (16). For this chapter I have used Samuel Richardson, *Pamela: or, Virtue Rewarded. In a Series of Familiar Letters from a Beautiful Young Damsel, To her Parents*, ed. T. C. Duncan Eaves and Ben D. Kimpel, and refer to it as Part I. For references to Richardson's "sequel" I have used the first edition of volumes 3 and 4 of *Pamela: or, Virtue Rewarded. In a Series of Familiar Letters from a Beautiful Young Damsel To her Parents: And afterwards, In her Exalted Condition, between Her, and Persons of Figure and Quality, upon the most Important and Entertaining Subjects, In Genteel Life* and refer to it as Part II.

3. See Samuel Richardson, *A Collection of the Moral and Instructive Sentiments*.

4. Richardson uses the phrase "to the moment" both in one of Lovelace's letters (Letter 224, *Clarissa*, ed. Angus Ross, 721) and in the preface to *Sir Charles Grandison*, ed. Jocelyn Harris, 4. For analysis of this technique see Ball, *Samuel Richardson's Theory of Fiction*, esp. 23–25; Gopnik, *A Theory of Style and Richardson's 'Clarissa,'* esp. 66–67; Watt, *The Rise of the Novel*, 191–96. For a succinct but informative account of the relation between fiction, epistolarity, and gender see Perry, *Women, Letters, and the Novel*; she is especially helpful on the economic aspects of the nuclear family in relation to women and letters (27–62), referring to Richardson

throughout. For comparisons and indebtedness of Richardson to Defoe see Ermarth, *Realism and Consensus in the English Novel*, 95–143; Kinkead-Weekes, *Samuel Richardson*, 469–80; Moore, "Daniel Defoe: Precursor of Samuel Richardson," 351–69. Though Richardson never printed any of Defoe's fiction, he did print *The Complete English Tradesman, A New Family Instructor, Religious Courtship, New Voyage around the World*, and *A Tour thro' the Whole Island of Great Britain*. See Eaves and Kimpel, *Samuel Richardson*, 37, 71.

5. For further discussions of the role of audience and readers in Richardson's fiction see Brady, "Readers in Richardson's *Pamela*," 164–76; Iser, *The Implied Reader*, 65–83; Preston, *The Created Self*, 38–93; Spacks, *Imagining a Self*, 208–18.

6. On the public implications of Pamela's conduct see Morris Golden, "Public Context and Imagining Self in *Pamela* and *Shamela*," 311–29.

7. Roy Roussel has pointed out the way in which distance operates in Richardson's novel, arguing that the metaphor of keeping one's distance both in the physical sense (keeping space between oneself and one's antagonist) and in the symbolic sense (keeping to one's social place) accounts for the use of epistolarity in the novel. The letters themselves initially afford the means of preserving distance; later, of course, they activate the very means by which that distance is diminished. When Mr. B. reads Pamela's collection he is morally and socially transformed. See Roussel, "Reflections on the Letter," 375–99.

8. For a similar account of how the concept of the self deconstructs itself in *Pamela* see Patricia McKee, *Heroic Commitment in Richardson, Eliot and James*, 51–96.

9. The word "self" plays a significant role in Pamela's discourse, especially at the beginning, when she is constantly being reminded to remember her self, or, in other words, remember her social standing: "I hope I shan't be so proud as to forget myself. Yet there is a secret Pleasure one has to hear one's self prais'd. ... Lady Davers ... has taken great Notice of me, and given me good Advice to keep myself to myself" (Part I, 29). But the word has ontological relevance apart from the class context.

10. On the manipulation in *Pamela* of words like "honesty" and "virtue" see Spacks, *Imagining a Self*, 210–13; McKeon, *The Origins of the English Novel*, 364–69. For a study of the politics of modesty see Yeazell, *Fictions of Modesty*, 83–101.

11. See Lévi-Strauss, *The Elementary Structures of Kinship*; Rubin, "The Traffic in Women," 157–210.

12. The phrases "Freedom of Conversation" and "Freedom of Speech" play pivotal roles in the arguments between Pamela and Mr. B. He uses them ironically when referring to the freedoms that he thinks his servant

has taken with his family's reputation. For Pamela, though, such phrases have deep symbolic meaning, and for Richardson they perhaps echo deeply rooted political beliefs about the consequences of the Revolutionary Settlement (1701). See Doody, "Richardson's Politics," 113–26; Hill, *The Century of Revolution*, 235–68; J. H. Plumb, *The Growth of Political Stability in England*, 112–75. For a cogent discussion of the political subtext in Pamela's conversations with Mr. B. see Kay, *Political Constructions*, 141–59.

13. The spatial dimensions of Pamela's situation have often been commented upon, and the distribution of figures within confined domestic spaces (houses, closets, summerhouses, carriages, walled gardens, bedrooms) have been seen as psychological representations of the self. When Pamela retreats to a private and seemingly autonomous space (her private closet) she inevitably defines herself as a dependent object within a community. That her family correspondence lies so close to her body and that the extremest space of privacy to which she retreats in order to compose herself by writing those letters is the closet, itself a personal space contiguous with and defined by the structure of a larger domestic enclosure, articulates the complex deviation of metaphors required to express the subsistence of "self." On the relevance of space to Pamela's psychology see Bullen, *Time and Space in the Novels of Samuel Richardson*, 34–55; Fisher, "'Closet-work': The Relationship between Physical and Psychological Spaces in *Pamela*," 21–37; Folkenflik, "A Room of Pamela's Own," 585–96; C. Gillis, *The Paradox of Privacy*, 122–23, 130–35. On the way voyeurism also complicates the narrative's identification of private space with personal autonomy see Straub, "Reconstructing the Gaze," 66–81.

14. See Castle, *Clarissa's Ciphers*; Eagleton, *The Rape of Clarissa*; Warner, *Reading Clarissa*.

15. On modes of impersonation in Richardson's narrative see Conboy, "Fabric and Fabrication in Richardson's *Pamela*," 81–96; Kahn, *Narrative Transvestism*.

16. Both Pamela and Mr. B. engage in a textual struggle according to which verbal authority is manifested by close reading. When he interprets some of Pamela's letters in the light of his own views, for example, she replies by challenging his hermeneutic skill: "Well, Sir, said I, that is your Comment; but it does not appear so in the Text" (Part I, 200). On the subject of authority in *Pamela* see Cruise, "*Pamela* and the Commerce of Authority," 342–58; McKeon *The Origins of the English Novel*, 357–81.

17. On Richardson's depiction of the female body see Aikins, "Re-Presenting the Body in *Pamela II*," 151–77; Flynn, "Running Out of Matter," 147–85; Gwilliam, "Pamela and the Duplicitous Body of Femininity," in *Samuel Richardson's Fictions of Gender*, 15–49.

18. For example, note these remarks by Mr. B.: "She will not write the

Affairs of my Family purely for an Exercise to her Pen and her Invention" (Part I, 39); "I am very much displeased with the Freedoms you have taken with my Name to my House-Keeper, as also to your Father and Mother; and you may as well have real Cause to take these Freedoms with me, as to make my Name suffer for imaginary ones" (Part I, 41); "I find I am likely to suffer in my Reputation by the Perverseness and Folly of this Girl. She has told you [Mrs. Jervis] all, and perhaps more than all; nay, I make no doubt of it; and she has written Letters; for I find she is a mighty Letter-writer! to her Father and Mother, and others, as far as I know" (Part I, 45). In these comments Mr. B. is responding (though unfairly) to a contemporary domestic problem recounted by, among others, Daniel Defoe in *The Great Law of Subordination Consider'd; or, the Insolence and Unsufferable Behaviour of Servants in England duly enquir'd into* (1724). As Lawrence Stone notes in *The Family, Sex and Marriage in England*, "the increasing stress laid upon personal privacy" in upper-class architectural design in the seventeenth and eighteenth centuries was predominantly aimed at providing "the family itself with some escape from the prying eyes and ears of the ubiquitous domestic servants, who were a necessary evil in every middle-class and upper-class household" (169–70). Mr. B., of course, reverses this historical condition, since he is the ubiquitous voyeur invading the privacy of his domestic servant.

19. Just as *Robinson Crusoe* exploits paradigms of mastery and subjugation, especially in the relation between Crusoe and Friday, *Pamela* depends on the opposition of master and slave and on how, in Hegelian terms, the master becomes ontologically relevant only in the presence of the slave. Like so many other forms of literature, the early novel is largely constituted by figures of domination and submission.

20. When Pamela puns on the "presents" of her master, she plays on a complicated set of distinctions, all related to her function within the B. household and the gifts she receives there. In the parcel scene, she divides these gifts into three categories, each of which represents a stage in her development as a person; the two parcels she rejects as not really belonging to her correspond to the two meaningful relationships she establishes outside of the family of origin. One set constitutes the clothes she receives from Lady B., the other those from Mr. B. The clothes she considers her own are the ones she originally brought from home or made herself through her own labor. Taken together, these parcels represent her status as daughter, as servant, and finally and most problematically as both servant and mistress to Mr. B. Narratively, Pamela's problems and the difficulties she faces in trying to decipher the domestic arrangements in the B. household begin with two related acts of gift giving. On the one hand, Lady B. urges her son to accept Pamela as the favored servant and to care for her as she has

done. In fulfilling this obligation, Mr. B. presents some of his mother's clothing to Pamela, but the intimacy of this act and the nature of the apparel suggest that Mr. B.'s designs are of a different nature. Pamela's father quickly perceives the real basis of the gesture and warns his daughter to leave the new house as soon as possible, a warning that Pamela slowly begins to take seriously. Her interpretation of the presents indicates that she is learning to distinguish the material basis of family politics. For a discussion of sartorial meaning in Richardson's work see McIntosh, "Pamela's Clothes," 89–96.

21. In Part II, Mr. B. goes into a long explanation of his early attraction to and jealousy of Pamela. He says he noted at a very early stage his mother's partial treatment and admiration of the young girl, speaks of a secret decision he made to foil his mother's plans for Pamela by seducing her, and describes his tactics for getting her to succumb, including a version of the first rape attempt. In everything he says, the mother's favoritism toward Pamela seems somehow to be at the root of his sexual motivation. See *Pamela*, Part II, 3, 185–212.

22. On the relation of Pamela's story to fairy-tale analogues see Muecke, "Beauty and Mr. B.," 467–74; Utter and Needham, *Pamela's Daughters*.

23. See, for example, Kinkead-Weekes, *Samuel Richardson*, 96–100.

24. On Mr. B. as both hero and villain see Dobson, *Samuel Richardson*, 35. For an account of how this doubling effectively conveys a greater complexity and interest to Mr. B.'s character than is customarily acknowledged see Needham, "Richardson's Characterization of Mr. B.," 433–74.

25. On Pamela's stasis see, for example, Ermarth, *Realism and Consensus*, 103, 109.

26. Pamela's attraction to Mr. B. is indicated from the beginning when he gives her and Mrs. Jervis gifts: "He gave these good Things to us both with such a Graciousness, as I thought he look'd like an Angel" (Part I, 31). Richardson continues to supply evidence of her secret feelings (to which Pamela is oblivious) until she recognizes them herself. See Kinkead-Weekes, *Samuel Richardson*, 111–13.

27. This is a point also made by Terry Castle: "She 'moves' others to regeneration by her own 'immoveable' goodness." Castle, *Masquerade and Civilization*, 141.

28. See A. Hamilton, *The Family of Love*; Marsh, *The Family of Love in English Society, 1550–1630*.

29. On the ideological implications of carnival atmosphere see Stallybrass and White, *The Politics and Poetics of Transgression*, 27–79, 171–90.

30. For a different reading of the masquerade see Castle, *Masquerade and Civilization*, 130–76.

31. On Pamela's birthing and rearing of children see Chaber, "Child-Bearing in Richardson's Novels," 1698–1701; Erickson, *Mother Midnight*; Hilliard, "*Pamela*: Autonomy, Subordination, and the 'State of Childhood,'" 201–17; Peters, "The Pregnant Pamela," 432–51; D. Rogers, "Eighteenth-Century Literary Depictions of Childbirth," 305–24. On Richardson's treatment of Locke see Chaber, "From Moral Man to Godly Man," 213–61.

32. Pamela is painfully aware of her obscurity. At one point after her marriage to Mr. B., when she is about to enter his carriage, she regrets that she has no "Arms to quarter with my dear Spouse's" (Part I, 399). At other times, however, she is able to voice the same arguments Defoe used in *The True-born Englishman* to attack the notion of privilege: "Many of these Gentlefolks, that brag of their ancient Blood, would be glad to have it as wholsome, and as really untainted, as ours!" (Part I, 222).

33. The final installment in Pamela's rendition of her family history appears when Lady Davers finally accepts her. Appropriately, it is at this moment of triumph that Pamela justifies her rise in stature by giving the fullest and most flattering account of her parents' background: "Madam, said I, they are the honestest, the lovingest, and the most conscientious Couple breathing. They once lived creditably; brought up a great Family, of which I am the youngest; but had Misfortunes, thro' their doing beyond their Power for two unhappy Brothers, who are both dead, and whose Debts they stood bound for, and so became reduced, and, by harsh Creditors, (where most of the Debts were not of their own contracting) turn'd out of all; and having, without Success, try'd to set up a little Country School, (for my Father understood a little of Accompts, and wrote a pretty good Hand) forced to take to hard Labour; but honest all the Time" (Part I, 375).

Chapter 5

1. For a précis of each of these works see Schofield, *Eliza Haywood*, 103–15.

2. On the relation between fiction and instruction in Haywood's work see Koon, "Eliza Haywood and the *Female Spectator*," 43–55; Shevelow, "Re-Writing the Moral Essay: Eliza Haywood's *Female Spectator*," 19–28.

3. See, for example, Schofield, *Eliza Haywood*, 9; and Todd, *The Sign of Angellica*, 146. Extended critical work devoted to Haywood's fiction is sparse. See Ballaster, *Seductive Forms*, 153–95; Nestor, "Virtue Rarely Rewarded," 579–98; Richetti, *Popular Fiction Before Richardson*, 153–210; Schofield, "'Descending Angels,'" 186–200; Schofield, "Exposé of the Popular Heroine," 93–103; Schofield, *Quiet Rebellion*; J. Spencer, *The Rise of the Woman Novelist*, 147–53. Specific analyses of *Miss Betsy Thoughtless* of

note include D. Ross, *The Excellence of Falsehood*; Schofield, *Masking and Unmasking the Female Mind*, 101–7; Tadmor, "Dimensions of Inequality," 303–34.

4. Quoted in Todd, *The Sign of Angellica*, 146. For an insightful account of the parallels between Haywood's fiction, biography, and conduct writing see D. Ross, *The Excellence of Falsehood*, 7–71. Ross notes Haywood's "self-portrait" in the opening number of *The Female Spectator* and compares it to Betsy's profile as a "heroine in a reformed state."

5. On the movement indoors of saturnalia and masquerade see Castle, *Masquerade and Civilization*, 119.

6. See, especially, Lukács, *The Theory of the Novel*, 66–67, 121; Bakhtin, *The Dialogic Imagination*, 224–36.

7. For a classic account of the rape victim as instigator see Brownmiller, *Against Our Will*, 350–58.

8. Despite their seeming randomness, the narrative juncture of circumstances, which begins with a disagreement between the two lovers about Forward and concludes with Trueworth's false supposition of Betsy's sexual history (and that run seamlessly from pages 84 to 208 of the second volume), reflects Haywood's purposeful structuring of complementary events. They include all of the key characters in Betsy's life (except for her first husband, who, in any event, she marries largely as a result of these circumstances). Arguably, this rapid sequence of events constitutes the key development of the text, in which Betsy's history—her past, present, and future—coalesces.

9. The narrator painstakingly notes "several footmen with wedding favors in their hats"; "three coaches in six"; one coach "filled by four maid servants, and the two valet of chambres"; "a great deal of luggage before and behind"; the wedding party's "extreme rich riding habits"; and eleven "spruce" footman in "new liveries"; and concludes that "the whole cavalcade altogether made a very genteel appearance" (3: 285–86).

10. The brothers maintain this viewpoint because they recognize their culture's insistence on the irredeemable failure of the fallen woman, who ruins patriarchal economy by casting doubts on paternity and lineage, and hence, the proper transference of material wealth from father to son. The theme of irrecoverable female sin is reiterated throughout Haywood's novel. See 2: 92, 104; 3: 108.

11. For an excellent account of how marriage and estate management tended to limit women's financial freedom see Okin, "Patriarchy and Married Women's Property," 121–38. Part of Okin's aim is to dismantle Lawrence Stone's argument that the "sentimental nuclear family of Western society . . . was significantly less patriarchal than its predecessor, in its rela-

tions both between husbands and wives, and between parents and children" (121).

12. For background on Haywood's life, much of which still remains highly speculative because of the scarcity of facts, see Blouch, "Eliza Haywood and the Romance of Obscurity," 535–51; Schofield, *Eliza Haywood*, 1–9, 82–83; Spender, *Mothers of the Novel*, 81–111; Whicher, *The Life and Romances of Mrs. Eliza Haywood*. Haywood was constantly derided for the "moral indiscretion" of living apart from her husband by writers like Pope (who attacked her in *The Dunciad* [2: 137–48 and 163–70; 3: 149–53]), and Richard Savage (who, though once a friend, seems to have turned against her after her censure in *The Dunciad*). On the difficulties eighteenth-century women faced when seeking a separation from their husbands see Okin, "Patriarchy and Married Women's Property," 137–38.

13. Some nineteenth-century novels, Anthony Trollope's *Phineas Finn* and *Phineas Redux*, for example, approximate this plot, but even these are rare and frequently involve a secondary character rather than the main heroine. In any event, when the plot involves a main character, as in the Trollope novels, the nineteenth-century novel rarely allows the separated woman to remarry; Lady Laura Kennedy, nee Standish, simply absconds to Dresden in order to avoid her husband's attempt to force her back legally; when he goes mad and then dies before altering his will, she retires—prematurely aged, her love unreciprocated by Phineas—to her husband's estate.

14. See Okin, "Patriarchy and Married Women's Property," 137.

15. Several critics have argued that the narrative pattern in novels, particularly ones in which intensifying crises are marked by attempts of seduction and rape, imitates, in part, the rhythms of sexual intercourse. This would appear to be an essentially male prototype of storytelling. As Joseph Allen Boone suggests in *Tradition Counter Tradition*, "the erotic dynamic of the traditional love-plot, however much it may play to female desire, nonetheless would seem to encode at the most elementary level of narrative a highly specific, male-oriented norm of sexuality fostering the illusion that all pleasure (of reading or of sex) is ejaculatory" (72). The prolonged nature of the novel, however, would seem to make this claim somewhat self-flattering to male readers and writers. Moreover, the tendency in novels to describe a series of crises and resolutions (that is, a number of climaxes) would, if anything, produce the opposite conclusion—in which one would associate the novel with a conventional, highly specific, female-oriented norm of sexuality. Novels would then express, depending on the disposition of the reader or writer, either male-oriented fantasies about matching the purported sexual capacity of women or female-oriented desires for an alternative pleasure that was not limited by the demands of male satisfac-

tion. Even when narrative is so limited, the fact that it "creates" and "fosters" characters might suggest another way in which novels reproduce or co-opt female capacities. But the relation of narrative form to sexual activity seems dubious to me. At best, it accounts for only a small part of narrative inspiration. It might be more profitable to argue that novels construct an erotics of reading that exploits a number of variables based on conventional and (occasionally) unconventional notions of gender. The complexity of how male and female sexual attributes structure a specific novel will then depend on the inclinations and sensitivities of both writer and reader.

16. Radway refers in these comments to Ann Douglas's suggestion that women who read rape narratives are "enjoying the titillation of seeing themselves, not necessarily as they are, but as some men would like to see them: illogical, innocent, magnetized by male sexuality and brutality," but seeks to establish a more complex reading (71).

17. As Richetti states of the novelist Penelope Aubin: "perhaps the most important and certainly the most obvious sign of her integrity (or better, since I wish to avoid ethical judgements, her homiletic efficiency) is the alacrity with which her protagonists are married, or, at least, linked by legal and proper desire, right at the very beginning of the chaos of events which makes up the novel. This marriage or commitment to marriage remains throughout the tangle of disasters a guiding and saving simplification, like the protagonists' faith in Providence" (Richetti, *Popular Fiction Before Richardson*, 220–21).

18. As Dale Spender notes: "The growth and development of the novel can be illustrated with reference to the writing of this one woman, who reveals an extraordinary creative ability, who freely experiments with form and style, and who produces an unprecedented and perhaps unparalleled range of novels. Every enduring and exemplary feature of the new genre is to be found in her writing, and yet she has never been given the credit for her contribution" (Spender, *Mothers of the Novel*, 83).

Chapter 6

1 See, for example, Foucault, *Discipline and Punish*, 218–28.

2. Recent work that suggests this includes Bruhm, *Gothic Bodies*; Castle, *The Female Thermometer*; Cavaliero, *The Supernatural and English Fiction*; Clery, *The Rise of Supernatural Fiction*; Day, *In the Circles of Fear and Desire*; *Gothic Fictions: Prohibition/Transgression*, ed. Kenneth W. Graham; Haggerty, *Gothic Fiction/Gothic Form*; Howard, *Reading Gothic Fiction*; Massé, *In the Name of Love*; Mishra, *The Gothic Sublime*; Wolstenholme, *Gothic (Re)visions*; Wiesenfarth, *Gothic Manners and the Classic English Novel*.

3. Particularly useful on the gothic sublimation of family relations are

Clery, *Supernatural Fiction*, 77–79; Ellis, *The Contested Castle*; Harfst, *Horace Walpole and the Unconscious*; Kieley, *The Romantic Novel in England*, 27–42; Moers, *Literary Women*, 90–110; Pinch, *Strange Fits of Passion*, 111–36; Watt, "Time and the Family in the Gothic Novel," 159–71; Wilt, *Ghosts of the Gothic*, 3–95. Of particular interest is Pinch's argument that the excessive repetition of "extravagant feelings" may be aligned with their overdetermination in some psychoanalytic and feminist social analysis.

4. Walter Benjamin, discussing epic theater, describes this process as a form of alienation in which the audience discovers the existing conditions of life through the startling interruptions of events, and he exemplifies it through the effect of a "primitive" family scene on an astonished spectator: "The mother was just about to seize a bronze bust and hurl it at her daughter; the father was in the act of opening the window in order to call a policeman. At that moment the stranger appears in the doorway. This means that the stranger is confronted with the situation as with a startling picture: troubled faces, an open window, the furniture in disarray. But there are eyes to which even more ordinary scenes of middle-class life look almost equally startling" (150–51). With slight alteration, this is also the fantastic scene of the gothic, and of *The Castle of Otranto* specifically. A father or grandfather may be the figure hurling the family's cherished work of art, and a mother the one who calls for the policeman (customarily a priest in the gothic); the daughter, however, is indeed almost always the target of violent parental emotions. The house (invariably a castle) usually indicates the aristocratic origins of the gothic family, but it suspiciously complements the disordered middle-class domain described by Benjamin. In the gothic, moreover, domestic objects serve, as they do in Benjamin's short tale, as intensely emotive signs; in disarray they suggest a phenomenological rupture in the spatial intimacy for which family and house seem particularly designed. See Benjamin, *Illuminations*.

5. See Fenn, "*The Castle of Otranto* for Children," quoted in *Horace Walpole: The Critical Heritage*, ed. Peter Sabor, 82. On the tension in gothic fiction between didactic and speculative strains see P. Lewis, "Beyond Mystery," 7–13; and P. Lewis, "Fearful Lessons," 470–84.

6. For an assessment of Manfred's character, particularly in relation to rationalism and tyranny, see Dole, "Three Tyrants in *The Castle of Otranto*," 26–35.

7. See Eagleton, *Ideology*, 4. On the complicated issue of the gothic's connection to revolutionary politics in the second half of the eighteenth century—largely because of its scenes in which familial, political, and cognitive order are massively overturned—see Howells, *Love, Mystery, and Misery*, 6; Paulsen, "Gothic Fiction and the French Revolution," 532–54; Punter, *The Literature of Terror*, 127–28, 425–26. On the political ramifica-

tions of gothic literature see Bernstein, "Form and Ideology in the Gothic Novel," 151–65; Samson, "Politics Gothicized," 145–58. Jacques Blondel, in "On 'Metaphysical Prisons,'" 133–38, argues that the gothic challenged the rational ideas of the Enlightenment. See also Byrd, "The Madhouse, the Whorehouse, and the Convent," 268–78; Butler, *Romantics, Rebels, and Reactionaries*, 20–38; Solomon, "Subverting Propriety," 107–16. For a fascinating discussion of the destabilizing of masculine ideology in a romantic context see M. Ross, *Contours of Masculine Desire*.

8. Troy Boone, for instance, argues that Walpole's story "associates the supernatural, that which is most other to Manfred's masculine rationalism, with a counterforce of feminine or feminized characters who are aligned with power and authority at the end of the novel ("Narrating the Apparition," 173–89, esp. 185).

9. For accounts of *The Castle of Otranto*'s dramatic nature see Bedford, "'This castle hath a pleasant seat': Shakespearean Allusion in *The Castle of Otranto*," 415–35; Burney, "Shakespeare in *Otranto*," 61–64; Holzknecht, "Horace Walpole as Dramatist," 174–89. On the gothic novel's relation to drama generally, see Evans, *Gothic Drama from Walpole to Shelley*; and M. Booth, *English Melodrama*.

10. On the gothic's destabilizing of literary conventions and structures in general, see Sedgwick, "The Character in the Veil," 255–70; Doody, "Deserts, Ruins and Troubled Waters," 529–72; Novak, "Gothic Fiction and the Grotesque," 50–67; Hilliard, "Desire and the Structure of Fiction."

11. For compelling accounts of these ruptures in Sterne's work see Alter, *Partial Magic*, 30–56; H. Brown, *Institutions*, 116–37; M. Brown, "Sterne's Stories," in *Preromanticism*, 261–300; Burckhardt, "Tristram Shandy's Law of Gravity," 70–88; Iser, *Laurence Sterne: 'Tristram Shandy'*; Lamb, *Sterne's Fiction and the Double Principle*; Lanham, *'Tristram Shandy': The Games of Pleasure*; Lukács, *Soul and Form*, 124–51; Rothstein, *Systems of Order and Inquiry in Later Eighteenth-Century Fiction*, 62–108; Seidel, *Satiric Inheritance*, 250–62.

12. On the problematic issue of *Tristram Shandy*'s ending, see Allentuck, "In Defense of an Unfinished *Tristram Shandy*," 145–55; W. Booth, "Did Sterne Complete *Tristram Shandy*?" 172–83; Brissenden, "Trusting to Almighty God: Another Look at the Composition of *Tristram Shandy*," 258–69; Loveridge, "Stories of COCKS and BULLS: The Ending of *Tristram Shandy*," 35–54; and Swearingen, *Reflexivity in 'Tristram Shandy,'* 203–10. On issues relating to birth see Erickson, *Mother Midnight*.

13. For an account of the critical importance of Jenny as a sign of Tristram's developing appreciation of the pragmatic effects of female sensibility, see Noakes, "On the Superficiality of Women," 339–55. See also Rivers, "The Importance of Tristram's 'Dear, Dear Jenny,'" 1–9.

14. The classical and Renaissance models of instruction on which Walter bases his manual (particularly Xenephon's *Cyropædia*, Giovanni della Casa's *Galateo*, and Obadiah Walker's *Of Education*) are finished works, though, admittedly, they move from the Greek economy of Xenephon to the "scattered Counsels and Notions" that Walker garners from "Observation" and "some *Italian Writers*." See Walker, *Of Education*, quoted in New and others, eds., vol. 3, *Notes*, 445.5–9, 364. On authority as a theme in Sterne's narrative see Cruise, "Reinvesting the Novel: *Tristram Shandy* and Authority," 215–35.

15. For a compelling reading of feminist elements in *Tristram Shandy* that stress Sterne's subtle endorsement of maternal order and creativity see Ehlers, "Mrs. Shandy's 'Lint and Basilicon,'" 61–75. See also Benedict, "'Dear Madam,'" 485–98; Loscocco, "Can't Live Without 'Em: Walter Shandy and the Woman Within," 166–79; New, "Job's Wife and Sterne's Other Women," 55–74.

16. On male impotence, as opposed to female fecundity, see Spacks, *Imagining a Self*, 129–34; Towers, "Sterne's Cock and Bull Story," 12–29. For a contrasting account, see Carol Kay's discussion of "remasculinization" in *Political Constructions*, 230–46. For a deconstructive reading of Sterne's sexual allusiveness see Allen, "Sexuality/Textuality in *Tristram Shandy*," 651–70. On the body in Sterne see Flynn, "Running Out of Matter," 147–85; McMaster, "'Uncrystalized Flesh and Blood': The Body in *Tristram Shandy*," 197–214.

17. See Locke, *Some Thoughts Concerning Education*, especially the following passages: "That the Difference to be found in the Manners and Abilities of men is owing more to their Education than to any Thing else, we have reason to conclude, that great Care is to be had of the forming Children's Minds, and giving them that Seasoning early, which shall influence their Lives always after" (20); "The little, or almost insensible Impressions on our tender Infancies, have very important and lasting Consequences: And there 'tis, as in the Fountains of some Rivers, where a gentle Application of the Hand turns the flexible Waters in Channels, that make them take quite contrary Courses; and by this Direction given them at first in the Source, they receive different Tendencies, and arrive at last at very remote and distant Places" (1). Ever the good husbandman, Locke compares the course of the mind's development in utilitarian terms: the implication of the river analogy is that minds should be made to serve the land.

18. The best critical examinations of *The Wrongs of Woman* include C. Johnson, *Equivocal Beings*, 58–69; Langbauer, *Women and Romance*, 93–126; Poovey, *The Proper Lady and the Woman Writer*, 94–113; Todd, *Women's Friendship in Literature*, 192–208.

19. In general, when Paine speaks of the family in the *Rights of Man*, it

is as a pejorative aristocratic institution. He rarely describes domestic government in its positive application, using it once to contrast primogeniture and egalitarian family principles (82) and once to allegorize religious toleration (271). By thus muting ideal family structure Paine avoids the difficulties Locke had in reconciling political and domestic liberalism.

20. While *The Wrongs of Woman* was composed during the relatively stable period a year and a half before her death, in which Wollstonecraft accepted William Godwin as a lover and then married him, it was nonetheless written in the wake of severe disappointments in personal and political affairs in the preceding years. These disappointments intersected with two issues in which she was also invested as a professional writer: sentiment and political rights. The narrative was begun after Wollstonecraft returned from France, following the various reprisals of the Revolutionary government (including the September Massacres and the Terror), and the humiliation, trial, and execution of Louis XVI. While in France she had given birth to her daughter, Fanny, and upon her return to England discovered that the father, Gilbert Imlay, had been unfaithful. She attempted suicide twice in 1795 as the result of the broken relationship with Imlay. For the best biographical accounts of this period see Flexner, *Mary Wollstonecraft: A Biography*, 187–224; Tomalin, *The Life and Death of Mary Wollstonecraft*, 167–94; and Wardle, *Mary Wollstonecraft: A Critical Biography*, 215–57.

21. On the political dimensions of Wollstonecraft's writing see Barker-Benfield, "Mary Wollstonecraft: Eighteenth-Century Commonwealth-woman," 95–115; Johnson, *Equivocal Beings*, 23–46; V. Jones, "Women Writing Revolution," 178–99; Poovey, *The Proper Lady and the Woman Writer*, 48–81; Rajan, "Wollstonecraft and Godwin: Reading the Secrets of the Political Novel," 221–51; Sapiro, *A Vindication of Political Virtue*.

22. On the relation between didacticism and fiction in Wollstonecraft's work see MacCarthy, *The Later Women Novelists*, 189–96; Myers, "Pedagogy as Self-Expression," 192–210; and Myers, "Reform or Ruin," 199–216.

23. On the incompleteness of Wollstonecraft's narrative see Myers, "Unfinished Business," 107–14.

24. Several critics generally conclude either that *The Wrongs of Woman* implies Wollstonecraft's conviction that an exclusive community of women can transcend the material and political conditions of female oppression or that Wollstonecraft's model of motherhood vitiates the feminist intentions of her work. I read it, in contrast, as a somber account of the minimal, and mostly private, effect of such solidarity on the present and future lives of women. I have tried to avoid, on the one hand, the wholesale (and somewhat ahistorical) condemnation of Wollstonecraft's representation of maternity voiced in such works as Cole, "(Anti)Feminist Sympathies," 107–40; Landes, *Women and the Public Sphere in the Age of the*

French Revolution, 129–38; Barker-Benfield, *Culture of Sensibility*, 279–86, and, on the other hand, the determinedly positive readings of maternal ideology in Langbauer, *Women and Romance*, 95–107; and Wilson, "Mary Wollstonecraft and the Search for the Radical Woman," 88–101.

25. On Wollstonecraft's use of the gothic see Butler, "The Woman at the Window," 128–48.

26. On the reader's function in *The Wrongs of Woman* see Maurer, "The Female (as) Reader," 36–54.

Afterword

1. This is not to say, then, that national concerns about succession and heredity disappear—the '45 Rebellion is indeed striking evidence to the contrary—but fictional references to such matters suggest that they had become diminished in importance. Perhaps the most famous literary instance, *Tom Jones*, introduces the '45 Rebellion only to swerve away from it as the hero consciously decides to pursue his romantic and domestic destiny by following the road to London rather than joining the British Army on its journey north to confront the Young Pretender. The narrative's engagement in ordinary family history is simply divorced from what becomes an ancillary plot about an obsolete political crisis over the genealogical basis of monarchical authority.

Works Cited

Abelove, Henry. "Some Speculations in the History of 'Sexual Intercourse' During the 'Long Eighteenth Century' in England." *Genders* 6 (1989).

Adams, Percy G. *Travel Literature and the Evolution of the Novel.* Lexington: University Press of Kentucky, 1983.

Aikins, Janet E. "Re-Presenting the Body in *Pamela II.*" In *New Historical Literary Study: Essays on Reproducing Texts, Representing History.* Ed. Jeffrey N. Cox and Larry J. Reynolds. Princeton, N.J.: Princeton University Press, 1993.

Allen, Dennis W. "Sexuality/Textuality in *Tristram Shandy.*" *SEL* 25 (Summer 1985).

Allentuck, Marcia Epstein. "In Defense of an Unfinished *Tristram Shandy.*" In *The Winged Skull: Papers from the Laurence Sterne Bicentenary Conference.* Ed. Arthur H. Cash and John M. Stedmond. Kent, Ohio: Kent State University Press, 1971.

Allestree, Richard. *The Whole Duty of Man.* London: John Eyre, 1741 [1658].

Alter, Robert. *Partial Magic: The Novel as a Self-Conscious Genre.* Berkeley: University of California Press, 1975.

Anderson, Michael. *Approaches to the History of the Western Family 1500–1914.* London: Macmillan, 1980.

———. *British Population History: From the Black Death to the Present Day.* Cambridge: Cambridge University Press, 1996.

Andrews, Miles Peter. *The Mysteries of the Castle.* London: W. Woodfall for T. N. Longman, 1795.

Ariès, Philippe. *Centuries of Childhood: A Social History of Family Life.* New York: Knopf, 1962.

Aristotle. *Aristotle's Politics.* Trans. Benjamin Jowett. New York: Modern Library, 1943.

Armstrong, Dianne. "The Myth of Cronus: Cannibal and Sign in *Robinson Crusoe*." *Eighteenth-Century Fiction* 4 (April 1992).

Armstrong, Nancy. *Desire and Domestic Fiction: A Political History of the Novel*. New York: Oxford University Press, 1987.

Armstrong, Nancy, and Leonard Tennenhouse. *The Imaginary Puritan: Literature, Intellectual Labor, and the Origins of Personal Life*. Berkeley: University of California Press, 1992.

Ashcraft, Richard. "Locke's State of Nature: Historical Fact or Moral Fiction?" *American Political Science Review* 62 (1968).

———. *Revolutionary Politics and Locke's 'Two Treatises of Government.'* Princeton, N.J.: Princeton University Press, 1986.

Astell, Mary. *A Serious Proposal to the Ladies, Wherein a Method is Offer'd for the Improvement of their Minds*. London: R. Wilkin, 1697 [1692].

Bachofen, Johann Jakob. *Das Mutterrecht* (Mother Right). Basel: Schwabe, 1948.

Baker, Ernest. *The History of the English Novel*. 10 vols. New York: Barnes and Noble, 1950.

———. "Introduction." In *The Novels of Mrs. Behn*. London: Routledge, 1913.

Bakhtin, Mikhail Mikhailovich. *The Dialogic Imagination: Four Essays*. Trans. Caryl Emerson and Michael Holquist. Austin: University of Texas Press, 1981.

Ball, Donald L. *Samuel Richardson's Theory of Fiction*. The Hague: Mouton, 1971.

Ballaster, Ros. "Pretences of State: Aphra Behn and the Female Plot." In *Rereading Aphra Behn: History, Theory, and, Criticism*. Ed. Heidi Hutner. Charlottesville: University Press of Virginia, 1993.

———. *Seductive Forms: Women's Amatory Fiction from 1684–1740*. Oxford: Clarendon Press, 1992.

Bannet, Eve Tavor. "The Marriage Act of 1753: 'A most cruel law for the Fair Sex.'" *Eighteenth-Century Studies* 30 (Spring 1997).

Barker-Benfield, G. J. *Culture of Sensibility: Sex and Society in Eighteenth-Century Britain*. Chicago: University of Chicago Press, 1992.

———. "Mary Wollstonecraft: Eighteenth-Century Commonwealthwoman." *Journal of the History of Ideas* 50 (January/March 1989).

Bedford, Kristina. "'This castle hath a pleasant seat': Shakespearean Allusion in *The Castle of Otranto*." *English Studies in Canada* 14 (December 1988).

Behn, Aphra. *The Fair Jilt* [1688]. In Vol. 5 of *The Works of Aphra Behn*. Ed. Montague Summers. New York: Phaeton, 1967.

———. *The Lucky Chance; or, An Alderman's Bargain* [1687]. In Vol. 3 of

The Works of Aphra Behn. Ed. Montague Summers. New York: Phaeton, 1967.

———. *The Ten Pleasures of Marriage, and the Second Part, The Confession of the New Married Couple.* New York: William Godwin, 1933.

———. *The Younger Brother; or, The Amorous Jilt* [1696]. In Vol. 4 of *The Works of Aphra Behn.* Ed. Montague Summers. New York: Phaeton, 1967.

Beizer, Janet. *Family Plots: Balzac's Narrative Generations.* New Haven, Conn.: Yale University Press, 1986.

Bell, Ian A. "King Crusoe: Locke's Political Theory in *Robinson Crusoe.*" *English Studies: A Journal of English Language and Literature* 69 (February 1988).

Bender, John. *Imagining the Penitentiary: Fiction and the Architecture of Mind in Eighteenth-Century England.* Chicago: University of Chicago Press, 1987.

Benedict, Barbara M. "'Dear Madam': Rhetoric, Cultural Politics and the Female Reader in Sterne's *Tristram Shandy.*" *Studies in Philology* 89 (Fall 1992).

Benjamin, Walter. *Illuminations.* Ed. Hannah Arendt. New York: Schocken, 1968.

Bentham, Jeremy. *Bentham's Theory of Fictions.* Ed. C. K. Ogden. London: Kegan Paul, Trench, Trubner, 1932.

Berkenhout, John. *A Volume of Letters from Dr. Berkenhout to His Son at the University.* Cambridge: J. Archdeacon, 1790.

Bernbaum, Ernest. "Mrs. Behn Biography a Fiction." *PMLA* 28 (1913).

Bernstein, Stephen. "Form and Ideology in the Gothic Novel." *Essays in Literature* 18 (Fall 1991).

Birdsall, Virginia Ogden. *Defoe's Perpetual Seekers: A Study of the Major Fiction.* Lewisburg, Penn.: Bucknell University Press, 1985.

Black, F. G. *The Epistolary Novel in the Late Eighteenth Century: A Descriptive and Bibliographical Study.* Eugene: University of Oregon, 1940.

Blewett, David. *Defoe's Art of Fiction: 'Robinson Crusoe,' 'Moll Flanders,' 'Colonel Jack' and 'Roxana.'* Toronto: University of Toronto Press, 1979.

Blondel, Jacques. "On 'Metaphysical Prisons.'" *Durham University Journal* 32 (March 1971).

Blouch, Christine. "Eliza Haywood and the Romance of Obscurity." *SEL* 31 (1991).

Boardman, Michael M. *Defoe and the Uses of Narrative.* New Brunswick, N.J.: Rutgers University Press, 1983.

Bonhote, Elizabeth. *The Parental Monitor.* London: V. Lane, 1788.

Boone, Joseph Allen. *Tradition Counter Tradition: Love and the Form of Fiction.* Chicago: University of Chicago Press, 1987.

Boone, Troy. "Narrating the Apparition: Glanvill, Defoe, and the Rise of Gothic Fiction." *The Eighteenth Century: Theory and Interpretation* 35 (Spring 1994).

Booth, Michael R. *English Melodrama.* London: Herbert Jenkins, 1965.

Booth, Wayne C. "Did Sterne Complete *Tristram Shandy?*" *Modern Philology* 48 (1951).

Bourdieu, Pierre. "Marriage Strategies as Strategies of Social Reproduction." In *Family and Society: Selections from the Annales, Economies, Sociétés, Civilisations.* Ed. Robert Forster and Orest Ranum. Trans. Elborg Forster and Patricia M. Ranum. Baltimore: Johns Hopkins University Press, 1976.

Bowers, Toni. *The Politics of Motherhood: British Writing and Culture, 1680–1760.* Cambridge: Cambridge University Press, 1996.

Brady, Jennifer. "Readers in Richardson's *Pamela.*" *English Studies in Canada* 9 (1983).

Braithwaite, Richard. *Ar't Asleep Husband?* London, 1640.

Braudel, Fernand. *The Structures of Everyday Life.* 3 vols. Trans. Siân Reynolds. New York: Harper and Row, 1981.

Braudy, Leo. "Daniel Defoe and the Anxieties of Autobiography." *Genre* 6 (1973).

Braverman, Richard Lewis. "Crusoe's Legacy." *Studies in the Novel* 18 (Spring 1986).

———. "Locke, Defoe, and the Politics of Childhood." *English Language Notes* 24 (September 1986).

———. *Plots and Counterplots: Sexual Politics and the Body Politic in English Literature, 1660–1730.* Cambridge: Cambridge University Press, 1993.

Briffault, Robert. *The Mothers: A Study of the Origins of Sentiments and Institutions.* New York: Macmillan, 1927.

Brissenden, R. F. "Trusting to Almighty God: Another Look at the Composition of *Tristram Shandy.*" In *The Winged Skull: Papers from the Laurence Sterne Bicentenary Conference.* Ed. Arthur H. Cash and John M. Stedmond. Kent, Ohio: Kent State University Press, 1971.

Broderick, Carlfred B. "Family Process Theory." In *Fashioning Family Theory: New Approaches.* Ed. Jetse Sprey. Newbury Park, Calif.: Sage, 1990.

Brown, Homer Obed. "The Displaced Self in the Novels of Daniel Defoe." *ELH* 38 (1971).

———. *Institutions of the English Novel from Defoe to Scott.* Philadelphia: University of Pennsylvania Press, 1997.

Brown, Laura. "The Romance of Empire: *Oroonoko* and the Trade in Slaves." In *The New Eighteenth Century: Theory, Politics, English Litera-*

ture. Ed. Felicity Nussbaum and Laura Brown. New York: Methuen, 1987.

Brown, Marshall. *Preromanticism.* Stanford, Calif.: Stanford University Press, 1991.

Brown, Roger Lee. "The Rise and Fall of Fleet Marriages." In *Marriage and Society: Studies in the Social History of Marriage.* Ed. R. B. Outhwaite. New York: St. Martin's Press, 1981.

Brownmiller, Susan. *Against Our Will: Men, Women and Rape.* New York: Bantam Books, 1981.

Bruhm, Steven. *Gothic Bodies: The Politics of Pain in Romantic Fiction.* Philadelphia: University of Pennsylvania Press, 1994.

Bullen, John Samuel. *Time and Space in the Novels of Samuel Richardson.* Monograph Series 12. Logan: Utah State University Press, 1994.

Burckhardt, Sigurd. "Tristram Shandy's Law of Gravity." *ELH* 28 (1961).

Burguière, André, and François Lebrun. "The One Hundred and One Families of Europe." In *The Impact of Modernity.* Vol. 2, *A History of the Family.* Ed. André Burguière and others. Trans. Sarah Hanbury Tenison. Cambridge, Mass.: Belknap Press of Harvard University Press, 1996.

Burke, Edmund. *Reflections on the Revolution in France.* New York: Penguin, 1968.

Burney, E. L. "Shakespeare in *Otranto.*" *Manchester Review* 12 (Spring 1972).

Butler, Marilyn. *Romantics, Rebels, and Reactionaries: English Literature and Its Background, 1760–1830.* Oxford: Oxford University Press, 1982.

———. "The Woman at the Window: Ann Radcliffe in the Novels of Mary Wollstonecraft and Jane Austen." *Women in Literature* 1 (1980).

Byrd, Max. "The Madhouse, the Whorehouse, and the Convent." *Partisan Review* 44 (1977).

Cameron, William J. *New Light on Aphra Behn: An Investigation into the Facts and Fictions Surrounding Her Journey to Surinam in 1663 and Her Activities as a Spy in Flanders in 1666.* Auckland: University of Auckland Press, 1961.

Carlisle, Countess Dowager of. *Thoughts on the Form of Maxims Addressed to Young Ladies on their First Establishment in the World.* London: Reid, 1789.

Castamore [pseud]. *Conjugium Languens: or, The Natural, Civil, and Religious Mischiefs Arising from Conjugal Infidelity and Impunity.* London: R. Roberts, 1700.

Castle, Terry. *The Apparitional Lesbian: Female Homosexuality and Modern Culture.* New York: Columbia University Press, 1993.

————. *Clarissa's Ciphers: Meaning and Disruption in Richardson's 'Clarissa.'* Ithaca, N.Y.: Cornell University Press, 1982.

————. *The Female Thermometer: Eighteenth-Century Culture and the Invention of the Uncanny.* New York: Oxford University Press, 1995.

————. "Lab'ring Bards: Birth Topoi and English Poetics, 1660–1820." *Journal of English and Germanic Philology* 78 (1979).

————. *Masquerade and Civilization: The Carnivalesque in Eighteenth-Century English Culture and Fiction.* Stanford, Calif.: Stanford University Press, 1986.

Cavaliero, Glen. *The Supernatural and English Fiction.* Oxford: Oxford University Press, 1995.

Chaber, Lois A. "Child-Bearing in Richardson's Novels: 'This Affecting Subject.'" *Studies on Voltaire and the Eighteenth Century* 305 (1992).

————. "From Moral Man to Godly Man: 'Mr. Locke' and Mr. B. in Part 2 of *Pamela.*" *Studies in Eighteenth-Century Culture* 18 (1988).

Chapone, Hester. *Letters on the Improvement of the Mind, Addressed to a Young Lady.* London: H. Hughs for J. Walter, 1773.

Cheal, David. *Family and the State of Theory.* New York: Simon and Schuster, 1991.

Chernaik, Warren L. *Sexual Freedom in Restoration Literature.* Cambridge: Cambridge University Press, 1995.

Clark, J. C. D. *English Society 1688–1832: Ideology, Social Structure and Political Practice During the Ancien Regime.* Cambridge: Cambridge University Press, 1985.

Clery, E. J. *The Rise of Supernatural Fiction, 1762–1800.* Cambridge: Cambridge University Press, 1995.

Cobbett, William. *Advice to Young Men and (Incidentally) to Young Women.* Oxford: Oxford University Press, 1980 [1830].

Cohen, Paula Marantz. *The Daughter's Dilemma: Family Process and the Nineteenth-Century Domestic Novel.* Ann Arbor: University of Michigan Press, 1991.

Cole, Lucinda. "(Anti)Feminist Sympathies: The Politics of Relationship in Smith, Wollstonecraft, and More." *ELH* 58 (1991).

The Complete Family-Piece: and Country Gentleman and Farmer's Best Guide. London: Longman, 1736.

Conboy, Sheila C. "Fabric and Fabrication in Richardson's *Pamela.*" *ELH* 54 (Spring 1987): 81–96.

Cordier, Jean. *La famille saincte.* In *Family and Sexuality in French History.* Ed. Robert Wheaton and Tamara K. Hareven. Philadelphia: University of Pennsylvania Press, 1980.

Cother, Edward. *A Serious Proposal for Promoting Lawful and Honourable Marriage.* London: W. Owen, 1750.

Crossman, Samuel. *The Young Man's Calling; or, the Whole Duty of Youth.* London: T. James for N. Crouch, 1678.

Cruise, James. "*Pamela* and the Commerce of Authority." *Journal of English and Germanic Philology* 87 (July 1988).

———. "Reinvesting the Novel: *Tristram Shandy* and Authority." *The Age of Johnson: A Scholarly Annual* 1 (1987).

Crump, Michael. "Stranger Than Fiction: The Eighteenth-Century True Story." In *Searching the Eighteenth Century: Papers Presented at the Symposium on the Eighteenth Century Short Title Catalogue in July 1982.* Ed. Michael Crump and Michael Harris. London: British Library, 1983.

Curtis, Laura Ann, ed. *The Versatile Defoe: An Anthology of Uncollected Writings.* Totowa, N.J.: Rowman and Littlefield, 1979.

Daly, James. *Sir Robert Filmer and English Political Thought.* Toronto: University of Toronto Press, 1979.

Darrell, William. *The Gentleman Instructed, In the Conduct of a Virtuous and Happy Life.* London: E. Smith, 1716 [1704].

Darwin, Charles. *The Descent of Man, and Selection in Relation to Sex.* London: J. Murray, 1871.

Davis, Lennard. *Factual Fictions: The Origins of the English Novel.* New York: Columbia University Press, 1983.

Day, William Patrick. *In the Circles of Fear and Desire: A Study in Gothic Fantasy.* Chicago: University of Chicago Press, 1985.

Defoe, Daniel. *Conjugal Lewdness; or, Matrimonial Whoredom. A Treatise concerning the Use and Abuse of the Marriage Bed.* Gainesville, Florida: Scholars' Facsimiles and Reprints, 1967 [1727].

———. *Defoe's Review.* New York: Columbia University Press, 1938 [1704–13].

———. *The Family Instructor.* 2 vols. New York: AMS, 1973 [1715].

———. *The Farther Adventures of Robinson Crusoe* [1719]. Vol. 8, pts. 2 and 3 of *The Shakespeare Head Edition of the Novels and Selected Writings of Daniel Defoe.* Oxford: Basil Blackwell, 1927–28.

———. *The Fortunes and Misfortunes of the Famous Moll Flanders* [1722]. Vol. 6, pts. 1 and 2 of *The Shakespeare Head Edition of the Novels and Selected Writings of Daniel Defoe.* Oxford: Basil Blackwell, 1927–28.

———. *The History and Remarkable Life of the Truly Honorable Colonel Jacque, Commonly Call'd Colonel Jack* [1722]. Vol. 2, pts. 1 and 2 of *The Shakespeare Head Edition of the Novels and Selected Writings of Daniel Defoe.* Oxford: Basil Blackwell, 1927–28.

———. *The Life, Adventures, and Piracies of Captain Singleton* [1720]. Vol. 1 of *The Shakespeare Head Edition of the Novels and Selected Writings of Daniel Defoe.* Oxford: Basil Blackwell, 1927–28.

———. *The Life and Strange Surprizing Adventures of Robinson Crusoe*

[1719]. Vol. 8, pts. 1 and 2 of *The Shakespeare Head Edition of the Novels and Selected Writings of Daniel Defoe.* Oxford: Basil Blackwell, 1927–28.

―――. *Roxana; or The Fortunate Mistress* [1724]. Vol. 3, pts. 1 and 2 of *The Shakespeare Head Edition of the Novels and Selected Writings of Daniel Defoe.* Oxford: Basil Blackwell, 1927–28.

―――. *Serious Reflections During the Life and Surprizing Adventures of Robinson Crusoe* [1720]. Vol. 3 of *The Works of Daniel Defoe.* New York: Jensen, 1907.

―――. *The True Born Englishman* [1701]. In *The Shortest Way With Dissenters and Other Pamphlets.* Vol. 9 of *The Shakespeare Head Edition of the Novels and Selected Writings of Daniel Defoe.* Oxford: Basil Blackwell, 1927–28.

―――. *The Versatile Defoe: An Anthology of Uncollected Writings.* Ed. Laura Ann Curtis. Totowa, N.J.: Rowman and Littlefield, 1979.

Descartes, René. *The Meditations and Selections from The Principles.* Trans. John Veitch. La Salle, Ill.: Open Court, 1968.

Dobson, Austin. *Samuel Richardson.* Detroit: Gale, 1968.

Doddridge, Philip. *Family Expositor: or, a Paraphrase and Version of the New Testament.* London: G. Virtue, 1739–1756.

Dodsley, Robert. *The Oeconomy of Human Life.* Poughkeepsie, N.Y.: P. Potter, 1816 [1751].

Dole, Carol M. "Three Tyrants in *The Castle of Otranto.*" *English Language Notes* 26 (September 1988).

Donzelot, Jacques. *The Policing of Families.* Trans. Robert Hurley. New York: Pantheon, 1979.

Doody, Margaret Anne. "Deserts, Ruins and Troubled Waters: Female Dreams in Fiction and the Development of the Gothic Novel." *Genre* 10 (Winter 1977).

―――. *A Natural Passion: A Study of the Novels of Samuel Richardson.* Oxford: Clarendon Press, 1974.

―――. "Richardson's Politics." *Eighteenth-Century Fiction* 2 (January 1990).

―――. *The True Story of the Novel.* New Brunswick, N.J.: Rutgers University Press, 1996.

Doran, John. *Annals of the English Stage from Thomas Betterton to Edmund Kean.* London: W. H. Allen, 1865.

[Douglas, F.?]. *Considerations on the Cause of the Present Stagnation of Matrimony.* London: T. Spilsbury for J. Ridley, 1772.

Dryden, John. *The Letters of John Dryden.* Ed. Charles E. Ward. Durham, N.C.: Duke University Press, 1942.

Duffy, Maureen. *The Passionate Shepherdess: Aphra Behn 1640–89.* London: Methuen, 1989.

Durkheim, Emile. *The Division of Labor in Society.* Trans. W. D. Halls. New York: Free Press, 1984.

———. *Incest: The Nature and Origin of the Taboo.* Trans. Edward Sagarin. New York: L. Stuart, 1963.

Eagleton, Terry. *Ideology: An Introduction.* London: Verso, 1991.

———. *The Rape of Clarissa: Writing, Sexuality, and Class Struggle in Samuel Richardson.* Minneapolis: University of Minnesota Press, 1982.

Earle, Peter. *A City Full of People: Men and Women of London, 1650–1750.* London: Methuen, 1994.

Eaves, T. C. Duncan, and Ben D. Kimpel. *Samuel Richardson: A Biography.* Oxford: Clarendon Press, 1971.

Editor, Melmoth [pseud]. *Domestic Happiness Portrayed: Or, A Repository for Those Who are and Those Who are Not Married.* New York: Charles Hubbell, 1835.

Edwards, Charles S. *Hugo Grotius, The Miracle of Holland: A Study in Political and Legal Thought.* Chicago: Nelson-Hall, 1981.

Egan, James. "Crusoe's Monarchy and the Puritan Concept of the Self." *Studies in English Literature* 13 (1973).

Ehlers, Leigh A. "Mrs. Shandy's 'Lint and Basilicon': The Importance of Women in *Tristram Shandy*." *South Atlantic Review* 46 (1981).

Ellis, Kate Ferguson. *The Contested Castle: Gothic Novels and the Subversion of Domestic Ideology.* Urbana: University of Illinois Press, 1989.

Engels, Friedrich. *The Origin of the Family, Private Property, and the State.* New York: International Publishers, 1972.

Erickson, Robert. *Mother Midnight: Birth, Sex, and Fate in Eighteenth-Century Fiction (Defoe, Richardson, and Sterne).* New York: AMS, 1986.

Ermarth, Elizabeth Deeds. *Realism and Consensus in the English Novel.* Princeton, N.J.: Princeton University Press, 1983.

Evans, Bertrand. *Gothic Drama from Walpole to Shelley.* Los Angeles: University of California Press, 1947.

Faller, Lincoln. *Turned to Account: The Forms and Functions of Criminal Biography in Late Seventeenth- and Early Eighteenth-Century England.* Cambridge: Cambridge University Press, 1987.

Ferguson, Moira. "*Oroonoko*: Birth of a Paradigm." *New Literary History* 23 (1992).

Fielding, Henry. *The History of Tom Jones, a Foundling* [1749]. Ed. Martin C. Battestin and Fredson Bowers. The Wesleyan Edition of the Works of Henry Fielding. Middletown, Conn.: Wesleyan University Press, 1975.

Fisher, J. W. "'Closet-work': The Relationship Between Physical and Psychological Spaces in *Pamela*." In *Samuel Richardson: Passion and Pru-*

dence. Ed. Valerie Grosvenor Myer. Totowa, N.J.: Barnes and Noble, 1986.

Flanders, Austin. *Structures of Experience: History, Society, and Personal Life in the Eighteenth-Century British Novel*. Columbia: University of South Carolina Press, 1984.

Fleetwood, William. *The Relative Duties of Parents and Children, Husbands and Wives, Masters and Servants*. London: C. Harper, 1705.

Fletcher, Anthony. *Gender, Sex and Subordination in England 1500–1800*. New Haven, Conn.: Yale University Press, 1995.

Flew, Antony. "Locke and the Problem of Personal Identity." In *Locke and Berkeley: A Collection of Critical Essays*. Ed. C. B. Martin and D. M. Armstrong. Garden City, N.Y.: Anchor Books, 1968.

Flexner, Eleanor. *Mary Wollstonecraft: A Biography*. New York: Coward, 1972.

Fliegelman, Jay. *Prodigals and Pilgrims: The American Revolution Against Patriarchal Authority, 1750–1800*. New York: Cambridge University Press, 1982.

Flint, Christopher. "'The Family Piece': Oliver Goldsmith and the Politics of the Everyday in Eighteenth-Century Domestic Portraiture." *Eighteenth-Century Studies* 29 (Winter 1996).

Flynn, Carol Houlihan. "Defoe's Idea of Conduct: Ideological Fictions and Fictional Reality." In *The Ideology of Conduct: Essays on Literature and the History of Sexuality*. Ed. Nancy Armstrong and Leonard Tennenhouse. New York: Methuen, 1987.

———. "Running Out of Matter: The Body Exercised in Eighteenth-Century Fiction." In *The Languages of Psyche: Mind and Body in Enlightenment Thought*. Ed. G. S. Rousseau. Publications from the Clark Library Professorship 12. Berkeley: University of California Press, 1990.

Folkenflik, Robert. "*Pamela*: Domestic Servitude, Marriage, and the Novel." *Eighteenth-Century Fiction* 5 (April 1993).

———. "A Room of Pamela's Own." *ELH* 39 (1972).

Fordyce, James. *Addresses to Young Men*. Boston: Robert Hodge for William Green, 1777.

———. *Sermons to Young Women*. London: A. Millar and T. Cadell, 1768 [1765].

Foucault, Michel. *Discipline and Punish: The Birth of the Prison*. Trans. Alan Sheridan. New York: Vintage, 1979.

———. *The History of Sexuality: Volume I: An Introduction*. Trans. Robert Hurley. New York: Random House, 1978.

Fourier, Charles. *Harmonian Man: Selected Writings of Charles Fourier*. Garden City, N.Y.: Doubleday, 1971.

Franklin, Julian H. *John Locke and the Theory of Sovereignty: Mixed Monar-*

chy and the Right of Resistance in the Political Thought of the English Revolution. Cambridge: Cambridge University Press, 1978.

Freud, Sigmund. "The Dissection of the Psychical Personality." In Vol. 22
of *The Standard Edition of the Complete Psychological Works of Sigmund
Freud.* Trans. and ed. James Strachey in collaboration with Anna Freud,
assisted by Alex Strachey and Alan Tyson. London: Hogarth Press and
the Institute of Psycho-Analysis, 1959.

Furbank, P. N., and W. R. Owens. "The 'Lost' Continuation of Defoe's
Roxana." *Eighteenth-Century Fiction* 9 (April 1997).

Gallagher, Catherine. *Nobody's Story:* The Vanishing Acts of Women Writers in the Marketplace, 1670–1820. Berkeley: University of California
Press, 1994.

Gally, Henry. *Some Considerations upon Clandestine Marriages.* London: J.
Hughes, 1750.

Gauthier, David. "The Role of Inheritance in Locke's Political Theory."
Canadian Journal of Economics and Political Science 32 (1966).

Gee, Edward. The *Divine Right and Original of the Civil Magistrate From
God.* London, 1658.

The Gentleman's Magazine 7 (September 1738).

Gilbert, Sandra M., and Susan Gubar. *The Madwoman in the Attic: The
Woman Writer and the Nineteenth-Century Literary Imagination.* New
Haven, Conn.: Yale University Press, 1979.

Gillis, Christina Marsden. *The Paradox of Privacy: Epistolary Form in
'Clarissa.'* Gainesville: University Presses of Florida, 1984.

Gillis, John R. "Conjugal Settlements: Resort to Clandestine and Common
Law Marriage in England and Wales, 1650–1850." In *Disputes and Set-
tlements: Law and Human Relations in the West.* Ed. John Bossy. Ithaca,
N.Y.: Cornell University Press, 1983.

———. *For Better, for Worse: British Marriages, 1600 to the Present.* New
York: Oxford University Press, 1985.

———. "Making Time for Family: The Invention of Family Time(s) and
the Reinvention of Family History." *Journal of Family History* 21
(January 1996).

Gisborne, Thomas. *An Enquiry into the Duties of Men in the Higher and
Middle Classes of Society in Great Britain, Resulting from their Respective
Stations, Professions, and Employments.* London: B. and J. White, 1797
[1794].

———. *An Enquiry into the Duties of the Female Sex.* London: T. Cadell,
Jr., and W. Davies, 1797.

Godwin, William. *Caleb Williams.* Oxford: Oxford University Press, 1982
[1794].

Goffman, Erving. *Frame Analysis: An Essay on the Organization of Experience.* Cambridge, Mass.: Harvard University Press, 1974.

Golden, Morris. "Public Context and Imagining Self in *Pamela* and *Shamela.*" *ELH* 53 (Summer 1986).

Goldsmith, Oliver. *The Vicar of Wakefield.* In Vol. 4 of *Collected Works of Oliver Goldsmith.* Ed. Arthur Friedman. Oxford: Clarendon Press, 1966.

Goode, William J. *World Revolution and Family Patterns.* New York: Free Press, 1963.

Goody, Jack. "The Evolution of the Family." In *Household and Family in Past Time: Comparative Studies in the Size and Structure of the Domestic Group over the Last Three Centuries in England, France, Serbia, Japan and Colonial North America, with Further Materials from Western Europe.* Ed. Peter Laslett and Richard Wall. Cambridge: Cambridge University Press, 1972.

Gopnik, Irwin. *A Theory of Style and Richardson's 'Clarissa.'* The Hague: Mouton, 1970.

Goreau, Angeline. *Reconstructing Aphra: A Social Biography of Aphra Behn.* New York: Dial, 1980.

Gottlieb, Beatrice. *The Family in the Western World from the Black Death to the Industrial Age.* New York: Oxford University Press, 1993.

Gouge, William. *Of Domesticall Duties.* London: Edward Brewster, 1634 [1622].

Graham, Kenneth W., ed. *Gothic Fictions: Prohibition/Transgression.* New York: AMS, 1989.

Grant, Ruth W. *John Locke's Liberalism.* Chicago: University of Chicago Press, 1987.

Green, Katherine Sobba. *The Courtship Novel, 1740–1820: A Feminized Genre.* Lexington: University Press of Kentucky, 1991.

Grotius, Hugo. *De Jure Belli Ac Pacis: Libri Tres: Prolegomena.* Trans. Francis W. Kelsey. Oxford: Clarendon Press, 1925.

Guffey, George. *Two English Novelists: Aphra Behn and Anthony Trollope: Papers Read at a Clark Library Seminar, May 11, 1974.* Los Angeles: Clark Library, 1975.

Gwilliam, Tassie. *Samuel Richardson's Fictions of Gender.* Stanford, Calif.: Stanford University Press, 1993.

Haakonssen, Knud. *Natural Law and Moral Philosophy: From Grotius to the Scottish Enlightenment.* Cambridge: Cambridge University Press, 1996.

Haggerty, George E. *Gothic Fiction/Gothic Form.* University Park: Pennsylvania State University Press, 1989.

Hamilton, Alastair. *The Family of Love.* Cambridge: James Clarke, 1981.

Hamilton, Elizabeth. *Letters on the Elementary Principles of Education.* Alexandria, Va.: Cottom and Stewart, 1803.

Hareven, Tamara. "Cycles, Courses, and Cohorts: Reflections of Theoretical and Methodological Approaches to the Historical Study of Family Development." *Journal of Social History* 12 (1978).

———. "Family History at the Crossroads." In *Family History at the Crossroads: A Journal of Family History Reader.* Ed. Tamara Hareven and Andrejs Plakans. Princeton, N.J.: Princeton University Press, 1987.

———. "Modernization and Family History: Perspectives on Social Change." *Signs* 4 (1979).

Hareven, Tamara, and Andrejs Plakans, eds. *Family History at the Crossroads: A Journal of Family History Reader.* Princeton, N.J.: Princeton University Press, 1987.

Harfst, Betsy P. *Horace Walpole and the Unconscious: An Experiment in Freudian Analysis.* New York: Arno Press, 1980.

Hargreaves, Henry A. "New Evidence of the Realism of Mrs. Behn's *Oroonoko.*" *Bulletin of the New York Public Library* 74 (September 1970).

Harris, Ian. *The Mind of John Locke: A Study of Political Theory in Its Intellectual Setting.* Cambridge: Cambridge University Press, 1994.

Harris, Jocelyn. Introduction to *Sir Charles Grandison,* by Samuel Richardson. Oxford: Oxford University Press, 1986.

Harris, Olivia. "Households and Their Boundaries." *History Workshop Journal* 13 (1982).

Harth, Erica. "The Virtue of Love: Lord Hardwicke's Marriage Act." *Cultural Critique* 9 (1988).

Haywood, Eliza. *The Female Spectator.* Ed. Mary Priestley. London: John Lane, The Bodley Head, 1929 [1745].

———. *The History of Miss Betsy Thoughtless.* 4 vols. New York: Garland, 1979 [1751].

———. *The Wife; and The Husband. In Answer to the Wife.* London: Printed for T. Gardner, 1756.

Hill, Christopher. *The Century of Revolution, 1603–1714.* New York: Norton, 1980.

Hilliard, Raymond F. "Desire and the Structure of Fiction." In Vol. 9 of *Studies in Eighteenth-Century Culture.* Ed. Roseann Runte. Madison: University of Wisconsin Press, 1979.

———. "*Pamela*: Autonomy, Subordination, and the 'State of Childhood.'" *Studies in Philology* 83 (Spring 1986).

Hobbes, Thomas. *Leviathan or the Matter, Forme and Power of a Commonwealth Ecclesiasticall and Civil.* Ed. Michael Oakeshott. Oxford: Basil Blackwell, 1946 [1651].

Holzknecht, Karl J. "Horace Walpole as Dramatist." *South Atlantic Quarterly* 28 (April 1929).

Hornbeak, Katherine. "Richardson's *Familiar Letters* and the Domestic Conduct Books: Richardson's Aesop." *Smith College Studies in Modern Languages* 19 (1939).

Howard, Jacqueline. *Reading Gothic Fiction: A Bakhtinian Approach*. Oxford: Clarendon, 1994.

Howells, Corall Ann. *Love, Mystery, and Misery: Feeling in Gothic Fiction*. Atlantic Highlands, N.J.: Humanities Press, 1979.

Hume, David. "Of Polygamy and Divorces." In Vol. 3 of *The Philosophical Works of David Hume*. Boston: Little, Brown, 1854.

———. *A Treatise of Human Nature*. Ed. L. A. Selby-Bigge. Oxford: Clarendon Press, 1978.

Hume, Robert D. "The Conclusion of Defoe's *Roxana*: Fiasco or Tour de Force?" *Eighteenth-Century Studies* 3 (1970).

Hunter, J. Paul. *Before Novels: The Cultural Contexts of Eighteenth-Century English Fiction*. New York: Norton, 1990.

———. *The Reluctant Pilgrim: Defoe's Emblematic Method and Quest for Form in 'Robinson Crusoe.'* Baltimore: Johns Hopkins University Press, 1968.

Hutner, Heidi, ed. *Rereading Aphra Behn: History, Theory, and, Criticism*. Charlottesville: University Press of Virginia, 1993.

Iser, Wolfgang. *The Implied Reader: Patterns of Communication in Prose Fiction from Bunyan to Beckett*. Baltimore: Johns Hopkins University Press, 1974.

———. *Laurence Sterne: 'Tristram Shandy.'* Cambridge: Cambridge University Press, 1988.

Jacobs, Naomi. "The Seduction of Aphra Behn." *Women's Studies* 18 (1991).

JanMohamed, Abdul R. "The Economy of Manichean Allegory: The Function of Racial Difference in Colonialist Literature." *Critical Inquiry* 12 (Autumn 1985).

Jenkins, Ralph E. "The Structure of *Roxana*." *Studies in the Novel* 2 (1970).

Jephson, Robert. *The Count of Narbonne, a Tragedy*. London: T. Cadell, 1781.

Johnson, Claudia. *Equivocal Beings: Politics, Gender, and Sentimentality in the 1790s: Wollstonecraft, Radcliffe, Burney, Austen*. Chicago: University of Chicago Press, 1995.

Johnson, Samuel. *Johnson's Dictionary: A Modern Selection*. Ed. E. L. McAdam, Jr. and George Milne. New York: Pantheon, 1963.

Jones, Ann Rosalind. "Nets and Bridles: Early Modern Conduct Books and Sixteenth-Century Women's Lyrics." In *The Ideology of Conduct: Essays* on *Literature and the History of Sexuality*. Ed. Nancy Armstrong and Leonard Tennenhouse. New York: Methuen, 1987.

Jones, Vivien. "Women Writing Revolution: Narratives of History and Sexuality in Wollstonecraft and Williams." In *Beyond Romanticism: New Approaches to Texts and Contexts, 1780–1832*. Ed. Stephen Copley and John Whale. Syracuse, N.Y.: Syracuse University Press, 1991.

Jonnes, Denis. *The Matrix of Narrative: Family Systems and the Semiotics of Story*. Berlin: Mouton de Gruyter, 1990.

Kahn, Madeleine. *Narrative Transvestism: Rhetoric and Gender in the Eighteenth-Century English Novel*. Ithaca, N.Y.: Cornell University Press, 1991.

Karl, Frederick. *The Adversary Literature; The English Novel in the Eighteenth Century: A Study in Genre*. New York: Farrar, Straus and Giroux, 1974.

———. "Moll's Many-Colored Coat: Veil and Disguise in the Fiction of Defoe." *Studies in the Novel* 5 (1973).

Kavanagh, Thomas M. "Unraveling Robinson: The Divided Self in Defoe's *Robinson Crusoe*." *Texas Studies in Literature and Language* 20 (1978).

Kay, Carol. *Political Constructions: Defoe, Richardson, and Sterne in Relation to Hobbes, Hume, and Burke*. Ithaca, N.Y.: Cornell University Press, 1988.

Ketcham, Michael G. *Transparent Designs: Reading, Performance, and Form in the 'Spectator Papers.'* Athens: University of Georgia Press, 1985.

Kieley, Robert. *The Romantic Novel in England*. Cambridge, Mass.: Harvard University Press, 1972.

Kinkead-Weekes, Mark. *Samuel Richardson: Dramatic Novelist*. Ithaca, N.Y.: Cornell University Press, 1973.

Koon, Helene. "Eliza Haywood and the *Female Spectator*." *Huntington Library Quarterly* 42 (1978).

Kowaleski-Wallace, Beth. *Their Fathers' Daughters: Hannah More, Maria Edgeworth, and Patriarchal Complicity*. New York: Oxford University Press, 1991.

Kropf, Carl R. "Theme and Structure in Defoe's *Roxana*." *SEL* 12 (1972).

Lacan, Jacques. *Écrits: A Selection*. New York: Norton, 1977.

Lamb, Jonathan. *Sterne's Fiction and the Double Principle*. Cambridge: Cambridge University Press, 1989.

Landes, Joan. *Women and the Public Sphere in the Age of the French Revolution*. Ithaca, N.Y.: Cornell University Press, 1988.

Langbauer, Laurie. *Women and Romance: The Consolations of Gender in the English Novel*. Ithaca, N.Y.: Cornell University Press, 1990.

Lanham, Richard A. *'Tristram Shandy': The Games of Pleasure*. Berkeley: University of California Press, 1973.

Lasch, Christopher. *Haven in a Heartless World: The Family Besieged.* New York: Basic Books, 1977.

Laslett, Peter. *The World We Have Lost: England Before the Industrial Age.* London: Methuen, 1971.

———, ed. Introduction to *Two Treatises of Government,* by John Locke. Cambridge: Cambridge University Press, 1963.

Laslett, Peter, and Richard Wall, eds. *Household and Family in Past Time: Comparative Studies in the Size and Structure of the Domestic Group over the Last Three Centuries in England, France, Serbia, Japan and Colonial North America, with Further Materials from Western Europe.* Cambridge: Cambridge University Press, 1972.

Lautman, Françoise. "Differences or Changes in Family Organization." In *Family and Society: Selections from the Annales, Economies, Sociétés, Civilisations.* Ed. Robert Forster and Orest Ranum. Trans. Elborg Forster and Patricia M. Ranum. Baltimore: Johns Hopkins University Press, 1976.

Law, William. *A Serious Call to a Devout and Holy Life.* London: W. Innys, 1729.

LePlay, Frédéric. *Ouvriers Européens.* Tours: A. Mame et fils, 1877–79.

———. *La réforme sociale en France déduite de l'observation comparée des peuples européens.* Paris: Dentu, 1867.

Leslie, Charles. *The New Association.* London, 1703.

Letters on Love, Marriage, and Adultery. London: J. Ridgway, 1789.

Lévi-Strauss, Claude. *The Elementary Structures of Kinship.* Ed. Rodney Needham. Trans. James Harle Bell and John Richard von Sturmer. Boston: Beacon, 1969.

Lewis, Matthew Gregory. *The Castle Spectre; a Drama.* London: J. Bell, 1797.

Lewis, Paul. "Beyond Mystery: Emergence from Delusion as a Pattern in Gothic Fiction." *Gothic* 2 (June 1980).

———. "Fearful Lessons: The Didacticism of the Early Gothic Novel." *College Language Association Journal* 23 (1980).

Link, Frederick M. *Aphra Behn.* New York: Twayne, 1968.

Locke, John. *An Essay Concerning Human Understanding.* Ed. Peter H. Nidditch. Oxford: Clarendon Press, 1975 [1690].

———. *Some Thoughts Concerning Education.* Ed. John W. and Jean S. Yolton. Oxford: Clarendon Press, 1989 [1693].

———. *Two Treatises of Government.* Ed. Peter Laslett. Cambridge: Cambridge University Press, 1963 [1690].

Loscocco, Paula. "Can't Live Without 'Em: Walter Shandy and the Woman Within." *The Eighteenth Century: Theory and Interpretation* 32 (Summer 1991).

Lovejoy, Arthur. "The Supposed Primitivism of Rousseau's *Discourses on Inequality.*" In *Essays in the History of Ideas.* New York: Capricorn, 1960.

Loveridge, Mark. "Stories of COCKS and BULLS: The Ending of *Tristram Shandy.*" *Eighteenth-Century Fiction* 5 (1992).

Lukács, Georg. *Soul and Form.* Trans. Anna Bostock. Cambridge, Mass.: MIT Press, 1974.

―――. *The Theory of the Novel: A Historico-Philosophical Essay on the Forms of Great Epic Literature.* Trans. Anna Bostock. Cambridge, Mass.: MIT Press, 1971.

Macauley [Graham], Catherine. *Letters on Education.* London: C. Dilly, 1790.

MacCarthy, Bridget G. *The Later Women Novelists, 1744-1818.* Cork, Ire.: Cork University Press, 1941.

―――. *Women Writers: Their Contribution to the English Novel, 1621-1744.* Cork, Ire.: Cork University Press, 1944.

Macfarlane, Alan. *Marriage and Love in England: Modes of Reproduction, 1300-1840.* Oxford: Basil Blackwell, 1986.

Macheray, Pierre. *A Theory of Literary Production.* Trans. Geoffrey Wall. Boston: Routledge and Kegan Paul, 1978.

McIntosh, Carey. "Pamela's Clothes." In *Twentieth-Century Interpretations of 'Pamela.'* Ed. Rosemary Cowler. Englewood Cliffs, N.J.: Prentice-Hall, 1969.

Mack, Arien, ed. *Home: A Place in the World.* New York: New York University Press, 1993.

McKee, Patricia. *Heroic Commitment in Richardson, Eliot and James.* Princeton, N.J.: Princeton University Press, 1986.

McKeon, Michael. *The Origins of the English Novel, 1600-1740.* Baltimore: Johns Hopkins University Press, 1987.

McKillop, Alan Dugald. *Samuel Richardson: Printer and Novelist.* Chapel Hill: University of North Carolina Press, 1936.

McLennan, John Ferguson. *Primitive Marriage: An Inquiry into the Origin of the Form of Capture in Marriage Ceremonies.* Ed. Peter Rivière. Chicago: University of Chicago Press, 1970.

McMaster, Juliet. "'Uncrystalized Flesh and Blood': The Body in *Tristram Shandy.*" *Eighteenth-Century Fiction* 2 (1990).

Macpherson, C. B. *The Political Theory of Possessive Individualism: Hobbes to Locke.* Oxford: Clarendon, 1962.

Maine, Henry Sumner. *Ancient Law: Its Connection with the Early History of Society, and its Relation to Modern Ideas.* New York: Scribner, 1864.

Malinowski, Bronislaw. *Sex, Culture, and Myth.* New York: Harcourt, Brace, 1962.

Malthus, Thomas Robert. *An Essay on the Principle of Population.* In Vol. 1

of *The Works of Thomas Robert Malthus*. Ed. E. A. Wrigley and David Souden. London: Pickering, 1986.

Marks, Sylvia Kasey. *Sir Charles Grandison: The Compleat Conduct Book*. London: Associated University Presses, 1986.

Marriage Promoted in a Discourse of its Ancient and Modern Practice. London: Richard Baldwin, 1690.

Marsh, Christopher W. *The Family of Love in English Society, 1550–1630*. Cambridge: Cambridge University Press, 1994.

Martin, John. *Public and Domestic Devotion United*. London, 1779.

Mascuch, Michael. "Social Mobility and Middling Self-Identity: The Ethos of British Autobiographers, 1600–1750." *Social History* 20 (January 1995).

Mason, John E. *Gentlefolk in the Making: Studies in the History of English Courtesy Literature and Related Topics from 1531 to 1774*. Philadelphia: University of Pennsylvania Press, 1935.

Mason, Shirlene. *Daniel Defoe and the Status of Women*. St. Alban's, Vt.: Eden, 1978.

Massé, Michelle A. *In the Name of Love: Women, Masochism, and the Gothic*. Ithaca, N.Y.: Cornell University Press, 1992.

Maurer, Shawn Lisa. "The Female (as) Reader: Sex, Sensibility, and the Maternal in Wollstonecraft's Fictions." *Essays in Literature* 19 (1992).

Miller, Nancy. *The Heroine's Text: Readings in the French and English Novel, 1722–1782*. New York: Columbia University Press, 1980.

Mishra, Vijay. *The Gothic Sublime*. Albany: State University of New York Press, 1994.

Moers, Ellen. *Literary Women*. Garden City, N.Y.: Doubleday, 1976.

Moore, John Robert. "Daniel Defoe: Precursor of Samuel Richardson." In *Restoration and Eighteenth-Century Literature: Essays in Honor of Alan Dugald McKillop*. Ed. Carroll Camden. Chicago: University of Chicago Press for William Marsh Rice University, 1963.

Morgan, Lewis Henry. *Ancient Society, or Researches in the Lines of Human Progress from Savagery through Barbarism to Civilisation*. London: McMillan, 1877.

Morris, David. "Gothic Sublimity." *New Literary History* 16 (Winter 1985).

Mount, Ferdinand. *The Subversive Family: An Alternative History of Love and Marriage*. New York: Macmillan, 1992.

Muecke, D. C. "Beauty and Mr. B." *SEL* 7 (1967).

Myers, Mitzi. "Pedagogy as Self-Expression in Mary Wollstonecraft: Exorcising the Past, Finding a Voice." In *The Private Self: Theory and Practice of Women's Autobiographical Writings*. Ed. Shari Benstock. Chapel Hill: University of North Carolina Press, 1988.

———. "Reform or Ruin: 'A Revolution in Female Manners.'" *Studies in Eighteenth-Century Culture* 11 (1982).

———. "Unfinished Business: Wollstonecraft's *Maria.*" *The Wordsworth Circle* 11 (1980).

Needham, Gwendolyn B. "Richardson's Characterization of Mr. B. and Double Purpose in *Pamela.*" *Eighteenth-Century Studies* 3 (1970).

Nelson, T. G. A. *Children, Parents, and the Rise of the Novel.* Newark, Del.: University of Delaware Press, 1995.

Nestor, Deborah J. "Virtue Rarely Rewarded: Ideological Subversion and Narrative Form in Haywood's Later Fiction." *SEL* 34 (Summer 1994).

New, Melvyn. "Job's Wife and Sterne's Other Women." In *Out of Bounds: Male Writers and Gender(ed) Criticism.* Ed. Laura Claridge and Elizabeth Langland. Amherst: University of Massachusetts Press, 1990.

New, Melvyn, and others. *The Notes.* Vol. 3 of *The Life and Opinions of Tristram Shandy, Gentleman,* by Laurence Sterne. 3 vols. Ed. Melvyn and Joan New. Gainesville: University Press of Florida, 1978–84 [1759–67].

Noakes, Susan. "On the Superficiality of Women." In *The Comparative Perspective on Literature: Approaches to the Theory and Practice.* Ed. Clayton Koelb and Susan Noakes. Ithaca, N.Y.: Cornell University Press, 1988.

Novak, Maximillian. *Defoe and the Nature of Man.* London: Oxford University Press, 1963.

———. *Economics and the Fiction of Daniel Defoe.* New York: Russell and Russell, 1976.

———. "Gothic Fiction and the Grotesque." *Novel* 13 (Fall 1979).

Nussbaum, Felicity. *Torrid Zones: Maternity, Sexuality, and Empire in Eighteenth-Century English Narratives.* Baltimore: Johns Hopkins University Press, 1995.

Okin, Susan Moller. "Patriarchy and Married Women's Property in England: Questions on Some Current Views." *Eighteenth-Century Studies* 17 (Winter 1984).

Orr, Leonard. *A Catalogue Checklist of English Prose Fiction, 1750–1800.* Troy, N.Y.: Whitston, 1979.

Paine, Thomas. *Rights of Man.* New York: Penguin, 1984.

Paulsen, Ronald. "Gothic Fiction and the French Revolution." *ELH* 48 (Fall 1981).

———. "The Pilgrimage and the Family: Structures in the Novels of Fielding and Smollett." In *Tobias Smollett: Bicentennial Essays Presented to Lewis M. Knapp.* Ed. G. S. Rousseau and P.-G. Boucé. New York: Oxford University Press, 1971.

Percival, Thomas, *A Father's Instructions to His Children*. London: J. Johnson, 1775.

————. *Further Observations on the State of Population in Manchester, and other Adjacent Places*. Manchester, 1774.

————. *Observations on the State of Population in Manchester, and other Adjacent Places*. N.p., 1773.

Perry, Ruth. *Women, Letters, and the Novel*. New York: AMS, 1980.

Peters, Dolores. "The Pregnant Pamela: Characterization and Popular Medical Attitudes in the Eighteenth Century." *Eighteenth-Century Studies* 14 (Summer 1981).

Philogamus [pseud]. *The Present State of Matrimony: Or, The Real Causes of Conjugal Infidelity and Unhappy Marriages*. London: John Hawkins, 1739.

Pinch, Adela. *Strange Fits of Passion: Epistemologies of Emotion, Hume to Austen*. Stanford, Calif.: Stanford University Press, 1996.

Piozzi, Hester Lynch Thrale. "Letter to a Gentleman newly Married." In *A Series of Letters on Courtship and Marriage*. Trenton, Eng., 1813 [1796].

Plato. *The Republic of Plato*. Trans. Francis MacDonald Cornford. Oxford: Oxford University Press, 1975.

Platt, Harrison. "Astrea and Celadon: An Untouched Portrait of Aphra Behn." *PMLA* 49 (1934).

Plumb, J. H. *The Growth of Political Stability in England, 1675–1725*. Boston: Houghton Mifflin, 1967.

Pocock, J. G. A. *The Machiavellian Moment: Florentine Political Thought and the Atlantic Republican Tradition*. Princeton, N.J.: Princeton University Press, 1975.

Polin, Raymond. "John Locke's Conception of Freedom." In *John Locke: Problems and Perspectives; a Collection of New Essays*. Ed. John W. Yolton. London: Cambridge University Press, 1969.

Pollak, Ellen. "*Moll Flanders*, Incest, and the Structure of Exchange." *The Eighteenth Century: Theory and Interpretation* 30 (Spring 1989).

Pollock, Linda A. *Forgotten Children: Parent-Child Relations from 1500–1900*. Cambridge: Cambridge University Press, 1983.

Poovey, Mary. *The Proper Lady and the Woman Writer: Ideology as Style in the Works of Mary Wollstonecraft, Mary Shelley, and Jane Austen*. Chicago: University of Chicago Press, 1984.

Pope, Alexander. *Imitations of Horace*. In Vol. 4 of *The Poems of Alexander Pope*. Ed. John Butt. London: Methuen, 1953.

Poster, Mark. *Critical Theory of the Family*. New York: Seabury Press, 1979.

Preston, John. *The Created Self: The Reader's Role in Eighteenth-Century Fiction*. New York: Barnes and Noble, 1970.

Price, Richard. *An Essay on the Population of England, from the Revolution to the Present Time.* London: T. Cadell, 1780 [1779].

Propp, Vladimir Akovlevich. *Morphology of the Folktale.* Austin: University of Texas Press, 1968.

Punter, David. *The Literature of Terror: A History of Gothic Fictions from 1765 to the Present Day.* London: Longman, 1980.

Radway, Janice A. *Reading the Romance: Women, Patriarchy, and Popular Literature.* Chapel Hill: University of North Carolina Press, 1984.

Ragussis, Michael. *Acts of Naming: The Family Plot in Fiction.* New York: Oxford University Press, 1986.

Rajan, Tilottama. "Wollstonecraft and Godwin: Reading the Secrets of the Political Novel." *Studies in Romanticism* 27 (Summer 1988).

Ramsaran, J. A. "*Oroonoko:* A Study of the Factual Elements." *Notes and Queries* 205 [new ser. 7] (1960).

Rapaczynski, Andrzej. *Nature and Politics: Liberalism in the Philosophies of Hobbes, Locke, and Rousseau.* Ithaca, N.Y.: Cornell University Press, 1987.

Razi, Zvi. "The Myth of the Immutable English Family." *Present and Past* 140 (1993).

Reiss, Timothy J. *The Discourse of Modernism.* Ithaca, N.Y.: Cornell University Press, 1982.

Richardson, Samuel. *The Apprentice's Vade Mecum.* In *Richardsoniana 1.* New York: Garland, 1974 [1732].

———. *Clarissa: or, the History of a Young Lady.* Ed. Angus Ross. Harmondsworth, Eng.: Viking, 1985 [1748].

———. *A Collection of the Moral and Instructive Sentiments: A Facsimile Reproduction.* Delmar: Scholars' Facsimiles and Reprints, 1980 [1755].

———. *Pamela: or, Virtue Rewarded. In a Series of Familiar Letters from a Beautiful Young Damsel, To her Parents.* [Part 1.] Ed. T. C. Duncan Eaves and Ben D. Kimpel. Boston: Houghton Mifflin, 1971 [1740].

———. *Pamela: or, Virtue Rewarded. In a Series of Familiar Letters from a Beautiful Young Damsel, To her Parents: And afterwards, In her Exalted Condition, between Her, and Persons of Figure and Quality, upon the most Important and Entertaining Subjects, In Genteel Life.* [Part II.] 4 vols. London: Samuel Richardson, 1741.

———. *Sir Charles Grandison.* Ed. Jocelyn Harris. Oxford: Oxford University Press, 1986 [1753–54].

Richetti, John J. *Defoe's Narratives: Situations and Structures.* Oxford: Clarendon Press, 1975.

———. "The Family, Sex, and Marriage in Defoe's *Moll Flanders* and *Roxana.*" *Studies in the Literary Imagination* 15 (Fall 1982).

———. *Popular Fiction Before Richardson: Narrative Patterns 1700–1739.* Oxford: Clarendon Press, 1969.

Riley, Patrick. "On Finding an Equilibrium Between Consent and Natural Law in Locke's Political Philosophy." *Political Studies* 22 (December 1974).

Rivers, William E. "The Importance of Tristram's 'Dear, Dear Jenny.'" *Interpretations: A Journal of Ideas, Analysis, and Criticism* 13 (Fall 1981).

Rogers, Deborah. "Eighteenth-Century Literary Depictions of Childbirth in the Historical Context of Mutilation and Mortality: The Case of *Pamela*." *Centennial Review* 37 (Spring 1993).

Rogers, Katherine M. "Fact and Fiction in Aphra Behn's *Oroonoko*." *Studies in the Novel* 20 (1988).

Rogers, Pat. "Crusoe's Home." *Essays in Criticism* 24 (1974).

Rogers, Timothy. *The Character of a Good Woman, Both in a Single and Marry'd State.* London: J. Harris, 1697.

———. *Early Religion: or, The Way for a Young Man to Remember his Creator.* London: J. Robinson and J. Dunton, 1683.

Ross, Deborah. *The Excellence of Falsehood: Romance, Realism, and Women's Contribution to the Novel.* Lexington: University Press of Kentucky, 1991.

Ross, Marlon. *The Contours of Masculine Desire: Romanticism and the Rise of Women's Poetry.* New York: Oxford University Press, 1989.

Rothstein, Eric. *Systems of Order and Inquiry in Later Eighteenth-Century Fiction.* Berkeley: University of California Press, 1975.

Rousseau, Jean Jacques. *Emile.* London: Dent, 1911.

Roussel, Roy. "Reflections on the Letter: The Reconciliation of Distance and Presence in *Pamela*." *ELH* 41 (1974).

Rubin, Gayle. "The Traffic in Women: Notes on the 'Political Economy' of Sex." In *Toward an Anthropology of Women.* Ed. Rayna R. Reiter. New York: Monthly Review Press, 1975.

Sabor, Peter, ed. *Horace Walpole: The Critical Heritage.* London: Routledge and Kegan Paul, 1987.

Said, Edward. *Beginnings: Intention and Method.* New York: Columbia University Press, 1975.

Salzman, Paul. *English Prose Fiction, 1558–1700: A Critical History.* Oxford: Clarendon Press, 1985.

Samson, John. "Politics Gothicized: The Conway Incident and *The Castle of Otranto*." *Eighteenth-Century Life* 10 (October 1986).

Sapiro, Virginia. *A Vindication of Political Virtue: The Political Theory of Mary Wollstonecraft.* Chicago: University of Chicago Press, 1992.

Schellekens, Jona. "Courtship, the Clandestine Marriage Act, and Illegitimate Fertility in England." *Journal of Interdisciplinary History* 25 (1995).

Schochet, Gordon. *The Authoritarian Family and Political Attitudes in 17th-Century England: Patriarchalism in Political Thought.* New Brunswick, N.J.: Transaction, 1975.

Schofield, Mary Anne. "'Descending Angels': Salubrious Sluts and Pretty Prostitutes in Haywood's Fiction." In *Fetter'd or Free? British Women Novelists, 1670–1815.* Ed. Mary Anne Schofield and Cecilia Macheski. Athens: Ohio University Press, 1986.

———. *Eliza Haywood.* Boston: Twayne, 1985.

———. "Exposé of the Popular Heroine: The Female Protagonists of Eliza Haywood. *Studies in Eighteenth-Century Culture* 12 (1983).

———. *Masking and Unmasking the Female Mind: Disguising Romances in Feminine Fiction, 1713–1799.* Newark, Del.: University of Delaware Press, 1990.

———. *Quiet Rebellion: The Fictional Heroines of Eliza Fowler Haywood.* Washington: University Press of America, 1981.

Schonhorn, Manuel. *Defoe's Politics: Parliament, Power, Kingship, and 'Robinson Crusoe.'* Cambridge: Cambridge University Press, 1991.

Schücking, Levin L. *The Puritan Family: A Social Study from the Literary Sources.* Trans. Brian Battershaw. New York: Schocken Books, 1970.

Scott, Walter. "Introduction to *The Castle of Otranto.*" In *Horace Walpole: The Critical Heritage.* Ed. Peter Sabor. London: Routledge and Kegan Paul, 1987.

Sedgwick, Eve Kosofsky. "The Character in the Veil: Imagery of the Surface in the Gothic Novel." *PMLA* 96 (March 1981).

Seidel, Michael. "Crusoe in Exile." *PMLA* 96 (1981).

———. *Satiric Inheritance: Rabelais to Sterne.* Princeton, N.J.: Princeton University Press, 1979.

Shanley, Mary. "Marriage Contract and Social Contract in Seventeenth-Century English Political Thought." In *The Family in Political Thought.* Ed. Jean Bethke Elshtain. Amherst: University of Massachusetts Press, 1982.

Sheffey, Ruth T. "Some Evidence for a New Source of Aphra Behn's *Oroonoko.*" *Studies in Philology* 59 (1962).

Shevelow, Kathryn. "Re-Writing the Moral Essay: Eliza Haywood's *Female Spectator.*" *Reader: Essays in Reader-Oriented Theory, Criticism, and Pedagogy* 13 (Spring 1985).

Shklovsky, Victor. "Art as Technique." In *Russian Formalist Criticism: Four Essays.* Trans. and ed. Lee T. Lemon and Marion J. Reis. Lincoln: University of Nebraska Press, 1965.

———. "Sterne's *Tristram Shandy*: A Stylistic Commentary." In *Russian Formalist Criticism: Four Essays.* Trans. and ed. Lee T. Lemon and Marion J. Reis. Lincoln: University of Nebraska Press, 1965.

Shorter, Edward. *The Making of the Modern Family*. New York: Basic Books, 1975.

Sill, Geoffrey M. "Crusoe in the Cave: Defoe and the Semiotics of Desire." *Eighteenth-Century Fiction* 6 (April 1994).

Sim, Stuart. "Interrogating an Ideology: Defoe's *Robinson Crusoe*." *British Journal for Eighteenth-Century Studies* 10 (Autumn 1987).

Simmons, A. John. *The Lockean Theory of Rights*. Princeton, N.J.: Princeton University Press, 1992.

Smith, Adam. *An Inquiry into the Nature and Causes of the Wealth of Nations*. Ed. R. H. Campbell and others. Oxford: Clarendon Press, 1976.

Solomon, Stanley J. "Subverting Propriety as a Pattern of Irony in Three Eighteenth-Century Novels: *The Castle of Otranto*, *Vathek* and *Fanny Hill*." *Erasmus Review* 1 (1971).

Spacks, Patricia Meyer. *Desire and Truth: Functions of Plot in Eighteenth-Century English Novels*. Chicago: University of Chicago Press, 1990.

———. *Imagining a Self: Autobiography and Novel in Eighteenth-Century England*. Cambridge, Mass.: Harvard University Press, 1976.

Spencer, Herbert. *Principles of Sociology*. New York: Appleton, 1893.

Spencer, Jane. *The Rise of the Woman Novelist from Aphra Behn to Jane Austen*. New York: Basil Blackwell, 1986.

Spender, Dale. *Mothers of the Novel: 100 Good Women Writers Before Jane Austen*. London: Pandora, 1986.

———, ed. *Living by the Pen: Early British Women Writers*. New York: Teachers College Press of Columbia University, 1992.

Sprey, Jetse. "Theoretical Practice in Family Studies." In *Fashioning Family Theory: New Approaches*. Ed. Jetse Sprey. Newbury Park, Calif.: Sage, 1990.

———, ed. *Fashioning Family Theory: New Approaches*. Newbury Park, Calif. Sage, 1990.

Stallybrass, Peter, and Allon White. *The Politics and Poetics of Transgression*. Ithaca, N.Y.: Cornell University Press, 1986.

Stanley, Maria Josepha Lady. *The Early Married Life of Maria Josepha Lady Stanley*. Ed. Jane H. Adeane. London: Longmans, Green, 1899.

Starr, George A. *Defoe and Casuistry*. Princeton, N.J.: Princeton University Press, 1971.

———. *Defoe and Spiritual Autobiography*. Princeton, N.J.: Princeton University Press, 1965.

Stennet, Samuel. *Discourses on Domestic Duties*. Edinburgh: J. Ritchie, J. Ogle, M. Ogle and R. Ogle, 1800.

Stenton, Doris. *The English Woman in History*. New York: Schocken, 1977.

Stephanson, Raymond. "Defoe's *Roxana*: The Unresolved Experiment in Characterization." *Studies in the Novel* 12 (1980).

Sterne, Laurence. *The Life and Opinions of Tristram Shandy, Gentleman.* Ed. Graham Petrie. Harmondsworth, Eng.: Penguin Books, 1967 [1759–67].

———. *A Sentimental Journey Through France and Italy.* Harmondsworth, Eng.: Penguin Books, 1979 [1768].

Stewart, Susan. *On Longing: Narratives of the Miniature, the Gigantic, the Souvenir, the Collection.* Durham, N.C.: Duke University Press, 1993.

Stone, Lawrence. *The Family, Sex and Marriage in England 1500–1800.* New York: Harper and Row, 1977.

Straub, Kristina. "Reconstructing the Gaze: Voyeurism in Richardson's *Pamela*." In *Gender: Literary and Cinematic Representation: Selected Papers from the Eleventh Annual Florida State University Conference on Literature and Film.* Ed. Jeanne Ruppert. Gainesville: University Presses of Florida, 1994.

———. *Sexual Suspects: Eighteenth-Century Players and Sexual Ideology.* Princeton, N.J.: Princeton University Press, 1992.

Strauss, Leo. *Natural Right and History.* Chicago: University of Chicago Press, 1953.

Summers, Montague. "Introduction: Memoir of Mrs. Behn." In Vol. 1 of *The Works of Aphra Behn.* Ed. Montague Summers. New York: Phaeton, 1967.

Swearingen, James. *Reflexivity in 'Tristram Shandy': An Essay in Phenomenological Criticism.* New Haven, Conn.: Yale University Press, 1977.

Swetnam, Joseph. *The Araignment of Lewd, Idle, Froward, and Unconstant Women: or the Vanitie of Them.* London: Edward Allde for Thomas Archer, 1615.

Tadmor, Naomi. "Dimensions of Inequality Among Siblings in Eighteenth-Century English Novels: The Cases of *Clarissa* and *The History of Miss Betsy Thoughtless*." *Continuity and Change* 7 (1992).

Tanner, Tony. *Adultery in the Novel: Contract and Transgression.* Baltimore: Johns Hopkins University Press, 1979.

Tarcov, Nathan. *Locke's Education for Liberty.* Chicago: University of Chicago Press, 1984.

Tawney, R. H. *Religion and the Rise of Capitalism: A Historical Study.* New York: Harcourt, Brace, 1926.

Taylor, A. E. "The Ethical Doctrine of Hobbes." In *Hobbes Studies.* Ed. K. C. Brown. Oxford: Blackwell, 1965.

Temple, William. *Miscellanea.* London, 1680.

Thorp, William. "Henry Nevil Payne, Dramatist and Jacobite Conspirator." In *Essays in Dramatic Literature: The Parrott Presentation Volume.* Ed. Hardin Craig. Princeton, N.J.: Princeton University Press, 1935.

Tobin, Patricia Drechsel. *Time and the Novel: The Genealogical Imperative.* Princeton, N.J.: Princeton University Press, 1978.

Todd, Janet. *The Sign of Angellica: Women, Writing and Fiction, 1660–1800.* New York: Columbia University Press, 1989.

———. *Women's Friendship in Literature.* New York: Columbia University Press, 1980.

———, ed. *Aphra Behn Studies.* Cambridge: Cambridge University Press, 1996.

Tomalin, Clare. *The Life and Death of Mary Wollstonecraft.* New York: Harcourt, Brace, 1974.

Tomashevsky, Boris. "Thematics." In *Russian Formalist Criticism.* Trans. and ed. Lee T. Lemon and Marion J. Reis. Lincoln: University of Nebraska Press, 1965.

Tournier, Michel. *Friday.* Trans. Norman Denny. New York: Pantheon, 1969.

Towers, A. R. "Sterne's Cock and Bull Story." *ELH* 24 (1957).

Tribe, Keith. *Land, Labour, and Economic Discourse.* Boston: Routledge and Kegan Paul, 1978.

Trumbach, Randolph. *The Rise of the Egalitarian Family: Aristocratic Kinship and Domestic Relations in Eighteenth-Century England.* New York: Academic Press, 1978.

Turner, Mark. *Death Is the Mother of Beauty: Mind, Metaphor, Criticism.* Chicago: University of Chicago Press, 1987.

Tyrrell, James. *Patriarcha Non Monarcha: The Patriarch Unmonarch'd: Being Observations on a Late Treatise and Divers Other Miscellanies.* London: R. Janeway, 1681.

Uphaus, Robert W. *The Impossible Observer: Reason and the Reader in Eighteenth-Century Prose.* Lexington: University Press of Kentucky, 1979.

Utter, Robert P., and Gwendolyn B. Needham. *Pamela's Daughters.* New York: Macmillan, 1936.

Vermillion, Mary. "Clarissa and the Marriage Act." *Eighteenth-Century Fiction* 9 (July 1997).

Veylit, Alain. *A Statistical Survey and Evaluation of the 'Eighteenth-Century Short-Title Catalog.'* Ph.D. diss., University of California, Riverside, 1994.

Wall, Richard. "Mean Household Size in England from Printed Sources." In *Household and Family in Past Time: Comparative Studies in the Size and Structure of the Domestic Group over the Last Three Centuries in England, France, Serbia, Japan and Colonial North America, with Further Materials from Western Europe.* Ed. Peter Laslett and Richard Wall. Cambridge: Cambridge University Press, 1972.

Walpole, Horace. *The Castle of Otranto*. Ed. W. S. Lewis. Oxford: Oxford University Press, 1982 [1764].

———. *Yale Edition of Horace Walpole's Correspondence*. 28 vols. Ed. W. S. Lewis and others. New Haven, Conn.: Yale University Press, 1940–1960.

Wardle, Ralph M. *Mary Wollstonecraft: A Critical Biography*. Lincoln: University of Nebraska Press, 1966.

Warner, William Beatty. *Reading Clarissa: The Struggles of Interpretation*. New Haven, Conn.: Yale University Press, 1979.

Warrender, Howard. *The Political Philosophy of Hobbes: His Theory of Obligation*. Oxford: Clarendon Press, 1957.

Watt, Ian P. "Time and the Family in the Gothic Novel: *The Castle of Otranto*." *Eighteenth-Century Life* 10 (October 1986).

———. *The Rise of the Novel: Studies in Defoe, Richardson and Fielding*. Berkeley: University of California Press, 1957.

Weber, Max. *The Protestant Ethic and the Spirit of Capitalism*. Trans. Talcott Parsons. New York: Scribner, 1976.

Westermarck, Edward. *The History of Human Marriage*. London: Macmillan, 1891.

Whately, William. *A Care-cloth: or, A Treatise of the Cumbers and Troubles of Marriage*. London: F. Kyngston for T. Man, 1624.

Whicher, George Frisbie. *The Life and Romances of Mrs. Eliza Haywood*. New York: Columbia University Press, 1915.

Wiegman, Robyn. "Economies of the Body: Gendered Sites in *Robinson Crusoe* and *Roxana*." *Criticism* 31 (Winter 1989).

Wiesenfarth, Joseph. *Gothic Manners and the Classic English Novel*. Madison: University of Wisconsin Press, 1988.

Williams, Raymond. *Keywords: A Vocabulary of Culture and Society*. New York: Oxford University Press, 1983.

Wilmot, John, Earl of Rochester. "Like a Great Family." In *The Complete Poems of John Wilmot, Earl of Rochester*. Ed. David M. Vieth. New Haven, Conn.: Yale University Press, 1968.

Wilson, Anna. "Mary Wollstonecraft and the Search for the Radical Woman." *Genders* 6 (1989).

Wilt, Judith. *Ghosts of the Gothic: Austen, Eliot, and Lawrence*. Princeton, N.J.: Princeton University Press, 1980.

Winch, Donald. *Adam Smith's Politics: An Essay in Historiographic Revision*. Cambridge: Cambridge University Press, 1978.

Wolff, Cynthia Griffin. *Samuel Richardson and the Eighteenth-Century Puritan Character*. Hamden, Conn.: Archon, 1972.

Wollstonecraft, Mary. *A Vindication of the Rights of Woman*. Ed. Carol H. Poston. New York: Norton, 1975 [1792].

————. *A Wollstonecraft Anthology*. Ed. Janet Todd. New York: Columbia University Press, 1990.

————. *The Wrongs of Woman* [1798]. In *Mary and The Wrongs of Woman*. Ed. Gary Kelley. New York: Oxford University Press, 1976.

Wolstenholme, Susan. *Gothic (Re)visions: Writing Women as Readers*. Albany: State University of New York Press, 1993.

Woodcock, George. *Aphra Behn: The English Sappho*. Montreal: Black Rose, 1989.

Woodward, Josiah. *The Young Man's Monitor*. London, 1706.

Wright, Louis B. *Middle-Class Culture in Elizabethan England*. Ithaca, N.Y.: Cornell University Press, 1958.

Wrigley, E. A., and R. S. Schofield. *The Population History of England, 1541–1871: A Reconstruction*. London: Edward Arnold, 1981.

Wycherley, William. *Miscellany Poems*. Vol. 3 of *The Complete Works of William Wycherley*. Ed. Montague Summers. Soho, Eng: Nonesuch Press, 1924.

Yeazell, Ruth Bernard. *Fictions of Modesty: Women and Courtship in the English Novel*. Chicago: University of Chicago Press, 1991.

Yolton, John W. "Locke on the Law of Nature." *Philosophical Review* 67 (1958).

The Young Lady's Own Book. London: T. T. and J. Tegg, 1833.

The Young Man's Own Book. London: T. T. and J. Tegg, 1833.

Zaretsky, Eli. *Capitalism, the Family, and Personal Life*. New York: Perennial Library, 1986.

Zimmerman, Everett. *Defoe and the Novel*. Berkeley: University of California Press, 1975.

Zomchick, John P. *Family and the Law in Eighteenth-Century Fiction: The Public Conscience in the Private Sphere*. Cambridge: Cambridge University Press, 1993.

Zonabend, Françoise. "An Anthropological Perspective on Kinship and the Family." *Distant Worlds, Ancient Worlds*. Vol. 1, *A History of the Family*. Ed. André Burguière and others. Trans. Sarah Hanbury Tenison and others. Cambridge, Mass.: Belknap Press of Harvard University Press, 1996.

Index

In this index an "f" after a number indicates a separate reference on the next page, and an "ff" indicates separate references on the next two pages. A continuous discussion over two or more pages is indicated by a span of page numbers, e.g., "57–59." *Passim* is used for a cluster of references in close but not consecutive sequence.

Library of Congress Cataloging-in-Publication Data

Flint, Christopher, 1957– .
   Family Fictions : narrative and domestic relations in Britain,
1688–1798 / Christopher Flint.
      p.   cm.
   Includes bibliographical references and index.
   ISBN 0-8047-3072-5 (alk. paper)
   1. English fiction—18th century—History and criticism.
2. English fiction—early modern, 1500–1700—History and
criticism. 3. Domestic fiction, English—History and criticism.
4. Family in literature. 5. Narration (Rhetoric). I. Title.

PR858.F29F58   1998
823.009'355—dc21   97-39162
                                                          CIP

This book is printed on acid-free, recycled paper.

Original printing 1998
Last figure below indicates year of this printing:
07   06   05   04   03   02   01   00   99   98